L. SCOTT KELLUM

PREACHING THE FAREWELL DISCOURSE

AN EXPOSITORY WALK-THROUGH OF

John 13:31-17:26

ACADEMIC
NASHVILLE, TENNESSEE

Preaching the Farewell Discourse:
An Expository Walk-through of John 13:31–17:26
Copyright © 2014 by L. Scott Kellum
Published by B&H Publishing Group
Nashville, Tennessee
All rights reserved
ISBN: 978–1–4336–7376–4
Dewey Decimal Classification: 251

Subject Heading: PREACHING \ BIBLE. N.T. JOHN 13–17 \ JOHN, APOSTLE

Unless otherwise noted, Scripture quotations are by L. Scott Kellum.

Scripture quotations marked HCSB are taken from the Holman Christian Standard Bible ®, Copyright © 1999, 2000, 2002, 2003, 2009 by Holman Bible Publishers. Used by permission. Holman Christian Standard Bible®, Holman CSB®, and HCSB® are federally registered trademarks of Holman Bible Publishers.

Scripture quotations marked ESV are taken from The Holy Bible, English Standard Version Copyright © 2001 by Crossway Bibles, a division of Good News Publishers. Used by permission. All rights reserved.

Printed in the United States of America

Dedication

For my Mom,

who went to be with the Lord in 2010,

the year of my greatest loss,

and to the dad she temporarily left behind.

We are all still learning to move on without forgetting.

"Seldom does one encounter a book that blends the disciplines of hermeneutics, discourse analysis, biblical exposition, and homiletics. In *Preaching the Farewell Discourse* my friend and colleague Scott Kellum does exactly that, and he does it well. In the future when I prepare to preach from John 13–17, this book will be ready at hand. It is an excellent resource for any pastor committed to rightly dividing the Word of Truth."

—*Daniel L. Akin, president, Southeastern Baptist Theological Seminary*

"*Preaching the Farewell Discourse* is a faithful bridge between the past world of the New Testament and our present situation. This book is informationally grounded, connecting each sermon to the narrative discourse with expertise. It's also formationally challenging to the heart of a disciple today. The content is theologically robust, weaving together the biblical themes of John. It sets the preacher up to preach to a particular place and people in their current context. Each of our four live preachers at our campuses has put this book to immediate and fruitful use in our preaching and teaching."

—*Daniel Montgomery, lead pastor, Sojourn Community Church, Louisville, Kentucky*

"A beautiful medley of hermeneutical, exegetical, and homiletical insight. For the preacher preparing sermons on the Farewell Discourse (John 13:31–17:26), this volume will prove invaluable."

—*Robert L. Plummer, professor of New Testament Interpretation, The Southern Baptist Theological Seminary*

"In *Preaching the Farewell Discourse*, Scott Kellum challenges pastors and students to explore the contribution of discourse analysis to the exegetical process. Adopting the well-established methodology of semantic and structural analysis, he breaks down each pericope of Jesus' final words to his disciples into suggested units for preaching. Kellum provides a thorough interaction with the commentary literature including discussion of major textual variants, yet he is not afraid to make his own views known. Regardless of whether one ultimately adopts Kellum's approach, readers will greatly benefit from his years of dedicated study and careful exegesis of the Greek text."

—*Steven E. Runge, scholar-in-residence, Logos Bible Software*

"It has been rightly said that if a man is going to stand up and say, 'Thus saith the Lord,' then he had better know what the Lord saith. As both a New Testament scholar and a faithful preacher, Scott Kellum affirms and models the indispensability of contemporary sermons being derived from and driven by a right understanding of God's counsel as recorded in the biblical text. *Preaching the Farewell Discourse* is a clinic on how to start with a text of Scripture and allow it to give birth to relevant, prophetic sermons that maintain the integrity of speaking on God's behalf. This is the heart of authentic expository preaching. Additionally, Kellum's laboratory of John 13:31–17:26 offers rich insight into both the expositional process and some of our Lord's most intimate, practical, and profound instructions to his followers. Pastors, teachers, and all who love God's Word will benefit from this work."

—*Jim Shaddix, professor of Preaching, Southeastern Baptist Theological Seminary; pastor of teaching and training, The Church at Brook Hills*

"Like Augustine's *De Doctrina Christiana* written more than 1,500 years ago, Scott Kellum's *Preaching the Farewell Discourse* brings together in an inextricable unity both the *content* of hermeneutics and the *contour* of homiletics. The reader is escorted into the sermonic laboratory of this New Testament biblical scholar and effective homiletician to learn the *what* and the *how* of expository preaching, being greatly assisted by practical sermon examples provided from the author's pulpit work. The one who reads this volume will unquestionably be informed by its matter, inspired by its manner, and enriched in not only preaching the Farewell Discourse of Jesus but also the whole counsel of God."

—*Robert Smith Jr., professor of Christian Preaching, Beeson Divinity School*

CONTENTS

Acknowledgments	ix
Abbreviations	xi
Introduction	1
1. An Expository Theory	5
2. Analyzing Literary Structure and Flow of Thought	41
3. Opening Movements	67
4. Unit 1: Commands that Comfort (14:1–31)	89
5. Unit 2: Commands that Unite (15:1–16:4c)	131
6. Unit 3: Advantages of Jesus' Departure (16:4d–33)	161
7. Unit 4: The Final Prayer	199
Conclusion	219
Appendix 1: Preparing Your Study	229
Appendix 2: A Sermon Series through the Farewell Discourse	239
Select Bibliography	331
Name Index	337
Subject Index	341
Scripture Index	345

Acknowledgments

I would like to take a few moments to thank the special people who helped me produce this work. First, I would like to thank my precious bride, Cathy Kellum, who puts up with me while I write, re-write, and write again. She is a precious gift, and I was blessed when the Lord put her in my life. Hannah, Joshua, Rachel, and Elijah get some props in this hour as well.

I would also like to thank those in my office complex for their help. My secretaries who spent time proofing this document are deserving of double honor. Carol Thompson was first, then Laura Reid finished up. Both caught errors and made suggestions that vastly improved this work. Laura did yeoman's work in having to proof the whole document. I am especially grateful for her "eagle-eyes." I assure the reader that any remaining errors are completely my own. My colleague David Beck also reviewed the conclusion for me, and his selfless attention has made be a better professor and writer.

Finally, I would like to thank President Danny Akin, the trustees, administration, and faculty of Southeastern Baptist Theological Seminary, who provide a God-honoring, stimulating environment of learning and preparation.

ABBREVIATIONS

AB	Anchor Bible
ABD	*Anchor Bible Dictionary*
BBR	*Bulletin of Biblical Research*
BDAG	Bauer, W., F. W. Danker, W. F. Arndt, and F. W. Gingrich, *Greek-English Lexicon of the New Testament and Other Early Christian Literature* (Chicago, 1961)
BECNT	Baker Exegetical Commentary on the New Testament
Bib	*Biblica*
BSac	*Bibliotheca Sacra*
BT	*The Bible Translator*
BWANT	Beiträge zur Wissenschaft vom Alten und Neuen Testament
CH	*Church History*
CTR	*Criswell Theological Review*
Enc	*Encounter*
ETL	*Ephemerides théologicae lovanienses*
EGGNT	Exegetical Guide to the Greek New Testament
FRLANT	Forschungen zur Religion und Literatur des Alten und Neuen Testaments
HCSB	Holman Christian Standard Bible
ICC	International Critical Commentary
Int	*Interpretation*
ITQ	*Irish Theological Quarterly*
JBL	*Journal of Biblical Literature*
JSNTSup	Journal for the Study of the New Testament: Supplement Series
NAC	New American Commentary

NCB	New Century Bible
Neot	*Neotestamentica*
NICNT	New International Commentary on the New Testament
NIV	New International Version
NovTSup	Supplements to Novum Testamentum
NTS	*New Testament Studies*
NTSup	New Testament Studies Supplement
ÖTKNT	Ökumenischer Taschenbucher-Kommentar zum Neuen Testament
PNTC	Pillar New Testament Commentaries
SBJT	*Southern Baptist Journal of Theology*
SBLDS	Society of Biblical Literature Dissertation Series
SBLMS	Society of Biblical Literature Monograph Series
SIL	Summer Institute of Linguistics
SNTSM	Society for New Testament Studies Monograph Series
SP	Sacra pagina
TBT	*The Bible Today*
TDNT	*Theological Dictionary of the New Testament*. Edited by G. Kittel and G. Friedrich. Translated by G. W. Bromiley. 10 vols. Grand Rapids, 1964–76
TNTC	Tyndale New Testament Commentary
TynBul	*Tyndale Bulletin*
WBC	Word Biblical Commentary

INTRODUCTION

THE book that you hold is the culmination of many years of thinking, practice, and writing on the topic of the practical application of the study of the New Testament. In 1985 I began a journey as a twenty-one year-old graphic design student who left that career path to undertake God's calling in ministry. I started taking Greek in the University of Mississippi's classics department to prepare for seminary as I finished up college. I took all the Greek and Hebrew I could in my seminary career because I was convinced that it was necessary to preach the Word of God.

As I transitioned from student to pastor, the question of how to use the Hebrew and Greek without boring my people to tears or constantly appealing to "secret knowledge" became a priority for me. At first, I was attempting to be a running commentary—offering lots of content without much application. I have preached through books of the Bible serially—that is, each sermon was but on the text in sequence—but not really covering the book as a whole. I have done word studies, theological studies, and the occasional topical study, all in the pursuit of preaching the Word of God. It was always my intent that while I may not have a lot of amusing anecdotes and great illustrations, my people would get the content of the Bible. I believed, and still do, that cute without content serves no one. But how do you preach an expository sermon? I didn't really have a rigorous way to preach one when I was pastoring churches.

My next transition was to doctoral studies to pursue a calling in teaching. I continued to preach and teach in churches, and I was very interested in taking what I do as a professor of New Testament and Greek and applying it in the pulpit. Now my answer to the question, "What is an expository sermon?" has grown over the years. For a sermon to be an exposition of the text, everything about the text must be reflected in the sermon. The main idea and purpose of the text should be the main idea and purpose of the sermon. Furthermore, the major movements of the text ought to be the major movements of the sermon. In other words, the structure of the text should also be the structure of the sermon. Evangelicals are particularly adept at three-point sermons, but not every text has three points. Evangelicals are particularly adept at "how-to" sermons, but very few texts are actually procedural texts. We can do better if we can be shown, at least, a place to begin and a procedure to follow, adapt, and perfect. This book intends to be a place to begin.

I intend to take you through the hermeneutical process to the shaping of an outline of an expository sermon. I will not spend a great deal of time on the domain of the homiletician in the body of the book, for that is outside of my expertise. However, I do intend to show a way to take a certain genre of Scripture and craft an outline that matches the outline of the text. Our job in preaching is to discover the outline, not come up with one. In a way, this book is a "walk-through" for pastors and teachers of the Word.

I have chosen to narrow our focus to the Farewell Discourse of John's Gospel for space reasons. This section was chosen because I have been working in it for years. My doctoral dissertation was an investigation of author attribution in the Fourth Gospel. Many of the structural arguments in chapters 3–6 are a revision of parts of my dissertation. Many of the spiritual insights the Lord gave me in the deep study of that passage were not appropriate for that project. I am thrilled to find a place for them here.

In the pages that follow, I will show you how I employ discourse analysis to analyze a text and to shape a sermon outline. Chapter 1 is a description of my expository theory and some foundational tools to begin the journey from text to exposition. I will lay out a process to go from text to sermon outline. These steps do not have to all be done in the sequence I outline, but they should be done by any serious exegete who is not faced with crushing time constraints.

Chapter 2 is a description of how I employ discourse analysis to a hortatory document (like the Farewell Discourse). I have adapted the "semantic and structural analysis" (SSA) of the Summer Institute of Linguistics (the academic branch of Wycliffe Bible Translators) to analyze this genre of text. It is detailed and the analyses can be daunting to view, but when we look at it one step at a time it is really very simple. I have found it extremely helpful in discovering the meaning and structure of a text. The presentations in the body of the book are simplified to define the major movements of the text and to make them easier to grasp. I always suggest looking at the left side of the SSA to see the major movements.

Chapters 3–7 are the actual implementation of the theory on the Farewell Discourse of John's Gospel. I express the overall process in three sections: Analyzing the Text (where we look at the structure of the text), Interpreting the

Text (where we do the spade-work of hermeneutics), and Preaching the Text (where we produce the sermon sketch). It is my hope that these will be valuable illustrations of the process I am advocating.

Finally, two appendices include (1) my suggestions for preparing your study with reference resources and (2) detailed outlines for a sermon series through the Farewell Discourse that includes application and illustration. Scripture translations throughout are my own unless otherwise indicated (usually HCSB).

At the end of the day, it is my purpose to encourage you to preach and teach biblically. It is my hope that you will digest, appropriate, and adapt the process I describe to preach and teach the Bible clearly. I have become a better man for the study; I pray the process benefits the reader as well.

Soli Deo Gloria
L. Scott Kellum
Wake Forest, North Carolina

Chapter 1

An Expository Theory

THERE is an unmistakable and disturbing gap between our hermeneutics and our preaching. We see this clearly in Christian publishing. Most commentaries are not bought by the professor in the ivory tower but by the professional in the work place. I dare say preachers and students training to be preachers buy most of the commentaries published. Yet, most of these commentaries (especially academic commentaries) never seem to have in mind the need for preachers to present the text to an audience—that is, the preaching moment.[1] We seem to be writing for each other. Preaching commentaries may be a rich mine for illustrations and outlines but often do not offer the depth for serious students of the Word. The value of these commentaries diminishes in proportion to their slim handling of the Word. An outline that "will preach," but is imposed on the Word, is still poor handling of the Word of God.

Similarly, most hermeneutics textbooks do not deal with the preaching moment. They discuss general hermeneutics (theory in general) and special hermeneutics (dealing with different genres and covenants), but rarely does one find a treatment of how to express the text's meaning in a sermon.[2] To be fair, preaching the text is not usually one of the objectives of a hermeneutics textbook. In like manner, most homiletic textbooks do not treat the exegesis of the text in any great detail. For example, Haddon Robinson's *Biblical Preaching*—standard in the field—is an excellent work that has had profound

---

[1] An exception to this is the Exegetical Guide to the Greek New Testament (EGGNT) series from B&H Academic. Each volume provides a detailed analysis of the Greek text and also offers homiletical helps for preachers.
[2] The recent work by my mentor Andreas J. Köstenberger includes a chapter I wrote at the end of the book to deal with this need. See A. J. Köstenberger and J. Patterson, *Invitation to Hermeneutics* (Grand Rapids: Kregel, 2011). The Zondervan volumes *Grasping God's Word* (2005) and *Preaching God's Word* (3rd ed., 2012) are also a welcome exception although hindered by a strict reliance on the TNIV.

influence in our pulpits.³ Furthermore, a great deal of what follows in this book agrees substantially with Dr. Robinson's work. Yet, the gap between hermeneutics and homiletics is still evident. His book only devotes one chapter to the study of the text and a scant four pages to the nuts-and-bolts of exegesis. Likewise, Stephen Olford's fine book *Anointed Expository Preaching* does more (about thirty pages), but the gap (while narrower) is still present.⁴

Neither hermeneutic textbooks nor homiletic textbooks are designed to be one-stop shops for the preacher. Each is dependent on the other to complete the task, but it is disturbing that seldom do they work in tandem. The hermeneutics writer and the homiletics writer may not have similar exegetical philosophies, homiletical philosophies, or even core beliefs. This mismatch may be substantial or minimal, but it is inevitable between independent individuals. This bifurcation is also evident in our seminaries and Bible colleges. We have Bible experts and preaching experts who teach their respective courses but seldom collaborate. Such distance has inevitably led to a similar problem in Christian pulpits. This is, of course, nothing new. A generation ago, Walt Kaiser noted this gap.⁵

The Present Need in Christian Preaching/Teaching (Bridging the Gap between Hermeneutics and Exposition)

In 1954, Merrill F. Unger made a plea for expository preaching:

> The greatest single need of the contemporary church is undoubtedly the strengthening of the local pulpit. This fact is not difficult to realize in the light of distressing present-day conditions in this phase of the Christian ministry and in view of the key place pastoral preaching holds in the carrying out of the divine program. The progress of God's work depends primarily on the local church, and the local pastor has the most strategic position for weal or woe in this important activity. In no way can the individual pulpit be strengthened for its momentous task than by a diligent return to the Bible injunction: "Preach the Word." The benefits of such a ministry are incalculable.⁶

Dr. Unger goes on to list several benefits to the church and the preacher of an expository sermon. He was obviously attempting to persuade his audience to be expository in their preaching.

---

[3] Haddon Robinson, *Biblical Preaching: The Development and Delivery of Expository Messages* (Grand Rapids: Baker, 1980).
[4] Stephen F. Olford with David L. Olford, *Anointed Expository Preaching* (Nashville: B&H, 1998).
[5] Walter C. Kaiser Jr., *Toward an Exegetical Theology: Biblical Exegesis for Preaching and Teaching* (Grand Rapids: Baker, 2004), 18–20.
[6] Merrill F. Unger, "Expository Preaching," *BSac* 111 (1954): 325.

So, what do I mean by "expository"? It is not topical (i.e., a moral encouragement not necessarily based on specific Scripture) nor theological (i.e., a description of biblical theology based on numerous passages). By "expository" I mean a pastor/teacher (as in Eph 4:11) teaches his audience the meaning intended by the author (as would be understood by his original audience) of a specific text of Scripture and then applies it to the present situation.

The good news is that Dr. Unger, and those like him, seem to have convinced conservative evangelicals of the primary place of such preaching in the pulpits. Unfortunately, few do it well. Forty-five years after Unger's work, Thomas Schreiner noted, "It seems that almost everyone trumpets the importance of expositional preaching, and yet genuine and powerful expository preaching seems to be in short supply."[7]

I concur with both Unger and Schreiner in this regard. Expository preaching is best for the steady diet of the believer, and those who do it with skill and power are few and far between. So what is the cause of this gap between what we believe and what we produce? Several reasons come to mind beyond the impasse in publishing previously mentioned.

First, we confuse sermons based on the Bible for expository preaching. This is a matter of definition. Preaching verse-by-verse does not make a sermon expository. Honestly, a passage can be dismembered verse-by-verse just as well as any other method. This happens in both interpretation and application. Regarding the former, we all have seen an interpreter miss the point of a passage (verse-by-verse). I have personally developed quite a list of passages that are routinely preached out of context. Hebrews 4:12 immediately comes to mind. How many times have we heard a preacher defending the power of the Word of God by citing Hebrews 4:12 by memory? Quite often, I would imagine. However, if we read it in context, it is not an abstract defense of the power of the Word but a concrete basis for a warning. We are laid bare and exposed before the Word of God. When we reduce it to a convenient prooftext, we domesticate the text and make it serve our purposes. This is quite an indictment for a people who claim to have a high view of Scripture!

We also can dismember the application of a passage. To be fair, it usually happens as a result of poor exegesis. I have heard sermons that were spot-on regarding interpretation but then moved into questionable applications. Can we preach Matthew 28:18–20 and then apply it only to meeting the goal of a global missions offering? We can, and have, but it is certainly not the only (or even the best) application of the passage.

---

[7] Thomas R. Schreiner, "A Plea for Biblical Preaching," *SBJT* 3 (1999): 3.

We can even preach through a whole book without preaching a single expository sermon. The problem here is that we preach serially through a book without any regard to the bigger picture. No single passage in the Bible is an isolated entity. Each passage works toward the book's larger purpose literary structure (beyond sermon-appropriate sections). How many sermons have been preached on Nicodemus in John 3 apart from those who "believe but don't really believe in John 2:23–25?"[8] I dare say most of them. However, Nicodemus is the prototypical example of one who believes but does not have a saving faith. "Rabbi," Nicodemus says, "we *know* that You have come from God . . ." (John 3:2, emphasis mine). Even worse, we almost never contrast Nicodemus with the woman at the well in John 4. The whole section actually highlights what saving faith truly is, but because we never look at how the larger structures work together, we lose a grand opportunity. Yes, we can preach the whole book without preaching a book, but a series of sections. When we do this we, at the very least, teach our people to read the Bible in a way certainly not intended.

Some err in another direction. They preach a running commentary on the text. They parse every verb, comment on textual variants, do word studies from the *TDNT*,[9] and even cite academic commentaries. Some of these preach verse-by-verse until time runs out and then close the service with "We'll pick up verse 12 next week." The problem is that this is not a sermon but a commentary. In other words, it may be expository, but it certainly ignores the preaching mandate to apply the text and call for a response. Definition, expectation, and application go hand in hand to produce a gap.

The second way we display a gap between what we believe and what we produce involves a lack of skill in biblical interpretation. Here the problem is not about our assumptions but our abilities. The problem is multifaceted. Some preachers really do not have a good grasp of how to interpret a book of the Bible. This person simply has no clue about the Bible as a work of ancient literature. This fellow is rarely a seminary graduate. He does exist, however. Far more common is the man who relies completely on English resources to interpret his text. He may have taken Hebrew and Greek, but for whatever reason (whether through neglect or never really learning the languages) he never looks at the original languages while composing his sermon. As will be seen in the pages that follow, I am no proponent of spouting off this or that Greek word and giving the

---

[8] The HCSB renders πιστεύω at 2:23 as "trusted." This is undoubtedly to have a consistent rendering of the Greek word used at both 2:23 and 24. They "trusted in His name," but Jesus did not entrust himself to them. John is clearly making a play on words here that is difficult to express in English.

[9] Gerhard Kittel, Geoffrey Bromiley, and Gerhard Friedrich, eds., *Theological Dictionary of the New Testament*, 10 vols. (Grand Rapids: Eerdmans, 1964); and Colin Brown, ed., *The New International Dictionary of New Testament Theology* (Grand Rapids: Zondervan, 1975).

"technical meaning" (more often such language means the interpreter is squeezing a word for more than it can bear). Nor am I suggesting that we all sight-read our Greek New Testaments. What I am suggesting is that we should be proficient enough in Hebrew and Greek to use intelligently the basic tools to craft our sermons. When we were building our house, I was surprised that the plumber spoke to his hispanic employees in Spanish. He took time to learn Spanish because he considered it vital for his work. His example should inspire us. Basic skill at Greek and Hebrew is vital to the preacher's task of exegesis. Let's take the time to use it well in the work. Great expositors are good grammarians.

I suggest, finally, a third reason for the gap between our intentions and our product is the constant demand on our time. The Lord's Day pursues the preacher like a bloodhound. It may only come once a week, but it is relentless in its pursuit. Sunday is always coming, but the schedule is not always consistent. Chaos can happen at any moment. Deaths, sicknesses, and family emergencies rarely are scheduled in advance. A time-consuming outreach project can chew up time scheduled for sermon preparation. We will not even mention conflict, crisis, and complex administrative needs. On top of all this is the truth that good exegesis alone takes time; to shape the exegesis into an expository message, even more. There are those who have forty hours a week to work on their sermons, but few of us are pastors of mega churches who have multiple staff members to help carry the load. In fact, most pastors are the only staff at their churches. They do all the funerals, visitations, education, and some poor souls must even lead the congregation in worship. In this environment it is very tempting to have a few "sermons-you-can-preach" books on the shelf (or links to favorite websites!).[10] When overwhelming need meets crushing constraints, the temptation to preach someone else's study can be powerful.

That is not to say that there is something wrong with studying other people's sermons. There is everything right with listening to sermons or reading the great preachers of the past to get suggestions or insights for your own sermon. There is everything wrong with preaching their sermons as your own. I well remember a youth group trip to a neighboring state when I was a youth minister in Vidalia, Louisiana. Being good Baptists we picked one of the mega churches to attend that Sunday morning. As we attended Sunday school, the regular teacher introduced a guest speaker. This guest preacher stood up and preached a sermon that I recognized. It was Robert G. Lee's "Payday Someday" (one of the most influential sermons of the twentieth century). I remember being shocked as much by the speaker's hubris as the fawning praise of the adult hearers.

---

[10] I am well aware that there are quite a number of subscription services to deliver sermons to pastors with the intent that they are preached wholesale. We will not stoop to listing them here.

So what's wrong with preaching another person's work? Well, for starters it robs the hearers of a preacher who has drunk deeply from the wells of Scripture and has grown spiritually from the exercise. The fellow borrowing the sermon has not wrestled with discovering the outline or the structure of the text. He has not been convicted by the Word of God about his own failures. Consequently, passion for the topic of the Scripture is nearly impossible to express. It is in every sense of the word, stale.

Another problem is that the Scripture is not applied to his local situation. I remember listening to a fine example of an expository sermon by W. A. Criswell from the 1950s. I was somewhat amused that the application dealt with tithing, social drinking, and dancing. I remember thinking, "I wish that social drinking was the biggest problem we had." There is only one meaning to the Scripture but many specific applications. As time, location, and culture change, the application of a text is going to change even though its meaning will not. Preaching another's sermon often involves taking an irrelevant application to your hearers.

Yet another problem is the dishonesty of the matter. Are we really comfortable standing before our people and presenting another person's sermon as our own construction? Are we going to steal their glory for our own? Does it not foster laziness and dependence on another's study (or lack thereof)? Let us remember that the false prophet preaches other men's messages (Jer 23:30). Our commitment should be to do the best we can in the time we have.

I say these things not to shame my brothers but to encourage steadfastness. Exegesis is a skill like any other. The more proficient we are with Greek and Hebrew, the more we are familiar with good reference works, the more we prepare sermons, and the more we walk with God, the less trial and error we go through. Practice will speed things up. Stick with it. An oak tree started as an acorn.

The Aim and Theory of This Book

The book that you hold is intended to start filling the gap between hermeneutics and exposition. In the pages that follow I will take a beloved passage of Scripture (the Johannine Farewell Discourse) and lead us from interpretation to exposition. In terms of the gamer, it is a "walk-through." I will examine each section of John 13:31–17:26 verse-by-verse and suggest the meaning of the text. Then, I will transition from interpretation to exposition. I will suggest a sermon outline based on the outline of the text. Sometimes I will offer several possible outlines. It is not my intent to produce a series of sermons for you to preach, but to show you how to exegete faithfully a passage and to convert that study to an expository sermon.

At this point, I think a disclaimer is warranted. I do not consider myself a preaching guru—far from it! My expertise is in biblical studies: specifically the New Testament, Greek, and hermeneutics, among a variety of other academic interests. This is why I will not deal particularly much with the development of the sermon beyond the outline. I will leave that to the homiletic experts.

That is not to say that I am a stranger to preaching. I have been steadily preaching as both pastor and pulpit-mercenary for over twenty-five years. This involvement has led to the desire to put my experiences to paper. I do not particularly consider my sermons to be all that great (my former parishioners will attest to that!). My enunciation may not be the best (foiled by a southern accent), my projection could be better, and my delivery could be vastly improved (I tend to read my notes more than I should), among a host of other things that are in the preacher's domain. These things are important; the preacher should not get in the way of his message. Stumbling, mumbling, and boring your people certainly do that.

However important these things are, it is a mistake to allow them to trump biblical content. Frankly, I have experienced more than one sermon (some I preached!) that was "cute without content." It was plainly evident that the speaker spent more time attempting to force some illustration, make a dramatic object lesson (like a dirty shirt under a dress coat), or play an amusing YouTube video to make a point than he spent wrestling with the content of the text. Avant-garde, cutting edge, or cute is only helpful if it supports legitimate content that we communicate.

This is a lesson that Hollywood has learned. Multimillion-dollar blockbusters full of CGI special effects, explosions, and world-class monster effects do not guarantee a good movie. If the story is poorly executed, the movie will most-likely flop. The same is true for the sermon. The bells and whistles do not make the sermon. When I am sitting in the pew, I am looking for a few things from my preacher. I am looking for quality exegesis of the text, passion for Christ and his people, and a man who has wrestled with the implications of the text in his own life. Bells and whistles are only useful when I find these.

We should dwell at the point of faithful biblical content. The Word of God will change lives. Will a person's life be changed if we make them laugh? I long to see them tremble. Will a person's life be changed if we stave off boredom for thirty minutes? I long to see them hunger for the Word of God. Will a person's life be changed if he thinks we are great preachers? I would rather see a transformed life than hear "I enjoyed the sermon, Preacher." Let us cast off the desire to entertain as if it were a jacket infested with lice.[11] We have only one thing to offer that is life changing: the Word of God. Our time, our effort, our highest prioritized goal should be a faithful exposition of the Word of God. Then we capture the attention to point to the meaning of the Word. To this end, this book is humbly offered.

I am of the conviction that the majority of evangelical preachers aspire to be expository in the main of their preaching. Occasionally, a visionary series (describing the mission or vision of the church) or a series through this or that topic of biblical theology would lend itself to other forms of preaching. In the main, however, men who aspire to be expository preachers fill our pulpits. This is a great encouragement to me, and I hope the work that follows will be a great help.

From Text to Sermon

In an expository sermon everything about the text should drive the framework of the sermon (in both structure and concept). By this I mean that the outline of the text should be the outline of the sermon. The purpose of the text should be the purpose of the sermon. If our text is deductive, our sermon should be deductive (i.e., arguing from general to specific). If our text is inductive, our sermon should be inductive (arguing from specific to general), and so forth.

So where do we begin? For most of us it is a familiar place, interpreting the text correctly.[12]

The study of the New Testament is the study of documents written thousands of years ago to people who have long since died. The distance between a modern reader and the ancient text is sometimes quite a space, whether it be cultural, chronological, or even covenantal. The job of the interpreter of Scripture is to interpret the message correctly so that even though we may not enter the mind of the writer we may attempt to understand the text as well as any other contemporary reader would. We must infer the meaning from the linguistic clues the writer used. Admittedly, this requires us to understand the cultures, languages, and literary canons of antiquity. The preacher of God's Word must first have a clear understanding of the hermeneutical task that

---

[11] This entertainment mentality has infected almost every area of our worship. A person to lead in worship who really understands a theology of worship is hard to find because (1) we do not train our young people in this (and model it) and (2) we confuse musical talent for skill in leading worship. Frankly, most of the worship wars that have erupted in our churches are about entertainment and personal preference rather than about authentic worship.

[12] This begins with gathering good information. To this end, I have compiled some suggestions in an appendix: Preparing Your Study.

underlies his message. Below, I will briefly sketch the task of interpretation rather broadly for the sake of space.

What Are We Looking For?
The interpreter's first task is to understand for what he/she is searching. In other words, where is the location of meaning—the author, the text, or the reader? Hans-Georg Gadamer introduced something of a revolution in hermeneutics with his book *Truth and Method*.[13] The basic contours of his theory are as follows: Truth cannot reside in the reader's attempt to get back to the author's meaning because being in the past cannot be being in the present. The reader and the text are both autonomous; meaning comes in the fusion of the horizons of the text and the reader. As the reader interacts with the ancient text, he runs along the hermeneutical circle to create meaning in his own horizon. Since there are multiple "fusions" (i.e., readers' contexts), multiple valid meanings will arise. Since Gadamer a host of hermeneutical theories have grown up that decry propositional truth in favor of interpreting communities that deconstruct the text through the interplay of words. As a result, the evangelist encounters people who will appeal to "my truth" and "your truth." When giving our testimony we hear people respond, "I'm glad that worked for you." In other words, we live in a postmodern society that is trying to embrace individualized truth, usually dressed up in shortsighted pragmatics.[14]

The apologist has a duty to answer the challenges brought by postmodern approaches to life, but what about the preacher of God's Word? Without presenting a full-fledged retort to the new hermeneutic, let me give two fundamental reasons to reject it. In doing so, we will clarify and sharpen our understanding of the task of the preacher.

My first problem with locating meaning in the reader is found in the realm of universal human experience. Writing is an act of communication. When people communicate with one another, they use language (a series of linguistic conventions) to communicate ideas, instructions, praise, rebuke, and much more. Simply put, communication does not happen when the receiver misses the intent of the sender.[15] My oldest daughter is mildly autistic. One of the major struggles she has involves communicating her ideas to us. The difficulty is that she employs language in ways that those hearing her do not understand.

---

[13] Hans-Georg Gadamer, *Truth and Method* (New York: Seabury, 1975). Gadamer was highly influenced by his professor at Marburg, Martin Heidegger, and his existentialist philosophy that embraced the validity of nonhistorical meaning in the individual.
[14] I once had an encounter with a Buddhist "evangelist" that illustrates the pragmatic nature of many. He adamantly declared that his philosophy of life "really worked!" My response was a bit of propositional truth: it only "works" if it leads to eternal life.
[15] This begs the question why a deconstructionist would ever write anything.

So, for example, when asked a question that requires a yes or no answer, she, more often than not, answers, "I know." It has taken us years to figure out that she is not claiming knowledge but she means, "no." We have come to the conclusion that she does not navigate homonyms very well. Because of these kinds of "wiring" difficulties, communication with Hannah can be very difficult. Sometimes we have no idea what she is saying. Because she uses words in an autonomous way, communication is difficult, if not impossible. I do not deny that the gap between the writer and the reader creates two horizons. The question is what do you do with the phenomenon? It does not seem reasonable to make the horizon of the reader the magistrate over meaning because it undermines communication.

My second problem builds on the former but adds the dimension of who and what is the object of our investigation. God (the Who) inspired the Word of God (the What) to communicate to human beings (revelation). The idea of an autonomous text and the lack of propositional truth that accompanies many versions of it fly in the face of the doctrine of revelation (which is why we preach and teach the Bible in the first place). The divine, omnipresent, omniscient, transcendent God stands outside of human interpreting communities. He is the ultimate truth, the ultimate proposition, if you will. It stands to reason, then, that his Word that reveals his person, works, and desire does not have a plurality of meaning. Revelation as communication demands a coherent and concrete expression of the truth. If meaning resides in the fusion of horizons between the reader and the text, conflicting results are inevitable.

That is not to say that there is not a horizon of the reader. The classic defense of authorial intent as the location of meaning will help us to understand the horizon of the reader. In his 1967 book, *Validity in Interpretation*, E. D. Hirsch Jr. describes verbal meaning as "whatever someone has willed to convey by a particular sequence of linguistic signs and which can be conveyed (shared) by means of those linguistic signs."[16] He was describing the communication event involved in writing. We use words (linguistic signs) to convey what we mean. In this transference of meaning the reader does have a part to play beyond understanding the meaning. It is to apply the meaning to his/her own context. Thus, perhaps Hirsch's greatest contribution is his distinction between meaning and significance.[17] The meaning of a text cannot change; it is what the author intended. Significance, however, can and does change from individual to individual, from context to context. Significance is the meaning based on the message communicated by the author. Thus, as we exegete a text

---

[16] E. D. Hirsch Jr., *Validity in Interpretation* (New Haven, CT: Yale University Press, 1967), 31.
[17] Ibid., 8.

we understand there is but one valid interpretation (meaning) but many specific applications (significances). The horizon of the reader is about application, not meaning.

So then the first task of the preacher is receptive, not creative. That is, we do not create meaning; we receive it. We are to understand the intent of the author as can be inferred in the text. Kevin Vanhoozer offers a definition of "text" that might be helpful for us: "A text is a complex communicative act with *matter* (propositional content), energy (illocutionary force), and purpose (perlocutionary effect)."[18] In other words, the author uses words, sentences, paragraphs, etc. (propositional content) to perform something ("illocutionary force," including asserting, promising, excommunicating, exclaiming in pain, inquiring, or ordering) in order to achieve a purpose (perlocutionary effect).

We have to admit that certain things may not be totally available to us. For example, what exactly was the heresy at Colossae? Who exactly was the writer of Hebrews, or for that matter, the recipients? How exactly did the Gospel writers depend on previous Gospels? Did Q really exist? There are other questions whose answers are informed guesses but nothing more. How can we look for authorial intent in this environment? Our lack of knowledge should not bother us at all. What we do have is what is essential for our life and godliness.

Furthermore, the history of interpretation is filled with those who thought they absolutely knew the mind of the biblical writer. Fortunately, the thesis that we should know the writer better than he knows himself has been exposed for the overreaching that it is.[19] Instead, we should seek to read the text as well as any informed first-century reader would understand the text.

How Do We Find What We Are Looking For?

So, how do we go about this understanding? My procedure is a list of the basic tasks to complete. I have put them into a logical, though not rigid, order. Furthermore, as you preach a series some tasks have already been done (like reading the whole book) that do not need to be repeated. I have arranged the process into four major movements: Examine Literary Context, Identify Historical Context, Identify Canonical Context, and Proclamation. The first three involve hermeneutics while the last one concerns homiletics.

We shall begin with the investigation of meaning. There are three basic contexts that the interpreter of Scripture should understand: the literary context, the historical context, and the canonical context. I prefer not to use

---

[18] Kevin J. Vanhoozer, *Is There Meaning in This Text? The Bible, The Reader, and the Morality of Literary Knowledge* (Grand Rapids: Zondervan, 1998), 228.

[19] Friedrich Schleiermacher, *Hermeneutics and Criticism, and Other Writings*, trans. and ed. Andrew Bowie (Cambridge: Cambridge University Press, 1998).

commentaries until I am deep into the literary context of a passage. More often than not I will not look at a commentary until after I have made my provisional translation and understand, at least in general contours, the literary context—though occasionally something perplexing will send me scrambling for help before that. There is no hard and fast rule regarding when to use resources. As a rule of thumb, do your own investigation and then look at the commentaries. Far too often we substitute reading a favorite commentary over the Scriptures themselves. Let's avoid that error.

Examine Literary Context

The literary context should be the dimension of the text where you spend most of your time. Here we ask and answer all the most important questions regarding the author's message. This includes establishing the text, the text-type, genre, and how the author uses it to produce the message of the whole book. This is where we apply much of what we teach in seminary. To investigate the literary dimensions of a passage is to seek to understand the author's goals in communicating. There are five basic tasks to complete in this step. The literary context comprises the first five steps in our process. They are as follows.

LITERARY CONTEXT

Basic Tasks to Complete

1. Cursory reading of the whole text (the whole book). Identify the text-type.
2. Identify the genre of your section (narrative, hortatory, expository, or procedural).
3. Pragmatic translation (establish the text; parse and identify verbal forms; syntactical analysis; basic provisional translation).
4. Identify the macrostructure (boundary features, including internal cohesion; internal fit)
5. Identify the flow of thought (semantic structure analysis of an expository/hortatory text).

1. Cursory reading of the whole text. We begin with a cursory reading of the whole book. This is a major step that we often neglect for a variety of reasons. Regardless of the reason for neglect, we should make it our first goal to read afresh the entire book. As we read the book, we ought to be looking to identify first the text-type of the book. This is often called the genre of the book, but I prefer "text-type" to separate it clearly from a later category.

In the New Testament, there are three basic "text-types": epistolary, narrative, and apocalyptic. Identifying a book as one of these text-types is easy and intuitive. Letters fall in the category of *epistolary*, books relating a historical sequence of events are *narratives*, and the book of Revelation is the only *apocalyptic* book in the New Testament. Understanding the book's text-type tells us what literary conventions we might expect and, perhaps, helps us to avoid some serious errors in how we approach the text. Our text is the Gospel of John. We can easily see that it is a narrative—it is telling a story. We will expect to see sequences of events that (sometimes subtly) make a theological point rather than just relating bare events.

2. *Identify the genre of your section.* Assuming we are interpreting a distinct passage instead of the whole book, we should now identify the genre of that section. In a narrative text-type the writer will employ a variety of forms to make his/her points. These are really embedded genres within a larger framework. Within the larger framework of "narrative" we can see imbedded genres to compose the larger story. For example, a major figure may make a speech, engage in conversation, tell a parable, or perform certain acts.

A book's text-type sets up a series of expectations. For example, if we read "once upon a time" at the beginning of a text, we expect the text to follow the conventions of a fairy tale. Unicorns, fairies, leprechauns, and the like would be normal. They would be abnormal, however, in a book that purported to be a historical narrative. In other words, a piece of literature will employ a series of conventions that would be familiar to the reader. This familiarity will also spawn some "genre-bending" as a writer breaks or bends the conventions to make a point. The convention is, in these instances, the point of departure for the writer to bend the genre's rules (often with quite a bit of significance).

For simplicity's sake I call these forms within a text-type genres. They fall into four broad categories: narrative, hortatory, expository, and procedural. A narrative genre is often called a pericope in Gospel studies. It is a self-contained story, narrative of an event, or a series of events. A hortatory genre is when a writer/speaker is giving a series of commands to elicit a response or action from his/her hearers. For example, the epistle to the Hebrews is often called a hortatory letter because it is a call for endurance. Likewise, many speeches in the Gospels are hortatory. An expository genre argues a thesis, which is often intended to cause the hearer/reader to act. This can cause confusion with the hortatory genre. The difference between the genres is in the writer/speaker's method for causing the reader/hearer to act. Is it a series of commands or a carefully plotted argument that demands a response? The former is hortatory; the latter is expository. Finally, there are procedural genres. These are step-by-step instructions on how to do something. An example would be the instructions on the tabernacle in the Old Testament. Procedural genres are rare in the Bible and do not occur in the New Testament. As a result, we can focus our attention on the first three when we are identifying genres in the New Testament.[20]

A careful—often repetitive—reading of the section under consideration is necessary to identify its genre. The Farewell Discourse of Jesus in the Gospel of John is best described as hortatory.[21] It is a speech of Jesus reported by the evangelist, in which the Lord does not simply argue a thesis but gives a series of commands to his disciples.

At this point in the process we have read the whole book again to gain familiarity and identify its text-type. We have also carefully read the section that we seek to interpret more closely. We then determine the specific genre of our text, which will lead us in interpreting it. Next we will dive deeper into our text.

3. *Pragmatic translation.* We begin our close inspection with a pragmatic translation of the text. I am assuming you have basic familiarity with Greek at this point. If you do not, we can still continue, but you must deal with these issues on a secondary level, depending on what others tell you about the text rather than seeing it for yourself. Use a conservative translation that employs a rather literal approach to the text. Translations like the NIV and the NLT have their place, but my experience has been that they are insufficient when closely examining the text. I prefer a more "formal equivalent" translation like the NASB or an "optimal equivalent" translation like the HCSB.

We are not producing a translation for public consumption. We are translating to see the text in its original language. We want to see the text's conjunctions, tenses, and syntax (i.e., classify participles, genitives, etc.). We want to be able to see the Greek text behind any translation, including our own. Bible software, websites, and classic language references are indispensable at this stage. At first this might take a long time, but the more you translate the quicker it will go.

---

[20] As evidence of the problem we have with preaching today, it is telling that we have preached hundreds of "how-to" sermons though there is not a single procedural genre in the whole NT!

[21] Often "Farewell Discourse" is described as a genre in itself. See my article "Farewell Discourse" in Joel B. Green, Jeannine K. Brown, and Nicholas Perrin, eds., *Dictionary of Jesus and the Gospels* (Downers Grove, IL: IVP, 2013). There I was following the literary convention of referring to the type of scene in which a heroic figure calls his disciples and gives final instructions as a "farewell genre." In essence, this is a scene within a narrative that is employing a hortatory genre. Here I am speaking in broader terms.

As we translate we should check for any significant textual variant in the UBS apparatus. We should make prayerful and informed decisions regarding what the original text was. A few caveats are in order here. First, the preacher should never discuss a textual variant from the pulpit. You don't have time for that, some people are not ready for that, and the ultimate decision is all that is important. That being the case, how do you handle a textual issue? I do one of two things. I either offer my own humble-but-accurate translation (without comment), or I use a version for that day that agrees with me. "Today," I might say, "I will use the NASB because I feel it translated my text more clearly." There are venues other than Sunday morning to handle textual variants in the manuscript tradition. The wise pastor will find time to inform his people on these matters at these other venues.

Second, weigh the importance of variant. Almost any stretch of text will have some sort of variant in the manuscript tradition. Most of them do not affect the meaning of the text in any significant way. Read through the options; if it is a matter of spelling, inclusion or omission of an article, uses of synonyms, or other matter that does not affect the meaning of the text, do not address it in the study.

After establishing the text, you should begin to translate it. As you do so, parse and identify all verbal forms. This will tell you a great deal of information about the prominence and type of action being portrayed. Sometimes it makes a great deal of difference whether an action is progressive, discrete, or perfective. Bible software will do this for you, but see the cautions above.

You should also watch carefully for any syntax issues that may affect interpretation. The difference between a subjective and objective genitive, for example, may have great significance for the meaning of a text.

It is here where you will also do any pertinent word studies. Word studies have been the preacher's shiny coin for many years. He will on occasion pull the coin out and dazzle his hearers with secret and esoteric knowledge. Unfortunately a great many of the word studies I have heard from pulpits have been poorly done and often poorly applied. I could pull example after example of abused Greek words, but space will not permit; instead let me give just a few guidelines.

First, avoid thinking in terms of a "technical sense" to certain words. There are only a few words in the Greek New Testament that appear to have a "technical sense," but even these may not *always* have this technical sense. Take, for example, πίστις ("belief") and its cognates. Yes, it is used in "a technical sense" at certain places for saving trust in Christ—but not in every place. In John 2:23–25 (and other places) there are those who believe but don't really believe. It is also likely that Titus 1:6 refers to "faithful children" (HCSB), not "children who believe" (NASB). The same is true of other words such as "justification" and "righteousness."

Second, avoid anachronisms. Many anachronisms are the result of overvaluing etymology. Don't think that the etymology (the component parts of the word) exposes its meaning. To be blunt, the etymology of the word is next to useless in determining a word's meaning. Furthermore, classical usage or modern usage of a word is also irrelevant for a study. Why? Because words change over time. So, when studying the New Testament, look for the meaning of the word roughly between 100 BC and AD 100.

Third, avoid dumping the entire semantic range of a word into a single instance in your text. You should instead choose the range of meaning that fits your context. Occasionally a writer will express double entendre, but it is rarer than usually preached.

Fourth, avoid English cognates. The Greek word δύναμις (*dunamis* "power") does *not* mean "dynamite," ποίημα (*poiema* "that which is made") does *not* mean "poem," and οὐρανός (*ouranos* "heaven") does *not* mean "uranium." Exposing such ignorance does not get us one step closer to a correct interpretation.

We could go on, but let's get to the point of word studies. Every Greek word of the original text is inspired. Occasionally a word employed by the author has a unique emphasis or nuance that is inexpressible in English. For example, in Hebrews 4:13, after describing the power of the Word of God as a sharp, two-edged sword, the writer warns that "all things are naked and exposed to the eyes of Him to whom we must give an account." The word "exposed" is a translation of the Greek word τραχηλίζω. It literally means to "*take hold of by the neck*; . . . , as a metaphor drawn from ancient custom, either of making an enemy face his conquerors by a sword fixed under his chin, of fastening a lock grip on an opponent in wrestling, or of bending back the head of a sacrificial victim, ready for the knife."[22] It is pronounced "*trachelizō.*" Can you hear "trachea" when you say it out loud? Here is powerful imagery unavailable in English. We are naked, and the Word of God has left us defenseless before God. This is indeed a powerful warning.

While it is probably important for the listeners to hear the Greek word in the example above, normally it will not be necessary to mention the actual Greek word in your sermon. More often than not you can simply say something like, "the imagery presented by the original is . . ." There is a great need to streamline our teaching to the information needed by the congregation. We

---

[22] Timothy Friberg, Barbara Friberg, and Nerva F. Miller, *Analytical Lexicon to the Greek New Testament* (Victoria, BC: Trafford, 2006), s.v. τραχηλίζω.

should resist the impulse to show our learning and/or intelligence; doing so is only self-promotion. Instead we feed his flock.

You should end up with a basic provisional translation of the text. It should reflect the choices you made in your establishment of the text, matters of aspect and verbal tense, and your syntactical analysis. It might be a bit wooden or not sound just right, but it should reflect your reading of the Greek text.

4. *Identify the macrostructure.* You want to accurately segment your text. By this, I mean we should accurately identify the beginning, ending, and major movements within our text. We do not want to "lop off" the head or the tail of our text. We are looking for the higher-level divisions above the paragraph. We lose major components of the text's meaning when we pick it up too late or break it off too soon. There are many times when the concluding portion of a macrostructure segment sets the meaning for the whole section. Poor work with macrostructure risks missing the message.

Every text is formed by adding blocks of text (constituent levels) that are arranged in a hierarchical structure. The author gives linguistic markers, or "boundary features," that indicate these changes. In Greek, major boundary features can be conjunctions (δέ, διό, καί, οὖν, τότε, etc.), markers of time or space, summary statements, introductory statements, rhetorical questions that introduce a new topic, sometimes a vocative, change of participant(s), changes in verb elements (tense, aspect, mood, or person), chiasm, inclusio, tail-head linkage, hook-words, and repeated noun phrases.[23] Some of these boundary features (such as conjunctions) often signal both higher- and lower-level boundaries (i.e., within a larger segment as well as between larger segments). Close attention to context is essential for recognizing boundary features.

In the next chapter I will describe my methodology for finding the macrostructure of a text. For now, we need to understand the importance of the overall structure. The context of a passage affects greatly its meaning, sometimes in terms of theological emphasis. The genealogy in Luke's Gospel, for example, is in an unusual place. Instead of being at the beginning (as in Matthew), it appears in chapter 3 after Jesus' baptism. Unlike Matthew's genealogy, which begins with Abraham and moves forward chronologically, Luke's genealogy begins with Jesus and goes backward to Adam. After the genealogy, Luke recounts the temptation narrative with the last two temptations reversed from Matthew's order. What do we make of this? In my opinion, Luke runs the genealogy backward in time to end with Adam, the son of God. We are thinking of the garden and the fall when Jesus, the Son of God, is driven into

---

[23] See, e.g., John Beekman, John Callow, and Michael Kopesec, *The Semantic Structure of Written Communication*, 5th revision (Dallas: SIL, 1981).

the wilderness for his temptation. The reordering of the temptation then mirrors the description of the fall in Genesis 3:6. As the fruit was "good for food, and that it was a delight to the eyes, and that the tree was desirable to make *one* wise" so too were Jesus' temptations aimed at appetite, possessions, and personal status. Putting the text in this context leads us to see Jesus as the last Adam, who reverses the fall for us.

Context can also affect the application of a passage. Both Matthew and Mark contain parable chapters (13 and 4 respectively). However, the order of parables is different. I think this is the case because the writers had different purposes. In Matthew, the explanation of the parable of the Sower is followed by the parable of the Tares. Reading the two together suggests Matthew intended an application of the former to be found in the latter. Namely, although there are some who only appear to be Christians, it is not our job to root them out, lest we harm someone unintentionally. When we read Mark, we find the parable of the Lamp under a Basket immediately follows instead. In this order, we contemplate the parable of the Soils in terms of our fruitfulness.

Needless to say, understanding how the writer organized the larger structures of the book is *very* important. We should work hard at clearly understanding the structure of a text.

5. Identify the flow of thought. Once you have divided your text into its basic macrostructure it is time to identify the structure of the text itself. By structure I do not mean the grammatical structures like independent and subordinate clauses, but how the writer employs these items to build a mental representation (communication) to change the mental state of the reader (purpose). This enterprise is often called "discourse analysis" or "textlinguistics." It involves identifying the flow of thought at the lower structures (clauses, sentences, paragraphs, etc.) so that you clearly understand what the author/speaker is communicating. Although it sounds complicated, cumbersome, and perhaps annoyingly time consuming, it is (after learning the process) one of the most useful tools for communicating the meaning of a biblical passage.

There are quite a number of ways to track the flow of thought and do discourse analysis. None are perfect, and a few are based on what I feel are suspect theoretical foundations. Even those from better theoretical foundations (Rhetorical Structure Theory, Arcing, and Semantic and Structural Analysis, to name just a few) have their issues. However, if we are going to do good discourse analysis, our method will have to address some basic issues.

First, good discourse analysis will address the three aspects of discourse: unity, prominence, and coherence. Unity, formed by "identifiable and isolatable semantic units," is the hierarchical structure of the text.[24] Any stretch of text is composed of a series of interrelated hierarchically arranged grammatical structures. The second aspect of communication is prominence. In the structural hierarchy there must also be a hierarchy of importance, if it is a well-formed discourse. The author usually highlights some constituent as important. This takes place on a variety of levels; the highlighting of the overall structure will be referred to as "peak." In lower-levels we'll refer to "emphasis" and "highlighting." The idea of prominence/emphasis is almost entirely missing in the pulpits today. The third aspect is coherence. "In general, by coherence is meant that the constituents of a unit will be semantically compatible with one another."[25] A good method will always seek to identify the unity, prominence, and coherence of any span of text.

Second, the individual constituents are identified in terms dealing with meaning and not only grammatical function or subordination. It is not enough simply to indent subordinate clauses and to line up major clauses. Grammatical diagramming is not much better in this matter. Because humans are clever, we may *do* things with what we say that are not necessarily the content of our words. This phenomenon is called "semantic skewing." For example, when we say, "If you touch that wire, you will be shocked," we are probably not describing a simple cause and effect relationship in a conditional sentence. What we are *doing* with our words is a command. "Don't touch that wire." In the other direction, if we say, "If you save your money, you will be wise," we are advocating saving. Both are actually imperatives in meaning, so we should identify them as such and not as conditional sentences. A sound approach to discourse analysis will take semantic skewing into account.

Third, discourse analysis interprets the text from the top down (higher structures to lower structures). When writers set out to communicate to their readers, they will have a topic in mind, an assignment to write on, a problem to address, etc. The writer then builds an outline of the text and tackles each component part. While it is organized from the larger to the smaller structures, it is composed line by line. It is this phenomenon that we will be tracking.

As mentioned in the introduction, I follow a methodology developed by translators called "semantic and structural analysis" (SSA). I will describe the theory in more detail in chapter 2. For now I want to describe briefly the theory and its benefits for preachers.

Developed by a group of translators for Wycliffe's research arm, the Summer Institute of Linguistics, an SSA identifies the relationships of meaning in

---

[24] Ibid., 20.
[25] Ibid., 21.

all levels of discourse (hence "semantic"). Beginning with the results of our observations regarding macrostructure, the section under consideration is broken into the building blocks of any discourse, propositions (roughly synonymous to clauses in English). M. Larsen states, "[P]ropositions group together into larger and larger units. . . . In narrative texts, for example, propositions unite to form propositional clusters; these clusters unite to form semantic paragraphs; semantic paragraphs unite to form episodes; episodes unite to form episode clusters; episode clusters unite into parts; and these unite to form a discourse."[26]

These linguistic elements relate to one another in a hierarchical structure. That is, there is a system of elevation and subordination that arranges the linguistic items into a meaningful expression. This hierarchy should be more than just noted (as simply indenting subordinate clauses does); we should define what they do in communication with a finite set of relations called "communication relations." At this stage the analyst assigns communication relations to the propositionalized sentences/clauses within the unit. These propositions will group together to form proposition clusters that will relate to one another with the same types of communication relations (because we are dealing with meaning, not simply grammar). We continue with this method through the higher levels until we have mapped the relational structure of the whole text under consideration.

What we generate by this process is a representation of the writer's rhetorical plan. This rhetorical plan will generate our sermon outline. Thus, instead of some intuitive understanding, what we have is an outline produced through close inspection with methodological rigor. With minimal effort this process can become second-nature to you and extremely helpful in sermon design.

Identify the Historical Context

At this point we have done quite a bit of work with our text and should have more than a basic idea of the meaning of the text. However, there is more work to do. Our second step is to identify the historical context. Ancient texts have a historical context to them that affects their interpretation. *When* something is said or done is often as important as *where* it is said. We need to investigate and be familiar with the historical milieu of the text and how that might influence the interpretation of the expressions in the text. The basic tools here are commentaries but especially background commentaries, atlases, encyclopedias, and dictionaries.

---

[26] Mildred Larson, *Meaning-Based Translation: A Guide to Cross-Language Equivalence*, 2nd ed. (Lanham, MD: University Press of America, 1997), 299.

Blomberg describes two areas of historical context: "perspective" and "mindset."[27] Perspective refers to the shared material between writer and reader. Mindset refers to a mental attitude or inclination. To this we will add a third area—historical events that may affect the interpretation.

HISTORICAL CONTEXT

Basic Tasks to Complete

1. Investigate perspective.
2. Investigate mindset.
3. Investigate historical events.

1. Investigate perspective. Here we ask, "What are the shared presupposition pools between writer and reader?" Writers have a series of expectations of their readers. Though these expectations are sometimes more ideal than specific, the writer expects recipients to have certain knowledge. This will shape how the author will address the reader. For example, if the author expects his readers not to know Aramaic, he might translate certain important words (as John does in the Fourth Gospel). On the other hand, if he expects the reader to know a certain language, then he may simply transliterate certain words (as Mark does with Latin terms in his Gospel). The author and the intended reader will also share a series of presuppositions. These are conventions, norms, events, well-known people, or assumptions shared between the author and the reader. For example, a newspaper article written in 2014 can refer to "the president" without identifying which president because all who read will understand the reference to Barack Obama. Likewise, a person writing in 2007 could make the same statement but refer to George W. Bush. The reader and the author share the same presupposition so a longer reference is unnecessary. This phenomenon is particularly acute when dealing with ancient texts because we must work to understand the shared presupposition pool and not import foreign ideas into it.

When references are unknown we must avoid any interpretation based on a guess of the intended referent. For example, I have heard, even from conservative pulpits, that the Colossian heresy was Gnosticism. Thus, when Paul states at 1:19 "That in Him all the fullness ($\pi\lambda\acute{\eta}\rho\omega\mu\alpha$) was pleased to dwell" and 2:9

---

[27] William W. Klein, Craig L. Blomberg, and Robert L. Hubbard Jr., *Invitation to Biblical Interpretation, Revised and Expanded* (Nashville: Thomas Nelson, 2004), 229–30.

"that in him dwells all the fullness (πλήρωμα) of the godhead bodily" he refers to a Gnostic belief. In certain types of Gnostic philosophy the highest god emits a series of emanations (aeons) that are increasingly less divine until the last aeon deposited the demiurge, the creator god. The pantheon of aeons was called the fullness (πλήρωμα). Thus, Paul is saying that Christ is the πλήρωμα, the fullness, filling the Gnostic doctrine with Christian meaning. Space prohibits discussion of all the problems; however, let us note that the Gnostic doctrine quoted in its fullest form is not known before the second century (many years after Colossians). Furthermore, Paul nowhere identifies the Colossian heresy. We have no grounds to say that Paul's use of the word πλήρωμα is informed by a Gnostic conflict. Do we not have enough in the statement, as it stands, to understand what Paul is saying? Absolutely. Christ is not a lesser god but the fullness of God in bodily form—as to that we do not have to guess at Paul's meaning. Guessing at an unknown referent usually leads to error.[28]

How do we know how to identify such shared presupposition pools? The rule of thumb is to be a minimalist rather than a maximalist. In other words, interpret from the most probable and leave the "likely" or "possible" alone.

2. *Investigate the mindset.* Here we ask, "What is the cultural environment? What are the relevant political, civic, and religious institutions and how would they affect the meaning of the text?" Sometimes the political world is directly mentioned. For instance, the Pharisees clearly are worried about Rome's response to Christ at John 11:48: "Then the Romans will come and remove both our place and our nation" (HCSB). At other times it seems to be the environment that may explain some matters. For example, Pilate is known from historical records to be brash, arrogant, and cruel. He seemed not to care what offended the Jews. Yet the Gospel records show him bending over backward and almost forced to crucify Jesus. Some have argued against the historicity of John for this reason. However, when we dig a bit deeper we see that Pilate had a very powerful patron in Rome, Sejanus, the captain of the Praetorian Guard who administrated the empire for Tiberius. At the beginning of Pilate's reign, he was acting under Sejanus's cover. Sejanus was put to death, however, for treason. Thus by the time of Christ's arrest the last thing Pilate wanted was civil uproar.[29]

Knowing how the Idumean Herod became King of Judea also puts the Magi's visit at Matthew 2 in a different light. Herod was appointed king by the Roman Senate in 40 BC. He won his kingdom by military force in 37

---

[28] To appeal to a Gnostic background here is to run the risk of interpreting Paul to mean that Christ is a lesser deity, since the πλήρωμα was not the substance of the unknowable, highest god.

[29] Paul L. Maier, "Sejanus, Pilate, and the Date of the Crucifixion," *CH* 37 (1968): 3–13.

BC.³⁰ It does not take much imagination to realize the shock of Persian wise men standing before an *appointed* king asking, "Where is he who is born king of the Jews?"

3. *Investigate historical events.* Next we ask, "What historical events may be affecting the text?" One of the biggest mistakes in interpretation on a scholarly level is to identify a reference in historical records with the "backdrop" of a passage or book. One of the most commonly cited references is the *birkhat ha minim*—"the blessings against the heretics"—and the council of Jamnia around AD 85. Some surmise that this council marks the formal split between Christianity and Judaism. Thus, almost anything that smacks of conflict between Christians and Jews in the NT is dated around or beyond AD 85, most notably the Gospels of both Matthew and John. Yet it is the height of speculation that this council exerted such influence or even existed.³¹ This is not to say that historical events have no influence on biblical texts; they do. However, the key is to exercise control and restrict ourselves to events to which the text directly alludes. Some of these historical events are recorded in the Bible. Sometimes these are scriptural allusions (such as a reference to the exodus), or it may be recorded in one of the Gospels or Acts (such as Paul's mentioning of the founding of the church at Thessalonica).

Identify the Canonical Context

Not only is there a macrostructure to the book as a whole; there is a canonical and theological structure that the book also fits into. This canonical context appears in two dimensions: covenant and theology. The major tasks to complete are to investigate these areas.

CANONICAL CONTEXT

Basic Tasks to Complete

1. Investigate covenantal dimensions.

---

³⁰ Andreas J. Köstenberger, L. Scott Kellum, and Charles L. Quarles, *The Cradle, the Cross, and the Crown* (Nashville: B&H Academic, 2009), 61.

³¹ See e.g., P. L. Mayo, "The Role of the Birkath Haminim in Early Jewish-Christian Relations: A Reexamination of the Evidence," *BBR* 16 (2006): 325–44; and J. P. Lewis, "Jamnia, (Jabneh) Council of," *ABD* 3:634–37. David Whenam notes: "The eschatological traditions of the gospels, especially of Mt. 24/Mk. 13/Lk. 21, may indicate that the events of 66–70 A.D. themselves (rather than the Jamnian Council) were seen by Christians as marking the decisive break with Judaism." David Whenam, "The Enigma of the Fourth Gospel: Another Look," *TynBul* 48 (1997): 152.

2. Investigate theological dimensions.

1. Investigate covenantal dimensions. The Bible is both old covenant and new covenant (the word "testament" should be translated "covenant"). Interpreting the different genres of the old covenant requires the Christian exegete to discover both the original meaning and the Christian appropriation of that meaning. In the new covenant (our subject) we are dealing with later progressive revelation, but in many ways it grows from the older covenant. Understanding the old covenant, therefore, helps in finding the correct interpretation. Sometimes understanding the context of an Old Testament quotation or an allusion benefits the interpretation. For example, one does not understand the book of Hebrews apart from the book of Numbers and the wilderness generation. At other times the New Testament reference is a specific fulfillment. When reading apocalypse, people should be prepared to saturate themselves in the Old Testament in order to understand apocalyptic allusions and symbolism. The New Testament is the fulfillment of the promises of the old covenant and is produced in the society that the old covenant generated. We do well to pay attention.

2. Investigate theological dimensions. At this point we should also investigate the theological dimension of our text. Because the biblical book is the work of God as well as a human author, the theology presented will agree across the canon. In the New Testament there exists diversity of perspective and emphases but not diversity of theology. The New Testament is best described as unity within diversity. Check your conclusions with other passages that deal with the same issues. If your conclusion conflicts with simple, direct propositions from other passages, modify your conclusions.

Proclamation

Now we start building a bridge from the exegesis to the exposition, from the text to the sermon. I suggest six major tasks to complete in the formation of the sermon. The first three tasks are transitional; they build the bridge from the world of the text to the world of the hearer. The main elements of the bridge are identify the main idea of the text (MIT); identify the purpose of the passage; convert the MIT into the main idea of the message (MIM). The first two are on the text side of the bridge; the last two are on the sermon side of the bridge. We'll begin on the text side.

PROCLAMATION

Basic Tasks to Complete

1. Identify the main idea of the text (MIT).
2. Identify the purpose of the passage.
3. Convert the MIT into the main idea of the message (MIM).
4. Use the MIM to develop the outline of the sermon from the outline of the text.
5. Develop each movement of the sermon by explicating, illustrating, and applying the text.
6. Write the conclusion and introduction.

1. Identify the MIT. Sermon textbooks have long suggested that the sermon should have a controlling idea, a point.[32] In an expository message the point of the sermon should be a result of your study and built off the point of the text. Thus, the bridge to the sermon begins with an accurate description of the main idea of your passage. We will call this the MIT.

The MIT should be a single sentence in the past tense that expresses the entire content of your passage. It should not be overly complicated or convey all the detail of the passage; instead, it should be a simple statement that encapsulates your passage. If you get this wrong, the entire sermon will be off kilter at best. Some of the hardest work of the sermon is to get this right.

2. Identify the purpose of the passage. The purpose of the passage should be in harmony with the MIT, but it is not exactly the same. You should be asking yourself, "What is the writer trying to get me to do?" Remember that communication has the intent to modify the state of the reader. So what is the attempt? Is the writer admonishing an action or attitude? Does he prohibit an action or attitude? Is the basic purpose to inform? What does the writer want us to do with the information? Keeping in mind the macrostructure of the whole book and how your passage works within that macrostructure will help keep you on track.

Let me illustrate with a common mistake (one I have committed myself). Luke 8:22–25 relates the familiar story of Jesus stilling the storm. Earlier in

---

[32] See, e.g., Daniel L. Akin, Bill Curtis, and Stephen Rummage, *Engaging Exposition* (Nashville: B&H Academic, 2011), 129–32, to whom I am also indebted for the terminology "MIT," "MIM" (below), and "Bridging." See also Olford, *Anointed Expository Preaching*, 75. He states: "To craft an expository sermon we must first crystallize the *theme* of the text or unit of Scripture under consideration. . . . We must capsulize the subject in one word, phrase, or sentence—'the big idea,' the core of the message, the sermon in a nutshell."

my preaching career, I preached this text from the point of view that Jesus cares about the "storms of your life." Thus, I declared, "Jesus will often still the child rather than the storm." What I did was twofold: (1) I missed the MIT and the purpose of the passage, and (2) I preached a refrigerator magnet's message rather than the text.

A closer inspection of the text and the surrounding text could have alleviated this disaster. By examining the text we see the payoff of the pericope comes in verse 25 when the disciples ask, "Who can this be? He commands even the winds and the waves, and they obey Him!" (HCSB). The point is that he has authority over nature. By examining the surrounding text this interpretation is borne out in the sequence of pericopes that follow. They all will comment on Jesus' authority over different dimensions of reality. The next passage is the story of the Gerasene demoniac: Jesus has authority over the supernatural. The next is the raising of a little girl and the healing of the woman with the matter of uncleanness: Jesus has authority over sickness and death. Who is this man? He is a man with the authority of God.

The MIT of Luke 8:22–25 should be, "Jesus displayed his divine authority." The purpose of the text was not to reassure Christians in trouble but to reveal who Jesus is. Thus the MIT is not simply a restatement of the event, "Jesus stilled a storm," but is a distillation of what point the text is making.

3. Convert the MIT into the MIM. On this bridge to the sermon we first convert the MIT into the MIM, a tool to help the preacher express the meaning of the text to the contemporary audience. It should provide the conceptual framework to develop the sermon outline. It should be a statement that is as simple as possible, in the present tense, and often appropriates the purpose of the passage.

In an expository message the MIM is more about expressing the sermon structure than developing it. In other models the preacher is asked to develop the sermon by asking heuristic questions of the MIM (how? what? etc.). I have no problem with this method if the text is actually answering those kinds of questions. More often than not, however, the resulting sermon is at best building off the text and at worst imposing pop religious advice on the text. The former has its place in Christian pulpits; the latter should be avoided. Our task is the expository sermon so the structure of the text is our outline. We simply need to package it for teaching and preaching.

Let's take, for example, the passage above (Luke 8:22–25). As we convert the MIT (Jesus displayed his divine authority) to the MIM we should appropriate what the author of the text wants us to do. In this case, Luke is telling the story to display Jesus' authority. While there are subthemes like Christ's care for his disciples, these are not the main point. The main point is that he is not merely a man; he displays authority over the wind and the waves . . . and they obey! This truth has implications regarding what we do with the information so that the message will have a strong emphasis on the implications of Christ possessing divine authority. I would state the MIM of Luke 8:22–25 as "People should embrace Christ's divine authority."

4. *Use the MIM to develop the outline of the sermon from the outline of the text.* If we have done our homework in studying the text we have already discovered the outline of our text. In expository or hortatory genres we use a semantic and structural analysis (or some other form of discourse analysis) to map the flow of thought of the argument or injunctions. It is my conviction that the major movements of the sermon (often called "points") should match the major movements of the text. Continuing with Luke 8:22–25, we should note that its genre is narrative, more specifically a simple problem-resolution story. As such, the outline is fairly simple, and a flow-of-thought diagram is not as helpful. As Young notes, the outline will be along these lines "Setting, Problem, (complicating factor), Resolution, Sequel."[33] I would describe the progression of events as follows:

8:22 Setting
One day He and His disciples got into a boat, and He told them, "Let's cross over to the other side of the lake." So they set out,

8:23 Problem
and as they were sailing He fell asleep. Then a fierce windstorm came down on the lake; they were being swamped and were in danger.

8:24 Resolution
They came and woke Him up, saying, "Master, Master, we're going to die!" Then He got up and rebuked the wind and the raging waves. So they ceased, and there was a calm.

8:25 Sequel
He said to them, "Where is your faith?" They were fearful and amazed, asking one another, "Who can this be? He commands even the winds and the waves, and they obey Him!" (HCSB).

---

[33] Richard Young, *Intermediate Greek: A Linguistic and Exegetical Approach* (Nashville: B&H Academic, 1992), 250.

I see three major movements after the introduction: the problem, the resolution, and the sequel (where the theological payoff is in this story). So, my sermon will have three points (or movements). Because the narrative genre unfolds the point, my sermon should as well. If we follow the outline of the text, we will naturally do so. The MIM (built off the MIT and the point of the passage) unfolds the sermon, just like the text unfolds the MIT. My outline of the text is as follows:

I. See the Plight of Man vs. Wild (8:23)
II. See the Might of Son of Man vs. Wild (8:24)
III. Embrace the Divine Authority of Christ (8:25)

At the *problem* and *resolution* stages of the pericope the narrator wants us to understand the situation of the disciples and note the solution that Christ brings. I chose to cover both ideas with the applicational verb "see." I could have just as easily used "understand" or some other verb of knowing, but I want the audience to have a mental picture of the events.

You will also notice that I borrowed from pop culture for the first two movements. Here is an attempt to connect with the everyday world of the audience (esp. ten-year-old boys and their dads) by playing off the title of one of the Discovery Channel's survival TV shows.

The last movement is the pay off. Christ asks them, "Where is your faith?" and the disciples ask themselves, "Who is this man?" Here's where we apply the MIM directly. In this movement it is a virtual restatement of the MIM, but it should not be the case in every movement. Sometimes each movement will develop some portion of the MIM. In this case, the text builds to it, so our sermon does as well. To embrace his divine authority is to exercise faith. For the lost, it begins with coming to Christ. For the redeemed it is exercising faith.

5. *Develop each movement of the sermon by explicating, illustrating, and applying the text.* There are a variety of ways to develop a sermon movement (point). I believe it helps to be as simple as possible. There are three basic elements to sermon development: explanation of the text, application of the text, and illustration of either the text or the application. To deal with these elements I use a method taught by my preaching professor called the "Text-Today" method. It will be how we generally develop sermons in this book. There are times, however, when the text itself makes the application of its movements. It would be redundant, then, to follow this way of development. Most often it works well, but it is important to experiment with developing skills in other methods as well.

In my basic approach, I explain the text in a "text" section. I will give a description of the text. In the case of Luke 8:23 (my first movement above), I describe the situation, the boat, and the weather patterns on the Sea of Galilee.

In the "today" section, I apply the movement to us today. Application is a tricky part of any sermon. I think it is best not to think of every situation to which the text would apply, but to give general areas and certain specifics and trust the Holy Spirit to make specific applications. For example, in the first movement above, "Plight of Man vs. Wild (8:23)," I make the application of human frailty. When it's man vs. wild, wild will eventually win. Then I unpack that statement in selected specific areas. For instance, we may prepare against natural disasters, but if enough of them come, or one comes at a strong enough force, we die. The same is true for health. We may have iron constitutions, or be health and exercise nuts, but eventually our bodies wear out. The general principle that we are finite creatures works for areas like retirement savings, vaccinations, and rainy day funds.

As for illustrations, they can enhance a sermon, but caution is needed because illustrations are like windows that allow light to enter a room. As House and Garland state, "Windows too large, or too many, can structurally weaken a building. Likewise, illustrations that are too extensive, elaborate, entertaining, or memorable can weaken a sermon."[34] By "illustration" I mean an example that brings your movement into sharp focus for your people. This can come in a variety of ways. You may want to illustrate with another biblical text. In the case above, the parable of the Rich Fool in Luke 12:13–21 is a good choice to illustrate the application. At times this is impractical because the secondary text requires a great deal of explanation. It may be that you could draw on news reports of those who trusted that they could outwit, outlast, and outplay the principle of entropy that pursues us all.

Other types of illustrations, such as biographies (I especially like missionary biographies) and parables (both from the Bible and elsewhere) are often powerful. When illustrations are not well crafted or presented well, however, they can be trite. I especially avoid poetry of all kinds (except biblical poetry, of course), but some find it useful. Specific historical events may also supply rich illustrative material. Finally, statistics have been overused in our pulpits and often have a chilling effect on the audience. We have all been subjected to misinformation given in the form of statistics. Most of us are familiar with the old saying "figures don't lie, but liars do figure." Be very careful when using statistics.[35]

---

[34] H. Wayne House and Daniel G. Garland, *God's Message, Your Sermon: Discover, Develop, and Deliver What God Meant by What He Said* (Nashville: Thomas Nelson, 2007), 85.

[35] See House and Garland's discussion. Ibid., 83–86.

The placement of a movement's illustration is not set in stone. You may want to illustrate the meaning of the text itself as a clarifying tool. You may, instead, want to illustrate the application. Whatever you do, you do not want to clutter your point with too many illustrations; one major illustration per movement is a good rule to follow.

Types of Illustrations

Biblical Texts
Anecdotes (including personal observations)
News Reports
Biographies
Parables (biblical and non-biblical)
Poetry (including songs)
Historical Lessons
Statistics

When using illustrations, be careful to document your source material. Furthermore, because some of the most memorable parts of the sermon are the illustrations, be sure you are illustrating the text. Be wary of forcing an illustration into service when it does not fit. It is better to have no illustration than the wrong one.

Repeat this development procedure for each section of the sermon. Although not a rigid rule, I feel it best to follow the same pattern throughout the sermon that you use in the first movement. Instead of "lather, rinse, repeat," it's "explain, apply, illustrate, repeat."

6. *Write the conclusion and introduction.* The next thing I do is write the conclusion of the sermon. A good conclusion ends the sermon with a powerful appeal so that the end of the sermon is the beginning of a life-changing decision. We do well to prayerfully compose a good conclusion, although as Carter, Duvall, and Hays note, "Unfortunately, sometimes preachers deplete all their energy, discipline, and time in the writing of the body of the sermon and then have nothing left to develop a solid, creative, and powerful conclusion."[36] Resist the temptation to "wing it." I have fouled up many sermons by an ill-crafted conclusion.

---

[36] Terry G. Carter, J. Scott Duvall, and J. Daniel Hays, *Preaching God's Word: A Hands-on Approach to Preparing, Developing, and Delivering the Sermon* (Grand Rapids: Zondervan, 2005), 32.

The conclusion should summarize the entire sermon and call for a decision by the hearers. If your outline has been applicational, you've been doing this through the whole sermon. Though I like an illustration that encapsulates the MIM, these are often the hardest to find. I quickly try to make a global application to both Christians and non-Christians in my audience.

In sermons where I have already applied and illustrated the main point, as in the sermon outline above, it would be redundant to find another global illustration and apply it. In these cases I move rather quickly into the invitation and appeal.

Finally, I write the introduction to the sermon. We should compose it last because only when we have completed the sermon do we know what we are introducing. We may have an idea of what we are going to do, but the actual composition should come last.

The introduction should be short. The major mistake most preachers make is spending more than half of their allotted time on the sermon's introduction to the sermon. Invariably this leads to rushing toward the end of the sermon, which is arguably more important.

There are three major components to a good introduction: (1) orienting your audience to the issue you are addressing, (2) communicating the MIT, and (3) presenting the MIM.

The orientation sets the stage for the rest of what you do. It can be something outside the preacher himself—a video clip, dramatic skit, or interpretive dance—but the transition from an external orientation to the sermon is difficult to accomplish and usually runs the risk of being excessively long and irrelevant. "Communicating the MIT" can be as short as a single statement. Finally, "presenting the MIM" makes the point of your sermon and usually transitions nicely to the body of the message.

Again, using Luke 8 above, the MIT is "Jesus Displayed His Divine Authority." The MIM is, "Everyone Should Embrace the Divine Authority of Jesus." To introduce the sermon, I want to orient my audience to the situation in which everyone finds themselves. To whom do they place the trust of their souls? I oriented the hearers with an illustration of people who had made the tragic error of misplaced trust, which can be disastrous.

SERMON SKETCH

TEXT: Luke 8:22–25
TOPIC: Life in the Wild
MIT: Jesus Displayed His Divine Authority
MIM: Everyone Should Embrace the Divine Authority of Jesus.

INTRODUCTION

1. Orientation: He lived in Crooked River Ranch, OR. His friends knew him as a young physician affiliated with Mountain View Hospital in Madras, OR. The young doctor convinced one of his friends to allow him to treat a minor problem at his home. It wasn't long until that friend recommended other friends to see this doctor. He would dispense medicine, treat infections and injuries, and performed at least one out-patient (minor) surgery. Three of the patients saw him in their own homes. I'm sure that these friends each thought it was a great deal. Imagine their surprise when the Redmond Police Department arrested the man. His crime? Impersonating a doctor. Specifically the charges were "one count of second-degree assault, two counts of identity theft and recklessly endangering another person, and a count of manufacturing or delivering a controlled substance."[37] These six people should have known better. First of all, the man pretending to be a doctor was only twenty-two years old—Doogie Howser was a TV character, not a real person. Second, physicians don't usually do house calls anymore. That's a quick trip to the malpractice lawsuit. One police officer put it this way, "How many times do you have a doctor at your home do surgery on you?"[38] Not only did the impersonator have no affiliation with Mountain View Hospital, he had no medical training whatsoever. They trusted their bodies to someone unqualified, with no authority by licensing boards to practice medicine and no professional training. This had all the makings of a disaster. In *whom* you trust matters.

---

[37] "Police: Fake Doctor Performed Surgeries" (1 May 2009). Cited 26 July 2011. Online: http://www.upi.com/Odd_News/2009/05/01/Police-Fake-doctor-performed-surgeries/UPI-67101241201956/#ixzz1TEDAy2cs.

[38] Patrick Cliff, "Man Did Surgeries as a Fake Doctor, Police Say," *The Bulletin* (30 Apr 2009). Cited 16 Jan 2014. Online: http://www.bendbulletin.com/apps/pbcs.dll/article?AID/20090430/NEWS0107/904300383/1004/NEWS01nav_category"NEWS01.

This is even more important in the matter of your soul. To whom or what have you entrusted your soul? The Christian answers, "In Christ." Christ did not just claim to be our Savior; he displayed his divine authority, his credentials. We find one of these demonstrations of divine authority in our text this morning, Luke 8:22–25.

2. MIT: In this text, Jesus displayed his divine authority by his command over nature. Surrounding texts will describe his authority over demons, disease, and death. Altogether his authority is shown to be God's authority.

3. MIM: Everyone should embrace the divine authority of Jesus. Let's look at the Bible to see how the story unfolds.

OUTLINE

I. See the Plight of Man vs. Wild (8:22–23)

A. Text

1. Storms raged on the Sea of Galilee.

2. Jesus fell asleep in the boat.

3. The disciples were struggling against the waves.

B. Today

1. In the struggle against nature we will lose.

2. We will lose physically (we will die).

3. We will lose spiritually (we will not be right enough to go to heaven).

C. Illustration

Ehow.com contains an article on how to cheat death (difficulty rating: easy).[39] The truth is that death is inevitable unless the Lord returns in our lifetimes. The wild waits at our window for the opportune moment, and it will eventually catch us. But we are not without help.

---

[39] "How to Cheat Death." Cited 1 August 2011. Online: http://www.ehow.com/how_2083549_cheat-death.html.

II. See the Might of Son of Man vs. Wild (8:24)

A. Text

1. The disciples were *not* asking for a miracle.

   Perhaps they wanted him to bail water! ("Here is water what doth hinder us from bailing?")

2. He displays his authority.

   The wind and the waves must obey him. There was calm.

B. Illustration: Types of Authority

1. Government (legitimacy—power is recognized).
2. Societal structures (a sanctioned power—voluntary to some degree).
3. Jesus' power is independent of human recognition. It is innate and overpowering.

C. Today

1. We tend to seek human solutions rather than the might of the Son of Man.
2. His ability/authority is beyond what we can ask or imagine (Eph 3:20).

   Transition: We act this way because we haven't fully come to grips with this truth. We should . . .

III. Embrace the Divine Authority of Christ (8:25)

A. Text

1. An embarrassing question: Where is your faith? (Suggests that embracing his divine authority is a matter of belief.)
2. An incomplete recognition.

B. Today

1. What would it look like if a believer fully embraced Christ's divine authority?

>   a. Doubt would be gone.
>
>   b. Faith would be regularly exercised.
>
>   c. Risk would be seen in the light of his sovereignty.
>
> 2. What would it look like if a non-believer embraced his divine authority?
>
>   a. He would turn from his sins.
>
>   b. He would make Christ the Lord of his life.
>
>   c. He would place his trust in Christ's sacrifice for his sins.

C. Illustration: A Fatal Lack of Trust

> The Great Fire of London began on the night of September 2, 1666. The fire devastated the city of London, which was already under siege from the black plague. The magnitude of the property loss was staggering. After burning for four days, some 430 acres—as much as 80 percent of the city proper—was destroyed, including 13,000 houses, 89 churches, and 52 guild halls. Thousands of citizens found themselves homeless and financially ruined. But, amazingly enough, only 16 people died in the fire (some say only six). It should have been less. The first death was completely unnecessary. The fire began "as a small fire on Pudding Lane in the bakeshop of Thomas Farynor, baker to King Charles II. At one o'clock in the morning, a servant woke to find the house aflame. The baker and his family escaped, but a fear-struck maid perished in the blaze." She refused to jump from an upper story window onto a neighboring roof and burned to death.[40]
>
> *Invitation:* Jump! Trust as if your life depended on it!

The above theory will be fleshed out as I walk us through the Farewell Discourse of John's Gospel. I will first describe my theory of literary structure and thought-flow analysis in more detail. This will be the content of the next chapter.

---

[40] Anniina Jokinen, "The Great Fire of London." Cited 1 August 2011. Online: http://www.luminarium.org/encyclopedia/greatfire.htm.

CHAPTER 2

Analyzing Literary Structure and Flow of Thought

BEFORE we begin our walk-through of Jesus' Farewell Discourse in the Gospel of John, we need to lay the groundwork for the methodology I will use for both the macro- and microstructure of the text. Each methodology is based on a fundamental understanding of human language I touched on in the previous chapter.

The Theory

My theory regarding a narrative text-type like the Gospel of John is that it is made up of constituent units that are not necessarily all narrative pericopes. Any text-type can have a variety of different genres. It might help to think of this with the term "macro-genre" for a text-type and "imbedded genre" for the major building blocks of the book.

For example, in a narrative text-type a wide variety of imbedded genres are at the author's disposal. He or she will certainly employ narrative discourse (the events of a story) but may also report an exchange of conversation, a parable, a speech, a poem, or even a song. A major book like the Gospel of John will be composed of a wide variety of these smaller genres, which will undoubtedly be arranged in varying levels of complexity.

These smaller constituents are arranged in a hierarchical order within the book's larger structure to impart meaning. The name and number of these microstructures vary according to the book's complexity. In the Gospel of John the largest unit is the entire book. Then there are two major constituents commonly called "books." These books are composed of different types of episodes. These episodes are composed of cycles. The cycles are composed of units. The units are composed of paragraph clusters. Paragraph clusters are made up of paragraphs. Paragraphs are made up of proposition clusters. Proposition clusters are made up of propositions.[1] When the writer sits down to write a book, he uses the larger units as an overall framework. Then the writer will compose the larger framework clause by clause, forming propositions, proposition clusters, paragraphs, paragraph clusters, etc. So, while the author writes the narrative from the bottom up, we should interpret it from the top down (i.e., from the higher structures to the lower).

This attention to literary structure is more than a literary exercise. It is an exercise in meaning and theology. This point is particularly missing in much biblical theology today. The arrangement of a book says a great deal about the theology and the purposes of the book. The interpreter of Scripture should be able to understand the entire book before he attempts to teach it. Again, I have failed here many times. I was committed to "preaching through a book," but all I did was preach serially (i.e., in a disconnected manner) through the book because I did not understand the larger structure.

Internal Divisions in the Fourth Gospel

Books
Episodes
Cycles
Units/scenes
Paragraph clusters
Paragraphs
Proposition clusters
Propositions

Discerning the Structure of a Whole Book

Familiarity with the whole book we are preaching is necessary. The following is presented in order both to understand the entire Gospel of John and how the Farewell Discourse completes the purpose of the Gospel and to illustrate the boundary features of a narrative text-type. Space will not allow a full

---

[1] We could, of course, descend to words, letters, and diacritical marks, but below the proposition we risk getting bogged down in minutiae that has little exegetical payoff. The proposition is roughly equivalent with the sentence but includes the clause. The English idea of a sentence does not exactly correspond to the ancient Greeks who thought in terms of colons (branches) or clauses.

description of all these boundary features, but we can illustrate them quickly enough in the Gospel of John.

The macrostructure of the Fourth Gospel is recognizable and generally agreed upon in scholarship.[2] It is made up of a prologue, two major "books," and an epilogue. We look briefly at the boundary features of these units to set the stage for our investigation, to illustrate the type of linguistic and literary markers to look for in these features, and to make our initial survey through the whole Gospel.

The Gospel begins with a well-defined prologue in 1:1–18. The first formal feature we see is an *inclusio*, a bracketing feature that marks the outer boundaries of a unit with a repeated word or thought. The repeated word is "word" (λόγος) in 1:1 and 14. In verse 14 begins a summary paragraph marked by broad, general statements that runs through verse 18. A shift in person, topic, time, and place begins at 1:19 and marks the beginning of a new section.

The Book of Signs

The first book (sometimes called the "Book of Signs") starts at 1:19. This section introduces the gospel story with a remarkable three days including the witness of John the Baptist and the gathering of the first disciples (1:19–51). The segment is marked by a shift in space/time and participants interacting with John (after whom Jesus takes over as the main character), and each shift is marked with the phrase "the next day" (ἐπαύριον). The chapter ends with the promise of seeing greater things, which foreshadows the content of the major section: seven signs as Jesus offers himself to Israel.

The Cana Cycle

The first set of signs is called the Cana Cycle because the first and last signs occur at Cana of Galilee. The beginning employs content and a linguistic marker that connects it to 1:19–51 but shows a movement to a new section. In content it shows continuity with "on the third day" (τῇ ἡμέρᾳ τῇ τρίτῃ; i.e. on the same day as previously mentioned). The linguistic marker is the "and" (καί) that begins the section by connecting to the previous section and beginning a new section. Verse 12 ends with a summary statement followed by another καί and an introductory statement to the temple cleansing (2:13–22). Conceptually the next two chapters hang together around the idea introduced in 2:23–25, those who believe but don't really believe. Nicodemus is an example of one such man. He believes Jesus (that Christ is a teacher come from God) but needs to be born again. The rest of chapters 3 and 4 deals with the

---

[2] See, e.g., Andreas J. Köstenberger, *John*, BECNT (Grand Rapids: Baker, 2005), 10–11.

issues surrounding salvation and true belief. Nicodemus is the foil for explaining the necessity of being born again, while John the Baptist (or the evangelist) describes the nature of true belief (3:35–36). The woman at the well and her Samaritan village are examples of true belief (approved by Jesus in 3:31–32). The section ends with the summary statement of 4:54 "Now this again was the second sign that Jesus did having come out of Judea into Galilee." These types of summary statements are common features at the ending of a constituent and help us note the beginning of the next. Also, note that the healing of the nobleman's son was at Cana of Galilee. Furthermore, the recall of the water being turned to wine groups these signs together (4:46).

The Festival Cycle

Chapter 5 begins with a common boundary feature in John, "after these things" (μετὰ ταῦτα). Three more signs follow through 10:42, each taking place at a religious festival, which explains why these events are often called "the festival cycle." Each of these signs involve rising opposition as Jesus reveals who he is. First, the healing of the lame man in chapter 5 is the catalyst to a Sabbath controversy with the Jews. Second, Jesus' statement that "My Father is still working, and I am working also" (5:17 HCSB) is a claim to deity. Third, as God works on the Sabbath (he is exempt to the Sabbath) so too does his Son, as 5:18 makes clear.[3]

"After these things" (μετὰ ταῦτα) introduces scenes in 6:1 and 7:1 as well.[4] 6:1 transitions to the feeding of the 5,000 with a change in location, space, and participants. John presents Jesus as the new Moses as many of the features are reminiscent of the wilderness wandering (the miraculous bread, sitting in "camps," the setting in the wilderness). A change in participants and setting takes place in 6:16–21 where Jesus walks across the water and stills the storm. Here the theological point also builds on OT texts. God is the One who "treads on the waves of the sea" (Job 9:8 HCSB).[5] The two scenes together set the stage for the Bread of Life Discourse that follows. Not only is Christ the prophet like Moses, he is divine. The key themes through the discourse are related to these propositions.

Instead of seeking free food (6:26) or signs (6:30), the people should eat the bread of life. Jesus defines the metaphors in verse 35: "eating" means coming to Christ, and "drinking" means believing in him. Thus, there are really more of those who come to him but don't "believe." Those who do believe

---

[3] See Craig S. Keener, *The Gospel of John: A Commentary* (Peabody, MA: Hendrickson, 2003), 1:646.
[4] Note, however, that not every use of μετὰ ταῦτα denotes a major break. See its occurrence at 5:14 that is used as a minor transition.
[5] The LXX reads "the one who walks on the sea, like it was ground." See Keener, *John*, 1:673.

in him have satisfaction and security in Christ (6:35–40). He emphasizes his heavenly origins (6:41–51) and concludes with the declaration that he is real food that leads to eternal life in contrast with the manna in the wilderness (6:52–58). The matter of God's selection and true belief come to a head when some of his "disciples" turn back (6:60–71). Yet, even though Peter affirms that they have no other place to go, "We have come to believe and know that You are the Holy One of God!" (John 6:69 HCSB), Jesus notes that there are those who don't believe (one—Judas Iscariot—is a devil).

The transition to the next unit is, as noted above, a change in place and time introduced by "after these things" (μετὰ ταῦτα). John will narrate the last six months of Jesus' public ministry in chapters 7–8.[6] The topic of unbelief continues through the brothers of Jesus (see 7:5) who demand he reveal himself at the Feast of Tabernacles. Jesus, however, is elusive with them, "For not even His brothers believed in Him" (7:5 HCSB). This question of belief sets the stage for the discussion at the festival, which is marked by conflict with the Judean leadership over the Sabbath healing in chapter 5 (7:14–24). It seems to be common knowledge that the leaders are seeking an opportunity to kill Jesus, even though they flatly deny it (cf. 7:20, 25). Jesus boldly proclaims that he is from the One they do not know (7:28). Insulted, they seek to arrest him but are divinely prevented (7:30). Jesus' activities accelerate through this chapter. He comes in secret (7:10), then he preaches openly (7:14), then he shouts loudly an invitation to those who thirst (7:37).[7] As a result, questions and misunderstandings abound regarding Jesus' messianic status (7:40–44). In 7:45–52, the temple guards must explain why they did not arrest Jesus. They question if the assistants have "been led astray," noting none of the rulers or Pharisees have believed in him. Nicodemus, who offers a plea for fairness, is accused of being a Galilean. The foundation for the leadership's rejection of Jesus is that "no prophet arises from Galilee" (7:52 HCSB). The truth is that several did (see e.g., Jonah and Nahum), and the child who was to be born in Isaiah 9:6 brings light in Galilee of the Gentiles. This provides a conceptual link to the discourse that begins at 8:12: Jesus is the light of the world.[8]

Chapter 8 continues the activities of Jesus at the festival and continues both his revelation of his identity and the discomfort it causes the Judean leadership. It is strongly connected to the previous vignette by "again, Jesus said

---

[6] Köstenberger, *John*, 224.

[7] Andreas J. Köstenberger, *A Theology of John's Gospel and Letters*, Biblical Theology of the New Testament (Grand Rapids: Zondervan, 2009), 217.

[8] I am assuming that the passage known as the *pericope de adultera* (7:53–8:11) was not original to the Gospel of John. However, the point is still valid that there are strong conceptual links if it was original. In my opinion, if included it disrupts the flow. However, it can be construed as an illustration of those who walk in darkness. So our main point is still valid whatever we think of this thorny textual issue.

to them . . ." (πάλιν οὖν αὐτοῖς ἐλάλησεν). Jesus presents himself as the light of the world, but this sparks a debate regarding the validity of his testimony (8:13–18) and the identity of his Father (8:19–20). The vignette closes with the notation (again) that by divine providence no one arrested him (8:21).

Another pericope is strongly connected to the previous by "Then He said to them again . . ." (Εἶπεν οὖν πάλιν αὐτοῖς). Jesus discloses his destination, the spiritual destination of his interlocutors. More questions ensue and Jesus' answer borders on a claim to divinity ("When you lift up the Son of Man, then you will know that I am" [ἐγώ εἰμι, 8:28]). The pericope is closed by the summary statement, "As He was saying these things, many believed in Him" (8:30 HCSB).

The next pericope opens with an address to those who "believe" in him. In actuality, it highlights the lack of belief in these Judeans. They deny their enslavement because they are the descendants of Abraham (8:33, 39). In truth they are the children of the father of lies, the Devil (8:44). In the following discussion Jesus clearly claims God as his Father (8:42, 54). He was seen by Abraham (8:56), and he existed before Abraham (8:58). The last statement, clearly using the absolute "I am" (ἐγώ εἰμί), sparks an attempt at stoning, fulfilling Jesus' words that they never denied: "But now you are trying to kill Me" (8:40 HCSB). The pericope ends with Jesus leaving the temple complex, again, with the suggestion that he was divinely protected by God.

The following narrative is joined to the previous by "and" (καὶ), suggesting that we are still reading scenes conceptually tied together, although there is a change in spatio-temporal elements marking the beginning of a new scene. We are still reading about signs in the midst of controversy. The second identification of Jesus as the light of the world (9:5), veiled references to Jesus' departure, and the controversy with the Pharisees regarding healing on the Sabbath provide more conceptual links to suggest that the larger literary unit continues. This scene reports the healing of a young man who had been born blind, by all accounts the sixth sign.[9] Oddly enough, Jesus himself is a background character in this scene. Once he heals the young man we do not see him again until 9:35.

After the healing, the young man is taken (perhaps better "dragged"[10]) to the Pharisees because he was healed on the Sabbath. In the interrogation that follows, the Pharisees are befuddled by the contradiction between their

---

[9] The contrast to the earlier Sabbath healing could hardly be stronger. The age of the men, their response to the Pharisees, and the response to Jesus is 180 degrees apart.

[10] Ἄγουσιν (present active indicative 3rd plural, to lead, or drag, hence "bring" or "brought" in certain contexts) may have an involuntary connotation here (see 18:28).

unbelief and the implication of this miracle.[11] No doubt, the obstinacy of the young man added to their frustration ("You don't want to become His disciples too, do you?" [9:27 HCSB]). The scene highlights and expands the questions about Jesus' messianic qualifications pondered by the crowd earlier. The young man is thrown out of the synagogue (not unexpected from 9:22), Jesus finds him, the young man calls Jesus "Lord," (9:38), and worships him. Jesus' comment in 9:39 (HCSB), "I came into this world for judgment, in order that those who do not see will see and those who do see will become blind," provides the commentary on the whole scene. The meaning of Jesus' words is not lost on the Pharisees who heard him. Their question "We aren't blind too, are we?" (9:40 HCSB) is the foil upon which the Good Shepherd Discourse that follows (10:1–40) is built. Here we change from a narrative imbedded genre to an expository genre (similar to the Farewell Discourse to follow interspersed with narrative portions).

The Good Shepherd Discourse is composed of two major scenes confirmed by the transition from the Festival of Tabernacles to the Festival of Dedication (10:22). In the first scene (10:1–21) Jesus expands an illustration from sheep herding. The Pharisees' sins remain (9:41) because they are trying to enter the sheepfold apart from the shepherd (10:1). Two of the famous "I am" statements follow and form twin planks to his argument. He is the door of the sheepfold (10:2, 7, 9) and the good shepherd (10:11, 14). He is the entrance to the flock of God (and those coming in another way are simply thieves), and as the good shepherd he dies for the flock. He makes a clear allusion to the resurrection in 10:17. The first scene is closed by a description of the response to Jesus' words. Those who hear are divided between belief and unbelief; the latter is quite derogatory of both Christ and those who follow him (10:20). This, again, highlights the mounting opposition in the second half of the Book of Signs.

The second scene of this unit is 10:22–39 (40–42 concludes the whole discourse). Although the scene has shifted to the winter months and the Feast of Dedication, the topic continues through the shepherd/sheep motif. The same question regarding Jesus' identity is still on the table. The exasperated statement "tell us plainly" leads Jesus to resume the discourse. Here the point is that they don't believe because they are not his sheep. In 10:30 Jesus declares "My Father and I are one," making explicit the implied claim of being the good shepherd (cf. Psalm 23). The reaction is to accuse him of blasphemy, which Jesus denies. Jesus withdraws to the place where John first baptized.

---

[11] Often called a "hard" miracle because of the intransigent nature of blindness from birth. See, Keener, *John*, 1:776, citing Sophocles, *Oedipus coloneus*.

The reference to John concludes the Festival Cycle and forms an *inclusio* with chapter 1 that introduced the Book of Signs. There is a finality about Jesus' revelation to Israel. John, who was introduced in chapter 1, is proven to have been correct about Jesus: "Everything John said about this man was true" (10:41 HCSB). Again, faith is emphasized with the note that many believed in him.

The Pivotal Sign: Raising Lazarus

The Book of Signs has one final sign, and it will be costly to Jesus. The ultimate sign is the raising of Lazarus. The last sign is a scene made up of five movements. Jesus receives the news of Lazarus and decides to return to Judea (11:1–16). His arrival at Bethany (a change in space and time) marks the new movement with Martha (11:17–27). Another change in place begins the third movement (11:28–44), where Mary is encouraged. Finally, a group goes to the tomb (another change of space) where Lazarus is called out of the tomb (11:38–44). Belief is again highlighted throughout the scene. In 11:15, it will be the result of the sign and Jesus is glad about it. Jesus' conversation with Martha is to move her to correct belief (cf. 11:26). It is also true of Mary (11:40). The result of the raising of Lazarus is both belief and unbelief. Many of the Jews believed, but some reported to the Pharisees what had happened. This leads to the decision to arrest and kill Jesus (47–57), making Lazarus the proverbial straw that broke the camel's back.

Chapter 12, composed of five scenes, finishes the Book of Signs. The first three scenes note that many believed through the witness of a living Lazarus. These scenes are a meal and an anointing with Lazarus present at Bethany (12:1–11), the triumphal entry (12:12–19), and the announcement of his hour (12:20–36). Note also that while many believe, the Jewish leadership wants Lazarus dead (12:10) and bemoan "the whole world has gone after Him" (12:19). The last two scenes form a formal conclusion to the Book of Signs. John notes the failure of the Jews to believe in him (12:37–43—cf. 1:12). See especially 12:37 that notes although they saw the signs, they did not believe. Finally, Jesus offers salvation one last time (emphasizing belief) (12:44–50).

The Book of Glory

The Book of Glory is the next major literary unit in the Gospel of John. It is composed of three major episodes: (1) Jesus with his disciples (13–17), (2) Jesus' "hour" (the arrest trial and crucifixion, 18–19), and (3) Jesus' glorification (the resurrection appearances, 20–21). I will not dwell on 13–17 here, for that will be the subject of the rest of the book. However, we will say now that the sustained scene of Jesus preparing his disciples for his absence will help us understand the purpose of the Gospel better.

The Arrest and Trials

Chapter 18 shows Jesus' arrest and three hearings. In the first two hearings Jesus appears before the Jewish leadership (18:1–27) and the Roman governor (18:28–33). In the midst of the Jewish phase a third "trial" belongs to Peter who denies that he knows the Lord.

18:1–14 shows Jesus' arrest by the Roman cohort and the temple officers. Jesus is clearly in control of both his fate and the situation. He identifies himself to the cohort, and they cannot help but to bow down. In doing so, he both fulfills Scripture (18:9) and provides a reason for Peter to stop resisting (18:11). The paragraph concludes with a subtle reminder of Caiaphas's prophecy that one man would die for the nation.

18:15–27 contains a series of cut-aways between Jesus' trial and Peter's less formal trial. Peter will fail utterly, but Jesus fulfills his duties perfectly. In 15:28, Jesus is taken to the Praetorium, to Pilate. Pilate declares him to be innocent of insurrection (his kingdom is not of this world—18:33–38) but lets the crowd select Barabbas for release.

Jesus' Death and Burial

The events surrounding Jesus' death and burial are narrated in chapter 19. In 19:1–16 Jesus' death sentence is completed. Pilate and the Jewish leadership exercise a legal tango to reach a death penalty. 19:17–24 relates Jesus' crucifixion. Next, 19:25–27 shows Jesus taking care of his last earthly responsibility—seeing to the care of his mother. 19:28–37 records the death of Jesus (note the fulfillment of OT prophecies here). And finally, 19:38–42 records the burial of Jesus.

The Resurrection Appearances

Chapter 20 of John concludes the main narrative in four scenes and a preliminary conclusion. In 20:1–10, the disciples find the tomb empty. John notes that they did not understand the Scripture that he must rise again from the dead, suggesting that faith has not yet happened. The second scene is 20:11–18 where Jesus reveals himself to Mary. In the third, 20:19–24, Jesus reveals himself to his disciples with the note that Thomas was missing.

20:25–29 records Jesus' encounter with Thomas, where the emphasis is on belief. Although Thomas has declared unless he has tactile contact with Jesus he will not believe, Jesus appears and offers that to him. Thomas's declaration "My Lord and my God" is the ultimate confession in the Gospel of John. After Thomas's confession of faith, Jesus, in a sense, addresses the reader through Thomas, "Because you have seen Me, you have believed. Those who believe without seeing are blessed" (20:29 HCSB). John applies this to the audience in 20:30–31, noting that belief is the purpose of the book ("that you may believe"). It is possible for those who have not seen or touched to believe.

The Epilogue
The final chapter is often suggested to be a later addition because 20:30–31 is such a natural conclusion. Yet, there is some unfinished business, namely the restoration of Peter and correction of misinformation regarding the beloved disciple.[12] Chapter 21 comprises two scenes and a final conclusion. The first scene, 21:1–14, shows Jesus' third appearance to the disciples. In 21:15–23, Peter is restored and told he will glorify the Lord in his death. One final matter of cleanup is the clarification about the perpetuity of the beloved disciple. Finally, 21:24–25 concludes the whole of the Gospel, glorifying the deeds of Christ.

This type of broad survey should be part of any preacher's "to do list" when preparing for a sermon series. The structure of the book informs the reader of the purpose of the book as well as any statements given by the author. In this case we have both. The given purpose in 20:30–31 is that "you believe." It has long been questioned just what "believe" means. Does it mean "come to believe" or "believe strongly" or perhaps both?[13] The answer ultimately lies in the structure of the book. We have seen the Book of Signs as Jesus' revelation to Israel, and they failed to believe the signs (see 12:37). Obviously, in the first half of the book "come to believe" is the main focus. Yet, the second half of the book focuses on Jesus' disciples.

Discerning the Structure of Your Passage

Once a general overview is completed and we have a good idea of the overall structure of the book, it's time to look at the specific section we are going to study. The initial survey, however formal, is a necessary step regardless of the number of sermons preached from the particular text.

Because the Farewell Discourse is a reported speech, it will fall into the hortatory or expository genre. Clearly John reports the speech to get his readers to do something. In this case, Jesus is preparing his disciples to thrive during his absence. Thus, this reported speech is best described as hortatory.

---

[12] See Köstenberger, *John*, 596. I will discuss the interchange between ἀγαπάω and φιλέω later. For now, I think clearly Peter is allowed to confess Christ three times to match the denials.

[13] The manuscripts show this deliberation through a small but notable variant. πιστεύω ("believe") is presented as a present subjunctive in some of the earliest Alexandrian manuscripts. This would suggest "believe continually." The aorist subjunctive reading (which has wider geographic support and early support) would suggest "come to believe." However, both tenses may be interpreted broadly, and as such an interpretation based solely on the tense is suspect.

Therefore, it is very important to track the flow of thought to understand what Jesus commands.

The method that I use to track this thought flow is called a semantic and structural analysis (henceforth SSA). It was developed by Beekman and Callow in their book, *The Semantic Structure of Written Communication*, to assist translators. Mildred Larson's book *Meaning-Based Translation* represents the most modern description of this method. What follows is my own adaptation of this method.[14]

Boundary Features

The preacher should begin by examining the scenes for major breaks that would naturally divide the text into its largest divisions. The Farewell Discourse is made up of units, paragraphs, propositional clusters, and propositions. The initial survey will not note breaks lower than the paragraph level.

Greek discourse, like all languages, signals to the reader/hearer the discourse boundaries. In Greek some of the more common discourse boundary features are represented in the following chart.[15]

Discourse Feature	Explanation	Example
Conjunctions	Structure words that bring a specific constraint on its context.	And, now, but, therefore, etc.
Indicator (deixis) of time or space	Phrases or words that introduce a new time or spatial setting. This may occur at the end or the beginning of the constituent.	John 13:30 (HCSB) "...And it was night."
Summary statements	Statements that generalize a great deal of information in a broad description. Normally marks the end of a constituent. The next passage is beginning a new section.	"So the church throughout all Judea, Galilee, and Samaria had peace, being built up and walking in the fear of the Lord and in the encouragement of the Holy Spirit, and it increased in numbers." Acts 9:31(HCSB)

---

[14] Mildred Larson, *Meaning-Based Translation: A Guide to Cross-Language Equivalence*, 2nd ed. (Lanham, MD: University Press of America, 1997).

[15] See, e.g., John Beekman, John Callow, and Michael Kopesec, *The Semantic Structure of Written Communication*, 5th revision (Dallas: SIL, 1981), 80; Stanley E. Porter, *Idioms of the Greek New Testament*, Biblical Languages 2 (Sheffield: Sheffield Academic Press), 301; Stephen Levinsohn, *Discourse Features of the Greek New Testament: A Coursebook on the Information Structure of the New Testament*, 2nd ed. (Dallas: SIL, 2000), 271–84; and George H. Guthrie, *The Structure of Hebrews: A Text-Linguistic Analysis*, repr., NovTSup 73 (Leiden: Brill 1994; Grand Rapids: Baker, 1998), 12.

Discourse Feature	Explanation	Example
Rhetorical questions introducing a new theme or topic	Questions that are not meant to get information but to make a statement.	"What then? Should we sin because we are not under law but under grace? Absolutely not!" Romans 6:15 (HCSB)
Vocatives	Nouns of direct address are often used (but not always) to introduce a new topic.	"Dear friends, let us love one another . . ." 1 John 4:7 (HCSB)
Change of participant	Someone else becomes the focal topic. In the example, one of the signals of a new unit is that the participant shifts from Philip to Saul.	"Philip appeared in Azotus, and he was traveling and evangelizing all the towns until he came to Caesarea. Meanwhile, Saul was still breathing threats and murder . . ." Acts 8:40–9:1 (HCSB)
Chiasm and inclusio structures	Inclusio is an instance of a reflexive parallelism that marks the beginning and end of a stretch of text. Chiasm, a reflexive parallelism in each clause (often an A-B-B'-A' pattern), is found in small clause structures, less often in larger structures.	Inclusio "In the beginning was the Word . . . The Word became flesh . . ." John 1:1 and 14 (HCSB) Chiasm "A-The Sabbath was made B-for man B'-not man A'-for the Sabbath"
Hook-words	A word near the end of one section that appears again at the beginning of the next.	"So He became higher in rank than the angels, just as the name He inherited is superior to theirs. For to which of the angels did He ever say . . ." Hebrews 1:4–5 (HCSB)
Redundant participant noun phrases	The previous main participant is "introduced" again.	"Jesus departed with His disciples to the sea . . ." Mark 3:7 (HCSB)

John employs conjunctions uniquely in his Gospel. The following table briefly illustrates how John uses conjunctions to connect higher level divisions.[16] The major conjunctions used to connect sentences are "therefore" (οὖν), "now" (nontemporal δέ), and "and" (καί). In addition to explicit conjunctions, John also employs asyndeton (the absence of a conjunction). Each brings a unique constraint on their context that the interpreter would do well to note.

---

[16] For similar studies including other Gospels, see Buth, *"oun, de, kai and asyndeton,"* 145; Levinsohn, *Discourse Features*, 70; and most recently, Runge, *Discourse Grammar*, 51.

Conjunction	δέ	οὖν	asyndeton	καί
Markedness (what the conjunction indicates, or "marks")	Development (moving the story/argument along) at both high and low levels.	Low-level development	Nothing	Addition
Meaning	The next important thing	Therefore (substantiation) Then (sequencer)	Default connective for narrative in John	And
Connection	Discontinuity	Local discontinuity	Contextually dependent	Continuity

An important feature often found at discourse boundaries is what Levinsohn calls a "point of departure." He states, "The term POINT OF DEPARTURE designates an element that is placed at the beginning of a clause or sentence with dual function: 1. It provides a starting point for the communication; and 2. It cohesively anchors the subsequent clause(s) to something which is already in the context (i.e., to something accessible in the hearer's mental representation."[17] "Point of departure" thus signals a local discontinuity and looks both forward and backward. It looks backward to relate its expression to a previous constituent, and it looks forward to provide a setting for the present statement. In an argument like the Farewell Discourse, "adverbial constituents expressing condition, reason, purpose, and other situational relations may also be placed initially in the sentence to act as points of departure."[18]

This point of departure may have one or more of the features in the chart above. One of the major features is the word order. One occurs in 13:31a to note a transition from the Last Supper scene to the speech itself. "When therefore he left . . ." ("Οτε οὖν ἐξῆλθεν) is placed before the main verb "He says" (λέγει) (called "fronting"). It provides continuity to the previous statement (by virtue of Judas's departure), but it also provides the setting for the discourse itself.

A second example offers perhaps a solution to one of the long-held problems of the Farewell Discourse: just where does one place a new unit after the vine and the branches unit? If one insists that "I have spoken these things" (ταῦτα λελάληκα) signals a discourse break or is a concluding formula alone, then the water is quite murky because the phrase (or some variation of it) is

---

[17] Stephen H. Levinsohn and Robert A. Dooley, *Analyzing Discourse: A Manual of Basic Concepts* (Dallas: SIL, 2001), 68.
[18] Levinsohn, *Discourse Features*, 8.

used four times in 16:1–7. The option defended below is that 16:4b begins the final unit. One of the reasons to begin the unit there is that it presents a significant point of departure. The fronted element, "Now, I did not speak these things to you from the beginning" (Ταῦτα δὲ ὑμῖν ἐξ ἀρχῆς οὐκ εἶπον) relates to the previous sentence while creating the setting for the present sentence. This usage indicates discontinuity that, combined with other factors, marks the beginning of a new unit. A point of departure does not necessarily demand a higher level break in discourse. It could very simply be, and often is, a local discontinuity, though when combined with other factors (like a switch in topic, tense, participant, etc.) could signal a much more significant break.[19]

Internal Divisions

The next step is to divide the largest units into their own hierarchical structure. Building blocks (usually paragraphs) comprise each of these units.[20] Each division relates to the others in a semantically unified whole that communicates the author's meaning. Typically, these paragraphs will relate to one another in one of three ways: (1) They support another paragraph. (2) They are supported by another paragraph. Or (3) they are equally prominent paragraphs. These support relations will be further defined below.

Propositions

The third step involves representing the Greek text as individual propositions in English. This is not a formal translation but an effort to represent the semantic force of the clause/sentence. For the most part, a literal translation suffices; however, occasionally a literal translation does not represent the proposition's rhetorical intent. In these propositions, the semantic intent is rendered. For example, at several places in the Farewell Discourse, Jesus employs a rhetorical question. The semantic force of these questions is not to ask a question but to state a matter prominently. To represent the force of rhetorical questions, I have marked them "(rhq)" and represented their semantic force (denial, command, etc.) as a direct statement. Thus, the rhetorical question in 16:31b, Ἄρτι πιστεύετε; ("Do you now believe?") is rendered "(rhq) you do not yet believe."

In the semantic and structural analysis that appears in the following chapters, I generally adhere to the clause structure of the text. This has been done for two reasons. First, according to the ancient rhetorical handbooks the discourse is structured in cola (i.e., "limbs" that are roughly equivalent to the

---

[19] See Levinsohn's cautions in this matter. Levinsohn, *Discourse Features*, 273–74.
[20] This is, of course, speaking in theoretical terms. In the real world of texts there is considerable skewing where what is ostensibly a propositional cluster might function as a short paragraph.

modern clauses).[21] Second, this method keeps the structure words (particles like "if," "although," "then," etc.) intact for a ready frame of reference that a more nuanced rendering often omits. The goal in the analysis below is not a smooth translation but an investigation into the semantic structure. For the present purposes, breaking down clauses into more minute constituents brings increasingly diminished returns.[22] Once the paragraphs are broken into clauses we will define the relationship between all constituents from the clauses level up with what is known as "communication relations."

Communication Relations

At this stage the interpreter identifies the communication relations between the propositionalized sentences/clauses within the unit. In doing so we are identifying the semantic relationship between clauses. In any meaningful text there is a semantic reason to add a clause, so when we identify the semantic relationship we define the reason and thus more closely identify meaning. A coherent text must relate to some previous item in the text by means of one of these relations because there is a hierarchy to human language. Even when presented with random clauses, we will attempt to interpret them in some meaningful way.

A couple of examples will be useful to show how the theory is practiced. Let's take a sentence made up of two clauses: "Talk of communication relations scares me because I think it will be difficult." There are two clauses that relate the reason for a fear. In the first clause fear is the *result* of the false notion of difficulty. The second clause (introduced by "because") states the reason for the fear. The communication relationship between the two clauses is RESULT-reason. We would display it as follows:

RELATIONAL STRUCTURE	CONTENTS
┌RESULT ────────	Talk of communication relations scares me
└reason ────────	because I think it will be difficult

Note that some words in this display and in the ones below are capitalized and some are not. The reason is that the display of communication relations also charts the phenomenon of natural prominence, the notion that some constituents are naturally more prominent than others. For instance, a command is

---

[21] Johannes P. Louw, "Discourse Analysis and the Greek New Testament," *Biblical Theology* 24 (1973): 104.

[22] See Richard J. Erickson, "The Damned and the Justified in Romans 5:12–21: An Analysis of Semantic Structure," in Stanley E. Porter, ed., *Discourse Analysis and the New Testament: Approaches and Results* (Sheffield: Sheffield Academic Press, 1999), 289.

more prominent than its grounds; a purpose clause is more important than its means. The text will display the naturally more prominent clause by the use of all caps. For example, two clauses that relate to one another in means-purpose (the first is the means of performing the purpose of the second) is displayed as means-PURPOSE.

A hortatory text like the Farewell Discourse is made up of more than simple two-clause relationships. These pairs may relate to other units in a variety of ways. Suppose we take our example above and add a third clause, "But I fear misinterpreting Scripture more." Now we have added a contrast to the mix and created a proposition cluster. We will note the semantic relation as follows:

RELATIONAL STRUCTURE	CONTENTS
┌HEAD ┌RESULT──────	Talk of communication relations scares me
│ └reason───────	because I think it will be difficult
└CONTRAST───────────	But I fear misinterpreting Scripture more.

In the display above, "HEAD" identifies the other equal constituent. In this case, it is the constituent to which the contrast is made ("HEAD" will also be used with other communication relations and simply marks the other constituent). It is contrasting both the first and second clauses not one or the other. Thus, "HEAD" is positioned between the two and connected by a bracket.

Now let us add another clause to our paragraph, "Therefore, I will study diligently." This clause/sentence will finish our paragraph. As we look at the semantic relationship between it and the surrounding context, it is best to understand it as the RESULT of the previous constituent (the reason). It is probably best to understand the "reason" to be the previous contrast. So then, the paragraph is a declaration of the intent to put forth a grand effort because the job is important. We would diagram it as follows:

RELATIONAL STRUCTURE	CONTENTS
┌reason┌HEAD ┌RESULT──────	Talk of communication relations scares me
│ │ └reason───────	because I think it will be difficult
│ └CONTRAST───────────	But I fear misinterpreting Scripture more.
└RESULT────────────────────	Therefore, I will study diligently.

Now let's suppose this paragraph is the beginning of a larger unit that describes the steps the speaker is going to take to study diligently. Let's further suppose that each of these steps are paragraph length texts. We would identify the semantic relations between the clauses that make up each paragraph then relate each of these paragraphs to our lead paragraph. Our lead paragraph would be labeled "GOAL" (i.e., to study diligently), and the paragraphs describing each component to achieve the goal (i.e., "steps") would be numerically ordered "STEP 1," "STEP 2," "STEP 3," etc.[23]

Mastering the communication relations is not particularly difficult for there is a finite set of communication relations. These relations ultimately derive from Beekman and Callow but have been modified over the years.[24] The following is a description of the major communication relations used in a hortatory discourse like the Farewell Discourse.

1. Relations with Equal Natural Prominence

In the larger structures it is sometimes more useful to use the generic term "HEAD" to describe large units that are equally prominent in the structure of the argument. In other words, these large units are used to make up a larger constituent. Within that larger constituent, the relationship between the largest segments are linear, i.e., equally prominent. Some of these will relate chronologically, whether sequentially or simultaneously. We would display them "SEQUENTIAL HEAD 1—SEQUENTIAL HEAD 2," or "SIMULTANEOUS HEAD 1," etc. If time is not in focus we call these "nonchronological" and will relate as either conjoining or alternating. The display then is "CONJOINING HEAD 1—CONJOINING HEAD 2" or "ALTERNATING HEAD 1," etc.

2. Relations with Unequal Natural Prominence (aka Support Relations)

a. Orientation[25]

(1) Orienter-CONTENT

"Orienter" is a word of feeling, thinking, or speaking. "Content" is the specific feeling, thought, or speech. This is most often seen in speech margins. The relationship is Orienter-CONTENT (with the content being naturally more prominent).

---

[23] This ordering feature can occur with any constituent. E.g., our reason-RESULT clause could conceivably have more than one reason or even multiple results (often compound clauses joined by "and"). These would be labeled "reason 1," "reason 2," etc.

[24] Beekman, Callow, et al., *Written Communication*, 112. Cf., Larson, *Meaning-Based Translation*, 297–378; and Peter Cotterell and Max Turner, *Linguistics and New Testament Interpretation* (Downers Grove: IVP, 1989), 109. The following descriptions are dependent upon these sources.

[25] Our chart of communication relations shows four, but since opening-BODY and introduction-HEAD are used in larger structures we will omit them for now.

Matthew 13:57 would be presented as follows:

```
┌ orienter ───── Jesus said to them
└ CONTENT ───── "A prophet is not without honor..."
```

(2) Circumstance-HEAD

Here the issue is the circumstance behind another event, which could be location, time, introduction, setting, or preliminary incident. Mark 1:14 would be presented as follows:

```
┌ circumstance ─── After John was put into prison
└ HEAD ─────────── Jesus went to Galilee
```

b. Chronological Relations

(1) Step-GOAL

Step-GOAL relations describe a series of events that culminate in an event. The main idea is that of intentional action. John 13:4–5 would be depicted as follows:

```
┌ step 1 ──── So He got up from supper
├ step 2 ──── laid aside His robe
├ step 3 ──── took a towel and tied it around Himself
├ step 4 ──── Next He poured water into a basin
├ GOAL 1 ──── and began to wash His disciples' feet
└ GOAL 2 ──── and to dry them with the towel tied around Him
```

(2) Stimulus-RESPONSE roles

Mostly used in conversation, stimulus-RESPONSE roles are constituents that generate a response/reaction. Unlike chronological relations, these are not always in strict sequence. Narrative roles are usually reserved for higher level constituents (above the paragraph) and will not be handled here. Those basic relations relate to sentences and paragraphs.[26]

(a) Question-ANSWER[27]

These relations are composed of a question and its answer.

Matthew 9:28 is an example of this relation:

```
┌ question ─── "Do you believe that I am able to do this?"
└ ANSWER ──── ..."Yes, Lord."
```

---

[26] These are culled from Larson, *Meaning-Based Translation*, 353–62. On the special case of conversation, Cotterell and Turner, *Linguistics*, 257–93, is very helpful.

[27] Each of the following relations in this section omits an imbedded Orienter-CONTENT ("they said, ..." etc.). For the sake of simplicity the communication relations are omitted and replaced by an ellipsis.

(b) Question-COUNTER QUESTION

In this communication relationship, the reply to the question is another question.

Look at the following simplified example from Matthew 21:23–25:

```
┌ question ─────────── By what authority are You doing these things?
└ COUNTER QUESTION ─── Where did John's baptism come from? From heaven or from men?
```

(c) Remark-EVALUATION

Here the first speaker makes a statement or remark, and this promotes an evaluation of the remark. In the example below, the evaluation is positive. However, it could just as well be a negative evaluation.

```
┌ remark ─────── "It's hot today"
└ EVALUATION ─── ..."yes, it is!"
```

(d) Remark-COUNTER REMARK

In this relationship, one speaker makes a remark. The second speaker, instead of making an evaluation, yea or nay, offers a remark that goes in another direction.

```
  remark ─────────── "The weather is really nice today."
  COUNTER REMARK ─── "It sure isn't normal for this time of year."
```

(e) Proposal-REPLY

Proposals are types of commands that offer a course of action to another (thus they stimulate a response). They may be exhortations, invitations, offers, prohibitions, suggestions, directions, challenges, etc.

```
┌ proposal ─── Come here.
└ REPLY ────── No, I don't want to.
```

c. Nonchronological Relations

(1) Restatement
(a) HEAD-equivalent

The essence of this relationship is pure restatement. The speaker/writer is saying the same thing, but (sometimes) in a different way. Luke 9:36 is described as follows:

```
┌ HEAD ─────────── They kept silent
└ equivalent ───── and in those days told no one
```

(b) HEAD-amplification

In this relationship, the essence is giving additional information, that is, expanding the knowledge and not just repeating it. The additional information may do things like clarify matters of participants, time, location, etc.

```
┌ HEAD ─────────── The postman was injured,
└ amplification ── the large brown dog had bitten him.
```

(c) GENERIC-specific

This relationship is similar to the previous in that more information is given, but this time the information is specifically related to something in the first clause. The example below specifically describes the injury (a generic term), while the example above describes how he was injured.

```
┌ GENERIC ──────── The postman was injured,
└ specific ─────── the bite severed tendons in his knee.
```

(d) HEAD-summary

"HEAD-summary" is usually used above the sentence level. Often a writer will summarize or condense general statements. The "HEAD" is usually the whole stretch of text. Summaries normally come at the end of a larger section, but may also appear at the beginning. (Cf. Matthew's familiar summary, "When Jesus had finished . . . ," which concludes a section at 7:28 but begins one at 13:53.)

(2) Clarification Relations
(a) HEAD-comparison

This indicates *a point of similarity* between two units being compared. English uses terms like "as," "like," or "than."

```
┌ HEAD ─────────── As Moses lifted the serpent in the wilderness
└ comparison ───── so must the Son of Man be lifted up
```

(b) HEAD-illustration

Usually used with relationships between larger units employing the comparison motif. An illustration is simply a large comparison. See John 16:20 (the HEAD unit) and 21 (the illustration).

[20] "Truly, truly, I say to you, that you will weep and lament, but the world will rejoice; you will grieve, but your grief will be turned into joy.

21 Whenever a woman is in labor she has pain, because her hour has come; but when she gives birth to the child, she no longer remembers the anguish because of the joy that a child has been born into the world."

(c) HEAD-manner

In these relations, the manner clarifies and supports the HEAD by providing information which answers a question, "In what way or how did the event take place?"

```
┌HEAD ────────── but the chief baker he impaled
└manner ──────── just as Joseph had predicted
```

(d) HEAD-contrast

Contrast happens when there are at least two points of difference between the two units and one point of similarity. One of the points involves an opposition. John 3:30 is a good example of this relationship.

```
┌HEAD ────────── He must increase,
└contrast ────── but I must decrease
```

(e) HEAD-comment

Occasionally, a writer will make a digression from the major point of a constituent. These digressions will be related to its target in a manner that is "off topic" from the rest of the larger unit. These may be as simple as a single line or as complex as several paragraphs. An example of the latter is Ephesians 3:2–13 where Paul interrupts his prayer for his readers with a long comment on his ministry. A shorter comment, Romans 1:25, is displayed below.[28]

```
┌HEAD ────────── and (they) worshiped and served something created instead of the Creator.
└comment ─────── who is praised forever. Amen.
```

(3) Logical Relations

The essence of logical relations is cause-and-effect. While there may be a temporal relationship/sequence, the issue is the type of cause and effect that is in view rather than time.

---

[28] Most who have described this relation also describe a HEAD-parenthesis relation. The difference is that "parenthesis" is more off topic than "comment." I have collapsed the two into one relation because the difference is not so significant that it is worth two relations. Furthermore, they place these relations under the major heading of "Association" appealing to the "off topic" nature of these relations (see, e.g., Beekman, Callow, and Kopesec, *Written Communication*, 107). I choose to place these as clarification relations because (1) the multiplication of categories is not always helpful and (2) they are in their essence clarification even if they are not strictly on topic. It makes no difference in actual exegesis.

(a) REASON-result

In this relation the proposition, which has the role of "reason," answers the question "why this result?" Often this is marked with words like "because," "so," and "therefore."

The following example is from Genesis 3:14

```
┌ reason ────────── Because you have done this,
└ RESULT ────────── cursed are you more than all cattle
```

(b) Means-RESULT

A means-RESULT relationship is one in which the means proposition answers the question "how did this result come about?" Often this is marked with words like "by" or "through." The main portion of Titus 3:5 would be diagrammed as follows:

```
┌ RESULT ────────── He saved us...
└ means ─────────── by the washing of regeneration...
```

(c) Principle-IMPLICATION

This relationship is a logical cause-and-effect relationship. It describes a principle and the implication of that principle. The following example is from 1 John 1:

```
┌ principle ─────────── God is light
└ IMPLICATION ───────── therefore His children walk in the light.
```

(d) Means-PURPOSE

The basic issue of the means-purpose relation is the question, "What was done in order to achieve this purpose?" A deliberate action is done to achieve a certain purpose. Intentionality takes center stage here. In English the words "in order that," "so that," and sometimes the infinitive indicate this usage. The following example is from Colossians 2:4:

```
┌ means ──────────── I say this
└ PURPOSE ────────── so that no one will delude you
```

(e) Grounds-CONCLUSION

The question answered is "What fact is this conclusion based on?" In English the conclusion typically uses the words "because," "so," and "must be."

```
┌ CONCLUSION ─────── it will rain soon
└ grounds ────────── the wind is blowing
```

(f) Condition-CONSEQUENCE

While a cause-and-effect relation, the condition is usually hypothetical or ambiguous. This is the familiar "IF-then" statement. The following example is from Hebrews 2:3.

```
┌CONSEQUENCE– how will we escape
└condition────── if we neglect so great a salvation
```

(g) Concession-CONTRAEXPECTATION

This relationship has an element of "unexpectedness." The expected effect has an unexpected result. In English this relation often employs the word "although."

```
┌concession──────────── the stone had been rolled away
└CONTRAEXPECTATION– although it was extremely large
```

(h) Grounds-EXHORTATION

While similar to the grounds-CONCLUSION relationship, the grounds-EXHORTATION relationship is always a command, though not all imperatives exhibit this relationship; some are means-PURPOSE. The following is Matthew 2:13:

```
┌EXHORTATION– flee to Egypt, and stay there until I tell you. ...
└grounds────── For Herod is about to search for the child to destroy Him.
```

(4) Delimitation Relations

Sometimes a proposition may relate to a concept within another proposition rather than the proposition as a whole. These are called "delimitation relations." Larson gives an example of this kind of relationship: "The man who came to town left quickly." There are two propositions here: "The man left quickly" and "who came to town." The second does not really relate to the entire first proposition but only "the man" as in, "which man." Leaving quickly has nothing to do with "who came to town." Quite often, though not always, such delimiting propositions are communicated with relative clause phrases. The propositions will either identify or describe.[29]

(a) HEAD-identification

An identification relation will distinguish one item from others. Larson's example above is identification, as is "Jesus Christ our Lord" in Romans 1:3–4.

```
┌HEAD────────── ...concerning His Son
└identification── ...Jesus Christ our Lord
```

---

[29] Larson, *Meaning-Based Translation*, 301.

(b) HEAD-description

"Description" does not identify; it gives more information about a concept in another proposition. It is often more "random" or "off topic" of the major theme of the HEAD proposition. Larson gives the example "John who was very tall, left quickly." "Who was very tall" is simply describing John and has nothing to do with leaving quickly.[30] At Romans 1:3–4 we also have two phrases that relate descriptively to "Son."

```
┌ HEAD ─────────── ...concerning his Son
├ description 1 ── who was a descendant of David...
├ description 2 ── and who has been declared to be the powerful Son of God...
└ identification ── ...Jesus Christ our Lord
```

After one learns the basic idea behind the communication relations it is often good to develop a brief chart for reference when attempting to identify communication relationships. The following chart displays the most common communication relations used in hortatory discourse.

EQUAL NATURAL PROMINENCE (i.e., no semantic hierarchy)
    Chronological
        SEQUENTIAL HEAD 1—SEQUENTIAL HEAD 2
        SIMULTANEOUS HEAD 1—SIMULTANEOUS HEAD 2
    Nonchronological
        CONJOINING HEAD 1—CONJOINING HEAD 2
        ALTERNATING HEAD 1—ALTERNATING HEAD 2
UNEQUAL NATURAL PROMINENCE (i.e., a semantic hierarchy)
    Orientation
        Orienter - CONTENT
        Circumstance - HEAD
    Chronological
        Step - GOAL
        Stimulus - RESPONSE roles
        Question - ANSWER
        Question - COUNTER QUESTION
        Remark - EVALUATION
        Remark - COUNTER REMARK
        Proposal - REPLY
    Nonchronological
        Restatement
            HEAD - equivalent
            HEAD - amplification

---

[30] Ibid.

GENERIC - specific
HEAD - summary
Clarification
   HEAD - comparison
   HEAD - illustration
   HEAD - manner
   HEAD - contrast
   HEAD - comment
Logical Relations
   REASON - result
   Means - RESULT
   Principle - IMPLICATION
   Means - PURPOSE
   Grounds - CONCLUSION
   Condition - CONSEQUENCE
   Concession - CONTRAEXPECTATION
   Grounds - EXHORTATION
Delimitation Relations
   HEAD - identification
   HEAD - description

A higher level discourse boundary may be proven to be out of order when examining communication relations. In other words, our initial assignment of paragraph structure may not fit and must therefore be adjusted. For example, something we thought was a conclusion may actually introduce the next section, or a cluster may be semantically connected to the previous paragraph rather than a part of the subsequent paragraph. We must not be afraid to make proper adjustments. We must be willing to "run up and down the ladder" to check our work and make adjustments when necessary, going from top to bottom and back again.

I have gone into all this for two reasons. First, I think it is helpful to track the flow of thought in a hortatory or expository text. Thus, in the pages to follow I will give a great deal of attention to a semantic structure analysis of the text. This helps me interpret the text but also means that I have an outline that can be faithfully rendered as the backbone of an expository message. I have discovered the outline rather than imposing it.

In the pages that follow I will display a simplified SSA for each section of the Farewell Discourse so that I can show clearly the text's major movements. The highest-level constituents of a section under consideration are the major movements of the text. These are generally the communication relations farthest to the left in our diagrams. These major movements of the text will become the major movements of our sermon. To make this more explicit I have simplified the SSAs to show mostly the higher levels.[31]

My second reason is that I hope readers will begin to track the thought flow of texts to craft messages/studies. It may be difficult at first to identify relationships and how to display them, but with practice the interpreter will gain skill in the method.

---

[31] My entire semantic and structural analysis of the Farewell Discourse is available as a PDF download at http://www.bhacademic.com/books.asp?p=9781433673764.

CHAPTER 3

Opening Movements

COMMENTATORS have generally accepted that chapters 13–17 form the Farewell Cycle of the Fourth Gospel. This cycle includes the foot washing episode (13:1–30), the farewell address (13:31–16:33), and the so-called high-priestly prayer of Jesus (17:1–26). Our focus deals with the discourse proper, that is, the farewell address itself that spans 13:31–17:26. I will defend this division below, but first a bit of orientation to a special problem regarding the Farewell Discourse.

Johannine scholars commonly suggest that this speech is actually a composite speech. Through the nineteenth century biblical scholars worked under the famous dictum of D. F. Strauss that the Fourth Gospel (including the Farewell Discourse) was (unlike the Synoptic Gospels) a seamless robe.[1] Over the years, however, this axiom has been challenged and virtually overturned. Today the opposite is the accepted paradigm, especially as it pertains to the Farewell Discourse. Simply put, most scholars see the Farewell Discourse as a redacted text. Segovia has stated it well; "Nowadays hardly any exegete would vigorously maintain that John 13:31–18:1 is a literary unity as it stands."[2] Approaching the discourse from this perspective can radically affect its interpretation, leading to a sort of redaction criticism whereby the exegete compares one version to the other version and the "editor's" redaction of the previous material. This often generates an understanding of the editor's purpose that is not readily apparent if one man wrote the text at one time. I do not believe that this view is accurate.

---

[1] David F. Strauss, *Gespräche von Ulrich von Hutten*, vol. 3 of *Ulrich von Hutten* (Leipzig: Brockhaus, 1860), xliii–iv.

[2] Fernando F. Segovia, *Love Relationships in the Johannine Tradition: Agape/Agapan in 1 John and the Fourth Gospel*, SBLDS 58 (Chico, CA: Scholars Press, 1982), 82.

My 2002 doctoral dissertation argues that the Farewell Discourse is the product of one writer at essentially one time.[3] I approached the question of unity by laying three planks: stylistic, structural, and procedural. The purpose of the stylistic plank was to test for evidence of more than one author at work. I examined the individual style-traits of the Fourth Gospel much like the FBI uses textual analysis to identify a criminal. The second structural plank was designed to investigate the possibility of a later redaction and expansion of the text. I used discourse analysis to demonstrate the coherence of the text as it stands, indicating that there is no reason to suggest multiple layers. Lastly, the procedural plank investigated the current theories that interpret a difficult transition as a literary seam (John 14:31 is the prototypical seam for many scholars).

My findings in all three planks affirmed the book's literary unity. The Farewell Discourse shows a discrete linguistic style in rather obscure criteria. It also demonstrates a meaningful semantic structure in terms of unity, prominence, and coherence. Finally, the procedure and assumptions that have led to the modern consensus of disunity have significant problems. Thus, not only does the text display a unity, but the reasons to posit disunity were insufficient to overturn the assumption of a single author producing a single product. Therefore, as my previous work has shown, there are no objective reasons to propose the literary disunity of the Farewell Discourse. With these preliminaries aside, let us now move on to interpreting and preaching the Farewell Discourse.

I will proceed through the rest of this book as if the first three steps to "Examine Literary Context" are completed. Essentially, I have already done these steps. They were (1) a cursory reading of the whole text, (2) identify the genre of our section (we have already identified it as a hortatory discourse), and (3) a pragmatic translation (you will see this as we progress). It is best to do this section by section in preparation for the sermon. The next step is that we must identify the largest sections of the whole discourse, i.e., the macrostructure.

Identifying the Macrostructure of the Farewell Discourse

In the last chapter we conducted a brief overview of the major contours of the Gospel of John. There we noted that the Book of Signs concludes with Jesus' offer of salvation at 12:44–50. The break to another major section is clear at 13:1. Here John introduces the Book of Glory but especially Jesus'

---

[3] L. Scott Kellum, "The Unity of the Farewell Discourse: The Literary Integrity of John 13:31–16:33" (Ph.D. Diss., Southeastern Baptist Theological Seminary, 2002). It has subsequently been published as *The Unity of the Farewell Discourse: The Literary Integrity of John 13:31–16:33*, JSNTSup 256 (London: T&T Clark, 2005).

time with his own: "Before the Passover Festival, Jesus knew that His hour had come to depart from this world to the Father. Having loved His own who were in the world, He loved them to the end" (HCSB). This is clear from the temporal markers "before the Passover Festival" (Πρὸ δὲ τῆς ἑορτῆς τοῦ πάσχα) and the change of topic (from invitation to loving his own).

The next major break occurs in 18:1. We noted earlier how John often organizes his narrative flow with "after these things" (μετὰ ταῦτα) or a similar sequencing reference, which we see in 18:1 (HCSB): "After Jesus had said these things" (ταῦτα εἰπὼν). There is an indication of change of location (from the garden to the Kidron Valley) and a change of genre (from prayer to a narrative of the arrest). Jesus is no longer with his own but is now moving to the end. Between 12:50 and 18:1 we see a long section that includes the narrative of the events around the Last Supper and Jesus' last words to his disciples. This stretch between 13:1 and 17:26 forms a major cycle that we will call "Jesus with his own in the world." Now we will examine this larger cycle to identify the smaller units of which it is constructed.

Most of the internal divisions within this chapter are easily identified. Two divisions, however, are more difficult to discern. The first question is where does the discourse actually begin, at 14:1 or 13:31? There are proponents on both sides of the issue (see below). The second question is similar to the first. At chapter 16, Jesus clearly transitions to the topic of the advantages of his departure, but where does that discussion begin? The transition is rather smooth and not easily discernible.

Our concern is a treatment of the discourse itself and not the whole cycle, so the first question we must answer is "where does it begin?" Most of chapter 13 contains the foot-washing scene that takes place in the Upper Room. The farewell speech itself clearly begins by chapter 14. The question is whether 13:31–38 ends the foot-washing scene or begins the Farewell Discourse.

A small group of commentators believe that these verses belong with the foot-washing scene (13:1–30) as the conclusion of the opening unit.[4] Another group holds that only a portion of 13:31–38 is the introduction to the farewell speech (generally those holding to chiasm theories).[5] However, the majority

---

[4] See, e.g., M. L. Lagrange, *Évangile selon Sain Jean* (Paris: Gabalda, 1927), 365–70; J. Marsh, *The Gospel of Saint John* (Baltimore: Penguin, 1968), 48; J. Beutler, *Habe keine Angst: Die erste johanneische Abschiedsrede (Joh 14)*, Stuttgarter Bibelstudien 116 (Stuttgart: Verlag Katholisches Bibelwerk, 1984), 9–11; Y. Simoens, *La Glorie d'aimer: Structures stylistiques et interprétatives dans le Discours de la cène (Jn 13—17)*, AB 90 (Rome: Biblical Institute, 1981), 100–104; F. J. Moloney, *The Gospel of John*, SP 4 (Collegeville, MN: Liturgical, 1998), 385; and Gerald R. Borchert, *John 12–21*, NAC 25B (Nashville: B&H, 2002), 96.

[5] Elsewhere I discuss in detail the reasons that a macro-chiasm must be rejected. See, Kellum, *Unity*, 63–71.

of commentators hold that 13:31–38 is the introduction to the entire Farewell Discourse.[6]

I prefer the last understanding for at least three reasons. The literary markers note a break between 13:30 and 31. John's literary style would suggest an introduction like 13:31–38. And finally, the content of the passage lends itself to such an understanding.

We will handle these in order starting with the linguistic markers. From the boundary features listed in the previous chapter we can see: (1) the use of the conjunction "therefore" (οὖν) often begins a new semantic unit in John. (2) John 13:30 and 31 have two time indicators, "and it was night" in 13:30 (ἦν δὲ νύξ) and "Therefore, when he departed" ("Ότε οὖν ἐξῆλθεν). These together mark a transition from the foot washing scene.[7] (3) ἐξῆλθεν is used in 13:30 making a hook-word with the use in 13:32. (4) There is also a change of participants from Judas to Jesus. Finally, (5) the monologue of chapter 14 develops from the disciple's questions linked to 13:3.

Thus, the shift from the rest of chapter 13 is impressive. Chapter 13, as the introduction to the Farewell Cycle itself, mentions Jesus' departure as the motivating incident for Jesus' actions at the meal. Having dismissed the betrayer (vv. 27–30), Jesus now turns his attention to the disciples. Formally, the conclusion of verse 30, ἦν δὲ νύξ, announces the sunset of Judas's time with the disciples and the setting of his dark act of betrayal. Jesus had previously warned the disciples that "night is coming" (9:4).[8] That ominous time has arrived (marking a thematic transition). So then, there is a strong linguistic break between 13:30 and 31 that leads me to understand 13:31–38 as the introduction of the discourse.

My second reason for suggesting that 13:31–38 is the introduction to the Farewell Discourse regards John's literary style. Most Johannine discourses of Jesus are introduced by dialogue that eventually turns to monologue.[9] The dialogue with Nicodemus introduces the New Life Discourse of chapter 3.

---

[6] See, e.g., Gary M. Burge, *John*, NIV Application Commentary (Grand Rapids: Zondervan, 2000), 37; Leon Morris, *The Gospel according to John*, NICNT (Grand Rapids: Eerdmans, 1995), 558; C. K. Barrett, *The Gospel according to John*, 2nd ed. (Philadelphia: Westminster, 1978), 449; D. A. Carson, *The Gospel according to John*, PNTC (Grand Rapids: Eerdmans, 1991), 476; H. A. Lombard and W. H. Oliver, "A Working Supper in Jerusalem: John 13:1–38 Introduces Jesus' Farewell Discourses," *Neot* 25 (1991): 357–77; and Raymond E. Brown, *The Gospel according to John*, AB 29A (New York: Doubleday, 1971), 608.

[7] The second is technically called a "point of departure" by Levinsohn. Stephen Levinsohn, *Discourse Features of the Greek New Testament: A Coursebook on the Information Structure of the New Testament*, 2nd ed. (Dallas: SIL, 2000), 7–28.

[8] Rekha M. Chennattu, *Johannine Discipleship as a Covenant Relationship* (Peabody, MA: Hendrikson, 2006), 99.

[9] D. H. Dodd, *The Interpretation of the Fourth Gospel* (Cambridge: Cambridge University Press, 1953), 400.

The long discourse of chapter 5 is preceded (in vv. 16–18) by dialogue that gives the charges against Jesus.[10] The Bread of Life Discourse in chapter 6 is introduced in verses 22–35, a section that is composed largely of dialogue in the form of questions and answers. John 9:35–41, which introduces the Good Shepherd Discourse in chapter 10, is also formed by dialogue. If John 13:31–38 is not the introduction to the Farewell Discourse, it is the only lengthy Discourse that begins without such an introductory dialogue. This is strong evidence that these verses are the introduction to the discourse.

Finally, the content of 13:31–38 functions as a specific introduction to the discourse that follows. The announcement of his glorification in 13:31–32 sets the agenda for understanding his departure, not in terms of sorrow, distress, or defeat, but joy, peace, and victory. Thus, although the narrator has set the stage for the entire discourse as his departure (see 13:1), this is the first time in this cycle that Jesus has openly declared his departure. Furthermore, the individual topics that are addressed in the discourse are announced here.

The three themes constantly developed are departure, a unique love among the ones remaining behind, and the disciples' need of the Paraclete.[11] These themes are developed in 13:31–38 in three brief paragraphs after Jesus first defines the parameters of his departure. The first theme developed is his departure (13:31–32), which is described as his glorification and the Father's glorification. This glorification is the reason for the discourse and the thread that runs throughout it (see especially 14:2–5, 18–19, 25–31; 15:26–27; 16:5–7, 16–24).

The second theme (remaining behind) is actually only part of the idea. The disciples' remaining behind in mission requires a tight bond among the disciples. Thus, it is the background for the new commandment found in 13:34 and 35. This command is expressly repeated in 15:12 and is the topic of 15:9–17. And although the command is not specifically mentioned, the reference of 14:15–24 "you will keep my commandments" (τὰς ἐντολὰς τὰς ἐμὰς τηρήσετε) may be inclusive.

The third theme, which is less overtly developed, is presented in 13:36–38: the disciples' inability to follow Jesus (i.e., their need for the Paraclete). John 13:36–38 uses the prediction of Peter's denials as the occasion to present Peter's defective love for Jesus, and in fact, a denial of Peter's claim to be able to follow Jesus immediately. In this way, these verses introduce the need that the Paraclete will fulfill. Jesus' highly dramatic response in 13:38 points out Peter's overestimation of the sacrifices he was willing to make for Jesus' sake and indicates his defective, though certainly real, love for Christ.

---

[10] Although the charges against Jesus are given in indirect discourse, the repartee between Jesus and the Jews is preserved by direct quotations from Jesus. See Carson, *John*, 246–47.
[11] Gordon Fee, "John 14:8–17," *Int* 43 (1989): 171.

Most commentators conclude that 14:1–31 forms the first unit within the farewell speech itself.[12] The beginning command controls the thought throughout 14:1–31. It is clear that a new unit within the discourse begins here. The shift in the person, tense, and mood of the verb signals a new addressee (all the disciples and not just Peter), and a new purpose (command, not prediction) also marks a shift in discourse boundary. Conceptually, it coheres to 13:31–38 in that Jesus' announcement of his departure, and thus (from their perspective) the imminent abandonment of the disciples, causes turmoil among them.[13] The command to depart at the end of the chapter signals the end of the speech by suggesting a change in time and space, thus bridging the gap between two units.

That 14:31 concludes the first major unit means, by definition, that 15:1 (the vine and the branch allegory) begins the next. This is universally conceded in the literature. The major debate concerns where the ending of the unit occurs. Three major options have surfaced. First, some posit that 15:1–16:4c make up the present unit with varying subdivisions.[14] Second, some view 15:1–17 alone as the second unit.[15] Finally, others suggest multiple breaks in smaller units.[16] A fourth, less attested option is that 15:1–16:33 is a single unit without major breaks.[17] Scholars generally concede that there are breaks (whether minor or

---

[12] One of the few exceptions is John L. Boyle who sees the first unit consisting of 13:31–15:10 based around the theme of mutual indwelling. Boyle's article is an example of how axiomatic multiple discourses have become. He denies the literary seam at John 14:31 but still assumes multiple discourses. John L. Boyle, "The Last Discourse (Jn 13,31–16,33) and Prayer (Jn 17): Some Observations on Their Unity and Development," *Bib* 56 (1975): 210–12.

[13] Some commentators suppose that μή + the present tense indicates "stop being in turmoil." See, e.g., G. R. Beasley-Murray, *John*, WBC 36 (Waco, TX: Word, 1987), 249; and Morris, *John*, 568. Although this is possible, the decidedly future-looking reference of the discourse suggests a customary prohibition rather than the cessation of present activities. The latter would restrict the untroubled heart to the disciples' present situation only when it is clear that a more gnomic sense is meant. The progressive aspect of the opposite command, "believe" (πιστεύετε), bears this out.

[14] So George Johnston, *The Spirit-Paraclete in the Gospel of John*, SNTSM 12 (Cambridge: Cambridge University Press, 1970), 165; Rudolf Schnackenburg, *The Gospel according to St. John*, vol. 3 (New York: Crossroad, 1982), 91–93; John Painter, *The Quest for the Messiah*, 2nd ed. (Nashville: Abingdon, 1993), 425; Simoens, *La glorie*, 132–39; and Moloney, *John*, 416. Moloney, as his custom, follows Simoens faithfully in his structure. In this case, both commentators take the unique position that 16:3 forms the outermost boundary of the second unit.

[15] Rudolf Bultmann, *The Gospel of John: a Commentary*, trans. G. R. Beasley-Murray, R. W. N. Hoare, and J. K. Riches (Philadelphia: Westminster, 1971), 421; Beasley-Murray, *John*, 269; Morris, *John*, 592–600 (Morris cautiously posits a break at 16); Fernando Segovia, *Farewell of the Word: The Johannine Call to Abide* (Philadelphia: Fortress, 1991), 125; Ben Witherington, *John's Wisdom* (Louisville, KY: WJK, 1995), 245; and Craig Blomberg, *The Historical Reliability of John's Gospel: Issues and Commentary* (Downers Grove, IL: InterVarsity, 2001), 205.

[16] So Edwyn Clement Hoskyns, *The Fourth Gospel*, ed. Francis Noel Davey, 2nd ed. (London: Faber & Faber, 1947), 471–76; Herman Ridderbos, *The Gospel of John: A Theological Commentary*, trans. J. Vriend (Grand Rapids: Eerdmans, 1991), ix.

[17] So R. H. Lightfoot, *St. John's Gospel: A Commentary* (Oxford: Oxford University Press, 1956), 255; Carson, *John*, 107; Brown, *John*, 2:546.

major) in 15:(10)11, (16)17. It is more debated whether there are breaks in 15:9 and 16:4c.

I believe that 15:1–16:4c are the boundaries to the second unit. This is borne out thematically, as the extended metaphor of the vine and the branches controls the thought through verse 16:4c. Structurally, the question is generally not the fact of a boundary at 16:4c, but what is the first paragraph break and how does 15:18–16:4c relate to its environment? Both the topic and the structure of these passages will be dealt with in detail below.

Three clear paragraph clusters make up this second unit. 15:1–11 and 12–17 develop two ancillary commands: abide and love one another. The third paragraph cluster (15:18–16:4c) develops the unavoidable result of the commands: the hatred of the world, which is introduced by the mitigated command "know." The obedience of the commands creates a new community that, because of its relationship to Jesus, will be hated by the world. Thus, the result is a clear example of Johannine dualism in which two disparate worlds are created and contrasted.

The final unit is composed of three semantic paragraphs that each describe an advantage to the departure of Jesus. The first paragraph is composed of 16:4d–15. The beginning boundary at 16:4d is not universally agreed upon. But I think that the phrase "I didn't tell you these things from the beginning, because I was with you," must begin the final segment for at least three reasons. First, the topic clearly changes from the hatred of the world to Jesus' departure in verse 5, signifying a new direction.[18] But, 16:5 cannot be the beginning because the continuity created by the contrast between "because I was with you" (v. 4) and "but now I am going away" (v. 5) suggests that at least part of verse 4 begins the new unit. Second, verse 4 uses certain developmental markers that are consistent with introducing a new line of thought.[19] Finally, the use of "these things" (ταῦτα) in both 16:4c and 16:4d (each the object of a verb of speaking) may also be an example of a hook-word that would indicate a transition as well. In 16:33, "I have spoken these things" (ταῦτα λελάληκα) as a summary statement of the previous speech marks the conclusion to the entirety of the discourse. The resulting transition from one unit to the next is rather subtle, but evident.

---

[18] The texture of the text also changes after this unit. Previously the backbone of the discourse is a series of injunctions. "Believe" and "love/obey" dominate chap. 14. Chapter 15 is dominated by "abide," "love one another," and "know." After the concluding formula of 16:4c there is not another imperative that appears in such a prominent role. Thus, the present paragraph's final boundary is best understood to be 16:4c.

[19] The use of the developmental marker δέ (translated here as "but") in 16:4b is in keeping with the use of δέ in material that backgrounds a new development. The clause stands in a Circumstance-HEAD relationship with v. 5 that is also introduced with δέ. The result is that the new unit is strongly marked for development.

The shift to prayer in chapter 17 with the indication that Jesus had finished speaking ("Jesus spoke these things") marks the beginning of a new unit. Its end is clearly indicated by the transition to Kidron in 18:1 with a similar concluding statement, "After Jesus had said these things . . ."

As we step back and take a look at the discourse we find that the movement from one unit to the next is marked not only by the linguistic and thematic markers that I have already noted, but the movement is also marked by something very subtle (and ingenious). Near the beginning of each unit except for the first unit and the last, motion is implied. Judas departs (13:31). Jesus and the disciples depart from the Upper Room (14:33). Jesus lifts his eyes (17:1). And Jesus and the disciples depart (18:1). It is not quite a universal marker for a division, but John does reinforce certain divisions by noting actual movement (however small). This use of movement to carry along a text is a common feature in John.[20]

What we found was that the Book of Glory is set up into two basic cycles, the Farewell Cycle (13–17) and the Passion Cycle (18–20), and chapter 21 is the epilogue to the whole book. This virtually mirrors the first half of the Fourth Gospel, which features a Prologue (1:1–18), then the Book of Signs, made up of the Cana Cycle (1:19–5:47) and the Festival Cycle (6:1–12:50). So then, our outline of the book would look as follows:

    I. Prologue (1:1–18)
   II. The Book of Signs (1:19–12:50)
      A. The Cana Cycle (1:19–5:47)
      B. The Festival Cycle (6:1–12:50)
  III. The Book of Glory (13–20)
      A. The Farewell Cycle (13–17)
         1. The Foot Washing (13:1–30)
         2. The Farewell Discourse (13:31–16:33)
         3. The Final Prayer (17)
      B. The Passion Cycle (18–20)
  IV. Epilogue (21)

A closer look at the Farewell Discourse divides it into its component parts. There are three major units within this episode. Each of these units takes on a topic related to Jesus' departure. These are comfort (14), unity between Jesus' followers (15:1–16:4c), and the advantages of Jesus' departure (16:4d–33). I would outline it in broad categories as follows:

---

[20] See Kellum, *Unity*, 230.

The Farewell Discourse (13:31–16:33)
a. Introduction (13:31–38)
b. Comfort (14:1–33)
c. Unity (15:1–16:4c)
d. Advantages (16:4d–33)

Now that we have a good idea of the macrostructure of our text, we are ready to start the formal exegesis of our text. This is to take up steps 5–7 of our exegetical program. We will identify the historical context, the canonical context, and the flow of thought of individual units.

Identifying the Historical and Canonical Context

This is a combination of our last two interpretational contexts. Regarding the Johannine Farewell Discourse there is at least one more global matter that is as much historical as it is literary.[21] It involves how the literary form of testament should influence our reading of the present speech. The ancients found great interest in the last words of a prominent person. The scene is so prevalent that "farewell discourse" (which is also known as a "farewell address," or "final discourse," or, more commonly, a "testament") has become a recognized genre of ancient literature. It features the last words of a dying figure to those intimately associated with the speaker.

The farewell scene varies in its component parts and complexities. Thus, it is better to avoid describing a monolithic fixed form and instead to describe a series of conventions that might be employed.[22] These features include announcement of death, parenetic (persuasive) sayings or exhortations, prophecies or predictions, retrospective accounts of the individual's life, the determination of a successor, a prayer, final instructions, and instructions for burial.[23]

The Johannine Farewell Discourse is clearly a farewell scene. It more closely resembles the Jewish testamentary literature than the Greco-Roman counterparts. Jewish testamentary literature differs from Greco-Roman examples

---

[21] For a fuller discussion of the Farewell Discourse Genre, see my recent article in the second edition of *Dictionary of Jesus and the Gospels* (L.S. Kellum, "Farewell Discourse," in *Dictionary of Jesus and the Gospels: A Compendium of Contemporary Biblical Scholarship*, 2nd ed., ed. Joel B. Green [Downers Grove, IL: InterVarsity, 2013], 266–69).

[22] Willliam S. Kurz, "Biblical Farewell Addresses," *TBT* 38 (2000): 71.

[23] Segovia, *Farewell of the Word*, 12. Greco-Roman examples of the scene include Plato's *Phaedo*; Plutarch's *Cato Minor* 66 and *Otho* 15–17; Diogenes's *Laertius Epicurus* 10:16–18. Examples in extrabiblical Jewish literature include *T. 12 Patr*, *1 Macc* 2:49–70; *Tob* 14:3–11; Philo, *Mos* 2:288–92; Josephus, *A. J.* 4.8.45–49 §§ 309–31, 12.6.3 §§ 279–84. Biblical examples include Deuteronomy 31–33; Joshua 23–24; 1 Sam 12:1–25; 1 Chronicles 28–29; Luke 22:21–38; John 13–17; Acts 20:17–38. William S. Kurz, "Luke 22:14–38 and Greco-Roman and Biblical Farewell Addresses," *JBL* 104 (1985): 262–63.

at important points. First, it emphasizes predictions or prophecies regarding the future from a monotheistic theological perspective (see, e.g., *Tob* 14:4–7), which is understandably uncommon in pagan sources. Second, Jewish examples of testamentary literature are longer. Greco-Roman farewell addresses tended to be short with only a few of any real length.[24] Third, many of the deaths in the pagan literature are suicides that provide an example of "how to die nobly" (*ars morendi*, again cf., Plutarch's *Cato Minor*). In the Jewish world, testamentary literature (derived from the biblical examples, especially Genesis 48–49) commonly focuses on the man of God who leaves words of instruction for his remaining followers (e.g., *Testament of the Twelve Patriarchs* leaves ethical instructions drawn from the examples of the patriarchs' lives).

Even a cursory reading of John's Farewell Discourse reveals that it deviates from the Jewish testaments at certain key points.[25] This may create a struggle for those who view genres as unbending forms. Rather than proposing new genres and sub-genres, Sheridan suggests reading the scene in light of the use of genre in ancient literature. Following Bakhtin, literary genres are not rigid forms that require one to seek another genre classification when a form deviates from the expected form (a taxonomic approach). Instead, a writer "employs" a genre rather than "belongs to" a given genre. Genres are open ended and can be modified by the writer within the general parameters that influence the possible interpretation.[26] Thus, divergences from the form can indicate specific theological emphases of the individual writers.

Ridderbos notes that it is easy to recognize some of the elements of the ancient genre "but John 14–17 is not simply a typical 'Farewell Discourse.'"[27] I would agree; the departure from the ancient form is quite remarkable. The sheer length of John 13:31–17 (almost 15 percent of the Gospel) is one of these divergences. There are also no strict rehearsals of the past, extended prophesies, or funeral preparations, and it contains an extended analogy (the vine and the branches). Thus, the Johannine Farewell Discourse is distinct in major ways from Jewish testamentary literature.

There are some points of similarity with Deuteronomy and the Mosaic farewell (Deuteronomy 31–33). Jesus' entreaty "let not your heart be troubled" immediately following the statement of departure is similar to Moses'

---

[24] Kurz, "Luke 22:14–38," 255, cf., *Cato Minor*, which is only thirty-two words long.
[25] Bammel lists nine points of departure for John. Ernst Bammel, "The Farewell Discourse of the Evangelist John and Its Jewish Heritage," *TynBul* 44 (1993): 111–19.
[26] Ruth Sheridan, "John's Gospel and Modern Genre Theory: The Farewell Discourse (John 13–17) as a Test Case," *ITQ* 75 (2010): 295.
[27] Ridderbos, *John*, 481.

"be strong and courageous" (Deut 31:7).[28] Furthermore, the final prayer of Jesus (John 17) may be reminiscent of the final blessing of Moses (Deuteronomy 33). But beyond this we are hard pressed to find *literary* similarities. Lacomara suggests, however, that there are a number of *conceptual* links with Deuteronomy (e.g., faith/love/obedience as the expression of love for Father/Christ, mutual love among believers, blessings for believers, and provision for propagating the covenant).[29] These links are compelling and suggest that the Johannine farewell flows out of the typology of Jesus as the new Moses (well established in Johannine scholarship) and the constitution and life of the people of God under the new covenant.

Typically the literary purpose of the farewell form in the Gospels focuses attention on the importance of the teaching.[30] The highly dramatic farewell form, the substantial length, and the position in the Gospel should also be taken into account as we investigate the purpose of the Gospel as a whole. John 20:30 states the purpose of the Gospel to be "that you may believe." Scholars debate whether that means "come to believe," "believe strongly," or both. If we take into account the structure of the Gospel, it would seem that John has both in mind. The first half of the Gospel is strongly evangelistic. The seven signs and the revelation of Jesus to Israel clearly are to describe who Jesus is and what saving faith in him really is. The second half—consisting mostly of the Farewell Discourse—clearly has in mind the life of the followers of Christ after his departure. In this light, "that you believe" seems to be more comprehensive than simply evangelism or discipleship. It is both.

From here we will unpack the Farewell Discourse section by section. In each section, we will address the remaining issues of our program. We will analyze the flow of thought, identify the historical context, and identify the canonical context. The historical context and canonical context we will handle together. Finally I will craft a sermon sketch that will incorporate what we have discovered. We will do this in three steps: analyzing the text, interpreting the text, and preaching the text. We will begin with John 13:31–38.

Introduction to the Farewell Discourse (13:31–38)

I track the flow of thought in expository/hortatory documents through a semantic and structural analysis (SSA) of each clause as described in the previous chapter. For our purposes, the SSA presented will be a simplified version. This simplification will describe mainly the larger structures of the text, which

---

[28] Craig S. Keener, *The Gospel of John: A Commentary* (Peabody, MA: Hendrickson, 2003), 2:931.
[29] A. Lacamara, "Deuteronomy and the Farewell Discourse (Jn 13:31–16:33)," CBQ 36 (1974): 65–84.
[30] Joel B. Green, *The Gospel of Luke*, NICNT (Grand Rapids: Eerdmans, 1997), 750.

will help us present the text's major movements in a way unencumbered with a clause-by-clause display. Furthermore, it will allow us to show the presentation at a size that is readable. I always build these off the complete diagram.[31] My simplified SSA of John 13:31–38 is presented below.

RELATIONAL STRUCTURE	CONTENTS
INTRO — circumstance	(13:31a-b) After Judas left...
— HEAD	(31c-32) "Now the Son of Man and God are glorified"
Theme 1 — HEAD	(33a) "I will soon depart from you"
— amplifi.	(33b-e) "And you will not be able to follow me"
Theme 2 — means — HEAD	(34a-b) "Love one another"
— compar.	(34c) "as I have loved you"
— RESULT	(35) "so that all will know you're my disciples"
Theme 3 — exchange 1 — question	(36a-b) Peter: "Why can't I follow you?"
— ANSWER	(36c-d) Jesus: "Not now, but you may later."
— exchange 2 — question	(37) Peter: "But, I will lay my life down for you!"
— ANSWER	(38) Jesus: "You'll deny me three times by morning."

Analyzing the Text

Structurally, 13:31–38 divides into four distinct segments (either sentences or small paragraphs but more properly called "propositional clusters") that are related around the fact of Jesus' imminent departure. The first segment, 13:31–32, forms a thesis statement that will drive the rest of the discourse. Judas's departure in 13:31 generates the speech to follow. Nevertheless, one should not simply think of this as a framing device. It has theological implications. Judas has gone to put the arrest and crucifixion of Jesus into motion.[32] Jesus' glorification is a loaded reference to his crucifixion and its results. So then, before he explicitly makes the statement of his departure, Jesus sets the parameters for understanding his departure—glorification. The use of the aorist passive for "glorify" (ἐδοξάσθη) is an unexpected form for this context. One would expect a forward-looking verb (e.g., "will glorify"). As such, the choice of the aorist is significant because it speaks of the event as a sure result. Wallace calls it a proleptic (futuristic) aorist.[33] Jesus' understanding of his death is not sorrow, pain, suffering, or the sad estate of all prophets—it is glory.

Three propositional clusters follow the verb; each is a theme of the latter discourse. The first theme is separated from 13:31–32 by a point of departure in 13:33. The phrase "Children, I am with you a little while longer" (τεκνία,

---

[31] My entire semantic and structural analysis of the Farewell Discourse is available as a PDF download at http://www.bhacademic.com/books.asp?p=9781433673764.
[32] Carson, *John*, 482.
[33] Dan Wallace, *Greek Grammar beyond the Basics: An Exegetical Syntax of the New Testament* (Grand Rapids: Zondervan, 1991), 563–64.

ἔτι μικρὸν μεθ' ὑμῶν; v. 33 HCSB) is fronted so that the main verb is the last constituent in the clause, therefore marking the beginning of a new theme (but not a new higher level unit). Of course, Jesus' departure is implied in the announcement of his glorification, but it is first explicitly told to the disciples here.

A similar structure appears in 13:34. The object, "a new commandment" (ἐντολὴν καινὴν), is placed in front of the verb as well, probably for emphasis. The topic turns from the bare fact of his departure to how the disciples are to relate to one another after his departure. Strongly implied is the continuing possibility of following Jesus as his disciples even after he has departed. As mutual love among the disciples is either the verb or the subject of the next two sentences, this theme runs through verse 35.

Finally, Peter's interruption resumes the topic abandoned by Jesus two verses earlier. This structure marks the beginning of a fourth short paragraph. It indicates a switch in subject matter by introducing a new participant. Through verse 38, the repartee between Jesus and Peter coheres to form the last theme introduced. Thus the structure of John 13:31–38 is divided into four small "paragraphs": 13:31–32, an introduction of the setting and overall theme of the discourse and 13:33, 34–35, and 36–38, which are subthemes that are developed in relation to Jesus' hour of glorification having arrived.[34]

Interpreting the Text

Setting the Themes (13:31–32)

The basic semantic relationship of the passage is rather straightforward. After some basic preliminary matters, essentially the "HEAD" statement in 31c is amplified twice in 31d and 32. The content, however, is more subtle. This type of simple construction with a deep substance is common in John. The interplay between three lexical items—"hour," "Son of Man," and "glorify"—supplies this deep substance. "Hour" refers obliquely to 13:1, which opens the farewell scene (and truly the whole final book) with a description of the "hour" (ἡ ὥρα). Often in the Gospel, "hour" is used simply as a descriptor of time (see e.g., 1:39 where the HCSB renders the Greek "it was about the tenth hour" [ὥρα ἦν ὡς δεκάτη] with "It was about 10 in the morning"). A few places employ "hour" as a cryptic reference to something more. Jesus refers to an hour unique to him (see, e.g., 2:4; 12:23, 27) or the narrator refers to "His hour" (see, 7:30; 8:20). John 13:1 explains that the "hour" is his time to depart.

---

[34] These are relations with equal natural prominence, but I have chosen to more closely define them here rather than labeling them merely "HEAD."

Clearly this is a reference to Jesus' death on the cross. The same chapters that refer to this hour usually refer to his departure and his purpose to glorify the Father or himself.[35] Now John clearly defines "hour" for us: the time to depart from this world. It is not surprising then that he begins the discourse with a reference to the purpose of his departure: the glory of the Son and the glory of the Father. There is no doubt he is referring to Jesus' death and frames it in terms of its results.

The second important lexical item is Jesus' self-reference as "the Son of Man." The phrase is used thirteen times in the Gospel of John (13:31 is the last appearance of it). As in the Synoptic Gospels, the term should not be seen in terms of humble self-deflection. Instead it should be seen in the light of the Old Testament reference in Daniel 7:13–14 where one like a son of man receives the everlasting kingdom from the Ancient of Days. The phrase is found in John in contexts where the Son of Man is the access to heaven or is from heaven (1:51; 3:13; 6:62), or in references to the cross (lifted up terminology—3:14; 8:28; 12:34[2x]), exercising judgment (5:27), or giving eternal life (6:27, 53; 9:35). It is no wonder then that the term is employed in 13:31 in connection with Jesus' looming death and resurrection. The only other reference to "Son of Man" in John combines all three terms: 12:23 "The hour has come for the Son of Man to be glorified" (HCSB). Thus, the cross, the resurrection, and the subsequent glorification are connected to Jesus' glorious rule described in Daniel 7.

The sheer repetition of the verb "glorify" (δοξάζω) identifies it as an important concept for understanding the purpose of Jesus' death. In this context, "glorify" refers to revealing the splendor of God and Christ. The statement in 13:31–32 is very similar to the voice of God in 12:28 where God affirms he will glorify his name in Christ. John 13:31 describes the glorification as an accomplished event (employing ἐδοξάθη—a proleptic/prophetic aorist). This glorification is a reciprocal glorification, "the Son of Man is glorified, and God is glorified in Him" (HCSB). Verse 32 has four instances of the third person pronoun (αὐτός) that may be taken in a variety of ways.[36] The best way to understand them is as follows: "If God is glorified in Him [Jesus], God will also [an adverbial use of καί] glorify Him [Jesus—matching the parallel structure with the previous clause] in Himself [God]." In this understanding, because Christ perfectly revealed God's splendor, God will, in turn glorify

---

[35] See, e.g., 8:12–59. His departure is mentioned at 8:14 and 21, his hour at 8:20, and his glory at 8:54. Likewise, see 7:30 for hour, 7:39 for glory, and 7:33–34 for departure. The exception is the mention of "hour" at 2:4.

[36] Because of the reciprocal nature between the Father and the Son, the ultimate sense is not dramatically affected one way or the other.

Christ in himself. It is reckless to suggest we can know all about the inner workings of how the Father glorifies the Son (exactly what does "in Himself" mean?); however, what we do clearly understand is a reciprocal glorification between the Father and the Son. Clearly, the Son's perfect obedience in life and his voluntary death on the cross glorify both the Son and the Father by revealing their splendor in the outworking of salvation. The Father, in turn, glorifies the Son in exaltation, revealing Jesus' splendor.[37] Carson states it well: "The Evangelist makes it clear that supreme moment of divine self-disclosure, the greatest moment of displayed glory, was in the shame of the cross."[38]

Theme 1: Jesus' Departure (13:33)

The first theme revealed in verse 33 regards Jesus' looming departure. That which is implied in 13:31–32 is now clearly stated. This seems to be the main purpose of verse 33. Although Jesus refers to his disciples as "children" (τεκνία), they will be in the same situation as the Jews who opposed Jesus earlier (7:33–35). They will seek him, but they will not be able to follow him. The reference to these Jews identifies where Jesus is going: back "to the One who sent Me" (7:33 HCSB). This topic functions as the revelation of the situation the disciples now face and will be addressed in the discourse that follows at several places (14:2–5, 19–20, 28–31; 16:5–7, 16–22, and 28). Jesus also does not repeat the warning to his dear children that he made to the Jews, "You will look for Me, but you will not find Me; and where I am, you cannot come" (7:34 HCSB). The promise of reunion is implicit; it will be made explicit in the discourse that follows.

Theme 2: The New Commandment (13:34–35)

The second topic that Jesus addresses here is found in 13:34–35. It is known as the new commandment as Jesus himself entitled it in 13:34 (ἐντολὴν καινήν). The grammar of 13:34–35 may be understood with certain distinct nuances. Most of the question revolves around how one understands the use of "that" (ἵνα) in 34b and 34d and, related to this, how one understands "just as" (καθώς) in 33c. The first use of ἵνα is clearly defining the content of the new commandment.[39] It is possible that the second ἵνα in 34d (often left untranslated) is employed in the same manner. If so, the second occurrence simply

---

[37] Keener, *John*, 2:921.
[38] Carson, *John*, 482. See also the detailed treatment by Peter Ensor, "The Glorification of the Son of Man: An Analysis of John 13:31–32," *TynBul* 58:2 (2007): 230–53.
[39] This is the epexegetical or explanatory use of ἵνα. BDAG explains that ἵνα can take the place of an explanatory infinitive (Frederick W. Danker, *A Greek-English Lexicon of the New Testament and other Early Christian Literature*, 3rd ed. [Chicago: University of Chicago Press, 2000], 476). This encroachment into the domain of the infinitive is typical of John's use of ἵνα.

repeats and expands the first by adding the element of Jesus' example.[40] Ridderbos translates the two occurrences, ". . . that you love one another and that, as I have loved you, you also love one another."[41] This use understands "just as" (καθώς) in a comparative sense. If so, the phrase describes the nature of the love disciples are to show to one another. While disciples cannot love exactly like Jesus (affecting salvation), they can love sacrificially, that is, above their own interests.

However, καθώς may be used in a causal sense. If so, the second occurrence of ἵνα functions as a purpose clause. In this sense the phrase forms the grounds for the new commandment. The meaning would be "A new commandment I give to you, that you love one another, because I loved you *so that* you would love one another."[42] While a little easier to translate into English, the interpretation suffers from at least two major contextual problems. First, it suggests the purpose of Jesus' love for his own is their mutual love. This promotes what is at best a related purpose to the main purpose, sidestepping his saving purpose (as indicated in the foot washing). Finally, and most importantly, in 15:12 the phrase "just as I have loved you" (καθώς ἠγάπησα ὑμᾶς) is identical to 13:34c and is clearly comparative.

The foundation for the brotherly love of the disciples is Jesus' example (in many ways an echo of 13:1, "Having loved His own who were in the world, He loved them to the end" [HCSB]). The expression in 13:34 is highlighted for significance by three literary devices. First, the expression "a new commandment," although the object of the verb "give," is placed before the verb in the original. It is also the very first phrase in the verse. Second, the command to love (ἀγαπᾶτε) is repeated. And, finally, the degree is heightened by the comparison to Jesus' love for his own disciples.

The command cannot be "new" in that brotherly love was commanded in the OT. Leviticus 19:18 says something similar, "Do not take revenge or bare a grudge against members of your community, but love your neighbor as yourself; I am the LORD" (HCSB).[43] The "newness" of the command must be related to the covenantal aspects noted earlier. As Chennattu notes, "The very idea of giving a commandment (ἐντολή) carries covenant overtones."[44] The

---

[40] So Morris, *John*, 562.

[41] Ridderbos, *John*, 476. Most English translations that take this option merely choose not to translate the second occurrence and express the last phrase as an imperative. See e.g., the ESV "A new commandment I give to you, that you love one another: just as I have loved you, you also are to love one another." Some, like the HCSB, omit both occurrences for they function like quotation marks: "I give you a new command: Love one another. Just as I have loved you, you must also love one another."

[42] See Bultmann, *John*, 525.

[43] See Barrett, *John*, 451–52.

[44] Chennattu, *Johannine Discipleship*, 96. Chennattu goes on to describe the "newness" of the command

people of God are now identified outside of Israel through a new covenant. It, then, can only be fulfilled when the disciples identify themselves and those in covenant with them as a new community. Without excluding love for the world,[45] Jesus introduces the theme of a fraternal love between the disciples. The result will be that this love is how the world will identify the members of this community (13:35). This makes mutual love a defining mark of what it is to be a Christian. I will develop the topic of mutual love more fully in the discourse that follows (15:12–17).

Theme 3: The Disciples' Lack of Readiness (13:36–38)

The last section is made up of two exchanges between Jesus and Peter. Each exchange is a question-answer stimulus-response role. Each question is asked by Peter and, given the highlighting of the new commandment, is somewhat impertinent. When Peter asks, "Lord, where are you going?" in 13:36, he brusquely returns to a previous topic, bypassing the love command altogether. This dramatically highlights the point of this paragraph: Peter (and later all the disciples) is not ready to follow Jesus. This is exactly the point Jesus makes as he answers the question in 13:36d. Jesus' statement identifies the topic of the paragraph for us and is neither overturned nor replaced in all that follows. Instead, all remaining propositions support it.

The second exchange begins with a rhetorical question by Peter in 13:37. As a rhetorical question, it is more of a statement than a real question. The question shows that Peter believed he was worthy of following Jesus immediately and needed more information to prove him wrong. It also has a persuasive tone to convince Jesus otherwise. It could be made into the indicative statement, "I am able to follow you now," without changing the meaning. This is demonstrated in that Peter does not wait for an answer but offers his qualifications as proof: "I will lay down my life for you." This claim, of course, Jesus rejects with the famous announcement of Peter's denial. Thus, in spite of his current beliefs, Peter is unprepared to follow Jesus. The Farewell Discourse repeatedly brings up this lack of preparation on the part of the disciples (see especially 16:29–32).

Discipleship cannot be accomplished apart from the accomplishment and application of Jesus' death and glorification. In Johannine terms, his hour must come before we may follow him. This implies a lack on the part of humans that

---

as (1) the aspect of reciprocity (i.e., "one another") and (2) that God is the source and Jesus is the model. The latter is certainly new, but the former does not take into account OT passages like Lev. 19:18.

[45] Burge notes that it is misdirected criticism to assume the command is a lesser command because it does not include love for the world. Such criticisms miss the salvation-historical aspect/setting of the command. Burge, *John*, 380.

must be remedied in the atonement. This is nothing new in the Fourth Gospel. Nicodemus was told that he must be born again to enter into the kingdom (3:3). This new birth is produced by the Spirit of God, (3:5) but it is appropriated by faith (3:14–18). This new birth, however, cannot happen until his hour is accomplished.

Furthermore, his hour must be accomplished before humans may follow him. The reader is not told in this introductory paragraph why Peter (and by extension, the rest of us) may not follow Christ now. However, what we see later is that it is the ministry of the Paraclete that mediates the presence of Christ in his absence (14:17–21): he reminds us of Jesus' teaching (14:26); he will give testimony about Christ in the midst of persecution (15:26); he will convict the world about sin, righteousness, and judgment (16:8); and he will guide the followers of Jesus in all truth about Christ (16:13). The ministry of the Paraclete is intimately connected with authentic discipleship. It cannot happen until the glorification of the Son. Thus, much of the Farewell Discourse is future for the Twelve, but a present reality for the people of God under the new covenant.

Preaching the Text

John 13:31–38 is a complete thought, although it clearly functions as the introduction to 14:1–16:32. When preaching a series through a text like the Farewell Discourse, we face the twin temptation either to brush over an introduction like this or to "overpreach" it and run the real risk of repeating ourselves when we have to deal with the same topics later. To avoid these pitfalls we should approach the text as it is presented to us.

First, we should identify the MIT. I always ask, "What is the text trying to communicate?" Here I look at how the three themes work together to communicate meaning in light of the introduction in 13:31–32. Jesus announced the arrival of his hour. It is his glorification, and it will glorify God, who will, in turn, glorify Christ. This describes the results of the hour; the three themes (departure, love command, and lack) flow out of it. It is tempting simply to describe the contents. Thus, some would describe the MIT as follows: "As Jesus' hour approached, he announced his departure, commanded mutual love, and exposed the disciple's inadequacy." However, this does not convey the purpose of the text as it introduces the entirety of the discourse. So I suggest the following as our MIT: "As Jesus' death approached, he prepared his disciples for life after his departure."

The MIM attempts to encapsulate the purpose of the text in the present; thus, I suggest the following MIM: "In light of our position, Christians should be prepared to live in a way that would glorify God."

Sermon Sketch

TEXT: John 13:31–38
MIT: As Jesus' death approached, he prepared his disciples for life after his departure.
MIM: In light of our position, Christians should be prepared to live in a way that would glorify God.
TOPIC: Jesus' Last Wishes

INTRODUCTION

Three themes are highlighted in 13:31–38: (1) He announced plainly his departure. (2) He gave the New Commandment—to love one another. And (3) in an exchange with Peter, he highlighted the disciple's innate disability apart from divine help (as illustrated by Peter). These three themes will show up throughout the discourse that follows. In fact, one could argue that Jesus elaborates these themes in the discourse that follows. In light of our position between his advents, Christians should be prepared to live in a way that would glorify God by addressing Jesus' concerns to our lives.

OUTLINE

I. **Live in Light of His Departure (13:31–33)**

   A. TEXT

   1. Jesus' departure is glorification (vv. 31–32).

   2. Jesus' departure is temporary (v. 33).

   B. TODAY: We need to see Jesus' departure in a similar way.

   1. It reveals the glory of the Father and the Son.

   2. It leads to a magnificent reunion.

II. **Live Loving One Another (13:34–35)**

   A. TEXT

   1. The Newness of the Commandment

a. The command to love your brother is not new (Lev 18:19).

b. The command is "new" because the people of God are composed in a new way.

2. The Substance of the Commandment

We love each other as Christ has loved us.

3. The Result of the Commandment

All men will know that we are his disciples when we love one another.

B. TODAY: Two major issues confront us in the New Commandment:

1. Your relationships with all Christians should reflect a Christ-like love.

2. Proclamation is dependent on how well you love.

III. Live Depending on His Resources (13:36–38)

A. TEXT

1. Through his overconfidence, Peter showed he was not ready to follow Christ.

2. Peter is not concerned with loving his brethren (v. 36).

3. Peter is not ready to hear displeasing news from Christ (v. 37).

4. Christ's departure prepares the way for the disciples to follow him (v. 36 cf. 21:19).

B. TODAY

Christians often live virtually dependent on themselves.

1. We make choices without seriously seeking God's will.

2. We do not even consider a sacrificial choice.

3. We are willing to believe patently false doctrines and interpretations if they are "beneficial to us."

4. It is a spiritual disaster that may well devastate us.

5. It is Christ's resources that make it possible to follow him.

CONCLUSION

The Farewell Discourse defines what it is to thrive between his departure and return.

Peter is not able to follow him now. However, after Jesus is glorified Peter will be able to follow him. In fact, Jesus tells him, "Follow me" (21:19). So now, from this side of Easter, the disciple of Jesus does not have to wait for him to be glorified. The disciple is able to follow Jesus, so we must follow in light of what his departure has accomplished, loving Christ and loving one another, and depending on his resources.

Other options for preaching the text are certainly possible. You may feel led to expand your treatment of John 13:31–38. One possible way is to preach a sermon on each of the movements of the passage. This would entail a sermon on the glorification of the Son by the Father, another sermon on Jesus' departure, another on the new command, and finally one on Peter's overconfidence. I would suggest, however, that there are at least two caveats to consider. First, make sure that your hearers understand your text as introducing what follows. You want to preach the text (including the purpose and/or literary function of the passage) and not just preach serially through the Farewell Discourse. Second, because these themes are repeated later in the discourse you run the risk of being redundant.

As we progress, we should keep in mind that this introduction to the Farewell Discourse begins to open up the world of new covenant discipleship for us. The discussion ahead will unpack and elaborate on the themes that are introduced here. Keeping in mind the big picture should help keep us from straying too far afield in the pages to come.

CHAPTER 4

UNIT 1: COMMANDS THAT COMFORT (14:1–31)

AS stated in the previous chapter, 14:1–31 is clearly the first of three single constituents that I pragmatically call a "unit" for the Farewell Discourse. The lead-in to the unit is a command not to be troubled (μὴ ταρασσέσθω ὑμῶν ἡ καρδία, to be comforted is its semantic equal). Two more commands related to the first form the backbone of the rest of the unit, and they result in the presence of Christ mediated through the Paraclete. Its structure can be summarized as, "Commands that Comfort." In the following paragraphs the disciples are commanded to believe (14:1–14) and to love/obey (14:15–31). Among other matters that will be discussed below, a new topic is clearly introduced in 14:15, "If you love Me, you will keep My commands," which isolates the start of the second paragraph.

Believe in Jesus (14:1–14)

Immediately following the announcement of Jesus' departure and the difficulty it poses for Peter, Jesus offers comfort against emotional turmoil (μὴ ταρασσέσθω). "Your heart must not be troubled" (HCSB; μὴ ταρασσέσθω) controls 14:2–31. Its repetition in 14:27 signals that Jesus does not leave the basic topic offered in 14:1. Like many imperatives, "Do not let your heart be troubled" is the ultimate purpose, developed by two means to accomplish the command. The first means is "believe" (14:1) and the second is "love/obey" (14:15–27). Therefore, in this first unit of the Farewell Discourse Jesus is telling the disciples the means to the untroubled heart in light of his absence.

As noted earlier, the language is the familiar language of covenant that is consistent with the Moses typology of the Fourth Gospel. Here, the new Moses (in the familiar context of the Last Supper where the new covenant is announced in the Synoptic Gospels) defines living (rather thriving) under the new covenant.[1] As Moses in Deut 31:6–7 and 23, Jesus offers comfort, only here in the form of a *litotes* (a negation), "do not let your heart be troubled."

The command to believe in God and Christ (the first means to the untroubled heart) is founded on three grounds in 14:2–14: (1) Jesus' own veracity (14:2–4), (2) Jesus' relationship to salvation (14:5–7), and (3) Jesus' relationship to the Father (14:8–14). There are a couple of ways to preach the text to reflect its structure. First, we may preach one sermon on 14:1–14. Our points then would be the three grounds. A good MIT would be "Christ exhorted us to have an untroubled heart based on his veracity, his relationship to salvation, and his relationship to the Father." A MIM that reflects this would be, "For disciples to have an untroubled heart, they should believe in Christ and God." Each of the grounds would be an individual point in the sermon.

I. Believe Because of Jesus' Own Veracity (14:2–4)
II. Believe Because of Jesus' Relationship to Salvation (14:5–7)
III. Believe Because of Jesus' Relationship to the Father (14:8–14)

I think, however, it would be irresistible for me to preach these points (grounds) as individual sermons for two reasons. First, the section is rather complex and deals with a variety of important theological themes, which makes it difficult to preach in a digestible time-period. Second, the structure of the text seems to divide into smaller structures that translate to the sermon well. Therefore, for 14:1–14, I will design three sermons around the grounds stated above.

---

[1] The question of John's knowledge of the Synoptics is frequent fare for Johannine scholars. It is my contention that John is fully aware of at least some of the Synoptic Gospels and chooses not to plow over familiar ground. See Andreas J. Köstenberger, *John*, BECNT (Grand Rapids: Baker, 2005), 17–18, for a brief summation. A more detailed defense can be found in D. A. Carson, *The Gospel according to John*, PNTC (Grand Rapids: Eerdmans, 1991), 49–58.

The First Ground for Faith: Jesus' Veracity (14:2–4)

Analyzing the Text

As usual we will begin with a simplified semantic and structural representation of the major movements of the text in question. The basic structure of this paragraph is EXHORTATION-grounds.

RELATIONAL STRUCTURE	CONTENTS
┌EXHORT─────────────	(14:1b) believe in me as you believe in God.
│ ┌HEAD────────────	(2) I go to prepare a place for you in my Father's house.
└grounds 1 ┼amplifi. 1────────	(3) And I will return to retrieve you.
▼ └amplifi. 2────────	(4) And you know the way to where I am going.

I am proceeding under the assumption that both appearances of "believe" (πιστεύετε) are imperatives. Because the present imperative ("believe") and indicative ("you believe") are identical in form, three identifications are possible. The form indicates either (1) two imperatives ("believe in God, believe also in me" [see, e.g., CSB, ESV, NIV, NASB, RSV]), (2) an indicative and an imperative ("you believe in God, also believe in me" [Vulgate, KJV, NKJV, NET]), or (3) two indicatives ("you believe in God, you also believe in me").[2] Because these verbs appear in close connection to an unmistakable imperative, "let it not be troubled" (μὴ ταρασςέσθω), at least one of them is best understood to be an imperative, ruling out option three.[3] No major translation has ever taken this option.

Of the other two possible options, option one is the most likely. The second verb is unambiguously an imperative, and nothing clarifies the first as an indicative (thus, most modern translations). Furthermore, the Old Italian and Syriac versions clearly understood the term to be an imperative.[4] Under both readings, the Christology is astonishingly high regardless of how one takes the grammatical forms.[5] Just as the Father is the proper object of our faith, so too is Christ.

The rest of the paragraph is a straight-forward HEAD with two amplifications. The statement of many rooms is amplified first by a conditional

---

[2] Also grammatically possible, but nonsense semantically, is to read the text as an imperative and indicative ("believe in God, you also believe in me").

[3] So C. K. Barrett, *The Gospel according to John*, 2nd ed. (Philadelphia: Westminster, 1978), 456.

[4] R. V. G. Tasker, *The Gospel according to John: An Introduction and Commentary*, TNTC 4 (Grand Rapids: Eerdmans, 1960), 170–71. By the time Jerome translated the Vulgate he chose "creditis... credite," preferring option three above. However, other forms could have been used if the writer had meant to be clearer. E.g., a perfect tense verb would also make sense here and grammatically clarify the intended difference.

[5] So, Carson, *John*, 488.

statement. The two consequences paired with the condition describe the result of the preparation (coming again) and the purpose (being with the Lord). The second amplification (4a), which forms the basis for the next paragraph, affirms that the disciples know the way. Taken in isolation, the second amplification carries little exegetical weight.

Interpreting the Text

The first matter of interpretation is to identify the intended nuance of "believe" in this context. Because he is speaking to the disciples it certainly does not mean "come to faith." Because the imperatives are equal constituents with coequal objects (God and Christ) the nuance is most certainly "trust": a temperament to rest in the providence of Christ. Grammatically, the present tense is appropriate for this situation as well. It suggests a progressive, ongoing trust. Jesus will offer three reasons to trust in him that each reveal grounds for belief but also reveal his person and his purposes for his own.

This first ground for belief (14:2–4) is on the surface related to Jesus' own veracity. The lead idea is "believe on me because I am faithful to my promises." This is clear even though translators differ on exactly how to translate the sentence. The heart of the issue is twofold. First, we must ask, "is the clause in 14:2c a question or an indicative statement?" This largely depends on the second issue, the translation of "that" (ὅτι) in 14:2d. Should we understand it as causal or indirect speech, or take the variant reading that is an omission of the word? If ὅτι is causal, the clause is an indicative, "I would have told you *because* . . ." If 14:2c is a question, the ὅτι clause is indirect speech, "Would I have told you that . . ." If the ὅτι is an insertion, 14:2d is either an affirmation of the disciples following later (cf. 13:36) or indirect speech.

The textual issue is not easy to adjudicate.[6] Raymond Brown makes a strong case for the originality of the omission.[7] It is both impressively early and widely distributed across the different text-types. In this reading, "I go to prepare a place for you" is new information, undergirding the purpose of Jesus' death and the many places in the Father's house. It also avoids a major problem of understanding the phrase as indirect speech (*vis.* Jesus referring to a statement not elsewhere in John). However, Brown's explanation that ὅτι was inserted to clear up John's lack of a conjunction is not very convincing.[8] If so, the scribe has produced a more difficult (even ambiguous) reading. This

---

[6] See, e.g., Craig S. Keener, *The Gospel of John: A Commentary* (Peabody, MA: Hendrickson, 2003), 2:937. He notes the difficulties but makes no decision.

[7] Raymond E. Brown, *The Gospel according to John*, AB 29A (New York: Doubleday, 1971), 2:619–20.

[8] Ibid., 619.

doesn't seem to be the most likely reason for the variant. It is more likely a scribe omitted the ὅτι (for whatever reason) rather than adding one.[9]

Therefore, I cautiously suggest it is best to interpret the ὅτι clause as indirect speech and a rhetorical question. "If not, would I have told you *that* I go to prepare a place for you?" While this exact phrase has not been used previously, it implies the promises of eternal life (assuming futurist eschatology) and, most recently, the promise of 13:36, "you will follow later."

This ground is introduced by a fronted prepositional phrase, "in my Father's house," that here signals the switch from injunction to argumentation. As often in John, the nuances the writer communicates are often both subtle and significant.[10] While the surface structure is the grounds for the exhortation, "believe," the content of the grounds is directly related to Jesus' purposes in going away and is the content of the words to which he has alluded. In essence it is a promise regarding the individual future of each disciple "in My Father's house."

It is popular to suggest that this means Jesus is in heaven preparing a marvelous place for his followers. It is more likely, however, that it is the going itself that prepares the place for the disciples. That is, his death, resurrection, and ascension open the way for the followers of Christ to go to heaven.[11] This implies that Jesus' purposes are to clear a way for the sinner to have permanent access to the Father.

Some have suggested that "the Father's house" is the temple.[12] Both James McCaffrey and Mary Coloe interpret "My Father's house" as the temple based on similar wording of John 2:16 that is then interpreted as Jesus' body. According to Coloe, the "abiding places" are not an eschatological destination, as traditionally interpreted, but the spiritual household of God. In the new temple, Jesus, the Father, the Spirit, and the believer dwell so that the believer enjoys the divine presence.[13] Thus, it is a vehicle to convey realized eschatology rather than futurist eschatology. However, this seems to be only partially correct.

It is likely that the reference is not a euphemism for "heaven" and that "My Father's house" may indeed refer to a temple, although the interpretation of Coloe and McCaffrey is not entirely convincing. Instead, more recent work

---

[9] Metzger wrote that the omission of ὅτι "is probably to be explained as a simplification introduced by copyists who took it as ὅτι *recitativum*, which is often omitted as superfluous." One wonders if it can be proven that all variants of ὅτι used with words of speaking are deletions. One man's omission is another's addition.

[10] The developmental marker δέ probably indicates a significant event cluster (the preparing of a place and returning to receive them joined by καί).

[11] Barrett, *John*, 457.

[12] James McCaffrey, *The House with Many Rooms: The Temple Theme of John 14:2–3* (Rome: Biblical Institute, 1988). See also, Mary Coloe, "Temple Imagery in John," *Int* 63 (2009): 368–81.

[13] Coloe, "Temple Imagery," 377.

suggests that the reference might be to language common in the Second Temple period referring to the eschatological destination for the people of God.

Steven M. Bryan makes a compelling case for the reference in John 14:2 to be to an eschatological temple, an idea that is current in both the Old Testament and Second Temple literature.[14] Bryan argues that building on Moses' promise of return to repentant Israel (Deut 30:4) lays a foundation for other references, such as points of contact between 2 Samuel 7:10 and Exodus 15:17—both refer to a place for the people of God (the latter a place established by God's hands). These texts were also read together as a reflection on the eschatological temple at Qumran (*4QFlorilegium*). "Whether together or apart, it is easy to see how these texts influenced the development of the idea that the Temple would be the eschatological dwelling place of God's people."[15] Influence can be seen in other Second Temple literature (see e.g., 2 Maccabees 1–2 and *1 Enoch*). At Qumran, the *Temple Scroll* refers to a temple in which rooms are provided for all Israel (clearly eschatological—11QT44:3–16). Furthermore, the Messiah was understood to be the builder of the eschatological temple as God produces a temple "not made by hands." The Sibylline Oracles speak of a "blessed man from the plains of heaven" who built the city God loved (Jerusalem) and fashions the sanctuary. Notably it is God who is "the sender of Thunder, the Creator of the great Temple" (*sib. Or.* 5.414–33). "John," Bryan asserts, "was speaking of a heavenly Temple that, though built by God, Messiah would prepare to be the eschatological dwelling of His people."[16] The consistent description is that human hands did not make this temple.[17]

To this we might add that a series of descriptions/criticisms of the Second Temple found in the New Testament was that it *was* "made by hands" (Mark 14:58; Acts 7:48; 17:24; Heb 9:11, 24). The language, "made by hands" is possibly an echo of the description of the eschatological temple current in Second Temple literature. Furthermore, Stephen in Acts 7:44 specifically cites the eschatological sanctuary (as does Heb 8:5 and 9:24). Both are straightforward interpretations of Exod 25:9 and 40: Moses was shown a pattern (suggesting a heavenly prototype). Thus, since a reference to the eschatological sanctuary is likely, there is no need to reject futurist eschatology regarding the reference to "my Father's house."

This interpretation helps us to understand the word *rooms* (μοναί). The word is a cognate of the more familiar *abide* (μένω), thus the popular translation of "abiding places." The image is of space reserved in the heavenly

---

[14] Steven M. Bryan, "The Eschatological Temple in John 14," *BBR* 15 (2005): 187–98.
[15] Ibid., 188.
[16] Ibid., 192.
[17] Ibid., 195.

sanctuary for the believer. Μονή itself is not a common word. It only occurs here and in 14:23 in the Greek New Testament. It can have the connotation of "a stay" or "continuing" (as a noun).[18] But here the reference is obviously to rooms in the heavenly temple, although permanence seems to be in play as well.

The popular interpretation of "mansions" fostered by the KJV and NKJV is taken from the Latin *mansiones* found in the Vulgate. While the Latin noun is an appropriate translation (merely a "staying" or "a stopover"), the English word was an unfortunate translation that in the American mind communicated not a place of intimacy and permanence in the eschatological temple but opulence and isolation in the abode of the dead.

A conditional statement regarding the veracity of Jesus' promise follows the promise of an abiding place. Jesus asks what amounts to a rhetorical question that asserts his veracity. If there were not many rooms would Christ have lied about it to his disciples? The expected response is, "of course not." But this is more than a simple assertion of his validity. It is a promise wrapped up in a condition. Jesus is going away to prepare a place for his followers. Then, assuming this is true, the statement is amplified by another promise: "I will return and receive you to myself." Jesus will not prepare a place and then sit down and wait for his own to find their own way there. He personally will return and usher his followers to their prepared place. Although John does not dwell on the cosmic nature but the personal consequences of his return, this promise is a very real event in the life of all followers of Christ, not just the ones alive at his return. For, as Paul puts it, "the dead in Christ will rise first. Then we who are still alive will be caught up together with them in the clouds to meet the Lord in the air and so we will always be with the Lord" (1 Thess 4:16–17 HCSB). The ultimate purpose, stated in 14:3e, is that the follower of Jesus would be with him forever. The promise of a place, then, is more than a reserved space (although it is that). It is also communion with the exalted Christ in that place. Given the connection between abiding (μενώ) and intimacy with God, and the nature of eternal life in the presence of Christ, the use of the cognate noun "abiding places" (μονή) seems rather appropriate.

The command to believe the truthfulness of Jesus' promises followed by a reiteration of those promises is wholly appropriate to the larger theme of having an untroubled heart.

Jesus concludes this ground with one more bit of information regarding this destination: the disciples know the way. Literally, this will transition to

---

[18] *TDNT*, 4:579–80.

the next grounds for the injunction to believe because it sparks Thomas's question regarding "the way."

Preaching the Text

The first sermon beginning the section 14:1–14 will be the first grounds for faith in Christ in 14:1–4. However, by necessity, we must cover the command to believe as the first means to the untroubled heart as an important part of this sermon. I will repeat the essence of this in each of the three sermons on why we should trust Christ. In this way we do not lose the point of the larger passage while preaching its component parts.

In this first sermon, my MIT is "So that they might have untroubled hearts, Jesus commanded his disciples to believe in him, because he is faithful to His word." The MIM, then, is an expression of this presented in present tense, with a sense of what should people do, based on the MIT: "To have untroubled hearts, people today should trust Christ because his word is true."

SERMON SKETCH

TEXT: John 14:1–4
MIT: So that they might have untroubled hearts, Jesus commanded his disciples to believe in him because he is faithful to his word.
MIM: To have untroubled hearts, people today should trust Christ because his word is true.
TOPIC: Believe Because His Word Is True

INTRODUCTION

On the eve of his departure Jesus had a message for his followers. His desire was that we thrive in Spirit until he returns. The first thing on his mind was that we should grasp the significance and the achievement of his departure. He wants our minds unclouded as we serve till he comes. So his first word is, "Let your heart not be troubled." Perhaps it would not be arrogance to paraphrase it "release your anxiety." The means of this untroubled heart is unfolded in the following chapter. It is twofold: to believe in Christ (14:1–14) and to love/obey him (14:15–31). Over the next few weeks we'll unpack the first of these means to the untroubled heart. Jesus asks us to believe in him, which is more than mere affirmation of Jesus. It is even more than coming to him for salvation, although it surely includes both. Here belief is aimed at his disciples. It must be a quiet disposition of trust in the person of Christ.

John 14:1: "Let not your hearts be troubled. Believe in God; believe also in me" (ESV).[19]

Jesus will give three reasons to believe in him in verses 2–14. Today we will look at the first of these reasons to believe. To have untroubled hearts, people today should trust Christ because his word is true. That is, he is faithful to his promises. So what does he promise?

OUTLINE

I. **He Promises Many Rooms (14:2)**

   "In my Father's house are many rooms. If it were not so, would I have told you that I go to prepare a place for you?" (ESV).

   A. TEXT

   1. "In My Father's House" = the heavenly sanctuary

   2. "Many rooms" = a place of intimacy with Christ for his own

   B. TODAY: The promise is powerful because of the implications for our present condition. The implications are . . .

   1. This world is not a permanent place.

   2. Our time here is limited by an act of his grace.

II. **He Promises a Personal Retrieval (14:3)**

   "And if I go and prepare a place for you, I will come again and will take you to myself, that where I am you may be also" (ESV).

   A. TEXT

   1. Retrieval refers to the second coming.

   2. It is the purpose of the going away.

   B. TODAY: The promise is powerful because . . .

   1. It describes the completion of this dysfunctional fallen world.

---

[19] Rather than go into all the issues regarding the translation of "ὅτι" in verse 2 that we covered above with a congregation, I usually simply choose a version that is acceptable to me. In this case the ESV does rather nicely.

2. It clearly establishes our resurrection and participation in his majestic return.

III. He Is Confident of a Clear Pathway (14:4)

A. TEXT:

"And you know the way to where I am going" (ESV).

Jesus is confident they know the way because . . .

   1. He is the way and they know him.

   2. He has cleansed them already.

B. TODAY: The clear pathway for people today is Jesus Christ.

   1. Salvation comes in believing in Jesus.

   2. Safekeeping comes in believing in Jesus.

   3. Security comes in believing in Jesus.

CONCLUSION

Belief in Christ begins with acknowledging the facts about him given in the Bible as true. But, that's not the end. We believe to be born-again. That is, we must turn from our sin and make him the Lord of our lives. We place our trust in what he did on the cross to cover our sin. Finally, there is everyday believing where we quietly and confidently trust his providence in our lives. You are somewhere on that continuum today. Christ calls you to progress to that quiet trust. You can do so today.

The Second Ground for Faith: Jesus Is the Way to the Father (14:5–7)

The next two grounds are in the form of dialogue between Jesus and two of his disciples. The first exchange (14:5–7) builds off the last statement of Jesus in verse 4, "You know the way to where I am going" (HCSB). The partner in the conversational exchange is Thomas, who will affirm rather prominently the substance of 14:5–7 when he proclaims in 20:28, "My Lord and my God!" (HCSB).

Analyzing the Text

RELATIONAL STRUCTURE	CONTENTS

The second grounds for the command at 14:1

- question ——————————— (14:5) Thomas: "How can we know where you are going?"
- ANSWER
  - HEAD ——————————— (6a-b) Jesus: "I am the way the truth, and the life"
  - amplifi. 1 ——————————— (6c) "no one comes to the Father except through me"
  - amplifi. 2 ——————————— (7a-b) "You neither know me or the Father now"
  - amplifi. 3 ——————————— (7c-d) "From now on you will know Him"

The major movements of the text (represented in the simplified diagram above) are that of a conversation exchange in the form of a Question-ANSWER. Thomas's question (14:5a–c) poses an inquiry based on the implications of an assumption: "We don't know the where so how can we know the way?" It is represented as a Grounds-CONCLUSION relationship.

Jesus' answer is a statement with three elaborations. The confession that he is the way leads to the further information that he is the only way (6c), he perfectly identifies and represents the Father (7a–b), and a promise of future intimacy (7c–d).

Interpreting the Text

Thomas complains (in the form of a question) that he does not know the place, much less the way. He obviously takes the metaphor of "way" (ὁδὸς, "road" or "path") literally, suggesting that at least he has not understood Jesus' metaphor of departure. In this way, John 14:5 is a classic example of misunderstanding in the Fourth Gospel. However, as Köstenberger notes, Christians certainly understood it by Acts 19 when they refer to themselves as "the Way."[20]

Just what Jesus means by the reference is debated. Those who hold to a realized eschatology understand the reference to be John's refashioning of futurist eschatology into the experience of the believer in the present. Jesus is the way to the *presence* of the Father as mediated in the present through the Holy Spirit.[21] Keener says something similar without the disavowal of all futurist content. Taking a moderating position, he suggests it is the way of the cross, which is embracing Jesus' identity and then sharing in his rejection by the world. It is ultimately the way "leading to the Father's presence."[22]

As is probably evident, the position taken on the identification of "my Father's house" plays a large part in the interpretation of "the Way." I have

---

[20] Köstenberger, *John*, 428. See, e.g., Acts 9:2; 19:9, 23; 22:4; 24:14, 22.
[21] See Ernst Haenchen, *John 2: A Commentary on the Gospel of John Chapters 7–21*, Hermeneia, trans. Robert W. Funk (Philadelphia: Fortress, 1984), 124–25.
[22] Keener, *John*, 2:939.

suggested that the house is most likely the eschatological sanctuary, i.e., the heavenly tabernacle. If so, there is no reason to interpret these verses devoid of futurist content. "The Way" is interlocked with Jesus' departure to prepare a place for his own.

Thomas's question is met with the "premier expression of the theology of this entire Gospel"[23]—John 14:6, "I am the way, the truth, and the life" (HCSB). It is the last, and most comprehensive, of the "I am" statements in the Gospel of John.[24] Here Jesus clarifies for Thomas that he is the center of all things salvation-historical. The leading thought is concerned about the way to God because that is Jesus' destination. Jesus is the way to God. Thus, when Jesus amplifies the statement, he describes it as "going to the Father." It is notable that he does not point to the way or show the way. He *is* the way. To go to the Father, one does not just follow the same way as Jesus. Jesus is the way to the Father.

Just how is this accomplished? This has been a theme throughout the Book of Signs. The nature of saving faith (illustrated by those who believe but do not really believe), the necessity of the new birth, Jesus as the sent Son, and other motifs all point to how one comes into the people of God. As John 6:35 records, "'I am the bread of life,' Jesus told them. 'No one who comes to Me will ever be hungry, and no one who believes in Me will ever be thirsty again'" (HCSB). We should note that "eating" and "drinking" are defined as "coming to" and "believing in" Jesus. There is really nothing to suggest in the expression itself that implies Jesus' cross and resurrection are also similar paths that followers of Jesus will take.[25] This truth is related elsewhere.

Jesus is not only the way to God, but he is the truth and the life. "Truth" is a frequent theme found in the Fourth Gospel. The noun ($\dot{\alpha}\lambda\acute{\eta}\theta\epsilon\iota\alpha$) and its cognates are used fifty-five times in the Gospel of John. The concept of truth is often connected directly to Christ. He is described by the narrator as being full of grace and truth (1:14) and the source of grace and truth (1:17), John testifies to the truth (5:33), Jesus is the true bread from heaven (6:32, 55), his judgment is true (7:16), he speaks the truth (8:40, 45, 46), his Spirit is the Spirit of truth (14:17; 15:26; 16:13), and those who are of the truth listen to him (18:37). He is truth *par excellènce*.[26] That he is the truth implies, at least, that those who

---

[23] Gary M. Burge, *John*, NIV Application Commentary (Grand Rapids: Zondervan, 2000), 392.
[24] Herman Ridderbos, *The Gospel of John: A Theological Commentary*, trans. J. Vriend (Grand Rapids: Eerdmans, 1991), 493.
[25] Contrary to Barrett, *John*, 458 and Keener, *John*, 2:939. Both do also claim that it is the way to the Father's presence that is described.
[26] Köstenberger, *John*, 429.

search for truth apart from Christ are doomed to fail at finding comprehensive religious truth, especially regarding the afterlife.

Finally, he is the life. Life is another major theme throughout the Gospel of John. Köstenberger notes there are "sixteen major clusters of references to 'life' in John's Gospel."[27] He goes on to claim that life is the subject of virtually every chapter in the first half of the Gospel. Nor is it missing in the second half, although the usage "thins out."[28] The various forms of the noun "life" (ζωή) are used thirty-six times in John. In those contexts in close connection to Christ, the word always has the connotation of eternal life. Eternal life is in Jesus (1:4; 3:15–16, 36; 4:14, 36; 5:24, 26, 40; 6:27, 33, 35, 40, 47, 53–54; 10:10, 28; 17:2; and 20:31), his Spirit gives life (6:63), he has the word of life (6:68), his followers walk in the light of life (8:12), he is the resurrection and the life (12:25), and eternal life is knowing God and his Christ (17:3).

In one sense, these three coequal terms are claims on the highest order of exclusivity. There is very little wiggle-room to suggest one might come to God another way than Jesus. He is not one of eight ways to heaven. He is the way. He does not just have some truth. He is truth incarnate. He does not point to eternal life. He is eternal life. If there is any doubt, Jesus amplifies his statement: "No one comes to the Father except through Me" (John 14:6 HCSB). Clearly, in the sense of how one gets to heaven, Jesus is an exclusivist. This is not a new idea in the Fourth Gospel. Jesus makes a very similar claim in John 6:44, "No one can come to Me unless the Father who sent Me draws him" (HCSB). Similarly in John 10:7 and 9, Jesus is the door for the sheep; those who try to enter the sheepfold another way are thieves and robbers (10:1).

The idea that Jesus is the sole road to heaven has at least two possible expressions outside of evangelical Christianity. The first is to suggest that John is wrong and dismiss the statement. Only the most radical critic would suggest so. However, the scandal of being exclusive in a pluralistic society leads some to be attracted to the second expression. For these people, Christ is indeed the way to heaven, but those outside of Christianity may be on this path without really knowing it; that is, they follow Christ anonymously. This is the view of much of the Roman Catholic Church following the teaching of Karl Rahner.[29]

---

[27] Andreas J. Köstenberger, *A Theology of John's Gospel and Letters*, Biblical Theology of the New Testament (Grand Rapids: Zondervan, 2009), 342.

[28] Ibid.

[29] One of the classic expressions can be found in Karl Rahner, "Anonymous and Explicit Faith," in *Theological Investigations*, vol. 16, *Experience of the Spirit: Source of Theology*, trans. David Morland (New York: Seabury, 1979), 52–59. Rahner, and those following him, affirm salvation is only through Christ. However, under certain conditions, a non-Christian (or even an atheist) may be understood to be in the church. What is required is that a person accepts his own radical transcendence that leads to God (even if he or she is not conscious of God in traditional terms). That person possesses "an anonymous faith." Ibid., 58–59.

Other theologians (including the occasional evangelical) outside the Catholic Church have also embraced such a thought.[30] The present text can hardly be understood in such a pluralistic manner.

Three subsequent statements amplify Jesus' statement in 14:6b, each adding depth to the HEAD statement. If, "I am the way, the truth, and the life" was not clear enough, Jesus clarifies that no one comes to the Father except through Christ. Yet this is not the problem for inclusivists, for they claim those with "anonymous faith" come to God through Christ, albeit ignorantly. The problem is in the second amplification. It first describes Christ's relationship to the Father. As such it hardly amplifies "no one comes to the Father . . ." It seems more reasonable to assume an identifying statement is amplifying an identifying statement (i.e., "I am the way . . ."). We might paraphrase "I am the way to God . . . to know Me is to know the Father." Coming to the Father, Jesus' equality to the Father, and knowing him are inseparably bound in their context. It is unquestionable that Jesus has in mind a personal relationship between him and his disciples. This personal relationship has an added dimension: to know Jesus is to know the Father. This presents the *non sequitur* for certain pluralist theories, "How does one *know* Jesus and the Father anonymously?"

To me there is also another *non sequitur* that is troubling. There is an unparalleled effort on the part of God to redeem mankind through Jesus Christ. The cost, the effort, and the anguish of doing so, is difficult (if not impossible) for us to understand fully. The cosmic struggle seems pointless if the ways of the other world religions were valid ways to God. Why go through all that?

The flip side of this argument is equally powerful for the exclusivist position. If God chose to go through all this anguish to redeem mankind, maybe it was the only way possible for God to do so. Could it be that God becoming man and dying for the sins of humanity is the only way that God could be just and the justifier (Rom 3:26)? I believe so.

Finally, Jesus reassures the disciples that they are on the right path. The words normally translated *from now* (ἀπ' ἄρτι), should be understood as a single word, ἀπάρτι, which means "certainly." Modern editions of the Greek New Testament have added accents and word spacing, though the manuscripts have neither. Furthermore, there is evidence in antiquity that the wording should be read in this way. For example, the Latin Vulgate translates the word

---

[30] E.g., John Hick, "The Non-Absoluteness of Christianity," in *The Myth of Christian Uniqueness: Toward a Pluralistic Theology of Religions*, ed. John Hick and Paul F. Knitter (Maryknoll, NY: Orbis, 1990), 16–36. Occasionally, "evangelicals" will respond to the siren call of pluralism. See, e.g., Clark Pinnock, *A Wideness in God's Mercy: The Finality of Jesus Christ in a World of Religions* (Grand Rapids: Zondervan, 1992), and most recently Rob Bell, *Love Wins: A Book about Heaven and Hell and the Fate of Every Person Who Has Ever Lived* (New York: HarperOne, 2011).

unambiguously as *utique*—"certainly." The meaning is an assurance that those who know Jesus have certainly known the Father and have seen the Father in Jesus. The upshot is that the paragraph provides the second reason why we should believe in Christ: there is no other way to God.

Preaching the Text

John 14:5–7 provides the second grounds for belief in Christ. The first was his veracity. This second is that humans ought to believe in him because he is the only way to the Father. It would be difficult to craft a better MIT than this statement. This leads to a very straightforward MIM: "You ought to believe on Christ because he is the only way to the Father."

The outline of the text should follow the structure of the text. Usually this means the structures farthest to the left of our diagram form the main points. The largest linguistic structures of this text are the question and its answer. However, the most prominent part is found in Jesus' answer. So, then, the best sermon outline would be structured around the HEAD-amplifications of verses 6–7. These verses give the meat of Jesus' response and should be the main treatment of our sermon.

SERMON SKETCH

TEXT: John 14:5–7
MIT: Jesus is the only way to the Father.
MIM: You ought to believe on Christ because he is the only way to the Father.
TOPIC: Jesus, GPS, and You

INTRODUCTION

Map errors have been the bane of travelers since the time of the first map. Today, something fascinating is occurring. We are fast becoming so utterly dependent on GPS devices that we believe them more than our own good sense. The fact of the matter is that who or what directs your path is incredibly important. A flawed guide will not direct you as you expect and may not get you to the destination you anticipate. It matters whom you trust. It matters even more to whom you trust your soul.

Our text today is the second reason one should believe in Jesus. In response to Jesus announcing his departure and his confidence that his own know the way he is going, Thomas declares, "Lord, . . . we don't know where You're going. How can we know the way?" (John 14:5 HCSB). Jesus' response is that he is the only way to the Father. This is perhaps the most important thing you will ever hear. You ought to believe on Christ because he is the *only* way to the Father.

OUTLINE

I. **The Lord's Claim Is Comprehensive (14:6)**
"I am the way, the truth, and the life" (HCSB).

A. TEXT

1. He is the way.

2. He is the truth.

3. He is the life.

B. TODAY

Humans were created for fellowship with God. The height of satisfaction comes from knowing him. Therefore, since Jesus Christ is the way, the truth, and the life . . .

1. Christ should be the object of our study;

2. Christ should be the object of our passions;

3. Christ should be the object of our communication.

II. **The Lord's Claim Is Exclusive (14:6)**

A. TEXT
"No one comes to the Father except through Me" (HCSB).

1. It does not allow for many paths.

2. It does not allow for unintentionally being on the path.

B. TODAY:
The implications are critically important.

1. Hopes that you may find eternal life apart from faith in Christ are unfounded.

2. Hope that the people of the world will live eternally apart from faith in Christ is unfounded.

3. Just getting off the wrong path does not insure salvation.

III. The Disciple's Certainty (14:7)

"If you know Me, you will also know My Father. From now on you do know Him and have seen Him" (HCSB).

A. TEXT

1. Christ promises intimacy with God[31] (to know Christ is to know the Father).
2. Christ is confident of the disciples' relationship to the Father.
   a. They had seen the Father without realizing it.
   b. "From now on" is really "certainly" (ἀπάρτι).

B. TODAY: Note the following implications:

1. The way is extraordinarily simple. You simply need to know Jesus.
2. You need no intermediary between you and God. You simply need to know Jesus.

CONCLUSION

In an act of complete selflessness Christ took the brunt of our sin. But beyond the scope of Christ's sacrifice, I want you to see the key difference. We threw the "grenade," if you will, before Christ, not the enemy. He died to take our sins away. It is offensive to propose that his is one way among many. It is foolishness to reject it for your own way to God.

---

[31] In this sermon I will develop the themes of intimacy and confidence (knowledge and certainty). The next passage develops the mutuality of the Father and the Son, so I would only mention it here.

The Third Ground for Faith: Jesus Is Equal to the Father (14:8–11)

Analyzing the Text

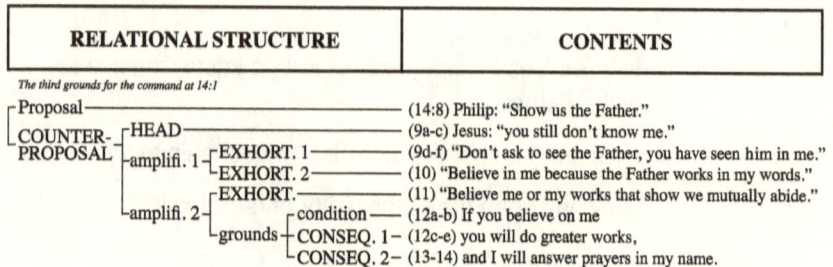

The third ground (and the second exchange) is again developed from the final clause of Jesus' statement in 7c. Jesus affirms, "and you certainly know Him, and have seen Him" (καὶ ἀπάρτι γινώσκετε αὐτόν, καὶ ἑωράκατε αὐτόν). The text is structured around a conversation exchange between Philip and Jesus along similar lines as the previous one with Thomas. Only this time it is more complicated.

Philip's proposal is the foil for Jesus' answer that forms a third ground for belief: Jesus' unique relationship to the Father. Jesus' response is a rhetorical question that must be interpreted as a statement (14:9b–c). It, in turn, is developed by two proposition clusters (14:10, 11–14). Each of these amplifications is an exhortation (cast, again as rhetorical questions) in light of the truth that the disciples don't quite grasp who Jesus is. The entire paragraph is developing the defense that Jesus and the Father are one (cf. John 10:31).

Interpreting the Text

The stimulus for the paragraph is Philip's request to see the Father. Given Old Testament revelation regarding the unmediated presence of God, Philip's request is at once laudable and audacious. Before we rebuke Philip, however, we should note that the desire to see God is praiseworthy. There is no higher human experience to be had than to be in the presence of God.[32] However pure his motivations are, Philip is audacious on two fronts. First, Jesus had just confirmed they had seen the Father. Philip's request must be seen as at least an implied denial of Jesus' statement, "You have seen Him" (John 14:7). Second, it is audacious because the request echoes Moses' request in Exodus 33:18.[33] Moses pleaded, "show me your glory" (LXX δεῖξόν μοι τὴν σεαυτοῦ δόξαν; cf.

---

[32] See Carson, *John*, 494.
[33] See Keener, *John*, 2:945.

Philip's question, δεῖξον ἡμῖν τὸν πατέρα). Philip's request casts the disciples in Moses' position when Jesus is the new Moses. Furthermore, Moses was allowed to see God's *glory* in Exodus 33 with a caveat. "'I will cause all My goodness to pass in front of you, and I will proclaim the name Yahweh before you. I will be gracious to whom I will be gracious, and I will have compassion on whom I will have compassion.' But He answered, 'You cannot see My face, for no one can see Me and live'" (Exod 33:19–20). This caveat permeates both testaments (see e.g., Gen 32:30; Exod 3:6; 24:8–11; Deut 4:33; 5:24, 26; Judg 6:22; 13:22; Isa 6:5; John 1:18; 5:37; 6:46; 1 Tim 6:16), yet Philip asks anyway, replacing "glory" with "Father." It is audacious for Philip to ask, perhaps expecting an exception to the caveat. Given the biblical record available to Philip and Johannine theology, we expect a rebuke from Jesus. The rebuke we get, however, is unexpected. It is foolish for Philip to ask, but it's foolish because Philip has already seen the Father in Jesus.

Jesus' initial reply is strictly a question, but it must be taken rhetorically; that is, more as a statement than a real question. This is the first of three rhetorical questions in this last paragraph alone (see also 14:9 and 10). The meaning of a rhetorical question is clearer when we convert it to a statement. If we make the conversion, we have, most likely, a Concession-CONTRAEXPECTATION relationship. This yields the meaning of "Although I have been with you [plural] for such a long time, you [singular] still do not know me, Philip."

Jesus then clarifies for Philip (and us), "The one who has seen Me has seen the Father" (John 14:9 HCSB). The clarification is more than the Jewish principle of representation of the messenger (the *šālîah*[34]), and more than simply intimacy with God.[35] Carson rightly notes the language of Sonship and Fatherhood that permeates the Gospel requires a stronger reference.[36] John's presentation simply outstrips any idea less than unity of essence. This is nothing new to the Fourth Gospel (see 10:30 and 12:45). Furthermore, in John 1:14, 18 Jesus is the bearer of God's glory on earth. He perfectly represents God to humanity. Thus, Jesus' claim of mutual indwelling with the Father, in context of Johannine theology, is very high Christology.

Jesus proceeds to give three commands. The first two are mitigated commands, framed as rhetorical questions. The last, "believe," is the only imperative by form, making it the more prominent command.

---

[34] See, Köstenberger, *John*, 432. *šālîah* is a messenger or an envoy; in the Mishnah, the envoy was considered intimately associated to the sender. Cf. *Berakoth* 5.5 "A man's agent is like to himself." Certainly more is intended here.

[35] Cf. Keener's citation of Profiat Duran (Isaac ben Moses Halevi) who suggested John was referring to intimacy not divinity. Keener, *John*, 2:944.

[36] Carson, *John*, 494–95.

The first two commands are closely connected and form the first amplification of Jesus' remark that the disciples still don't quite get it. The basis of the first exhortation in 9e is the statement in 9d: "The one who has seen Me has seen the Father" (HCSB). Therefore, asking to see the Father is not a proper request. The rhetorical question "How do you say . . ." is, in essence, a command. It carries the meaning of "Don't say, 'show us the Father.'" The second question/command follows on its heels. "Do you not believe . . . ?" (14:10a) is singular (aimed at Philip) and is another mitigated command. Here it has the force of "believe that I am in the Father and the Father is in Me." This implicit command is made explicit by the imperative in verse 11. The ground for believing is found in verse 10d–f. Believe because it is the Father who does his works in Jesus' words. Because it is the indwelling Father who does the works (Jesus' words), these works are evidence of the mutual indwelling of the Father and the Son. Jesus, then, is pointing to the divine source of his words, reinforcing the veracity of his claims. This seems to be an important point in his apologetic. In 10f the shift in agent (the Father who does the works) is marked for development by δέ. In conjunction with this, faith based on the Father's works in 11d is marked for development by another δέ.

The second amplification (14:11–14) is the more prominent of the two. It is linguistically marked for prominence in that "believe" (πιστεύετε) is the only imperative by form in the paragraph. The exhortation in 11a is also prominent in how it is developed. In the previous amplification, exhortation one (9e–f) and exhortation two (10b–c) are both paired with rather brief grounds. In this second amplification, the exhortation (11a) is developed with more complexity and length. Here, the "law of proportion" suggests a matter important to the writer/speaker.

Jesus' injunction to believe is not to believe in him (as in salvation), but to believe him that he and the Father mutually indwell.[37] The heart of the matter is Jesus' reliability. This mutual indwelling is also the content of "believe" in the rest of this verse. So, then, the meaning is something like, "Believe Me *when I say* that I am in the Father and the Father in Me, but if not, believe *that I am in the Father and the Father in Me*, because of the works themselves." Thus, he gives his own two options for faith in him; we can believe him for his own reliability or we can believe the works that also declare the mutual indwelling (10f). Lest we miss it, the point is the mutual indwelling.

---

[37] The construction at 14:11 (πιστεύετέ μοι) is different than the construction earlier (εἰς ἐμὲ πιστεύετε, 14:1). In the former, 14:11, "me" is the direct object of the verb. At the latter, 14:1, the construction employs a prepositional phrase that makes Jesus the place where we lay our faith. The concept of saving faith is clearly meant.

The connection between verses 11 "Believe me," and 12–14 illustrate one of the difficulties in describing the semantic structure of John. Does 12–14 conclude 1–11, or is it the grounds for the exhortation in 14:11?[38] One viable option is to see 12–14 as the conclusion to 1–11 because of a slight difference in the reference of "believe." The "believe" of 8–11 is an exhortation to accept the ontological nature of Christ as the grounds for faith in verse 1. The expression is "believe me" (πιστεύετέ μοι). In contrast, "believe" in verse 11 does not have a direct object but a prepositional phrase that is normal when describing saving faith: "believing on me" (πιστεύων εἰς ἐμέ). As such the referent is slightly different. Furthermore, Jesus' solemn announcement ("truly, truly . . .") highlights these verses as important. Furthermore, it introduces a heretofore-unmentioned point: the greater works of the believer and a new power in prayer.[39] Therefore, one could simply construe it as the conclusion to 1–11. If so, the constituent would function as a result of verse 1's "believe."

However, I think that the tight-knit connection between 11 and 12–14 requires them to be associated together. Verses 12–14 announce the grounds for the exhortation to believe Jesus in 11. Because the command in verse 11 is quite similar and part of the argument of the nuclear clause in verse 1, it is still proper to see this as concluding the present paragraph. In doing so, it gives the greater works of the believer as the grounds for believing (on the further grounds of his departure). The "and" (καί) that begins verse 13 conjoins it with verse 12d (both are consequences on the condition of belief). The believer, then, will do greater works and enjoys a new privilege in prayer. However, the promise is not to benefit the believer alone; its purpose is to glorify the Father (13c). Here begins a pattern that will be displayed in all but one paragraph in the Farewell Discourse: it concludes with a purpose clause (see 14:31; 15:11, 17; 16:4a, 33).

The two consequences of believing should be briefly explored. The first is found in 12c–d: the believer will not only do Jesus' works but greater works. It is amazing enough to contemplate doing Jesus' works, but the promise to

---

[38] John is often accused of having rough or bad transitions. (E.g., Wayne Meeks is often cited regarding the nature of Johannine transitions: "the major literary problem of John is its combination of remarkable stylistic unity and thematic coherence with glaringly bad transitions between episodes at many points." Wayne Meeks, "Man from Heaven in Johannine Sectarianism," *JBL* 91 [1972]: 48.) However, it is also true that John often has nearly seamless transitions, as is the case here. The topic "believe" smoothly guides us through this paragraph. It was reintroduced as a rhetorical question in 10a, then belief in his mutual indwelling with the Father is encouraged (10a, 11a) on the grounds of his veracity and the Father's work through him (11c) to finally the present promise to those who do believe (12b).

[39] Levinsohn points out that when ὅτι does not follow ἀμὴν ἀμὴν λέγω σοι/ὑμῖν (18/25 times) a new point is developed. Stephen Levinsohn, *Discourse Features of the Greek New Testament: A Coursebook on the Information Structure of the New Testament*, 2nd ed. (Dallas: SIL, 2000), 266. See also Stephen H. Levinsohn, "ὅτι *Recitativum* in John's Gospel: A Stylistic or a Pragmatic Device?", *Work Papers of the Summer Institute of Linguistics, University of North Dakota Session* 43 (1999): 1–14.

do greater works is staggering. Exactly what Jesus' works and "greater works" mean has been variously interpreted. It is not likely that the works are miraculous events like walking on water or changing water to wine. John prefers the word "signs" for these (although not all signs are miraculous). Nor does a reference to more spectacular works seem to be possible. What is more spectacular than Lazarus coming from the tomb? In light of this, some have suggested that, based on the book of Acts, the promise refers to converts.[40]

It is more likely that this verse may be understood in light of the believer's relationship with Christ. The conclusion in 12c and d is based on the fact that Jesus "is going to the Father." In other words, Jesus' death, resurrection, and exaltation provide the basis for the works. In this way, the setting for the works is thoroughly eschatological. That is, the new age and relationship founded through the accomplishments of Christ will facilitate Jesus' works through the disciple. Because of the believers' union with Christ, these works are Jesus' works. Furthermore, as Köstenberger states, "these works will be 'greater' than Jesus', since they will take place in a different, more advanced phase of God's economy of salvation."[41] They are not greater because of what they are or how many they are, but when they take place in salvation history. As Carson states, ". . . the works that the disciples perform after the resurrection are greater than those done by Jesus before his death insofar as the former belong to an age of clarity and power introduced by Jesus' sacrifice and exaltation."[42]

The second consequence of believing on Jesus is a promise regarding Jesus' response to their prayers in 14:13–14. The Christological implications of these statements are impressive. Not only does Christ expect to be the object of faith in the same way as God (14:1); now he also receives and answers the prayers of the disciples. However, not only does he answer prayers in his name, so does the Father (see 16:23). The mutual work of the Son and the Father is a theme that runs through the Farewell Discourse.[43] Clearly the Christology is of the highest order.

The phrase "in the name of *x*" is used in a variety of ways in the Scriptures. It could signal reputation (as in showing honor and avoiding shame—see Ps 29:2). In prayer, it can signal to whom the prayer is made (see Ps 9:2) and

---

[40] E.g., Barrett, while not dismissing the belief in miracles, understands the reference to be to the gathering of converts. Barrett, *John*, 460. See also Leon Morris, *The Gospel according to John*, NICNT (Grand Rapids: Eerdmans, 1995), 574.

[41] Andreas J. Köstenberger, "The Greater Works of the Believer according to John 14:12," Διδασκαλια (Spring 1995): 41.

[42] Carson, *John*, 496.

[43] Cf. e.g., 14:16 and 26. Both the Father and Son send the Paraclete. The controversy in the great schism of the eleventh century comes from the West appropriating the FD language and adding "and the Son" (Latin: *filioque*) to the Nicene Creed's reference of the progression of the Spirit from the Father. The East vigorously objected.

perhaps serve as a substitution for the divine name (see 1 Chr 13:6 LXX). It can be used to describe the authoritative representative, so that false prophets actually speak "in their own name" while claiming to speak for God. In John 5:43 we see this usage in Jesus speaking "in my Father's name" and another speaking "in his own name."[44]

The promise of effective prayers in Jesus' name is rather common in the Farewell Discourse (14:13–14; 15:7, 16; 16:23–24, 26), Johannine epistles (1 John 3:21–22; 5:14–15), and outside of Johannine literature as well (Matt 7:7–8; 18:19; 21:22 and pars.; Jas 1:5–6; 5:15). In the Farewell Discourse the usage refers either to the Paraclete who is sent in Jesus' name (14:26) or to the disciples' praying in Jesus' name. Regarding the latter, it is one of the purposes of the disciples' election (15:16) and is closely associated with the disciples' direct access to God (16:26–27). Jesus' declaration in 16:24 suggests that in the new era inaugurated by Jesus the people of God approach him in identification with Christ. Thus, the usage in John more closely resembles representing the deity. In this case, representation is based on the disciples' identification and union with Christ.

Elsewhere in Scripture many of the promises to hear such prayers carry caveats such as "according to His will" (1 John 5:14–15 HCSB) and "keeping His commandments" (1 John 3:21–22) among others. It is noteworthy that no such caveat or condition appears in 14:13–14. However, because the promise is closely connected to the greater works (a parallel consequence of believing), it is no stretch to see the greater works and the prayers of disciples in the same context. Far from being a magic incantation to get what one desires, prayers in Jesus' name are the prayers of believers who are in union with Christ (see e.g., 15:5). This would assume most of the caveats found elsewhere in Scripture (believing, obedience, according to the Father's will, etc.), and it explicitly states that these prayers are answered to glorify God. It is also no stretch to associate greater works with prayer in Jesus' name as well. The two naturally go hand in hand.

Preaching the Text

The MIT of this passage is "Christ declared that people should believe on him because of his unique relationship to the Father." As we bridge to the sermon, the MIM, then, is "Today we should believe on Jesus because of his unique relationship to the Father." Like the previous text, it is the content of Jesus' response to Philip's question that should form the heart of the sermon. In this case it is the counterproposal, more specifically, the development of the

---

[44] Keener, *John*, 2:949.

CONTENT starting in 14:9b. The three large elements (HEAD and two amplifications) that make up Jesus' response should be the points of the sermon.

SERMON SKETCH

TEXT: John 14:8–14
MIT: Christ declared that people should believe in him because of his unique relationship to the Father.
MIM: Today we should believe in Jesus because of his unique relationship to the Father.
TOPIC: Seeing God

INTRODUCTION

In Jesus' last formal lesson before his disciples, he teaches them about the things most near to his heart at the moment: how to enjoy his presence in spite of his absence. This is the essence of thriving spiritually between his going away and coming again. First he tells us at 14:1 not to have a troubled heart at his departure. Instead he will reveal the "secret" of the untroubled heart. It is to believe on him (14:1–14) and to love/obey him (14:15–25). We have been exploring the concept of believing in him in 14:1–14. We saw that we should believe in him because of his own veracity (14:2–4), because he is the only way to God (14:5–7), and today we will see that we should believe in him because of his unique relationship to the Father in 14:8–14.

The topic is introduced in 14:8 by Philip who asks Jesus to "show us the Father." This question is at once touching and startling. It is touching because there is no greater desire than to be in the presence of God. It is startling because Philip asks for a very dangerous thing, for no man can see God and live.

As we listen in to the conversation between Philip and our Lord, I want you to ask yourself a question. "Am I missing that greatest of all desires, to see God, by failure to believe in Jesus?"

I. The Desire of the Ages: The Longing to See God (14:8–9c)

"Lord," said Philip, "show us the Father, and that's enough for us." Jesus said to him, "Have I been among you all this time without your knowing Me, Philip?" (HCSB).

A. TEXT

1. Philip's Ambition

    a. The desire to see God is a person's highest ambition.

       i. The blessing of the righteous is that they will see God.

       "The pure in heart are blessed, for they will see God" (Matt 5:8 HCSB).

       ii. It was the confidence of Job.

       "Even after my skin has been destroyed, yet I will see God in my flesh. I will see Him myself; my eyes will look at Him, and not as a stranger. My heart longs within me" (Job 19:26–27 HCSB).

    b. It is noble.

       He is not hiding from God like Adam and Eve in the garden. In Philip's case there may very well be a sense of self-indulgence with the request.

2. Philip's Audacity

    a. It ignores (or rebukes) Jesus' previous statement.

    b. No man can see God and live.

       i. A desire to be like Moses? (cf. Exodus 34).

       ii. Expecting a special dispensation from God?

3. Philip's Exposure

    a. In 14:9 we expect a rebuke from Jesus.

    b. Jesus' statement is not a rebuke but revelation. It is best understood as "after all these years, you still do not know me."

    c. In other words, in Philip's desire to see God he missed perceiving God.

B. TODAY: A Form of Religion

Philip's problem is that he did not recognize Jesus' union with the Father. Shockingly, then, he's practicing religion without its power. It's far too common today.

1. We desire to do good things but seldom do lasting good.
2. We turn a relationship with God into something for personal gain.
3. We have a form of religion while not knowing the power of it.

It's time to be done with all that. Jesus' words to Philip are the cure. We must believe.

II. Belief in Christ: The Way to See God (14:9d–10)

"The one who has seen Me has seen the Father. How can you say, 'Show us the Father'? Don't you believe that I am in the Father and the Father is in Me? The words I speak to you I do not speak on My own. The Father who lives in Me does His works" (HCSB).

A. TEXT

Belief in Christ is how we will see God because seeing Jesus is actually seeing the Father.

1. Jesus identifies himself with the Father.

   A reciprocal (mutual) identification

2. Jesus commands belief in him (v. 10).
3. The words of Jesus are the Father's works.

   The words are the work of the Father who dwells in Christ.

B. TODAY

1. Authentic faith in Jesus identifies him with the Father.
2. Authentic faith in Jesus takes him at his word.

III. Belief in Christ: The Way to Glorify God (14:11–14)

"Believe Me that I am in the Father and the Father is in Me. Otherwise believe because of the works themselves. I assure you: The one who believes in Me will also do the works that I do. And he will do even greater works than these, because I am going to the Father. Whatever you ask in My name, I will do it so that the Father may be glorified in the Son. If you ask Me anything in My name, I will do it" (HCSB).

A. TEXT

1. Believe that Jesus is one with the Father.
   a. Believe because of Jesus' veracity.
   b. Believe because of Jesus' works.
   c. Both point to his Messiahship.
2. Believers will do greater works.
   a. Greater works are not more miraculous works.
   b. Greater works are not more numerous works.
   c. Greater works are the works associated with the new covenant.
3. Believers will enjoy effective prayer.
   a. What the promise is not:
      i. The promise is not a promise of a limitless genie.
      ii. It is not for personal gain.
      iii. The promise assumes many of the caveats elsewhere in Scripture.
   b. What the promise is:

   The means to glorify the Father

B. TODAY

1. Jesus expects his followers to do the greater works.
   a. Witnessing

      b. Mission trips

      c. Social ministry

  2. Jesus expects his followers to be effective pray-ers.

Much of the reason we are not is that we treat salvation as if it were all for us and not to glorify the Father.

CONCLUSION

Adam walked with God in the cool of the day, but since the fall of humanity we have not had the same privilege. Humanity is fallen and therefore distant from God. We hear his voice with difficulty and never see him in the same way. In fact, the fall is so devastating that if we could see God in all his glory, we would die for "no one can see Me and live" (Exod 33:20 HCSB). Yet, in Christ this horrid state of affairs is reversed. When we have seen him, we have seen the Father. Because of his identity with the Father, the results of the fall can be mitigated and ultimately reversed. In Christ, we may see God. Believe in him, for he is God.

John 14:1–14 forms a single semantic unit around the command to believe and the advantages that accompany belief. For the disciples to have untroubled hearts they must exercise faith in both God and Christ. This is not an exhortation to exercise faith without basis, as the exchanges between Christ and his disciples develop three grounds for exercising trust in him. The first reason that they must not be troubled but trust is that Christ prepares a place for them in his Father's house. The second reason is that he himself is the way to the Father. And the third reason is the relationship between Jesus and the Father: they are one. Thus, the ultimate destination, path, and authority for the disciples' subsequent journey are given as grounds for faith and not despair.

Loving Obedience (14:15–27)

In the last section I divided the command to believe into sermons based on the grounds for belief presented in the text. In the next command given to lead his disciples into comfort, Jesus enjoins loving obedience and its results. I will treat it as one textual unit for the sermon. The Reason-RESULT structure of the text could be treated as such, but I felt keeping the pairs together would avoid unnecessary repetition. Furthermore, the text length is well suited for the sermon setting.

Analyzing the Text

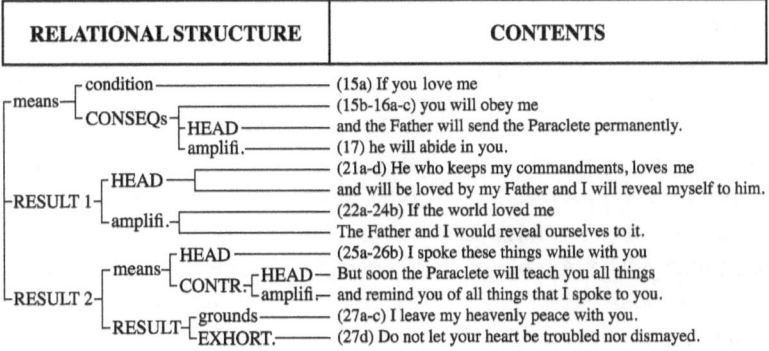

John 14:15–31 develops the second command in the first unit of the Farewell Discourse. The overall structure of 15–27 is means (indwelling), RESULT 1 (manifestation), and RESULT 2 (peace). This paragraph, in turn, makes a transition smoothly into the conclusion of the chapter (28–31) with backward looking references ("anaphora") to the previous unit. Many of the lower-level structures will be discussed in the interpretation below.

Interpreting the Text

The Promised Paraclete (14:15–20)

The first paragraph spans 14:15–20.[45] Here Christ promises the Paraclete to the ones who love and therefore obey Christ. This promise introduces the Paraclete as the indwelling Spirit of truth.[46] The Paraclete is "another" Paraclete. The Greek ἄλλος indicates "another of the same kind" and has Trinitarian implications.[47] The Paraclete is another being like Christ and, as we will see, will mediate the presence of Christ. The conditional sentence that begins the verse is actually a mitigated command (i.e., it is a bit softened) and is the means to the two results that follow.[48] The force is that of an imperative, "Love me and keep my commandments." The language of "love" and "obey" is typical of the OT regarding the duties of God's people to be faithful to the covenant. God's people are to love the Lord. Obedience, then, is the preeminent

---

[45] It has two movements (15–17 and 18–20) that some might want to call paragraphs. Pragmatically I am referring to them together as one paragraph because they relate so closely together.

[46] Dwight M. Smith, *The Composition and Order of the Fourth Gospel: Bultmann's Literary Theory* (New Haven, CT: Yale University Press, 1965), 169; cf. Barrett, *John*, 454.

[47] Jesus is the "paraclete" (i.e., "advocate") at 1 John 2:1.

[48] Barrett noted that the protasis "if you love me," ('Εὰν ἀγαπᾶτέ με) "controls the grammar of the next two verses (15–17a)." Barrett, *John*, 461; see also Carson, *John*, 498.

expression of love. The implication is that even under the old covenant obedience that comes from fear, duty, or guilt rather than love is not the heart of obedience. Covenant faithfulness and love are inseparable. This has not changed under the new covenant.

The gift of the Paraclete to those in covenant with Christ is for the purpose of a permanent divine presence in the life of the believer. This is quite different than the old covenant. In contrast to the world that cannot see or know the Spirit, the disciples do know him because he abides with them (παρ' ὑμῖν μένει). This is likely a reference to the presence of the Spirit through Christ's earthly ministry. The notable promise, however, is the promise of indwelling, "He will be in you" (ἐν ὑμῖν ἔσται). This indwelling fleshes out the nature of the permanent presence of the Paraclete noted in 16c.

This presence of the Paraclete is the way in which Jesus will not leave his own bereft like orphans. John 14:18–20 gives more detail about the promise just made. John has already noted that the Spirit will not come until he is glorified.[49] In 14:18–20, Jesus refers to his own resurrection appearance (19b "you will see me") to the disciples as the day of indwelling. The clause in 20d "and I am in you" hints that the Paraclete's indwelling in some way is manifesting the presence of Christ. This is made explicit in the next two paragraphs.

The Manifestation of Christ (14:21–24)

The paragraph in 14:21–24 is the first result of the indwelling Paraclete. Specifically, the Paraclete mediates the presence of God and Christ to the ones who are in covenant with him (notice the love/obey language is repeated in 14:21). This effectively defines how the giving of the Paraclete will fulfill Christ's proclamation to keep his disciples from being left without his presence. The gift of the Spirit is not based on the believer's obedience. Kruse rightly notes that the gift of the Spirit is not a matter of human effort in works; it is a commitment to follow him in love.[50] In contrast, the world that does not follow Jesus neither sees him nor knows him (i.e., the Paraclete). Jesus promises to send the Paraclete to be with the followers of Jesus forever.

Furthermore, this is not particularly a "second blessing" or reception of the Spirit after conversion, for this is strongly connected to the idea of being in the covenant relationship with God and Christ. Furthermore, in verses 20–21, Christ implies that this is an experiential indwelling. The disciples will know

---

[49] Referring to the promise of "rivers of living water," John explained, "He said this about the Spirit. Those who believed in Jesus were going to receive the Spirit, for the Spirit had not yet been received because Jesus had not yet been glorified" (7:39).

[50] Colin G. Kruse, *John: An Introduction and Commentary*, TNTC (Grand Rapids: Eerdmans, 2003), 304.

the indwelling of Christ in the Father and Christ in them. So then, the first result of the indwelling of the Paraclete is the manifestation of the Son. In other words, Jesus promises his continued presence in spite of his absence through the indwelling of the Paraclete.

Judas's question in 14:22 helps define what manifestation will include. Jesus will not manifest himself to the world because the world is not in a covenant relationship with him. They do not love him. Judas's question provides a foil for Jesus to describe what kind of manifestation he is promising. He does this in verse 23 by posing a what-if scenario. If they love him, he and the Father will make their abode with them. In other words, the manifestation is an inner indwelling.

Christ Leaves Peace (14:25–27)

The structure of 14:25–31 is probably the most difficult portion of the discourse to outline. Scholars have proposed at least four different options with minor variations. First, many hold that 25–31 begins a new paragraph and begins the conclusion to 14:1–24.[51] Second, others suggest that there is no major break here (i.e., 14:15–31 forms one unit of discourse).[52] Third, some agree that verses 25–26 belong to the previous paragraph but think that 14:27 (or some part of it) marks the beginning of the conclusion.[53] Finally, some think the conclusion of 14:1–31 begins in verse 28 and 25–27 belongs to the previous paragraph.[54] Coming to a decision is no easy feat.

I believe the last option is the best understanding of the structure of the text.[55] The phrase "I have spoken these things" (ταῦτα λελάληκα) in 14:25 is

---

[51] This is the most common opinion. So Brown, *John*, 2:652; Rudolf Bultmann, *The Gospel of John: a Commentary*, trans. G. R. Beasley-Murray, R. W. N. Hoare, and J. K. Riches (Philadelphia: Westminster, 1971), 625; Edwyn Clement Hoskyns, *The Fourth Gospel*, ed. Francis Noel Davey, 2nd ed. (London: Faber & Faber, 1947), 461; Morris, *John*, 582; F. J. Moloney, *The Gospel of John*, SP 4 (Collegeville, MN: Liturgical, 1998), 409; Ridderbos, *John*, 510; Barnabas Lindars, *The Gospel of John*, NCB 34 (London: Oliphants, 1972), 483; Rudolf Schnackenburg, *The Gospel according to St. John*, vol. 3 (New York: Crossroad, 1982), 3:82; and Thomas L. Brodie, *The Gospel according to John: A Literary and Theological Commentary* (New York: Oxford University Press, 1993), 458.

[52] Carson, *John*, 498; Gerald R. Borchert, *John 12–21*, NAC 25B (Nashville: B&H, 2002), 131; Craig Blomberg, *The Historical Reliability of John's Gospel: Issues and Commentary* (Downers Grove, IL: InterVarsity, 2001), 201.

[53] See, Keener, *John*, 2:982; Jürgen Becker, *Das Johannes nach Johannes: Kapitel 11–21*, ÖTKNT 4 (Würzburg: Echter, 1981), 475; Beasley-Murray, *John*, 245; A. Dettwiler, *Die Gegenwart des Erhöhten*, FRLANT 169 (Göttingen: Vandenhoeck & Ruprecht, 1995), 125; Ernst Haenchen, *A Commentary on the Gospel of John*, vol. 2, Heremeia, trans. Robert W. Funk (Philadelphia: Fortress, 1984), 128; and M. L. Lagrange, *Évangile selon Sain Jean* (Paris: Gabalda, 1927), 392–93.

[54] Fernando F. Segovia, *Love Relationships in the Johannine Tradition: Agape/Agapan in 1 John and the Fourth Gospel*, SBLDS 58 (Chico, CA: Scholars Press, 1982), 110; K. Scholtissek, "Abschied und neue Gegenwart: exegetische und theologische Reflexionen zur johanneischen Abschiedsrede 13, 31–17, 26," *ETL* 75 (1999): 335.

[55] This marks a small revision of my 2005 opinion but does not affect the thesis proposed there.

often seen as an indicator of a conclusion. However, this alone is not sufficient reason.[56] The context suggests a much broader reference of ταῦτα λελάληκα than just the present speech.[57] The paragraph 25–27 is best understood as the second result of the indwelling Paraclete: peace.

Jesus gives in 14:26 the fullest description of the Holy Spirit in this Gospel.[58] The Paraclete is explicitly identified as the Holy Spirit. His sending by the Father is "in my name." The Holy Spirit, then, is connected to Jesus' authority. We see this plainly in that the Spirit will teach the disciples all things (i.e., everything they need to know) and will remind them of Jesus' words.[59] As Köstenberger notes, the Spirit does not give new or independent revelation. His is a continuation of Jesus' ministry just as Jesus was not independent of the Father.[60]

Finally, Jesus concludes with the promise that he grants a unique peace to his disciples. It is common to note that "peace" (εἰρήνη) is the common Jewish greeting "shalom" (שָׁלוֹם). Jesus, however, clearly means more. He qualifies it as "my peace" (εἰρήνην τὴν ἐμὴν), and it is peace that is different than the world's. It is clearly more than a farewell, but a promise. While it is the aspiration of most people to "lead a tranquil and quiet life" (1 Tim 2:2 HCSB), Jesus describes something more. It, most likely, is a supernatural inner disposition of serenity. Paul describes the peace that "surpasses every thought" (Phil 4:7 HCSB). "Peace" is essentially equivalent to a heart "not troubled" (14:1)—this and the fact that Jesus repeats 14:1 nearly verbatim suggests an *inclusio* (whether it is a formal *inclusio* or not).[61] In the face of Jesus' looming absence, he affirms belief in him and that those in covenant with him will receive the gift of the Holy Spirit, whom the world cannot receive. The Holy Spirit will manifest the presence of Christ. The further ministry of the Spirit is to remind the disciples of Jesus' teaching. Ultimately he produces peace in the heart of the one in covenant with Christ.

---

[56] Contrary to Ridderbos, *John*, 511.

[57] Ταῦτα λελάληκα cannot be a reference to the present speech because the contrast is between the words which Jesus spoke while with the disciples and the Paraclete's future ministry of teaching/reminding. If ταῦτα λελάληκα refers to the present speech (as it must, if this is the conclusion to the speech), then the Paraclete can only amplify the present words of Jesus.

[58] Morris, *John*, 582.

[59] Ibid.

[60] Köstenberger, *John*, 442.

[61] In my 2002 dissertation I was not convinced of a strong separation between 14:27 and 28. At that time I concluded an *inclusio* is unlikely. However, I now am more inclined to think that it is a possibility. See, Segovia, *Farewell*, 65; Becker, "Die Abschiedsreden," 220–21; D. H. Dodd, *The Interpretation of the Fourth Gospel* (Cambridge: Cambridge University Press, 1953), 403; and J. Ramsey Michaels, *The Gospel of John*, NICNT (Grand Rapids: Eerdmans, 2010), 793. Even so, I stand by my contention then that it is a difficult decision here.

The secret to the untroubled heart is belief in Christ expressed in loving obedience. When this happens, the Paraclete manifests the presence of Christ in the believer, communicates Christ's word, and produces a supernatural peace in the believer. Surely no greater bulwark against a troubled heart could exist.

Preaching the Text

The major movements of the text are represented in the largest structures in our diagram "Analyzing the Text" on page 117. These three suggest a sermon with three major movements based on the Means-RESULT(s) structure of the text. The complication of the text makes it difficult to express it in a simple sentence, so my MIT is a little wordy: "The Paraclete mediates the presence of Christ and produces peace in the hearts of those who love him (expressed in obedience)." The MIM is a bit simpler: "Lovingly obedient believers can expect to experience the presence of God and the peace that passes understanding."

FOUNDATIONAL WORK

MIT: The Paraclete mediates the presence of Christ and produces peace in the hearts of those who love him (expressed in obedience).

MIM: Lovingly obedient believers can expect to experience the presence of God and the peace that passes understanding.

TOPIC: Finding Peace

INTRODUCTION

In the Farewell Discourse, Jesus has told us not to have a troubled heart. The first part of not being troubled is faith in him. In John 14:15 he picks up the second step; it comes from the Holy Spirit whom Christ calls the Paraclete. The Paraclete mediates the presence of Christ and produces peace in the heart of those who love him (expressed in obedience). Today I want you to find this priceless treasure. It is the lovingly obedient believer who can expect to experience the presence of God and the peace that passes understanding.

OUTLINE

I. Love and Obedience (14:15–20)

"If you love Me, you will keep My commands. And I will ask the Father, and He will give you another Counselor to be with you forever. He is the Spirit of truth. The world is unable to receive Him because it doesn't see Him or know Him. But you do know Him, because he remains with you and will be in you. I will not leave you as orphans; I am coming to you. In a little while the world will see Me no longer, but you will see Me. Because I live, you will live too. In that day you will know that I am in My Father, you are in Me, and I am in you" (HCSB).

A. TEXT

1. Love and obedience are an expression of a commitment to faithfully follow Christ.

   a. The language of love and obedience is covenantal language.

   b. It is closely related to faithfulness.

2. The result is the indwelling of the Spirit.

   a. His presence in Christ's absence.

   b. He is available after the resurrection.

   c. He will produce confidence in the disciples.

B. TODAY

1. Being in the new covenant is not simply believing.

2. It is a commitment to love him.

3. Love is defined in terms of a heartfelt obedience.

II. Presence (14:21–24)

"'The one who has My commands and keeps them is the one who loves Me. And the one who loves Me will be loved by My Father. I also will love him and will reveal Myself to him.'" Judas (not Iscariot) said to Him, 'Lord, how is it You're going to reveal Yourself to us and not to the world?' Jesus answered, 'If anyone loves Me, he will keep My word. My Father will love him, and We will come to him and make Our home with him. The one who doesn't love Me will not keep My words. The word that you hear is not Mine but is from the Father who sent Me'" (HCSB).

A. TEXT

1. The Paraclete mediates the presence of God and Christ to those who love him.
2. Jesus will not manifest himself to the world because the world is not in a covenant relationship with him.

B. TODAY

There are three degrees of the presence of Christ in our lives.

1. There is growth in his presence.

    We love him, and that is expressed in obedience. Those who are closest to Christ are the ones who love him in every aspect of life.

2. There is the stagnant Christian.

    We confess love for him, but the truth is that we have let either distraction, pleasure, or convenience choke out our obedience. Our confession of love falls on deaf ears.

3. There are those who don't love or know him.

    It is no wonder that the world struggles to perceive God. Why would he manifest himself to those who refuse to submit in love?

III. The Results of the Spirit's Indwelling (14:25–27)

"I have spoken these things to you while I remain with you. But the Counselor, the Holy Spirit—the Father will send Him in My name—will teach you all things and remind you of everything I have told you. Peace I leave with you. My peace I give to you. I do not give to you as the world gives. Your heart must not be troubled or fearful" (HCSB).

A. TEXT

1. The Spirit had reminding ministry among the disciples.

2. The grand result is peace.

   a. It is a cumulative process.

      i. Belief

      ii. Love/obedience

   b. Peace is a product of the Holy Spirit.

      i. Not an absence of war

      ii. His peace transcends the earthly realm.

B. TODAY

   1. The Spirit has an illuminating ministry among us today.

   2. The "peace that passes understanding" is for those who believe in and love Christ.

CONCLUSION

Christ asks you to make an investment. It is to believe in him and love him. It is not complicated. It can be difficult, but the payoff is immense. You receive the indwelling Spirit who will mediate the presence of Christ and bring peace to your heart. The investment is well worth making.

The Conclusion to the First Unit (14:28–31)

Analyzing the Text

RELATIONAL STRUCTURE	CONTENTS
┌HEAD┬circum.────────────────	(28a-b) I told you that I am going away and coming to you.
│ └HEAD┬RESULT────────────	(28c-e) If you loved me, you would rejoice
│ └reason────────────	(28f) because the Father is greater than I
│ ┌HEAD───────────────────	(29a-b) I have told you beforehand so that you will believe.
│ │ ┌conclusion────────	(30a) I do not much more to say to you
│ └amplifi.┴GROUNDS───────	(30b-c) for my time is short
└amplifi.┬ ┌HEAD────────────	(31a-b) But so that the world will know I love the Father
└CONTR.┬PURPOSE┴amplifi.─	(31c) and as the Father has commanded me
└means────────────	(31d) I do this.

A simplified structural analysis is presented above. This section is made up of two proposition clusters or small paragraphs, related in a HEAD-amplification relationship. Its role in the present unit is to conclude the unit and transition to the next. In doing so, Jesus makes it clear that the disciples are not yet in covenant with Christ (nor could they be) and announces difficult times for him and the disciples.

Interpreting the Text

Three elements suggest that this is the conclusion to the entire first unit. First, Christ makes the announcement of his departure. This backward reference includes both major sections of the first unit. Second, Christ shifts the subject matter from his presence to his departure (suggesting this section is separate from the previous). And finally, this section is a summary-type statement (he does as the Father commands). This suggests that we understand this section as distinct from the previous and concluding the present unit of the Farewell Discourse.

The major premise of verse 28 is shocking. The way that Jesus frames the condition is best understood as a "contrary-to-fact condition" so that the "if" clause is stating something that is not the case.[62] The evidence that they do not love Christ is that they do not rejoice in his return to the Father. Instead they grieve and sorrow. Their focus is on their loss, not on Jesus' ultimate gain. The source of the rejoicing they should have is in the Father's superior status: "The Father is greater than I." Jesus is not denying his deity but noting his rank. Jesus in noting his return to the Father assumes his sending. Keener notes that the sender is greater than the one sent in the Mediterranean culture of the time. Elsewhere, John affirms both Jesus' own deity and his distinctiveness from the Father, in terms of personhood. So our best understanding is that the Father is greater, not in essence (i.e., ontologically) but in position (i.e., functionally).[63] While this verse has sparked quite a wide variety of Trinitarian debates, the point is that the disciples do not yet love Christ. The deficiency of the disciples is common throughout the Farewell Discourse. It is seen first in Peter in 13:31–38 and then in Philip in 14:9 (not to mention the ignorance of Philip, Thomas, and Judas). The deficiency of the disciples is now seen among the group: they do not love Jesus. The implications are that they are not yet in a fully realized covenant relationship with Jesus. They do not love, so they also do not follow in obedience.

However, 14:29 makes it clear that Jesus' speech is for the purpose of enabling his disciples.[64] Since Christ has not yet been glorified, the ultimate expression is not yet available. But the implicit promise is that they will enjoy the new relationship with Christ when they see him again. At this point, the

---

[62] See, for example, Köstenberger, *John*, 444; Carson, *John*, 199; and Morris, *John*, 585, among others.

[63] See Keener, *John*, 2:983.

[64] Carson notes that Jesus also noted the treason of Judas Iscariot for the same reason in 13:19. Carson, *John*, 508.

disciples are deficient in both love and belief, the very two commands that form the structure of this unit. But as Köstenberger and Carson both note, this is not to shame the disciples but to encourage them for the future.[65]

Jesus' statement in 14:29 is amplified by 14:30–31d. Jesus will not speak much more to them because the time is nearly up; the ruler of this world is coming. The Devil is pictured as the offstage director manipulating his minions to do his dirty work. At first glance it is difficult to understand the contrast in 14:31a to "He has no power over Me" (HCSB).[66] The phrase, however, indicates that Jesus is not under the Devil's authority.[67] The Devil has no power over Jesus' death, even though the Devil is the "ruler of this world." The contrast highlights Jesus' control over his fate. He does as the Father commands so that the world will know that he loves the Father. He does not die under God's curse but at God's command.

The command in 14:31e "Get up; let's leave this place" (HCSB), has generated a great deal of compositional controversy that I have dealt with elsewhere. Its function in this unit is to close and transition to another unit. The motion is clearly implied. We envision getting up from the table, gathering supplies, and leaving to another location. Pragmatically, this slows down the narrative to highlight the next unit, the vine-and-the-branch allegory.

Preaching the Text

This text lends itself to a two-point sermon following the HEAD-amplification structure noted above. The purpose of the text is twofold. First, the literary purpose of the text is to conclude the present portion of the discourse and move on to the next. For the purpose of preaching we can set this purpose aside. The second purpose, which is more germane to the sermon, is that Christ is making it clear that the disciples do not yet believe regarding a covenant relationship. Furthermore, what is coming is not under the control of the ruler of this world but under God's control. It will be done because he loves the Father (in contrast to the disciples' incomplete love for him).

Thus my MIT is, "Jesus explained what is the nature of covenantal love for God." This converts rather easily into a MIM: "Believers should follow Jesus' example of loving obedience." My topic is "Perfect Love."

---

[65] Ibid. and Köstenberger, *John*, 445.
[66] Both the HCSB and the NIV decline to translate the conjunction καί (normally "and, even, also" but can be translated "but"). The content here suggests strongly a contrast even though καί is employed.
[67] See, Keener, *John*, 2:985, "Jesus dies exclusively at his Father's command." The phrase might be a Semitic idiom meaning "he has no claim on me" (so Carson, *John*, 508). Ridderbos suggests that it might simply be a function of ἔχειν "to have" and mean something like, "against me, he is powerless" (Ridderbos, *John*, 513). The meaning changes little under both understandings.

Foundational Work

MIT: Jesus explained the nature of covenantal love for God.
MIM: Believers should follow Jesus' example of loving obedience.
TOPIC: Perfect Love

INTRODUCTION

The disciples' reaction to Jesus' departure reveals a great deal about them. Furthermore, it reveals a great deal about how we should orient our hearts and thoughts. Thus, in our text, Jesus explained the nature of covenantal love for God. As we investigate the text we will learn that believers should follow Jesus' example of loving obedience.

I. Reject an Insufficient Love (14:28)

"You have heard Me tell you, 'I am going away and I am coming to you.' If you loved Me, you would have rejoiced that I am going to the Father, because the Father is greater than I" (HCSB).

A. TODAY

1. The disciples' self-absorbed sorrow

   a. They are sorrowful because he is leaving them.

   b. Their grief is for their loss not Jesus' gain.

2. The sorrow exposes their hearts.

   a. Theirs, at the moment, was a self-absorbed love.

   They loved having Jesus with them. They wanted the status quo to continue.

   b. They did not listen to what he was telling them.

B. TODAY

This should cause us to examine why we do what we do, especially in the church. The fundamental fact is that while we may never totally solve the motivation issue, it matters.

1. Why do we serve?

    2. Why do we give?

    3. Why do we go?

II. **Perfect Love (14:29–31)**

"I have told you now before it happens so that when it does happen you may believe. I will not talk with you much longer, because the ruler of the world is coming. He has no power over Me. On the contrary, I am going away so that the world may know that I love the Father. Just as the Father commanded Me, so I do. 'Get up; let's leave this place'" (HCSB).

A. TEXT

Jesus' actions contrast directly to the disciples' actions. They love themselves; he loves the Father and expresses it through obedience.

   1. Jesus' life is not taken from him; he gives it.

   2. It is the demonstration of his love for the Father.

   3. He tells the disciples so that they will believe.

B. TODAY

   1. We should love Christ more than our own lives.

   Let us make Revelation 12:11 our highest prayer, "They conquered him by the blood of the Lamb and by the word of their testimony, for they did not love their lives in the face of death" (HCSB).

   2. We should demonstrate our love in obedience.

   While it is rare that God calls on his children to be martyrs, it is not rare that he calls on us to be obedient.

CONCLUSION

Obedience is also the greatest expression of love that we may have for the Lord. Do you want to say to the Lord, "I love you"? Then find what he desires and do it as an expression of worship.

John 14:1–33 contains one of the premier promises to the believer. The secret of the untroubled heart is a matter of the right belief and the right response to that belief. It is a matter of being in a covenant relationship with Christ—that is, under the new covenant. The promise is like this: believe on Christ, love and obey him, and the Holy Spirit will manifest the presence of Christ in your life as a believer. The result is a peace that is unlike what the world can give. The promise does not only entail a cessation of hostilities, but it is also a promise of intimacy. Surely intimate fellowship with Christ will drive out any sense of an anxious and troubled spirit. As we move forward in the Farewell Discourse, the life and advantages of these in covenant with God are the subject on the Lord's mind as he approaches the cross.

CHAPTER 5

UNIT 2: COMMANDS THAT UNITE (15:1–16:4C)

THE second unit of the Farewell Discourse features three sections that focus on issues related to the disciples' unity. The first unit developed the themes related to the situation after the departure of Jesus, then the second unit takes the next step dealing with the disciples' orientation both to Christ and to other people, specifically between those in the community of faith and those outside.

Chapter 14 concluded with an indication of movement. "Arise and let us depart from here" signals a transition to the reader. In narrative time, the pace slows down, and we envision the movement of arising from the dinner. We might imagine the putting away of dinner supplies or the gathering of personal items. We might see the disciples putting on sandals and cloaks for travel at night. Regardless, the mind slows down as we transition. The abrupt statement at 15:1, "I am the true vine" (HCSB; ἐγώ εἰμι ἡ ἄμπελος ἡ ἀληθινὴ), marks a new direction as well. Then, as we continue reading, the genre shifts from reported speech to extended allegory.

At this point, I need to identify an important element as we look at a stretch of text like the Farewell Discourse. A key ingredient to a successful discourse is that it develops a point.[1] That is, it is not solely concerned with the mere act of communication, but the act of communicating something *specific*. Robert Longacre stated, "While a discourse has cohesion/coherence and prominence, it just as necessarily involves *progress*, i.e., a well-formed discourse is going somewhere. The progress of a discourse typically issues in some sort of

---

[1] Beekman and Callow humorously note that a politician often makes statements that are purposefully void of prominence. "The politician may not want to make any promise or pledge stand out, in order that he not be held accountable for it. So he may talk very fluently for half an hour without ever highlighting anything" (John Beekman, John Callow, and Michael Kopesec, *The Semantic Structure of Written Communication*, 5th revision [Dallas: SIL, 1981], 24).

climactic development (or developments) which I have been accustomed to term *peak(s)*."[2] Peak is different than prominence or salience in that it is purely involved in the overall structure of the discourse and not limited to lower-level structures. In other words, we are looking for the heart of the discourse.

I believe the peak of the Farewell Discourse is the vine-and-the-branches analogy. Several reasons support this identification. First, in 14:31 John creates a mental pause as he transitions between the first two units. As a transitional statement, 14:31 bridges the gap but also requires the mind to visualize the process described (departing). Because of this pause the text shows a change of pace immediately before its peak.

Another point in support of 15:1–17 as the peak is that it displays an unprecedented amount of rhetorical underlining. "Abide" (μένω), in one form or another, is used eleven times in 1–17, "abide *in Me*" (μείνατε ἐν ἐμοί) is repeated four times, and an additional two times the disciple is commanded to "abide *in My love*" (μείνατε ἐν τῇ ἀγάπῃ τῇ ἐμῇ). Furthermore, fruit (the result of abiding) is employed eight times in these verses. Finally, "love" (ἀγάπη) or its cognate verb is used nine times in this passage. This is perhaps the most important of the constituents that point to peak. Longacre notes, "The importance of rhetorical underlining must not be underestimated. It is one of the simplest and most universal devices for marking the important point not only of a narration but of other sorts of discourse as well."[3] It would seem that John wanted to mark the importance and the relationship of abiding, loving, and bearing fruit.

The text also displays signs of heightened vividness not employed elsewhere in the discourse. Its use of allegory (an embedded genre) marks it for prominence. As an allegory, the vividness and importance of the text is strengthened. Interlocked with this switch in genre is the introduction of one of John's famous "I am" (ἐγώ εἰμι) sayings. Certainly, it is marked for prominence by precedence elsewhere in the Gospel.

John 15:1–17 also displays a switch in verb tenses. Most notably is the almost complete absence of the future tense in 15:1–17. The text is both a hortatory and an eschatological discourse. Future tenses abound in 14:1–31 and 16:18–33, but only two appear in 15:1–17. Furthermore, the reappearance of multiple aorist verbs is also striking. The use of present and aorist tense verbs dominate this whole section of the Farewell Discourse. This is probably directly due to the switch in genre to an allegorical motif, which only serves to heighten the effect of the embedded genre.

---

[2] Robert E. Longacre, *The Grammar of Discourse*, 2nd ed., Topics in Language and Linguistics (New York: Plenum, 1996), 33.
[3] Ibid., 39.

In this regard, we should not overlook that this passage is the direct reference for the prominent command in 13:34–35. Because the command to mutual love is interlocked with abiding in Christ (via 15:10), it seems that the peak was identified in the introduction. The connection here to the Johannine epistles is striking.

This interlocking of abiding in Christ and loving one another functioning as the peak of the discourse is also evidenced in 1 John. Both Longacre and Sherman and Tuggy identify the peak of the first epistle to be approximately 1 John 4:7–21.[4] There the readers are repeatedly exhorted to love one another based on God's love for them (1 John 4:10) and told that abiding in Christ/God is predicated on loving him (1 John 4:11–12 and 16). These parallels are striking and support a strong coherence between 1 John and the Gospel.

As stated in the previous chapter, in 15:1–16:4c Jesus addresses topics that are all connected to life as a body. In 15:1–11 Jesus addresses the familiar vine-and-the-branch allegory to describe the unifying matter among believers. John 15:12–17 unpacks the new commandment stated in 13:34–35. Finally, in 15:18–16:4c Jesus addresses the relationship of the world to his disciples. In the next major unit (16:4d–33) Jesus describes the advantages of his departure. In this way, the discourse has moved on to another sustained theme that we will unpack in the next chapter. What we see in the present unit is a section comprised of three major movements. None of the movements are particularly long so our study will be to prepare an outline of three sermons.

---

[4] Robert E. Longacre, "Towards an Exegesis of 1 John Based on the Discourse Analysis of the Greek Text," in *Linguistics and New Testament Interpretation: Essays on Discourse Analysis*, ed. David Alan Black, Katherine Barnewell, and Stephen H. Levinsohn (Nashville: Broadman, 1992), 279; Grace E. Sherman and John C. Tuggy, *A Semantic Structure Analysis of the Johannine Epistles* (Dallas: SIL, 1994), 79. See also H. W. York, "An Analysis and Synthesis of the Exegetical Methods of Rhetorical Criticism and Discourse Analysis as Applied to the Structure of 1 John" (Ph.D. diss., Mid-America Baptist Theological Seminary, 1993).

Abide in Christ (15:1–11)

RELATIONAL STRUCTURE	CONTENTS
Illustration — GENERIC	(15:1a-b) I am the true vine and my Father is the vine-dresser
specifics — means	(2a-b) based on fruit, He removes or prunes every branch
PURPOSE	(2c) so that it might bear more fruit.
EXHORTATION — circumstance	(3) You are already clean because of my words.
HEAD — means	(4a) Abide in me and I in you.
PURPOSE	(4c-d) so that you may bear fruit.
grounds 1 — CONCL. — means	(5a-b) I am the vine; you are the branches
RESULT	(5c-d) the one abiding bears much fruit
grounds	(5e) because apart from me you are not able to do anything.
HEAD — grounds 2 — condition	(6a) Unless one abides in me
CONSEQs	(6b-f) he is cast aside, withered, burned, and destroyed.
HEAD — grounds 3 — condition	(7a-b) If you abide in me and obey me
CONSEQ	(7c-d) your prayers will be accomplished.
grounds 4 — means	(8a-b) In bearing much fruit my Father glorified,
RESULT	(8c) and you would (prove to) be my disciples.
grounds	(9a-b) I loved you just as the Father loved me
equiv. — EXHORT — means	(9c) Abide in my love.
RESULT — cond.	(10a-f) If you keep my commandments
CONSEQ	(10b-d) you will abide in my love, as I the Father's.
CONCL — means	(11a) These things I have spoken to you
PURPOSE	(11b-c) so that my joy would be fully in you.

Analyzing the Text

The diagram above is a simplified presentation of the present passage's structure. The first section builds off the presentation of a familiar metaphor. The vine-and-the-branch allegory was so effective that Christians have embraced it as the metaphor of the indwelling Christ. As we will see, it has a rich history in the OT as well. 15:1–2 presents the metaphor.[5] 15:3–10 develops the metaphor mainly through an EXHORTATION—"abide in me" (μείνατε ἐν ἐμοί, 15:4)—that is developed on four grounds. Each of the grounds except the last is introduced by a repetition of either the command to abide or the metaphor itself. The first ground is developed locally in 4c-d and developed as a grounds in 15:5. This cluster begins with a repetition of the vine-and-the-branches metaphor. The ground is that disciples cannot bear fruit unless they abide in Christ. The second ground is found in verse 6 in a conditional sentence (repeating the command to abide in a slightly different manner): nonabiding branches are withered and destroyed. The third ground is found in verse 7 (with another repetition of the command). The disciples are given the

---

[5] Richard Bauckham understands these verses to be very similar to 10:7–18 that is the interpretation of the παροιμία in 10:1–5. He suggests that the author dropped a true parable of Jesus because it was redundant after the interpretation. He further suggests this parable is found in *The Acts of Thomas*, 146. This parable also has echoes in *The Odes of Solomon* 38:17–19 and *The Gospel of Thomas*, 40. Richard Bauckham, "The Parable of the Vine: Rediscovering a Lost Parable of Jesus," *NTS* 33 (1987): 84–101. Carson finds such an omission "astonishing, not to say unprecedented" (D. A. Carson, *The Gospel according to John*, PNTC [Grand Rapids: Eerdmans, 1991], 512).

incentive of answered prayer as grounds for abiding. Finally, verse 8 returns to the ground of fruit bearing; only this time the point is the abundance of fruit.

Structurally, one of the most debated points is whether or not Jesus moves on to a new topic in 15:9. He commands his disciples to abide in his love. Thus, 15:9 either begins a new paragraph or modifies 15:1–8.[6] Those who divide chapter 15 into 15:1–8 and then 15:9–16 usually do so on the grounds that the topic shifts from the metaphor of abiding in Christ to "love."[7] Although this interpretation is not completely without merit, "love" in 15:9–11 is the divine love for the disciples; in 12–17 love is commanded between the disciples. This is surely connected thematically but not within the confines of a single paragraph. Furthermore, and more importantly, to make the break in verse 8 one must overlook (or undervalue) some important structural clues.

First, Jesus' "Abide in my love" (μείνατε ἐν τῇ ἀγάπῃ τῇ ἐμῇ, 15:9) is virtually a restatement of "Abide in me" (μείνατε ἐν ἐμοί, 15:4). Thus, "abide in me" and "abide in my love" are virtual synonyms.[8] This is borne out by the fact that "abiding" and "his word abiding in the disciples" are presented in a reciprocal arrangement in verse 7, and keeping his commandments is presented as the main ingredient to abiding in his love in verse 10. Therefore, keeping his word/commandments seems to be the bridge in the semantic overlap between abiding in Christ and abiding in his love.

Second, 15:11 signals the conclusion to the first paragraph by the use of "I have spoken these things" (ταῦτα λελάληκα; 15:11 HCSB) in combination with a purpose clause. The reference seems to be to the entirety of 15:1–10 and not just 9–10, as the latter is too brief to warrant such a clause.

Finally, there is a rather notable repetition involving 15:12, "This is My command: Love one another as I have loved you" (αὕτη ἐστὶν ἡ ἐντολὴ ἡ ἐμή, ἵνα ἀγαπᾶτε ἀλλήλους καθὼς ἠγάπησα ὑμᾶς; HCSB) and 15:17 "This is

---

[6] Clearly the majority prefers the former. See, e.g., Rudolf Bultmann, *The Gospel of John: a Commentary*, trans. G. R. Beasley-Murray, R. W. N. Hoare, and J. K. Riches (Philadelphia: Westminster, 1971), 529; Jürgen Becker, *Das Johannes nach Johannes: Kapitel 11–21*, ÖTKNT 4 (Würzburg: Echter, 1981), 2:229; Herman Ridderbos, *The Gospel of John: A Theological Commentary*, trans. J. Vriend (Grand Rapids: Eerdmans, 1991), 514; Fernando F. Segovia, *Love Relationships in the Johannine Tradition: Agape/Agapan in 1 John and the Fourth Gospel*, SBLDS 58 (Chico, CA: Scholars Press, 1982), 132; Craig Blomberg, *The Historical Reliability of John's Gospel: Issues and Commentary* (Downers Grove, IL: InterVarsity, 2001), 207; Ben Witherington, *John's Wisdom* (Louisville, KY: WJK, 1995), 255; and Giorgio Giurisato, "Der Weinstock und die Reben: Struktur und Botschaft von Joh 15,1–8," in *Lebendiges Kloster*, ed. Marcus Steiner, Festschrift Georg Holzherr (Freiburg, Schweiz: Paulus, 1997), 112. Carson sees a break in 15:9, but the two paragraphs together make one sub-unit (15:1–16) within 15–16. Carson, *John*, 108.

[7] So Ridderbos, *John*, 514, and Craig S. Keener, *The Gospel of John: A Commentary* (Peabody, MA: Hendrickson, 2003), 2:1002 (Keener starts a new section at 15:8). Giurisato's only stated reason is that the structure of 1–8 is an *inclusio* around "my Father" and "fruit-bearing." Giurisato, "Der Weinstock und die Reben," 112.

[8] Beasley-Murray states, "'To remain' in Jesus is also to remain in his *love*, just as Jesus throughout his life remained in the Father's love." G. R. Beasley-Murray, *John*, WBC 36 (Waco, TX: Word, 1987), 273.

what I command you: love one another" (ταῦτα ἐντέλλομαι ὑμῖν, ἵνα ἀγαπᾶτε ἀλλήλους; HCSB). This *inclusio* joins 15:12–17 as a single unit, making it impossible to see 9–17 as a single paragraph.[9] For these reasons, it is best to see 15:1–11 as the first paragraph on the command to abide. In this way 15:9 and 10 form a new propositional cluster that adds another dimension in the concept of abiding in Christ, namely keeping his commandments.[10]

As stated above, 15:11 signals the conclusion of the paragraph in the repeated formula "I have spoken these things" (ταῦτα λελάληκα; HCSB), for it sums up the previous paragraph employing a purpose clause. By virtue of its summary force, the propositional cluster takes the imbedded themes of vital union, loving, and obedience and ties them to full joy.

Interpreting the text

The Controlling Metaphor (15:1–2)

Jesus begins his statement with "I am the true vine" (Ἐγώ εἰμι ἡ ἄμπελος ἡ ἀληθινή; HCSB). Invoking the imagery of the vine and modifying it with "true" (i.e., "genuine") stirs up powerful imagery that is pregnant with meaning.

The vine imagery is common throughout antiquity, yet the most likely source for the imagery is the OT. Even with a cursory look, it is clear that the metaphor of Israel as God's planted vine is part of Israel's self-understanding.[11] Many feel that the metaphor is introduced in Isaiah 5:1–8.[12] There a parable is given that describes Israel as a vineyard that, in spite of meticulous care, yielded "worthless grapes" and is disciplined. This is consistent with much of the vine imagery in the OT.[13] In Isaiah, though, the story of the vine does not end with the judgment of Isaiah 5, but the restoration of the vine in Isaiah 27:2–6. Motyer states it well, "The vineyard song in verses 2–6 is complementary to 5:1–7. In the earlier passage the emphasis lay on what Israel-Judah made of the Lord's vineyard, but here it is on what the Lord will yet make of

---

[9] As stated above, mere repetition in the Farewell Discourse cannot mark an *inclusio*; there must be strong structural clues as well. In 12–17, these clues are both present and strong. The *inclusio* is well marked, as it begins in a point of departure after the expression, "Ταῦτα λελάληκα." The clear shift to the new topic in 15:18 substantiates the repetition in 15:17 as an *inclusio*.

[10] This is borne out by the fact that 15:9 is introduced by a fronted adverbial clause that forms a point of departure. This local discontinuity does not shift completely off topic (that is, it does not indicate a new unit) but adds the dimension of obedience and love into the topic.

[11] See, e.g., Ps 80:8–18; Jer 2:21; 6:9; 12:10–13; Ezek 15:1–8; 17:5–10; 19:10–14; Hos 10:1–2; 14:7. In other Second Temple literature see *2 Esdras* 5:23; *Sirach* 24:17–23; *2 Baruch* 36–39; and *3 Baruch* 1:2.

[12] Hugh G. M. Willamson, *Isaiah 1–27: Volume 1 (Isaiah 1–5)*, ICC (London: T&T Clark, 2006), 329, 343.

[13] Rodney A. Whitacre, "Vine, Fruit of the Vine," in *Dictionary of Jesus and the Gospels*, ed. Joel B. Green, Scot McKnight, and I. Howard Marshall (Downers Grove, IL: IVP, 1992), 868.

Jacob-Israel, his vineyard people."[14] The vineyard allegory in Isaiah is a narrative of creation, fall, and restoration. This restoration is "in that day" (mentioned twice in the passage), the referent of which is certainly eschatological and soteriological. As Thomas notes, "Within the context of Isaiah the book, restoration will be decidedly a work of God, who imbues the suffering servant with His spirit to accomplish this divine task (Isa 48:16–19; 49:1–13, esp. vv. 6, 8, 61:1–11)."[15] This especially may be the background for the vine imagery employed here.[16]

That Jesus calls himself the *true* vine suggests that, first, he replaces Israel as God's planted vine. This is consistent with John's motif seen throughout the Gospel that Jesus is the replacement of Israel. God's elect are found in Jesus. As Köstenberger states, "Thus, Jesus, the Messiah and Son of God, fulfills Israel's destiny as the true vine of God (Ps. 80:14–17)."[17]

The Father is identified as the farmer. Again consistent with OT usage, it is God who tends to his vine. The language refers to the common actions of a vinedresser who prunes fruitful vines and dislodges useless, unfruitful vines that are burned when they dry out.[18] The main point is that the farmer tends the vine so that it produces more fruit.

The Overarching Command: Abide (15:3–8)

Verses 3–4 form the main injunction of this passage: abide in Christ. Jesus first addresses the disciples and declares their status in the vine. That the branches are "in Me" suggests that he is building off the concept of mutual indwelling presented in 14:20—but he will not explicitly state that until later. In the present context, he has already described the Father's pruning of the individual branches. The word used there is literally "to clean" ($\kappa\alpha\theta\alpha i\rho\epsilon\iota$ [v. 2]). Jesus declares that the disciples are already "clean" ($\kappa\alpha\theta\alpha\rho o i$ [v. 3]). Thus, he announces their status as fruitful branches in him through Jesus' words. However, continued fruitfulness will not happen unless the "branches" abide in the vine. In other words, their vital connection to the vine is absolutely

---

[14] J. Alec Motyer, *The Prophecy of Isaiah: An Introduction and Commentary* (Downers Grove, IL: IVP, 1993), 220–21.

[15] Heath Thomas, "Building House to House (Isaiah 5:8): Theological Reflection on Land Development and Creation Care," *BBR* 21 (2011): 198.

[16] Special thanks goes to my Ph.D. student Grant Taylor who has enlightened me to the vine narrative in Isaiah.

[17] Andreas J. Köstenberger, "John," in *Zondervan Illustrated Bible Backgrounds Commentary*, ed. Clinton E. Arnold (Grand Rapids: Zondervan, 2001), 143. Psalm 80:14–17 (HCSB) states, "Return, God of Hosts. Look down from heaven and see; take care of this vine, the root Your right hand has planted, the shoot that You made strong for Yourself. It was cut down and burned up; they perish at the rebuke of Your countenance. Let Your hand be with the man at Your right hand, with the son of man You have made strong for Yourself."

[18] For a nice historical description see Köstenberger, *Backgrounds Commentary*, 144–45.

necessary for fruit bearing. Thus, he commands them to abide in him (the essence of which is disclosed in v. 9).

Four grounds support the command to abide. First, fruit bearing can only happen when the branch is connected to the vine. In 15:5a–b Jesus clearly identifies the components of the allegory. He is the vine and the disciples are the branches. They must continue to abide in him to bear fruit. The ability of the branch to produce fruit is not dependent on the branch but on the vine's life-giving properties. Likewise, the believer must abide in Christ before fruit bearing is possible. My simple definition of fruit is as follows: anything beneficial that God produces in us and through us. This may be the fruit of the Spirit (Gal 5:22), converts (Rom 1:13), or the fruit of righteousness (Phil 1:11), among other spiritual things.

The second ground for abiding in Christ is given in 15:6 as a condition with four consequences. The four consequences are integrated in a logical sequence (almost a step-goal pattern). By stating it in this way Jesus graphically describes the destruction of nonabiding branches. Branches that do not abide in the vine (and by extension do not bear fruit) are cut off and burned. It is this last element that causes some concern for believers because it could be interpreted to mean one can lose his salvation. As Carson rightly notes, this understanding pushes the analogy of "in Me" too far. He states, "The transparent purpose of the verse is to insist that there are no true Christians without some measure fruit."[19] Throughout the Gospel of John there is a thread regarding those who "believe" but do not really believe. For example, in John 2:23–25 some "believed" in him, but Jesus rejects their "belief" (see also the ones who "believe" in 8:30 who later attempt to kill him, 8:59). People have often, for a variety of reasons, joined themselves superficially to the people of God. These will produce no fruit (see Matt 7:16, 20). The ultimate example of this in the Fourth Gospel is Judas Iscariot.[20]

The third ground is powerful prayer. The condition here is twofold. First, the branch must abide. Given what has already been said, this implies a derived vitality that results in bearing fruit. Second, the words of Christ must dwell in the believer. This suggests the commands of Christ are internalized. This person has a new power in prayer. This is not a heavenly *carte blanche* or the keys to the mall, if you will. Modern Western Christians are far too quick to see the ability to manipulate their environment in these words. It really is an indictment of the materialistic human heart.

---

[19] Carson, *John*, 515.
[20] Ibid.

If we abide in Christ and we have internalized his words, then we are people who have bent our will to his revealed will. We would want nothing except what he sees as best. Our prayers are under his direction. As Barrett notes, "The prayer of a truly obedient Christian cannot fail, since he can ask nothing contrary to the will of God."[21] It would also seem to suggest intimacy on some level.

The final ground is that abiding and fruitfulness are the way to glorify God. Bringing glory to God is a major part of the introduction of the Farewell Discourse (see 13:31–32). The verb "glorify" (δοξάζω) is also mentioned in each of the first three units of the discourse with either God or Christ as the object, and sometimes both (see 14:13; 15:8; 16:14). It also appears no less than five times in the final prayer (17:1 bis, 4–5, 10). The noun "glory" (δόξα) occurs only in the final prayer (17:5, 22, and 24).

Fruitful branches glorify the Father because the vitality of the vine produces fruit in the branch. Humanity was created to glorify the Father. In Christ humans can fulfill their creation mandate, thus proving they are disciples.

Defining "Abiding" (15:9–10)

Abiding in Christ's love stands in the center between God and mankind. Love runs from the Father through Jesus to the disciples (the Father→Jesus→disciples). The disciples are to abide in the love of Christ. Abiding follows a reverse path in the text. The disciples are to abide as Jesus abides in the Father's love (the Father→Jesus→disciples). As elsewhere in this Gospel, the disciples' relationship to the Lord, in many ways, mirrors Jesus' functional relationship with the Father.[22]

I partially defended my thesis that "abide in me" and "abide in my love" are functional equivalents above. If this is the case, comparing 15:9–10 with elements of chapter 14 effectively defines "abiding in Christ." Thus, if "abiding in his love" is accomplished through keeping his commandments, we already have a statement on how followers of Jesus and disciples keep his commandments: through loving him (see 14:15, 21–24). So, because abiding is accomplished in obedience and obedience is accomplished through love, then abiding is loving Christ. So instead of a long list of dos and don'ts, Johannine sanctification is one major do: love Christ. This supremely positive command puts a whole new spin on how a believer approaches consecration. No

---

[21] C. K. Barrett, *The Gospel according to John*, 2nd ed. (Philadelphia: Westminster, 1978), 475. See also Carson, *John*, 515, and Andreas J. Köstenberger, *John*, BECNT (Grand Rapids: Baker, 2005), 455.
[22] See John 20:21, "As the Father has sent Me, I also send you" (HCSB).

longer negative and oppressive, it is, rather, positive and freeing. The essence of abiding in Christ is loving him.[23]

First John 2:5 supports this interpretation, "But whoever keeps His word, truly in him the love of God is perfected" (HCSB). Here the genitive τοῦ θεοῦ ("of God") is best understood as the believer's love for God (an objective genitive). If it were God's love for the believer, then obedience earns God's love, and this is simply not the case.[24] So then, our love for God produces sanctification. How does this relate to abiding? First John 2:6 (the very next verse) declares "whoever says he abides in him ought to walk in the same way in which He walked" (ESV). Loving God, obedience, and abiding are strongly connected.

I believe that the connection between loving and sanctification partially explains the choice of the word "abiding." Of course, the analogy of the vine and the branches plays a large part, but there is a subtle, deeper dimension to the choice as well. It is especially clear when we consider the antonyms. When we cease loving Christ, we wander from him.

Summary (15:11)

As stated above, "I have spoken these things" (ταῦτα λελάληκα) marks the conclusion of this first section of unit 1 and does more than simply conclude the section. Jesus declares the grand result of abiding in Christ. He has spoken these things regarding joy in two increasing steps. First, it is his joy. To abide in Christ is to know his love both subjectively and objectively. It is both to receive it and to reflect it back to him. It is a joyous thing. It is his joy that he purposed to be characteristic of his followers.

It is, however, more than that. Not only does he purpose that disciples have his joy, but it is the full measure of joy. There is a contrast between "My joy" (ἡ χαρὰ ἡ ἐμή) and "your joy" (ἡ χαρὰ ὑμῶν) in verse 11. He delivers his joy to us, and our joy becomes full (πληρωθῇ). Anything less is only partial joy. Morris describes it well, "It is no cheerless, barren existence that Jesus plans for his people. But the joy of which he speaks comes only as they are wholehearted in their obedience to his commands. To be half-hearted is to get the worst of both worlds."[25]

---

[23] See Ridderbos, *John*, 519, "The fellowship described in vss. 1–8 is thus further defined as a fellowship of love, specifically as a fellowship of the love that is represented by Jesus."

[24] See e.g., 1 John 4:10 and Rom 5:8 among others.

[25] Leon Morris, *The Gospel according to John*, NICNT (Grand Rapids: Eerdmans, 1995), 598.

Preaching the Text

The text is clearly hortatory as Jesus commands his followers to abide in him. The MIT then is, "Jesus commanded his followers to abide in him." Converting to a MIM is fairly simple as well, "Believers should abide in Christ."

Our commitment is to match the structure of the sermon to the structure of the text. This means the largest significant structures (marked on the left of a SSA) should mark the movement of our sermon. In this case the largest movements are 15:1–2; 15:3–10; and 15:11. These will constitute our three main points in the sermon brief below. Another possible arrangement is to take the largest central section and build the sermon around the EXHORTATION and four grounds. However, a five-point sermon becomes a bit burdensome to follow.

SERMON SKETCH

    TEXT: John 15:1–11
    MIT: Jesus commanded his followers to abide in him.
    MIM: Believers should abide in Christ.
    TOPIC: The Secret of the Vine

INTRODUCTION

In John 15:1–11 Jesus will command his disciples to abide in him. It is the single most important thing that a follower of Christ can do. Today we will hear our Lord describe our vital connection with him. He calls it "abiding." Our overall obsession is to be abiding in Christ.

OUTLINE

I. Hear a Well-Known Analogy (15:1–2)
"I am the true vine, and My Father is the vineyard keeper. Every branch in Me that does not produce fruit He removes, and He prunes every branch that produces fruit so that it will produce more fruit" (HCSB).

A. TEXT

    1. The allegory

a. Isaiah 5

b. Isaiah 27

The story of the vine in Isaiah is a narrative of disobedience, judgment, and an eschatological redemption.

2. The activity of the vinedresser

a. He removes unfruitful branches.

b. He prunes fruitful branches.

B. TODAY

1. The Father's activity is not always pleasant.

2. The Father's activity is always necessary.

3. Fruit is dependent on the Father.

II. Understand the Explanation and Application of the Analogy (15:3–10)

A. TEXT

1. The power of abiding (15:3–4)

"You are already clean because of the word I have spoken to you. Remain in Me, and I in you. Just as a branch is unable to produce fruit by itself unless it remains on the vine, so neither can you unless you remain in Me" (HCSB).

2. The grounds for abiding (15:5–8)

"I am the vine; you are the branches. The one who remains in Me and I in him produces much fruit, because you can do nothing without Me. If anyone does not remain in Me, he is thrown aside like a branch and he withers. They gather them, throw them into the fire, and they are burned. If you remain in Me and My words remain in you, ask whatever you want and it will be done for you. My Father is glorified by this: that you produce much fruit and prove to be My disciples" (HCSB).

3. Abiding defined (15:9–10)

Unit 2: Commands that Unite (15:1–16:4c)

"As the Father has loved Me, I have also loved you. Remain in My love. If you keep My commands you will remain in My love, just as I have kept My Father's commands and remain in His love" (HCSB).

B. TODAY

1. When we fail to love Christ, we forfeit fruit.

2. When we have no fruit, we have reason to doubt.

3. When we sin, we do so because we love ourselves over Christ.

III. Acquire the Effects of the Analogy (15:11)

"I have spoken these things to you so that My joy may be in you and your joy may be complete" (HCSB).

A. TEXT

1. Christ's joy;

2. Maximized joy;

B. TODAY

1. Nothing is more joyful than loving Christ.

2. There is no end to the supply of joy.

CONCLUSION

On October 8, 1984, *Sports Illustrated* published a story on George Foreman regarding the tenth anniversary of his epic boxing match with Mohammed Ali. The two men met at Ali's mansion in Los Angeles. George Foreman's message to Mohammed Ali was simple: "Tell me you love Jesus."[26]

Ever since I read that article as a sophomore at Ole Miss, Foreman's words have burned in my ears: "Tell me you love Jesus." Ali did not embrace Christ that day. What will you do? As a believer orient your life around loving obedience. "Tell me you love Jesus." If you need to come to Christ, take your first steps in love. "Tell me you love Jesus." And I, and all others, will know that you abide in Christ.

---

[26] Gary Smith, "After the Fall: Ten Years Ago This Month George Foreman and Muhammad Ali Met in the Ring in Zaïre. While Ali Won That War, It's Foreman Who Has Found Lasting Peace," *Sports Illustrated* (October 8, 1984), 64.

Love One Another (15:12–17)

This next section moves from our love for the Lord (abiding in Christ) and expressing that in obedience to the new command. It is noteworthy that Jesus' demand for obedience to him is expressed in a very prominent command to love one another. In this section, the Lord will also define our relationship to him as friends and not just servants, demonstrating that Jesus' demand for obedience benefits us all and is not only for his own sake.

Analyzing the Text

RELATIONAL STRUCTURE	CONTENTS
HEAD	(15:12a-c) love one another like I loved you
amplif. — generic — HEAD	(13a) No one has greater love than this
identification	(13b) so that it might bear more fruit.
SPEC. 1 — HEAD	(14a-b) You are already clean because of my words.
amplif. — RESULT	(15a-c) Abide in me and I in you.
reason	(15d-e) so that you may bear fruit.
SPEC. 2 — HEAD	(16a-b) I am the vine; you are the branches
means — means	(16c) the one abiding bears much fruit
PURP. 1	(16d) because apart from me you are not able to do anything.
amplif. — PURP. 2 & 3	(16e-f) Unless one abides in me
RESULT — means	(16g) he is cast aside, withered, burned, and destroyed.
RESULT	(16h) If you abide in me and obey me
equiv.	(17a-b) your prayers will be accomplished.

My simplified semantic and structural analysis is presented above. A new topic begins in 15:12. However, the thematic connection to verse 10 is maintained through the presentation of the topic of "my commandment" (ἡ ἐντολὴ ἡ ἐμή). The same concept is again addressed by the cognate verb "I obey" in 14b (ἐντέλλομαι). The substance of the command is to love one another. Thus, this section expands the love command given in the introduction (13:34–35). The commanded love for one another is predicated on Jesus' love for the disciples (καθὼς ἠγάπησα ὑμᾶς). This qualification defines the rest of the paragraph. 15:13–16 forms two specific examples of Jesus' love for his own. Internally, the first example (15:14–15) elaborates on the concept of being a friend of Jesus. 15:16, the second example, declares the origins of Jesus' love for his own. It was through his sovereign choice. Therefore, it is best to see verse 17 as the conclusion of this paragraph, as Jesus never truly left the concept of Christlike loving of one another.[27] The repetition of the command to love is a clear example of *inclusio* in the Farewell Discourse. As such it is likely that it marks the conclusion of the paragraph. This is further substantiated by the

---

[27] Contrary to Morris, who cautiously takes 15:17 as the start of the next paragraph. Morris, *John*, 601.

summary statement, "I command these things to you" (ταῦτα ἐντέλλομαι ὑμῖν). Here, Brown is undoubtedly correct when he states, "The 'This I command you' of vs. 17 is not only an inclusion with 12; it is also a variant of the refrain 'I have said this to you' with which, as we have seen, John closes several of the units or subdivision of the Last Discourse."[28]

Interpreting the Text

The Love Command (15:12)

15:12 strongly echoes 13:34–35. The major difference is that 13:34–35 introduces the love command as a "new commandment" (ἐντολὴν καινήν). In 15:12 it is simply "my commandment" (ἡ ἐντολὴ ἡ ἐμή). It is often supposed that the plural commands of 15:10 are now subsumed under the singular command to love one another.[29] While this seems structurally attractive, it is hard to imagine the real situation where love for one another is the overarching command that subsumes love for God. It seems better to understand that love for Christ and God is the environment in which this command is given.[30] Brown rightly refers to a chain of love found in 15:9–12, "The Father loves Jesus; Jesus loves the disciples; they must love one another."[31] The premier example of love is Jesus' love for the disciples. This love is exemplified in the next section.

Jesus' love for the disciples is elaborated upon (amplified in my SSA) with a generic statement (15:13). There is no higher love than to lay down one's life for his friends. Such a magnanimous offer was not expected of friends in antiquity, but it was lauded.[32] This is, of course, a reference to Jesus' own sacrifice for our sins.

Being Friends of Jesus (15:14–17)

The concept of "friends" is fleshed out in two "SPECIFICS." The disciples are friends of Christ if they keep his commandments. "Friends" implies a deeper relationship than a mere servant. However, we should note that kings and authorities were said to have friends who could speak freely to the king who clearly were not equals.[33] Perhaps we should recall Abraham and Moses were friends of God (Exod 33:11; 2 Chr 20:7; Isa 41:8). The disciples are

---

[28] Raymond E. Brown, *The Gospel according to John*, AB 29A (New York: Doubleday, 1971), 2:684. Here the agreement with Brown ends in that he thinks 15:18 marks the beginning of a major division within the Farewell Discourse.
[29] See, e.g., Morris, *John*, 598.
[30] Köstenberger, *John*, 457.
[31] Brown, *John*, 2:682.
[32] Keener, *John*, 2:1004.
[33] Ibid., 2:1006–07.

friends and not servants, for Christ has divulged to them what he is doing rather than simply giving orders. This disclosure has its ultimate source in the Father (15:15d–e). This is not, of course, complete disclosure.

The second specific illustration of Jesus' love for the disciples (i.e., their friendship) is that he chose them. The disciples did not choose Christ (as much as it may have appeared to be so!). Instead, Christ's election of the disciples was his alone. While this is clearly a statement of personal election, it also hearkens back to the idea of covenant community. In the OT God chose Israel because he loved them and for no other reason (Deut 7:7–8).

Jesus' choosing of his friends is for an appointed purpose. The purpose is threefold. First, it is that they would "go" (ὑπάγητε). Clearly, Jesus' intention for his friends would be that they would take the gospel to the nations. This is made clear in the second purpose, that they would bear permanent fruit. This fruit is clearly the fruit of converts but may include more because it is a general statement. The last two clauses of this second SPECIFIC (15:16g–h) are difficult. The most natural understanding is that 16g modifies "and your fruit remains." But it is difficult to see how this privilege in prayer modifies 16f alone. However, since 16f is in a series controlled by the same "that" (ἵνα) (16d, e, and f), "Whatever you ask" should be understood to modify the entire series. This would conform it to the similar promise in 15:7 that was based on Jesus' words abiding in the believer. The promise is related to going, being fruitful, and the fruit remaining, which are all related to the disciple's obedience. Essentially, then, it is a restatement of 15:7. 15:17 closes the section with a formal *inclusio* restating 15:12 almost verbatim.

Preaching the Text

The purpose of this text is not only to restate the new commandment but also (given the amount of space devoted to it) to develop Jesus' affection for his disciples. This makes developing a MIT that encapsulates both ideas a little tricky. Here both the new commandment and the nature of Christ's friendship must be incorporated. So I suggest something like the following: "Christ commanded brotherly love between disciples using his love for his disciples as the premier example." The MIM, then, is "believers must love one another with Christ as their example."

The structure of the sermon below is two-part. The commandment itself in 15:12–13 comprises the first point. The two examples on being the friend of Christ will make up the second point.

Sermon Sketch

TEXT: John 15:12–17
MIT: Christ commanded brotherly love between disciples using his love for his disciples as the premier example.
MIM: Believers must love one another with Christ as their example.
TOPIC: The Friend of God

INTRODUCTION

In John 15:12–17 Christ commanded brotherly love between disciples using his love for his disciples as the premier example. In this, he commands us to love one another and describes what it is to be the friend of God. Obviously the intent is that believers must love one another with Christ as their example.

OUTLINE

I. The Friend of Christ Keeps the New Commandment (15:12–13)

"This is My command: Love one another as I have loved you. No one has greater love than this, that someone would lay down his life for his friends" (HCSB).

A. TEXT

1. The New Commandment (15:12)

2. The Premier Example of Love (15:13)

B. TODAY

What does Christlike brotherly love look like today? We have an inspired description in 1 Corinthians 13.

1. Love is . . . patient; kind; rejoices in the truth; long-suffering; trusting; hopeful; enduring.

2. Love does not practice . . . envy; boasting; conceit; inappropriate things; keeping grudges; joy in hardships of others.

To our shame Christians often fail to love one another.

3. The secret, however, is abiding in Christ.

   (Remember we defined abiding as loving Christ). If we love Christ we will love what he loves. We look at another believer and we should see them as another who loves Christ. If we love the same thing, how difficult is it to love one another? If you love what I love, how difficult is it for me to love you?

II. Being the Friend of Christ (15:14–16)

"You are My friends if you do what I command you. I do not call you slaves anymore, because a slave doesn't know what his master is doing. I have called you friends, because I have made known to you everything I have heard from My Father. You did not choose Me, but I chose you. I appointed you that you should go out and produce fruit and that your fruit should remain, so that whatever you ask the Father in My name, He will give you" (HCSB).

A. TEXT

It was unusual to use the term *friend* in relationship to God in the OT. However, we do see two examples. Abraham is called the friend of God (2 Chr 20:7; Isa 41:8) and God speaks to Moses like a man speaks to his friend (Exod 33:11). Under the new covenant, however, there is a new kind of relationship. We may be his friends.

1. Christ describes his friends.

   a. The Lord's friends are obedient to him.

   b. The Lord's friends are his confidants.

   c. The Lord's friends are not his equals.

2. Christ describes the lives of his friends.

   a. He chose them (not just personal election but in a covenant relationship with Christ).

   b. He appointed them to go and bear lasting fruit.

   c. He gives them access in prayer.

B. TODAY: Who is the friend of Christ today?

1. Those who abide in Christ

2. Those who are on mission with Christ

3. Those who pray in Jesus' name

CONCLUSION

We know of Herod the Great mostly from the Bible (especially the birth narratives). He is known as the vicious butcher of Bethlehem. He would probably like it that his name is remembered (even in infamy). He, however, probably would have preferred to be remembered in another way. He did many major work projects. After all, the temple in Jerusalem was known as "Herod's Temple." Maybe he would have wanted to be known as a religious man. He also built a temple to Jupiter elsewhere in Palestine to curry favor with the Gentiles. So maybe he would want to be known as a tolerant man. He had a man-made harbor installed at Caesarea. He put "friend of Rome" on his inscriptions. But even this was not really characteristic of his life. You see, he did all these things as a master politician. He wanted to stay in power. That meant he must please Rome, keep the masses happy if not skittish, and keep his enemies terrified. He was a friend of Herod and Herod alone. Let us not be like Herod and wear Friend of Christ t-shirts merely for show or for religious expedience. Let us love him in truth and deed and each other as Christ loved us.

Expect Persecution (15:18–16:4c)

The commands to abide in Christ and to love one another, by definition, create separation from those who neither abide in Christ nor love believers. Thus, Jesus takes time to explain the animosity of the world. He also takes time to explain what should be our response to the hostility. Furthermore, his Spirit gives the power to do so.

Analyzing the Text

RELATIONAL STRUCTURE	CONTENTS
| ```
           ┌CONCL:─┬HEAD─────────────
           │       │         ┌reason─
           │       └amplification┤
           │                 └RESULT─
 ┌Concess.─┤         ┌RESULT─┬HEAD───
 │         │         │       │       ┌HEAD──
 │         │         │       └amplif.┤
 │         └grounds──┤               └CONTR.─
 │                   │
 │                   └reason─HEAD─────────────
 │                                          ┌HEAD  ┌conds.──
 │                                 ┌amplif.─┤means 1┤
 │                                 │        │      └CONSEQ.─
 │                                 │        │      ┌HEAD────
 │                                 │        └CONTR.┤
 │                                 │               └amplif.─
 │                                 │                ┌HEAD  ┌conds.──
 │                                 │                ┤      │
 │                                 └means 2─────────┤      └CONSEQ.─
 │                                                  └CONTR.────────
 │                                                  └PURPOSE───────
 │CONTRA-  ┌HEAD──────────────────────────
 │EXPECT.──┤
 │         └amplif.─────────────────────────
 │         ┌HEAD──────────────────────────
 │         │                    ┌HEAD──
 │         │           ┌HEAD────┤
 └CONCLUSION┤          │        └CONTR.─
            │   ┌HEAD──┤
            │   │      │        ┌HEAD──
            └amplif.───┤ amplif.┤
                │      │        └CONTR.─
                └CONTR.─────────────────
``` | (15:18a-b) Expect the world's hatred for my sake.<br>(19a-d) You are not like the world but chosen by me.<br>(19e) because of this the world hates you<br>(20a-c) Remember, the servant is not greater than His master<br>(20d-e) If they persecuted me, they will also persecute you.<br>(20f-g) if they kept my word, they will also keep yours<br>(21a-b) They will persecute you for my sake because they do not know God.<br>(22a-b) If I had not come and spoke to them<br>(22c) they would have no sin<br>(22d) but now they have no excuse for their sin<br>(23a) The one hating me also hates the Father.<br>(24a-b) if I had not done among them unique works<br>(24c) they would have no sin<br>(24d) But they have both seen and hated me and my Father.<br>(25a-c) so that Scripture might be fulfilled<br>(26a-d) When the Paraclete comes, He will testify about me.<br>(27a-b) You eyewitnesses must also testify.<br>(16:1) I said this so that you will not be shaken.<br>(2a) They will cast you out of the synagogue,<br>(2b-d) but soon the ones who kill you will think they serve God.<br>(3a) And they will do these things because they neither know the Father nor me.<br>(4a-c) But I said this so that when their hour comes you will remember |

The structure of 15:18–6:4c is more complicated than the previous paragraphs. Though simplifying it was difficult, the boundaries are readily recognizable. However, interpreting the exact ending has proven difficult. The question is generally whether this is a third unit within 15:1–16:4c or the beginning of a new unit or an even smaller unit within 15–16.[34] There is also a significant minority who see a major discourse boundary in the vicinity of 16:25.[35] Finally, a diverse group does not recognize a major discourse break in 16:4c and posits a larger unit.[36]

---

[34] For the first option see, e.g., Rudolf Schnackenburg, *The Gospel according to St. John*, vol. 3 (New York: Crossroad, 1982), 3:91–93; F. J. Moloney, *The Gospel of John*, SP 4 (Collegeville, MN: Liturgical, 1998), 427; Y. Simoens, *La Glorie d'aimer: Structures stylistiques et interprétatives dans le Discours de la cène (Jn 13—17)*, AB 90 (Rome: Biblical Institute, 1981), 145–46; George Johnston, *The Spirit-Paraclete in the Gospel of John*, SNTSM 12 (Cambridge: Cambridge University Press, 1970), 167–68; Gary M. Burge, *John*, NIV Application Commentary (Grand Rapids: Zondervan, 2000), 420. For the second see, e.g., J. Neugebaur, *Die eschatologischen Aussagen in den johanneischen Abschiedsreden: Eine Untersuchung zu Johannes 13–17*, BWANT 140 (Stuttgart: Kohlhammer, 1995), 76; Blomberg, *Historical Reliability*, 209–12; Beasley-Murray, *John*, 269; Segovia, *Farewell*, 170–78. For the third option, see, e.g., Brown, *John*, 2:546; and Carson, *John*, 107 (beginning with 17).

[35] See, e.g., Morris, *John*, 600–604; Edwyn Clement Hoskyns, *The Fourth Gospel*, ed. Francis Noel Davey, 2nd ed. (London: Faber & Faber, 1947), 479–86; Barrett, *John*, 478; and Ernst Haenchen, *John 2: A Commentary on the Gospel of John Chapters 7–21*, Hermeneia, trans. Robert W. Funk (Philadelphia: Fortress, 1984), 2:133–42.

[36] R. H. Lightfoot, *St. John's Gospel: A Commentary* (Oxford: Oxford University Press, 1956), 255; C. H. Dodd, *The Interpretation of the Fourth Gospel* (Cambridge: Cambridge University Press, 1953), 410; Becker, *Johannes*, 2:486–87; and Barnabas Lindars, *The Gospel of John*, NCB 34 (London: Oliphants, 1972), 486.
```

Unit 2: Commands that Unite (15:1–16:4c)

The thematic connection with the previous sections in unit 2 is achieved in 15:18–16:4c by way of contrast rather than elaboration. The metaphor of the vine-and-the-branches in 15:1–11 introduced the idea of a new identity based on a vital connection with Jesus Christ. Jesus then elaborated on the relationship between the branches (to continue the metaphor) as they participate in the new identity (vital union with Christ) in 15:12–17. By definition a part of humanity does not participate in this new identity. So then, by way of contrast, 15:18–16:4c develops the rest of the story: the relationship with the world (i.e., those not participating in the new identity).

Three clear items mark verse 18 as the beginning of a new discourse boundary. The verse begins with a conditional statement that introduces a new participant, the world (ὁ κόσμος), and the opposite of the verb of the previous sentence: hatred (μισεῖ). The concluding boundary is marked in 4a by the use of "these things" (ταῦτα λελάληκα). However, as this phrase occurs elsewhere (even with a purpose clause), it alone cannot be the only feature that would signal a discourse boundary. Other factors help in deciding the boundary in 16:4c. These factors are found in 16:4d and 5.

The first clue is that 16:4d employs a conjunction (δὲ) that is marked for development but not for close connection.[37] Furthermore, the clause stands in a Circumstance-HEAD relationship with verse 5 that is also introduced with δὲ. The result is that the new unit is strongly marked for development (i.e., the next important thing). Furthermore, and probably less esoteric, the topic clearly changes from the hatred of the world to Jesus' departure in 16:5. The continuity created by the contrast between "I was with you" and "and now I go" further strengthens the identification of a new unit of discourse.[38]

Furthermore, the verbal texture changes after this unit. Previously, the backbone of the discourse was a series of commands (either explicit or mitigated). "Believe" and "love/obey" dominate chapter 14. In chapter 15 it is "abide," "love one another," and, in the present section, it is "know." After the concluding formula of 16:4c there is not another imperative (mitigated or otherwise) that appears in such a prominent role. Thus, the present paragraph's final boundary is best understood to be 16:4c.

The semantic structure of the section is best described from the vantage point of the macrostructure. 15:18–25 develops the warning to expect the hatred of the world. This conclusion is grounded on 20–25. The world persecutes believers because the world hates Christ and the Father (fulfilling

---

[37] The use of the developmental marker δὲ in 16:4d is in keeping with the use of δὲ in material that backgrounds a new development.

[38] The use of ταῦτα in both 16:4c and 4d (each the object of a verb of speaking) may also be an example of a hook word that would indicate a transition as well.

Scripture, 16:25). When paired with 15:26–27, a command to testify Christ to the world, the relationship between 15:18–25 and 26–27 is best described as Concession-CONTRAEXPECTATION. The meaning then is something like "although the world will hate you" (concession) "bear testimony to them" (CONTRAEXPECTATION). This, then, is concluded with a call to endurance based on Christ's warning beforehand (16:1–4c).

Interpreting the Text

The Hostility of the World (15:18–25)
At 15:18–21 Jesus develops the reason for the hostility of the world against the disciples in a series of propositional clusters dominated by cause-and-effect relationships. The most notable of these are several pairs of conditional sentences fired in rapid succession. The first pair is developed in verses 18 and 19.[39] The second elaborates on the first.

Jesus' exhortation in 15:18 is another mitigated command like we saw in 14:15. Here however, the semantic force is to shed light on the situation that will shortly exist.[40] I would paraphrase it as "expect the world to hate you." Here, the world is that classic Johannine usage that describes the system of thought embodied in lost humanity that is hostile to Christ.

The reason for the hostility is given in 15:19. If the disciples found the essence of their being like the world (lit. ἐκ τοῦ κόσμου, "from the world"[41]), the world would embrace them. We should not make too much of the usage of ἐφίλει in 19b (see comments in 13:31–38). The world would naturally love those like them. The disciples are not "of the world" but "out of the world" by Jesus' election. This close association is the foundation of the world's hatred. Jesus will support this conclusion in the next two paragraphs (15:20–25).

Jesus reminds them that he had previously stated that the servant is not above his master. Jesus made the same statement in 13:16. Only there, the analogy was positive; the disciples should serve one another as Christ had served them. Here the truth is expressed with negative and positive application. Because the world is hostile to Christ, it will be hostile to those who follow

---

[39] The first is a first-class condition and the next a second class.
[40] This is taking γινώσκετε to be a PA Imp 2pl "know." In form it might be PA Ind 2pl "you know."
[41] Exactly what is the force of the preposition ἐκ is difficult to decide. Often in Johannine usage the use encroaches strongly on the function of the genitive alone. So then, the question is whether the usage here indicates source or description? i.e., is it "from the world" or "of the world"? Eventually both concepts are related so characteristic description seems to be more in view, but source certainly cannot be discounted. The mistake would be to elevate the concept of source apart from the characteristic implied. Also note that the preposition is used three times in this verse. The first two times the meaning is source/description. The last appearance is clearly separation. See Morris, *John*, 602.

him. But if they keep his word, they will keep the disciples' word. The last clause is refreshing in this rather frank disclosure. There will be some of the world who embrace their message. However, Jesus reiterates that the world's violence is on the basis that disciples know the Father.

The participle phrase describing the Father in verse 21 "the one who sent Me" (τὸν πέμψαντά με) alludes to the mission of Jesus. His mission to save humanity also exposes their condemnation because of their rejection of Christ. Verses 22–24 provide twin ways that the rejection of Jesus fulfilled Scripture. Both these means are couched in virtually parallel linguistic constructions and describe the rejection of both Jesus' words and his works. The symmetry between the clauses is quite stark. They both have identical apodoses. Both 22c and 24c are each marked for development by δὲ and reach the same conclusion: because Jesus both spoke and did unique things among them, the world is without excuse for their hatred of Christ, which is hatred for the Father. Ridderbos states, "The two 'both . . . and' constructions have a cumulative effect of bringing to expression in a single loaded sentence both the mystery and guilt of 'seeing' the works and nevertheless 'hating me and my Father.'"[42] In this sense it is reminiscent of the exhortation in 14:10–11. There, Jesus implores faith based on his words or his works. Here, the hearers among the Jews have rejected both. The phrase "they would have no sin" (ἁμαρτίαν οὐκ εἴχοσαν; repeated in 15:22 and 24) is somewhat confusing. We cannot take it to mean that apart from the incarnation, the Jews (used in the Johannine sense) were safe. This would contradict teaching elsewhere in the Gospel (see, e.g., 3:18 where the world is already condemned). Instead, since he came and declared the kingdom of God and did works impossible for men to do, those who saw his works and heard his words are without excuse. As Morris states, it is "the measure of guilt of those who rejected Him."[43] Thus, their hatred for Christ was not for some fault in Christ,[44] but it exposed their own hearts.

A Bold CounterAssault (15:26–27)

In my SSA above, I have identified 15:26–27 as a CONTRAEXPECTATION to the previous paragraphs. Given that the world exhibits extreme hostility against Christ and his followers, it might be expected that one might retreat in the face of such adversity. Instead, Christ demands a bold testimony. In

---

[42] Ridderbos, *John*, 529.
[43] Ibid., 604.
[44] Ridderbos notes that δωρεάν "freely" may have several usages, but here it clearly suggests "undeserved" (Ridderbos, *John*, 526). Jesus cites, most likely, Ps 69:4, "they hated me without a cause." Köstenberger notes that the same phrase was used in Ps 35:19, but that 69:4 was more likely because it was widely considered to be a Messianic Psalm (Köstenberger, *John*, 467).

15:26–27 Jesus elaborates on the entirety of 15:18–25 by describing the ministry of the Paraclete in this hostile environment (his appearance here assures the Paraclete's presence in each unit of the Farewell Discourse).[45] Furthermore, the Twelve are to have this same ministry.

Given that the world offers hatred and violence to believers, it is noteworthy that there is not an inch given to the notion of retreat. Keener calls Christ's disclosure, "a bold counteroffensive."[46] Instead of retreat, the powerful helping presence of the Holy Spirit is promised. It suggests that the follower of Jesus must respond to persecution and hatred by testimony. Jesus affirms the source of the Paraclete is ultimately the Father, but that Christ sends him. Thus, believers may be outnumbered, but they cannot be overpowered. The Lord notes that not only the Spirit will testify, but the Twelve do as well. If we understand μαρτυρεῖτε as a present imperative, then the disciples are commanded to be Christ's witnesses.[47] Thus, the eyewitness testimony of the Twelve is seen as an important foundation for the proclamation of the gospel.

The Degree of Hostility (16:1–4c)

The final paragraph, 16:1–4c, concludes this section of the second unit and the entirety of the second unit as well. Jesus reiterates much of what he said throughout the unit. Jesus first declares the reason for his disclosure (16:1): so that they would not be shaken. The verb used is a passive form of σκανδαλίζω. The only other appearance in John is in 6:61 where it is synonymous with "apostasy." Here, the "falling away" doesn't appear to be apostasy *per se*, but cowardice, which is why I translate it "shaken" in the SSA above. His words are to give boldness to the disciples in bearing testimony.

In this final paragraph Jesus ramps up the degree of hostility. He declares that they will cast the disciples out of the synagogue (which seems to be a summary of the persecution mentioned above), and they will add murder to their sins. He notes that they think they will be pleasing God when doing so. While Jesus has specifically Jewish opposition to Christianity in mind (as against James, Stephen, and Paul), by extension it applies to all forms of religious persecution against Christians. Jesus is quick to remind the disciples (16:3) that the persecutors do so *because* they know neither the Father nor Christ. In other words, their claims to worship God in the persecution are false.

Finally, Christ declares the purpose for telling these things. It is so that they would remember. Thus, Jesus' warning is more than just foretelling. It

---

[45] I take this feature as further confirmation of the boundaries of this second unit.
[46] Keener, *John*, 2:1021.
[47] By form it might be a present indicative, and some take it this way (see Keener, *John*, 2:1024). However one takes it, the statement has an imperative force.

is to help the persecuted followers of Christ endure persecution. He does so in two ways. First, he sends the Paraclete. We have already been told that the presence of God and Christ will be mediated by the Spirit. Surely, that is a great comfort in persecution. But here we are specifically told that the Paraclete will have a significant role in proclaiming the gospel in the midst of hostility. Presumably, the Paraclete will testify through faithful disciples. Second, Jesus tells the disciples ahead of time that hostility will occur. Surely knowing ahead of time lets the disciples know how to prepare for the high probability of persecution.

Preaching the Text

This section of unit 2 is a good example of the practical use of discourse analysis in preaching. Once the structure of the text has been identified, the once-daunting section is much easier to delineate. First, I identify a general MIT: "Jesus prepared the disciples for effective testimony in the midst of hostility." Second I will convert that into a MIM: "Christians should be prepared for effective testimony to Christ in the midst of hostility." Next, I identify the major movements of the text and convert those to the major movements (points) of my sermon. These are 15:18–25, 26–27, and 16:1–4c.

SERMON SKETCH

TEXT: John 15:18–16:4c
MIT: Jesus prepared the disciples for effective testimony in the midst of hostility.
MIM: Christians should be prepared for effective testimony to Christ in the midst of hostility.
TOPIC: The Hatred of the World

INTRODUCTION

We live in a fallen world. Nothing makes it more evident than the kind of violence of which people are capable. We, as a species, are not only capable of grotesque individual violence, but we are capable of practicing it on large scales. Some of us are content, rather glad, to eliminate whole races of people for the most trivial of reasons. Perhaps most disturbing is that some are willing to do so in the name of God. Surely this is a gross miscarriage of God's purpose in the world under the new covenant.

Throughout history Christians have provided examples of both the persecutors and the persecuted. Many of those who lift the sword merely claim Christianity. Many of our evangelical brothers and sisters are bearing hostility even as we speak. And now we in the West are being more and more reviled. Given our text today, I wonder why we are surprised. Jesus warned us that the world would hate us. In John 15:18–16:4c, Jesus prepared the disciples for effective testimony in the midst of hostility. It is not my point to preach a theology that venerates suffering. It is true that there is a special reward for those who pay the ultimate price for the sake of Christ. It is not true that we should venerate it or manipulate our surroundings to be martyred. Christians in the past have done just this thing. I find this act repulsive, for it selfishly manipulates someone into murder. It does not matter if you are the victim. If we say we love someone, how can we then want him or her to commit murder? Surely not. Instead of a morbid culture of suffering and death, Jesus wanted to prepare his disciples for inevitable hostility. Christians should be prepared for effective testimony to Christ in the midst of hostility.

OUTLINE

I. Expect Persecution (15:18–25)

A. Text

1. The world hates Christ and his followers (vv. 18–19).

    "If the world hates you, understand that it hated Me before it hated you. If you were of the world, the world would love you as its own. However, because you are not of the world, but I have chosen you out of it, the world hates you" (HCSB).

2. Because the world does not know God (vv. 20–21).

    "Remember the word I spoke to you: 'A slave is not greater than his master.' If they persecuted Me, they will also persecute you. If they kept My word, they will also keep yours. But they will do all these things to you on account of My name, because they don't know the One who sent Me" (HCSB).

3. They are without excuse (vv. 22–25).

    "If I had not come and spoken to them, they would not have sin. Now they have no excuse for their sin. The one who hates Me also hates My Father. If I had not done the works among them that no one else has done, they would not have sin. Now they have seen and hated both Me and My Father. But this happened so that the statement written in their scripture might be fulfilled: They hated Me for no reason" (HCSB).

B. TODAY

1. What were you expecting?

2. The absence of hostility may be a sign that something is wrong.

   After all, all those who live godly in Christ Jesus will suffer persecution (2 Tim 3:12).

3. Nobody needs to "volunteer" for persecution.

   a. By being quarrelsome

   b. By being inappropriate

   c. By being insensitive

   It is enough that you know Christ and live for him; that alone will be enough.

4. We must not think the worst of every non-Christian.

II. Employ the Paraclete's Empowerment (15:26–27)

A. TEXT

The response to the world's hatred (in all its manifestations) is witness. This is an unexpected response. It is not a retreat. It is a bold counteroffensive.

1. The Promise and Ministry of the Paraclete (v. 26)

   "When the Counselor comes, the One I will send to you from the Father—the Spirit of truth who proceeds from the Father—He will testify about Me" (HCSB).

2. The Disciple's Ministry (v. 27)

"You also will testify, because you have been with Me from the beginning" (HCSB).

B. TODAY: We are called to go on the bold offensive with Christ.

1. You are empowered to witness.

2. You are commanded to witness.

III. Evoke His Words (16:1–4c)

A. TEXT

Jesus promises three very real possibilities for the believer:

1. Confidence (v. 1)

"I have told you these things to keep you from stumbling" (HCSB).

2. Escalation (vv. 2–3)

"They will ban you from the synagogues. In fact, a time is coming when anyone who kills you will think he is offering service to God. They will do these things because they haven't known the Father or Me" (HCSB).

3. Remembrance (v. 4a–c)

"But I have told you these things so that when their time comes you may remember I told them to you" (HCSB).

B. TODAY: Our application is straightforward.

1. You can have confidence.

2. You should not be surprised by an escalation of hostility.

3. When it happens, remember these words.

CONCLUSION

We should respond to the world's hatred consistently. We should expect it (but not in a morbid, paranoid way). We should employ the Spirit's empowerment to witness at all times but especially these. We should evoke his words to encourage us to maintain a faithful witness.

We have completed two-thirds of our journey through Jesus' Farewell Discourse. We can now pause and look back at the overarching message to this point. First, in light of Jesus' departure, we should note that Jesus gives the secret of the untroubled heart. It is to believe in Christ and to love/obey him. In this environment, the Holy Spirit mediates the presence of Christ in spite of his absence. Because the language is specifically covenantal, unit 1 describes what is available to the believer based on Jesus' death, burial, and resurrection. More than that it must be foundational to what follows. Unless one is in a covenant relationship with Christ, abiding cannot happen.

The second stage beyond this is the believers' orientation among Christ, other believers, and the world. This is the content of the present unit. Our orientation to Christ is that of vital union: originated, confirmed, and maintained through loving obedience. Next, the believers' orientation to each other is that of brotherly love defined in terms that are reciprocal with Christ's love for us. Finally, the believers' orientation to the world is that of witness to and against hostile forces. The final unit, which is the subject of the next chapter, describes the advantages to the believer of Jesus' departure.

CHAPTER 6

UNIT 3: ADVANTAGES OF JESUS' DEPARTURE (16:4D–33)

THE shift between unit 2 and unit 3 is subtle and, as stated in the previous chapter, quite a bit of disagreement occurs among experts as to the exact location. Whatever the precise point, it is clear before one reads too far that a new line of thought has begun. Unit 3 is composed of three sections that each describe an advantage to the departure of Jesus. 16:4d–15 is the first section. The initial discourse boundary was described in the previous chapter in the discussion of the concluding boundary for the previous paragraph. The concluding boundary is seen in 16:15 at the last mention of the Paraclete.

The second section begins in 16:16 and extends through 16:24. The discourse boundary is marked in 16:16 by the switch in topic from the Paraclete to the emotional state of the disciples. The phrase "A little while and you will no longer see Me" (HCSB; μικρὸν καὶ οὐκέτι) is fronted and therefore suggests a new section has begun.[1]

It is also significant that this section reintroduces participants that have been offstage since chapter 14. The disciples are no longer mere hearers; they return to participate. This, in a sense, sets up this final unit as a return to where we began. This section also complicates the SSA through the use of conversation. In conversation I have found that the skewing between what is said and how the saying is used is difficult to navigate. The major theme of this section (grief turning to joy) is, furthermore, intricately bound to the departure of Jesus mentioned in 16:16. The section concludes with a purpose clause in 16:24.

---

[1] As mentioned earlier, linguists refer to this as a "point of departure." It is an adverbial element brought to the front of the clause or sentence to signal a discontinuity with the previous context.

The switch from imperative to indicative in 16:25 and the introduction of a new topic signals the beginning of the last section. The announcement of Jesus' abandonment by the disciples and the Father's presence bring the final paragraph to a close. In 16:33, "I have told you these things" (HCSB; ταῦτα λελάληκα) as a summary statement of the previous speech marks the conclusion to the entirety of the discourse.

This threefold division of the unit will be the structure of the series of sermons to follow. Although one could break it up further (as I did in 14:1–15), the length of text and degree of interlocking themes within the sections make that an unwieldy proposition. Instead, the three sections function well in both complexity and length as individual sermons. Each of three sections will describe a different advantage to the disciple because of Jesus' departure.

The Advantage of the Paraclete (16:4d–15)

The overall structure of the present section is complex though not overly so. And, as usual, John's tendency to avoid subordinating features and simply employ parataxis (pairing independent clauses) often leaves the exegete with more than one option in understanding the communication relations between constituents. So we tread carefully.

Analyzing the Text

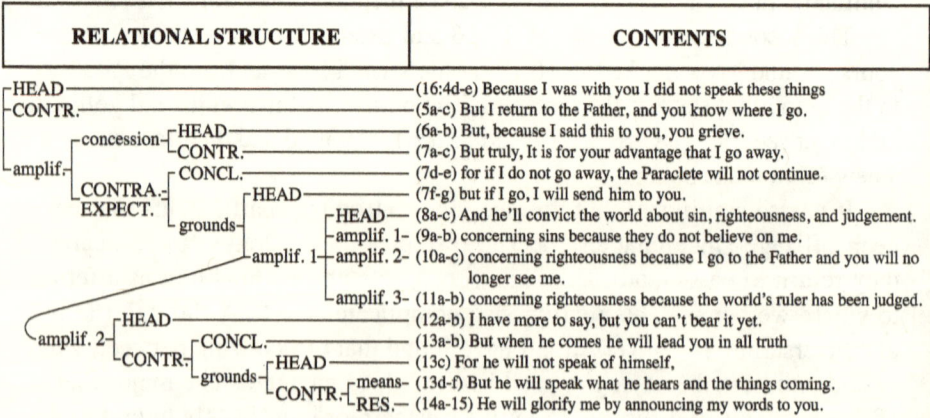

It is clear that by the time 16:4d opens, the disciples understand that Jesus is going away. In times past it has been suggested that 16:5 is evidence of disarrangement or other editorial activity because the disciples *have* asked the question.² This ignores both the present tense of the verb and the concerns of the immediate context.³ Jesus does not reprimand the disciples for their lack of concern but for their lack of discernment. The phrase contrasts, "Yet, because I have spoken these things to you, sorrow has filled your heart" (16:6 HCSB). This contrast indicates that they had correctly perceived the coming departure but had failed to understand its ramifications. In other words, Jesus does not seem concerned that no one has asked but that no one realizes the advantages of his departure. Grief had filled their hearts, but, contrary to their expectation, they will be far better off, for the advantages that stem from his departure outweigh the disadvantage of the departure. Again, in another contrast to the disciples' present situation, Jesus' announcement is highlighted by his declaration, "Nevertheless, I am telling you the truth" (16:7 HCSB). The content of 16:7b–c is that there are specific advantages if Jesus departs. These advantages dominate the rest of the discourse.

Although structurally prominent, semantically 16:4d–6 serves mainly to introduce Jesus' main proposition that lays out the section's major theme: the coming of the Paraclete is a distinct advantage for the disciples—and this cannot happen until Jesus departs.

This advantage is developed regarding the Paraclete's revelatory ministry to both the world and to the disciples. This ministry is developed by a twofold amplification of the arrival of the Paraclete as the basis for Jesus' conclusion that it is better for the disciples if he goes away. It is not, as some suggest, an independent fifth Paraclete saying.⁴ The first amplification (8a–11b) declares the Paraclete's conviction (ἐλέγξει) of the world. The theologically complex and varied debate on these verses will be discussed below.⁵

---

² See, e.g., Rudolf Bultmann, *The Gospel of John: a Commentary*, trans. G. R. Beasley-Murray, R. W. N. Hoare, and J. K. Riches (Philadelphia: Westminster, 1971), 558; Raymond E. Brown, *The Gospel according to John*, AB 29A (New York: Doubleday, 1971), 2:710; Rudolf Schnackenburg, *The Gospel according to St. John*, vol. 3 (New York: Crossroad, 1982), 3:126; G. R. Beasley-Murray, *John*, WBC 36 (Waco, TX: Word, 1987), 279; and Fernando F. Segovia, *Love Relationships in the Johannine Tradition: Agape/Agapan in 1 John and the Fourth Gospel*, SBLDS 58 (Chico, CA: Scholars Press, 1982), 227.

³ Carson is correct when he notes that "now" (νῦν) cannot indicate "no longer asking," for it does not clearly modify the verb of asking (ἐρωτᾷ) but "I am going away" (ὑπάγω). His solution that the question is rhetorical and carries the semantic meaning of protest is worthy of consideration (D. A. Carson, *The Gospel according to John*, PNTC [Grand Rapids: Eerdmans, 1991], 533). Likewise, Blomberg's contention is also intriguing. He suggests that the disciples should have been asking questions (in the didactic style of a rabbi and his disciples), and this mild rebuke is a signal to get them started. He points to the reintroduction of the questions at 16:17 and 29 as support, but the fact that these are not questions but statements (nobody ever really asks Jesus anything in this unit) should give pause to this idea.

⁴ See, e.g., Crinisor Stefan, "The Paraclete and Prophecy in the Johannine Community," *PNEUMA: The Journal of the Society for Pentecostal Studies* 27 (2005): 273.

⁵ For a more comprehensive survey see D. A. Carson, "The Function of the Paraclete in John 16:7–11," *JBL* 98 (1979): 547–66.

The second amplification begins in 16:11a. This second elaboration concerns more specifically the ministry to the disciples. When the Paraclete arrives, he will lead them into all truth. This truth is mediated by Jesus from the Father to the Paraclete and thus to the disciples. The first amplification fleshed out the revelation to the world of their own condition; this second describes the revelatory ministry to the disciples. Thus, the Paraclete's revelatory ministry, whether to the world or to the disciples, is an advantage that may only be appropriated after Jesus' departure.

Interpreting the Text

The Coming of the Spirit (16:1–7)
Jesus begins by noting that he did not refrain from telling them things in the past because he was being mysterious or elusive, but because there was no need to do so while he was with them. Now that his departure is near, he speaks.[6]

In the past, the point of 16:4–5 has been lost in the apparent contradiction of 16:5b, "and not one of you asks Me, 'Where are You going?'" (HCSB). Peter had already asked this in 13:36, and Thomas asked something similar in 14:5. The point, however, is not that none of them cared enough to ask, but now no one is asking because they get that Jesus is departing. Because they have grasped the implication of his words, a tremendous sorrow has filled the disciples' hearts. The disciples now understand that "departure" is a euphemism for death.

This is the second time that the sorrow of the disciples has been mentioned. In 14:28 it is expressed somewhat negatively as they did not rejoice at his departure. There, of course, the complaint was that the hearts of the disciples were heavy and troubled because they were not thinking of the advantages in Jesus going back to the Father. Now he encourages them to consider the advantages of his departure. In one sense, Jesus asks them to consider why his death is necessary.

In light of the sorrow that burdens the disciples, Jesus' statement in 16:7a is understandable. "Nevertheless, I am telling you the truth" is emphatic in both its content and its position. It serves to highlight the importance of what he is about to tell the disciples; it is to get their (and our) attention. It is the verbal equivalent of a parent saying, "look me in the eyes." With this verbal underlining Jesus emphasizes the advantage of the sending of the Spirit. If he

---

[6] So, Herman Ridderbos, *The Gospel of John: A Theological Commentary*, trans. J. Vriend (Grand Rapids: Eerdmans, 1991), 529.

does not go away, the Spirit will not be sent. Jesus must complete his purposes first. He must die for the sins of humanity and rise to the right hand of the Father before the Spirit will be sent.

The Ministry of the Spirit to the World (16:8–11)

The statement in 16:8–11 is simple in grammar but complex in theology. The elaboration in 9–11 is comprised of a single sentence employing a series of items in a simple μέν/δέ/δέ formulation. Our first duty is to understand how the verb translated "convict" (ἐλέγχω) is used in this passage. It is only expressed once, but by ellipsis it is assumed in all three amplifications in 9–11.

ἐλέγχω is used to express four semantic fields: (1) to scrutinize or examine carefully, in the sense of *expose*; (2) to bring a person to the point of recognizing wrongdoing, *convict, convince*; (3) to express strong disapproval of someone's action, *reprove, correct*; and (4) to penalize for wrongdoing, *punish, discipline*.[7]

Since the structure is relatively simple,[8] the interpretation should be relatively straightforward as well. This is supported by the fact that the author considered it unnecessary to elaborate beyond the amplifications of 9–11. For this reason, it is best to understand ἐλέγχω in the same sense in all three clauses.

Option 4 is clearly not in mind. In no sense does the Spirit punish the world in the present age. Likewise, option 3 does not seem to fit the context for it seems rather odd to declare that the Paraclete will disapprove of the world. This leaves option 1, "expose," and option 2, "convict, convince," as the only viable ranges of meaning to consider. Since "expose" seems to be rather mild in this context, option 3 "convict, convince" is the best option. Of the two glosses, "convict" seems the better choice.

The difficulty with this interpretation is that in 16:10 the grounds for "He will convict concerning righteousness" is that "you will no longer see Me" (HCSB). The "you" is ostensibly the disciples. However, one is constrained by the parallelism to understand "concerning righteousness" (περὶ δικαιοσύνης) in 16:10 on equal terms with "concerning sin and judgment" (περὶ ἁμαρτίας and περὶ κρίσεως), that is, in strictly negative connotations, either self-righteousness or unrighteousness.[9]

---

[7] BDAG, s.v. ἐλέγχω.
[8] So Ridderbos, *John*, 531, and Fernando Segovia, *Farewell of the Word: The Johannine Call to Abide* (Philadelphia: Fortress, 1991), 228.
[9] Admittedly only a nuanced difference exists between the two. For a good summary and methodological defense, see Carson, "Paraclete," 558–67; Carson, *John*, 533. The view here is essentially the same as Carson's. Cf. Craig Blomberg, *The Historical Reliability of John's Gospel: Issues and Commentary* (Downers Grove, IL: InterVarsity, 2001), 214; Andreas Köstenberger, *Encountering John: The Gospel in*

Therefore, the Paraclete will "convict concerning sin" because the world, by definition, does not believe on Christ. He will "convict concerning judgment" because the Devil is condemned. "Convict concerning righteousness" should be understood in the sense that the Son going to the Father is an example of *meronomy*—the part represents the whole. Thus, the reference is to the completion of the work of Christ on earth. The provision of a savior demands the admission that human beings are sinful and in need of righteousness. I believe the major arena of conviction is in the hearts of certain individuals, indicating that Christ refers to the inner working of the Spirit in service to evangelism.

People often overlook the major point in this conversation that the conviction of the world is an advantage to the disciples.[10] One is then compelled to see perhaps multiple benefits for the disciples in the conviction of the world (including evangelism and empowered ministry). In light of the hostility of the world in the previous passage, the role of the Paraclete in convicting the world is welcome information. The advantage to the disciples, then, is that their Paraclete is the prosecuting attorney in the court of the human heart, effectively arguing the truth against the world.

The Ministry of the Spirit to the Believer (16:12–15)

In 16:12–15 Jesus relates the second benefit from the arrival of the Paraclete: revelation. Jesus promises that the disciples have not heard all he has to say. But because he has not finished his work on earth, his followers are not yet ready to hear what he has to say. But God has made provision for this in the abiding presence of the Spirit.

The revelatory ministry of the Spirit is described in terms of the source of his revelation rather than the kind of revelation. That is, the specific kind of revelation and the specific manner of revelation are not disclosed. It does include the cryptic, "He will also declare to you what is to come" (HCSB) in 16:13. Many scholars see an expression of realized eschatology here. Bultmann, for example, held the "Spirit only states [Jesus' words] afresh. The Spirit will not bring new illumination, or disclose new mysteries; on the contrary, in the proclamation effected by him, the word that Jesus spoke continues to be efficacious."[11] This interpretation depends on the idea that new revelation *by definition* must be contrary to Jesus' words. Surely this is not *necessarily* so.

Historical, Literary, and Theological Perspective, Encountering Biblical Studies (Grand Rapids: Baker, 1999), 158; and essentially Smith, *John*, 294–95.

[10] This is mentioned by Beasley-Murray but not elaborated; *John*, 281.

[11] Bultmann, *John*, 575.

However, "the things that are coming" may refer to Christ's death and the period afterwards. In this view, the Holy Spirit explains the significance of the death of Jesus in the period to his disciples. In the context, the Holy Spirit will guide the disciples in all truth (because at the time of speaking they could not bear it). But the Spirit will not speak on his own but will report what he hears (ostensibly from God or Christ). Could "what is to come" (the neuter τὰ ἐρχόμενα) have an antecedent in "many more things" (neuter πολλὰ)? I think it is more than likely so, but to restrict it exclusively to the explanation of the death of Christ is not warranted. It certainly includes it, but the statement is general enough to include a modicum of futurist eschatology as well.

Others see the reference to predictive prophecy (the NT prophets like Agabus immediately comes to mind [cf. Acts 11:28 and 21:10]).[12] We should also mention that the book of Revelation, as Keener puts it, "could almost be read as a sequel work of the Paraclete in the Johannine Community."[13] The very idea of predictive prophecy was not rejected by either Jesus, his followers, or in modern times by evangelical Christians. Jesus' statement could include it here as well.

We should reject neither the realized nor the futurist dimensions of the statement. The truth is that the New Testament, and the Gospel of John in particular, embraces both. Therefore we should not dismiss one or the other interpretation based on prior commitments. The lack of specificity on *how* the Spirit reveals what is coming leaves open a wide variety of ways that the Spirit of truth may disclose his truth to Jesus' followers. Whether it is the illumination of Scripture, the inner promptings of the Spirit, or an application of the preaching moment, God has not lost his ability to know the future and to share it through the Spirit when the need arises. This must, of course, be cross-referenced with teaching in the rest of Scripture as we discern a biblical theology of revelation. Some aspects are clearly over (e.g., the inspiration of Scripture). Jesus' promise here, however, is that he will lead in all truth. He is purposefully vague, declining to specify it any further.

Finally 16:14–15 describes the result of the Spirit's ministry. Because Jesus is the source of the revelation, the Spirit of truth will glorify Christ. In other words, the Spirit does not operate apart from Christ. Furthermore, Christ does not operate independently of the Father. In 16:15a–b Jesus affirms that the Father is the ultimate source of Christ's information. However, Christ specifically is affirming his coequality with the Father while at the same time affirming the Father's functional superiority.

---

[12] Stefan almost exclusively so, but see his caveat that it may be used to refer to illumination of Scriptures. Stefan, "The Paraclete and Prophecy," 276.

[13] Craig S. Keener, *The Gospel of John: A Commentary* (Peabody, MA: Hendrickson, 2003), 2:1041.

Preaching the Text

The text displays three major movements. First, Jesus makes the declaration of the advantage in 16:4d–7 (see especially "HEAD" in 16:7 in the SSA above). This advantage (the giving of the Paraclete) is elaborated upon in the next two movements ("amplifications" in 16:8–11 and 12–15 in our SSA above). The first is the advantage of aid in evangelism (i.e., the conviction of the world). The second amplification is the advantage of the Spirit's revelatory ministry. This presents a simple three-point sermon built around these movements.

My MIT is as follows: "The first advantage of Jesus' departure is the sending of the Spirit of truth." The MIM then follows: "All believers should enjoy the advantage of the Spirit in their own ministries." I call my sermon, "The Believer's Secret Weapon."

SERMON SKETCH

TEXT: John 16:4d–15
MIT: The first advantage of Jesus' departure is the sending of the Spirit of truth.
MIM: All believers should enjoy the advantage of the Spirit their own ministries the advantage of ministry of the Spirit in their own ministries.
TOPIC: The Believer's Secret Weapon

INTRODUCTION

Our text this morning describes the believer's secret weapon. It is the Paraclete that we have discussed two other times through this series. We have seen that he mediates the presence of the Lord to those who love and obey Christ. ("But the Counselor, the Holy Spirit—the Father will send Him in My name—will teach you all things and remind you of everything I have told you" [John 14:26 HCSB]). And now he is promised to be our guide in this world.

In this text, Jesus enumerates several advantages to his departure for the believer. The first advantage of Jesus' departure is the sending of the Spirit of truth. My point today is that all believers should enjoy the advantage of the ministry of the Spirit in their own ministries.

Unit 3: Advantages of Jesus' Departure (16:4d–33)

OUTLINE

I. It Is Better for Us that Jesus Has Departed (16:4d–7)

A. TEXT

1. Jesus' departure filled the disciples with sorrow (vv. 4d–6).

   "I didn't tell you these things from the beginning, because I was with you. But now I am going away to Him who sent Me, and not one of you asks Me, 'Where are You going?' Yet, because I have spoken these things to you, sorrow has filled your heart" (HCSB).

   a. "Departure" is a euphemism for death.
   b. The disciples had asked before "where are you going?" But now they get it. He is going to die. In their experience, death is the chasm that is crossed only one direction.
   c. The thought of being separated from Jesus has filled them with sorrow.

2. Jesus goes away to benefit believers (v. 7).

   "Nevertheless, I am telling you the truth. It is for your benefit that I go away, because if I don't go away the Counselor will not come to you. If I go, I will send Him to you" (HCSB).

   a. Jesus had to die.
      i. The Holy Spirit could not come until salvation had been accomplished.
      ii. This was the Father's plan since before the foundation of the world.
   b. The Paraclete is our "secret weapon."

B. TODAY

1. What they feared, we face.

   Although we are on the other side of his death, burial, and resurrection, we too have longed to see, touch, and hear our Lord with our eyes and hands and ears. We think, at times, they had it better. They did not.

2. Because of the ministry of the Holy Spirit we are advantaged.

II. The Paraclete Leads in Ministry (16:8–11)

A. TEXT

"When He comes, He will convict the world about sin, righteousness, and judgment: About sin, because they do not believe in Me; about righteousness, because I am going to the Father and you will no longer see Me; and about judgment, because the ruler of this world has been judged" (HCSB).

The Paraclete is an advantage to us because he works in the world concerning the gospel.

1. The Ministry of the Paraclete involves the conviction of the world.

   a. Sin

   b. Righteousness

   c. Judgment

2. The Ministry of the Paraclete assumes the Christian's involvement in evangelism.

B. TODAY

1. A Christian not involved in evangelism is wasting a precious resource.

2. A Christian not involved in evangelism misses the opportunity to see God work.

3. A Christian involved in evangelism may rest in the Spirit's work.

4. We cannot convict or convert anyone. That is the Spirit's ministry. Ours is simply obedience.

III. The Paraclete Communicates the Will of God to Us (16:12–15)

A. TEXT

"I still have many things to tell you, but you can't bear them now. When the Spirit of truth comes, He will guide you into all the truth. For He will not speak on His own, but He will speak whatever He hears. He will also declare to you what is to come. He will glorify Me, because He will take from what is Mine and declare it to you. Everything the Father has is Mine. This is why I told you that He takes from what is Mine and will declare it to you" (HCSB).

1. The Spirit will guide in truth.

    a. Through illumination of God's Word

    b. Through inner promptings

    c. Through godly counsel

2. The Spirit will glorify Christ.

B. TODAY

1. We should not be afraid of the Holy Spirit.

2. We should look for him to guide us.

    a. Not ungodly "friends"

    b. TV show "counselors"

    c. self-help gurus

3. We should learn how to discriminate his "voice" from other inner influences.

    a. Knowing the Word of God

    b. Knowing what glorifies Christ

    c. Experience in walking with him

    d. Knowing the enemy (Devil, world, and flesh)

CONCLUSION

Beloved, if you love and obey Christ, you have a guide whom you can trust through life's foreign and confusing landscape. Christ has provided the Holy Spirit to indwell you, to mediate the presence of Christ for you. He is our secret weapon and our internal guide.

The Second Advantage: Abiding Joy (16:16–24)

This next section develops the second advantage for the disciples in Jesus' departure. It is both the announcement of the resurrection and an assurance for the disciples.

Analyzing the Text

RELATIONAL STRUCTURE	CONTENTS
┌remark─┬─HEAD───────────────	(16:16a) A little while and you will no longer see me
│ └─amplif.───────────	(16:16b) and again, in a little while you will see me.
├EVAL.─┬─orienter───────────	(17a) therefore some of his disciples said to one another,
│(quest.) └─CONT.────────────	(17b-18c) "We don't know what he is saying."
│ ┌─HEAD─┬─orienter────	(19a-c) Jesus knowing they wanted to ask said,
│ │ └─CONT.───────	(19d-g) "are you questioning one another about what I said?"
│ │ ┌─HEAD───────	(20a-c) Truly, you will weep and mourn but the world will rejoice
│ │ ┌─HEAD─┴─amplif. 1──	(20d-e) you will grieve but your grief will turn to joy.
│ │ │ ┌─HEAD───────	(21a-b) in childbirth a woman sorrows, for her hour has come.
│ ├amplif. 1─Illus.─┤ ┌─reason───	(21c) but when she gives birth to the child
│ │ └─CONTR.─┴─RESULT──	(21d-e) she no longer remembers her trouble for joy of a new child.
└ANSW.─┤ ┌─concession───────	(22a) And likewise you now have sorrow,
│ ─Comp.─┤ ┌─HEAD───────	(22b) But I will see you again
│   └CON.─┤   │
│ EXP. └─amplifs.───	(22c-d) and you will have permanent joy.
│ ┌─HEAD───────────	(23a) And in that day you will not ask me anything.
│ ┌─HEAD─┤ ┌─orienter──	(23b) Truly, truly I say to you,
│ │ └amplif.┴─CONT.────	(23c-d) Whatever you ask the Father in my name, he will grant it...
└amplif. 2─┤ ┌─HEAD───────────	(24a) Until now you did not ask anything in my name
└amplif.┤ ┌─means────	(24b-c) Ask and you will receive
└circumst.─┴─RESULT──	(24d) so that your joy might be full.

The structure of this section is simple in the general scheme but twists through a great deal of conversational material (thus the proliferation of "Orienter-CONTENT" even in the simplified SSA above). A new paragraph is indicated by the abrupt introduction of a new direction in the advantages topic that dominates unit 3. In the previous paragraph, Jesus had repeatedly mentioned his departure (16:5, 7 [*bis*] and 10) but not his return. Here the abrupt statement introduces the fact that not only will he send the Paraclete in a revelatory ministry, but his disciples will also see him again.[14]

The fronting of the temporal marker (called a "deixis") "a little while" (μικρὸν) structurally signals a local discontinuity and is corroborating evidence of a new paragraph. The opening movement of this section takes the form of remark (Jesus' statement), EVALUATION (the disciples' murmurings) that is also a question (the disciples' question is eventually publicly asked by Jesus), and ANSWER (Jesus' response). In Jesus' explanation of his opening comment

---

[14] So, Segovia, *Farewell*, 247.

it is clear that the point he wants to drive home is that the grief at his departure will be temporary. Joy will characterize their lives after his resurrection.[15]

This second advantage to the disciples is developed in two amplifications to the question posed by Jesus (which as a rhetorical question has the force of an indicative statement here: "You are asking one another . . ."). The first amplification is announced by Jesus' solemn double ἀμὴν statement (usually translated "truly, truly" but the HCSB opts for "I assure you," which catches the nuance well). Because it includes "that" (ὅτι—left untranslated by the HCSB), it does not introduce a new development but comments on given information. Consequently, the highly prominent formula is explaining the result of departure and resurrection. It is developed by a general statement that they will grieve over his departure, but the grief will be short-lived. This statement is illustrated by the metaphor of a woman in labor who has grief for a season but upon delivery has an abiding joy.[16]

Verse 22 explains and applies the illustration to the disciples' situation. Then verse 23 is, like verse 20, introduced by the prominent double ἀμὴν statement, which this time does not include a ὅτι. Thus, a new point is introduced that echoes 14:13 and 15:7 in that it describes a new relationship in prayer. This new relationship, however, is for a different purpose. Prayer is encouraged so that the disciples' joy would be full. Thus, the statement further elaborates on the joy that has risen from the ashes of grief. Therefore, not only will the disciples have joy at seeing Jesus again; they will have an abiding joy beyond the resurrection appearances in a newfound relationship through prayer.

It would be tempting to join this propositional cluster to the next one in 16:25–27 because they both are about prayer in the context of "in that day" (ἐν ἐκείνῃ τῇ ἡμέρᾳ repeated in 16:26). But another sharp turn in the topic of advantage occurs in 16:26. The advantage developed in 16:25–32 is direct access to God rather than the joy found in asking in Jesus' name. Furthermore, 16:24 concludes in a purpose clause utilizing ἵνα ("so that your joy may be complete," HCSB) that has signaled the end of many paragraphs throughout the Farewell Discourse. Finally, 16:25 begins with the summarizing statement,

---

[15] See, e.g., Schnackenburg who states, "In the 'consolatory' discourse of Chapter 16, the situation of sorrow (see v. 6) is once again made present and, at this point in the discourse, in order to express the fact that it will be changed into joy. The idea extends as far as v. 22 and then further to v. 24" (Schnackenburg, *The Gospel according to St. John*, 3:155).

[16] The illustration of the woman in labor is typical in the OT in eschatological situations. Köstenberger, *John*, 476. He lists Isa 13:8; 21:3; 26:17–18; 42:14; 66:7–13; Jer 4:31; 6:24; 13:21; 22:23; 30:6; 49:22–24; 50:43; Mic 4:9–10; cf. *2 Esdr (4 Ezra)* 16:38–39. Its use here, however, is primarily descriptive of the emotional situation the disciples now face. Surely, though, there are some eschatological overtones to its use here. Contrary Schnackenburg, *John*, 3:158. So, C. K. Barrett, *The Gospel according to John*, 2nd ed. (Philadelphia: Westminster, 1978), 493; Carson, *John*, 544; and Gerald R. Borchert, *John 12–21*, NAC 25B (Nashville: B&H, 2002), 2:172.

"I have spoken these things" (ταῦτα . . . λελάληκα) that has signaled a new paragraph in many of its occurrences. It is likely that the pattern continues.

Interpreting the Text

Jesus' Announcement (16:16–18)

In the SSA above, the communication relations in 16:16–18 is described as a Remark-EVALUATION. Jesus introduces a completely new topic. It builds off the subject of his departure and the sorrow it brings to the disciples that was background to the main point (the advantage of the Paraclete) of the previous section. The text is presented as a series of conversational exchanges with Jesus. In this way it is more like unit 1 (14:1–31) than it is unit 2 (15:1–16:4d). Jesus' announcement of the second "In a little while . . ." has been variously interpreted. Some see it as a reference to the return of Christ,[17] others the descent of the Spirit.[18] Some suggest that both the resurrection and the Parousia are in view.[19] The best interpretation is that the reference is to the death and resurrection of Christ.[20] The phrase "in a little while" has previously been used to refer to Jesus' death and return to the Father (7:33; the usage in 12:35 is more vague). It is unwise, however, to place a great deal of interpretive weight on a vague (albeit short) measure of time.

The thought that the statement refers to the coming of the Spirit has its foundation more in the scholar who is uncomfortable with Jesus' knowledge of the future than the basic meaning of the statements here.[21] As for the last—plenary—option, although eschatological overtones do exist in the text, nothing denies the reference to the resurrection. Furthermore, nothing demands the incongruity of a resurrection reference that would then demand that the second μικρόν be a reference to the Parousia.

---

[17] So Augustine, according to Brown, *John*, 2:729. Brown himself understood it to be a vague statement more historically accurate than the synoptic affirmations of resurrection. The latter, according to Brown, was an addition by the early church.

[18] In the context of the Gospel (not the historical setting), Brown believed the reference was to the gift of the Holy Spirit (ibid., 730).

[19] Barrett, *John*, 492.

[20] Carson, *John*, 543.

[21] See Brown's parenthetical statement on the view that μικρόν refers to the resurrection, "Obviously such an interpretation presupposes that Jesus knew in detail what would happen after his death, a presupposition that many scholars, Protestant and Catholic, would no longer make" (Brown, *John*, 2:729). Brown further objected by noting that seeing Christ would bring lasting joy and plenary understanding to the disciples is impossible simply from seeing the resurrection. I would disagree. Since the resurrection cannot be taken away, the joy it causes is permanent as well. As for the second, "plenary knowledge" will only happen in our resurrection. The reference at 16:23 surely has a less than "plenary" scope, for in the next verse Christ demands that we ask.

All this is not to say that the disciples understood what Jesus was saying. It seems clear that they understood that he was predicting his death (cf. 16:5). This produces the confusion regarding Jesus' statement. It is not just that their concept of "Messiah" did not include death before reigning, but that they did not understand especially the reference to the resurrection.[22] In 16:17 the disciples rephrase the statement with a curious addition, "'I am going to the Father?'"[23] Jesus has used this phrase several times in this discourse (13:33, 36; 14:4, 28; 16:5 and 10). If the disciples understood it as death (as 16:5 seems to indicate), then the confusion is, in part, over "seeing again" in the context of dying and going to the Father. This doesn't fit with their experience and probably conflicts with their messianic theology. Carson is often and rightly repeated in this context: "The disciples still have no category to allow them to make sense of a Messiah who would die, rise from the dead, and abandon his people in favour of 'another Counselor' (14:16)."[24] Nor would they, it appears, until after the resurrection.

Jesus' Clarification (16:19–22)
16:19 is a rhetorical question. Jesus is not mining for information. He is stating a fact. In effect, he is making the observation that he realizes they do not understand what he is saying. The use of the question format, among other things, provides the opportunity to repeat the statement. This fourth repetition signifies the importance of the concept. What is rather odd is that Jesus doesn't really answer the question plainly (notice the disciples near-relief response to Jesus' plain statement in 16:29). That is not to say he doesn't answer it. He does.

In 16:20 Jesus clarifies what he means in terms of the disciples emotional response to his departure. The terminology he uses is telling. Weeping and mourning was the standard practice at Jewish funerals.[25] So then, the weeping is in response to his death. The phrase "the world will rejoice" finally makes it clear that he is referring to his death. But that is not all; in 16:21–22 he will clarify that they will see him after his death. Presumably, they will see him alive. Their response will be joy.

Jesus uses the metaphor of a woman in labor to illustrate the disciples' emotions. The intense pain (so I'm told) of childbirth is immediately forgotten

---

[22] Contrary Ridderbos, *John*, 538.
[23] HCSB translates ῞Οτι as "because" most likely due to the use at 16:10. It is better understood as an ῞Οτι *recitativum*, an indicator of direct speech.
[24] Carson, *John*, 543.
[25] Blomberg, *Historical Reliability*, 217.

afterwards because of the mother's joy over the new life that is her child.[26] The metaphor, however, does have eschatological overtones. The childbirth metaphor was fairly common in the Old Testament. It was also employed in Second Temple literature to describe eschatological events. They used the term "the birth pangs of the Messiah" to describe the period immediately before the consummation of all things.[27] Also note the phrase "in that day" (v. 23a) is common in eschatological passages. This certainly does not mean the second "in a little while" refers to the eschaton. The asking that follows "in that day" is clearly the time between his departure and his second coming.[28] If there is an eschatological flavor, it suggests that the resurrection, clearly the reference, is an eschatological event.

Joy and Prayer (16:23–24)

The second amplification of the statement of his resurrection in 16:19 occurs in 16:23–24. At first it seems utterly disconnected from the previous context, for the topic is prayer. However, prayer is a means to an end. He desires for the disciples to have fullness of joy, so the connection comes at the end of the passage. There is far more to the significance of seeing Jesus alive after his death than joy. Jesus describes a new relationship in prayer. He has hinted at it three times previously (14:13–14; 15:7, 16).

The statement in 16:23a, "In that day you will not ask Me anything" (HCSB), seems to conflict with the rest of verses 23 and 24 that describes asking in Jesus' name. Much of the discussion among scholarship tries to tease out the nuance of ἐρωτάω ("ask") versus αἰτέω ("ask"). In classical usage the former normally suggested "to ask questions," the latter "to ask for something." However, in the *Koinē* period the two words were often used synonymously. Moreover, John consistently uses near synonyms in a single context without any discernable nuance. It is simply his style. In the context of 16:23, in verse 23a Jesus employs ἐρωτάω, while in verse 23c he employs αἰτέω in an "amplification" relationship. Surely no nuance of difference could be suggested. In the matter of prayer, both seem to be used in the sense of "to ask for something."

Instead, I believe that the key is the One to whom the disciple is directing the request. In verse 23a the request is made directly to Jesus. In verse 23b–c, it is to the Father in Jesus' name. In verse 24a, Jesus' "until now" suggests a

---

[26] It is probably the fact that the reference is resurrection that prompts the metaphor of childbirth. Jesus describes the child not as a "child" (παιδίον or τέκνον) but a "man" (ἄνθρωπος). This would be another difficulty in understanding the reference to be to the Parousia.

[27] Köstenberger notes 1QH 11:8–12 and Rev 12:2–5 as examples (Köstenberger, *John*, 476).

[28] Ridderbos, *John*, 539.

Unit 3: Advantages of Jesus' Departure (16:4d–33)   177

new order or dispensation is now in effect. When the disciples ask in Jesus' name, they may have direct access to the Father.[29] Asking "in my name" is to ask on the basis of Jesus' character and authority. This, of course, assumes the one asking is in covenant with and abiding in Christ and is, therefore, loved by the Father (14:21). Like the previous references to prayer in this portion of John's Gospel, inappropriate prayers (requests outside of the will of God) are not covered in the promise that the Father "will give it to you" (v. 23d HCSB).

The previous references to efficacious prayer in Jesus' name connect prayer to the rest of the elements Jesus has mentioned concerning following him. Believing, loving/obeying (i.e., abiding), loving one another, and praying in Jesus' name are the path to complete joy. Apart from these, the follower of Jesus will not experience lasting joy.

Lest we forget, we should note the structure one more time. These verses are the second amplification regarding the announcement of Jesus' resurrection. So then, these benefits are made possible by the Lord's completed work. It will not be available until Christ has been glorified. Joy links the resurrection and prayer in Jesus' name. We should not lose this fact. The first advantage of Jesus' departure is the gift of the Paraclete; the second is that because of the new dispensation inaugurated by Christ, the follower of Jesus may have full joy. The new nature of prayer will be the final advantage discussed as the discourse concludes in 16:25–33.

Preaching the Text

The structure of the text that is best for constructing an outline of a sermon is normally the largest elements. These are located at the far left of the SSA. Sometimes, however, this is not the case, as here. The largest structures are the remark (16:16a–b); EVALUATION (question) (16:17a–18c); and ANSWER (vv. 19a–24d). However, the remark and evaluation primarily set the stage for the more significant answer that Jesus gives. The most significant movements of the text are the constituents that comprise the ANSWER in verses 19a–24d. Thus, the major structural constituents that I will conform to the movements of the sermon are the HEAD (v. 19a–g), amplification 1 (vv. 20a–22d), and amplification 2 (vv. 23a–24d). Thus, my sermon will have three points dealing with the corresponding texts. The first point will cover the entirety of 16:16–19.

After finishing our survey of the meaning of the text, I suggest the MIT is, "The second advantage of Jesus' death is the promise of abiding joy to those who ask in his name because of his completed work." To convert this to a present-day application is a little more difficult to express without being

---

[29] Borchert, *John*, 2:176.

cumbersome. I suggest something like: "Today, abiding followers of Christ may experience complete joy when they ask the Father in Jesus' name."

SERMON SKETCH

TEXT: John 16:16–24
MIT: Jesus promised abiding joy to those who ask in his name because of his completed work.
MIM: Today, abiding followers of Christ may experience complete joy when they ask the Father in Jesus' name.
TOPIC: The Second Advantage: Complete Joy

INTRODUCTION

In our text today, Christ is finishing up his farewell address before his disciples. Because he has announced his upcoming death and they seem to understand it, he tells them that there are advantages for them if he departs. The first advantage we saw in the last sermon. It was the gift of the Paraclete. Today we will look at the second advantage: their grief will turn to joy. In our text, Jesus promised abiding joy to those who ask in his name because of his completed work. On this side of Easter, the application to believers is the same, except what was promised to the disciples is a reality for us. Today, abiding followers of Christ may experience complete joy when they ask the Father in Jesus' name. This joy begins when the disciples will see him again, that is, in the resurrection.

OUTLINE

I. The Resurrection Is the Foundation for Joy (16:16–19)

"A little while and you will no longer see Me; again a little while and you will see Me." Therefore some of His disciples said to one another, "What is this He tells us: 'A little while and you will not see Me; again a little while and you will see Me'; and, 'because I am going to the Father'?" They said, "What is this He is saying, 'A little while'? We don't know what He's talking about!" Jesus knew they wanted to question Him, so He said to them, "Are you asking one another about what I said, 'A little while and you will not see Me; again a little while and you will see Me'?" (HCSB).

A. TEXT

1. Jesus' announcement

   They will see him again after his departure.

2. Disciples' confusion

   They understood that "departure" meant death. The statement about seeing them again throws them into confusion.

3. Jesus is announcing his resurrection to his disciples.

B. TODAY

I expect the world to take extraordinary means to defy the resurrection, but why would those in the church do so? In many sectors resurrection might as well be in scare quotes for it has turned into code-speak for one of the above theories. I understand the enemies of Christ not embracing the bodily resurrection of Christ, but why do those who claim Christianity at times seem embarrassed by the doctrine?

There are no blanket reasons, but let me throw out a few.

1. Some of those who claim Christianity do not embrace Christ. They deny, or redefine, the new birth. We expect them to embrace a non-Christian worldview.

2. Some have drank deep in the wells of modernism, including the belief that miracles do not happen. We expect them to have difficulty with the resurrection.

3. Some are simply afraid of being branded as "unintelligent," "unscientific," or "religious nut" by the world.

4. Some, like Paul's opponents in Galatia, embrace false doctrine so they won't have to endure persecution.

Jesus affirmed that he would rise from the dead and that he would appear to his disciples. The born-again believer with courage and insight embraces the resurrection of Christ. But, as we will see, what they gain is joy in what the resurrection represents.

II. Joy Is Available in the Accomplishment of Salvation (16:20–22)

"I assure you: You will weep and wail, but the world will rejoice. You will become sorrowful, but your sorrow will turn to joy. When a woman is in labor she has pain because her time has come. But when she has given birth to a child, she no longer remembers the suffering because of the joy that a person has been born into the world. So you also have sorrow now. But I will see you again. Your hearts will rejoice, and no one will rob you of your joy" (HCSB).

A. TEXT

1. The disciples will be miserable over Jesus' death.

2. Their misery will be forgotten.

   The metaphor of the woman in labor

3. Their sorrow will be turned into an abiding joy.

   Because the resurrection cannot be taken away, neither can the joy associated with it.

B. TODAY

1. Like the disciples, we will know pain and, at times, suffering.

   a. It is part-and-parcel of living in a fallen world.

   b. In the providence of God, it is never for nothing.

   c. Jesus himself was no stranger to suffering.

2. Unlike the disciples, we live on the other side of the resurrection.

III. Joy Continues in the Relationship that Christ Establishes (16:23–24)

"In that day you will not ask Me anything. I assure you: Anything you ask the Father in My name, He will give you. Until now you have asked for nothing in My name. Ask and you will receive, so that your joy may be complete" (HCSB).

A. TEXT

Jesus describes a new relationship to the Father.

1. A new manner of prayer (v. 23a)

    a. It is now to the Father in Jesus' name.

    b. "Name" suggests the character and authority of Jesus.

2. A familiar promise of prayer (v. 23b–d)

    Three previous times (in every unit of the discourse) a promise regarding effectual prayer has been made.

    In 14:13–14 asking is connected to loving him, keeping his commands, and bringing him glory.

    In 15:7 it is connected to abiding in Christ (loving/obeying him) and fruit bearing.

3. A new result of prayer (v. 24)

    In 16:24 nothing new is added except the results. Those who pray to the Father in Jesus' name will have complete joy.

    The purposes of Jesus' coming are fulfilled, "in that day." He came to give abundant life (John 10:10, a life rich in the presence of the Holy Spirit and joy). He came to give us streams of living water flowing through us (John 7:38). That can be attained only after his glorification.

    Joy is dependent, however, upon abiding in Christ. The believer has tremendous potential to experience messianic joy. However, much of that is unmet in the average Christian.

B. TODAY

The text hints at a process that I want to make explicit for you who want to meet your potential in Christ.

1. Joy begins with belief.

    Faith is the starting point of the Christian life. It is also the matrix in which we operate our life after we come to Christ.

2. Joy is dependent on the love of/obedience to Christ.

After initial faith and then living faith, one must love Christ as expressed in obedience.

3. We must ask in Jesus' name.

Such asking implies an intimacy that was previously not available (see v. 24).

4. The result is joy.

CONCLUSION

Because of what the resurrection represents (the completed work of Christ), ask. Ask to glorify God in Christ. Ask to do his will. Ask to be more fruitful. Ask to lovingly obey him. Ask to have greater faith. Ask and it will be given to you so that your joy will be complete.

The Third Advantage: Direct Access in Prayer (16:25–32)

The advantage in present text is subtler than the other two advantages. The speech is also coming to an end, and Jesus is both concluding the speech and giving the third advantage of his departure. The specific advantage is direct access in prayer. However, Jesus is also making it plain that the disciples are not yet new covenant believers for he has yet to be glorified.

Analyzing the Text

RELATIONAL STRUCTURE	CONTENTS
remark — concession	(16:25a) I have spoken these things figuratively
CONTRA. — circum. — HEAD	(25b-c) soon I'll no longer speak figuratively
EXP. — CONTR.	(25d) but I will announce boldly to you about the Father
RESULT — HEAD	(26a) In that day you will ask in my name,
HEAD — amplif.	(26b-c) and I do not say that I'll ask the Father about you.
grounds — CONCL.	(27a) For the Father himself loves you
grounds	(27b-28d) because you love me and believe I came from God.
COUNTER- — grounds	(29a-c) disciples: you now speak boldly and not figuratively
REMARK — CONCL. 1 — orienter	(30a-b) Now we know that you know all things
CONTs.	(30c-d) and you have no need that someone should ask you.
CONCL. 2	(30e-f) We believe that you came from God.
EVAL. — CONCLUSION	(31a) Jesus: you believe now?
reason — concession	(32a-d) behold soon you will all be scattered.
CONTRA. — EXP.	(32e-f) But the Father is with me.

As usual, we will look at the overall structure of the section first with a simplified SSA. In 16:25, Jesus begins the third and last of the unit's theme of advantages for the disciples because of Jesus' departure. The surface structure of 16:25–31 is, again, relatively simple. It takes the form of remark (Jesus: 16:25–28)-COUNTERREMARK (disciples: 16:29–30)-EVALUATION (Jesus: 16:31–32). As in the last section, the conversational aspect of this section presents certain problems due to the skewing between what is said and how what is said is being used.

The referent for "I have spoken these things" (ταῦτα . . . λελάληκα) has been variously suggested as either 16:21,[30] 16:18,[31] a combination thereof,[32] the whole discourse,[33] or the whole of Jesus' teaching.[34] A further point of contention is whether the "veiledness" (i.e., the disciples' misunderstanding) is due to Jesus' intentional usage or the ability of the disciples to perceive what was said.[35] The question is important to how one understands this last section of the Farewell Discourse.

The referent for, "I have spoken these things" (ταῦτα . . . λελάληκα) must, by the rules of grammar, mean at least the recent discussion of Jesus with his disciples. By extension, there may be a reference to the whole of Jesus' teaching. Because he is still advocating the advantages of his departure, I feel it is best to see this as a reference to the present unit. However, there may be some "double usage" here as the discourse is winding down.

The statement itself sets up Jesus' disclosure of the third advantage, namely, direct access to the Father. The circumstance (25b–c), of which he will no longer speak elusively but plainly, leads to the statement of an unmitigated access in prayer (26a–c). This CONCLUSION is based on two reasons. First, the disciples have loved Christ (27b). And second, they have believed (27c–28d). It is tempting to assign these relations as RESULT-means. However, that classification would suggest a merit-based love from the Father. Ground-CONCLUSION avoids that error in that 27b–28d are evidence to support the conclusion of the Father's love.

---

[30] F. J. Moloney, *The Gospel of John*, SP 4 (Collegeville, MN: Liturgical, 1998), 453, and Brown, *John*, 2:734.

[31] Ridderbos, *John*, 540.

[32] See, e.g., Schnackenburg, *John*, 161, and Beasley-Murray, *John*, 286.

[33] See, e.g., Segovia, *Farewell*, 262.

[34] Most of the commentators who extend the reference to the whole of the discourse will ultimately extend it to the whole of Jesus' teaching. See, Segovia, *Farewell*, 262; Beasley-Murray, *John*, 286; Edwyn Clement Hoskyns, *The Fourth Gospel*, ed. Francis Noel Davey, 2nd ed. (London: Faber & Faber, 1947), 489–90; and Blomberg, *Historical Reliability*, 219.

[35] For the former see Ridderbos, *John*, 541; for the latter see Bultmann, *John*, 584; Schnackenburg, *John*, 3:161; and Jürgen Becker, *Das Johannes nach Johannes: Kapitel 11–21*, ÖTKNT 4 (Würzburg: Echter, 1981), 2:503.

16:29a–30f is the disciples' COUNTERREMARK to Jesus' remark in 16:25. They draw two CONCLUSIONS based on Jesus' avoidance of figurative language. First, 30a–d, Jesus knows all things. The second CONCLUSION is that they believe that Christ came from the Father.

Jesus' EVALUATION of the COUNTERREMARK is found in 16:31a–32f. The question in 31b is rhetorical in nature and should be classified like an indicative statement. In this case it is a CONCLUSION that they do not now believe (we'll discuss below the tension between Jesus' affirmation of belief in 27c and his denial of it here). The grounds for his CONCLUSION is that the hour has arrived when they will be scattered to their own homes (31c–32f).

Interpreting the Text

Jesus' Announcement (16:25–28)

The last advantage of Jesus' departure comes in Jesus' statement in 16:25–28. We have already identified the referent of "these things" as the present unit. He affirms that he is speaking figuratively. The choice of words is important to identify to what he refers. The manner of the speaking is specified by "in figures of speech" (ἐν παροιμίαις) that could signify a variety of narrative forms, including proverbial, comparative, or figurative language. Another option is that he is using veiled language.[36]

Beyond the lexical context of the word, two significant keys unlock the meaning of the noun in this context. The first key to understanding παροιμία is to note how it is used in 10:6: "Jesus gave them this illustration" (ταύτην τὴν παροιμίαν εἶπεν αὐτοῖς ὁ Ἰησοῦς). There the noun refers to a symbolic discourse laden with OT imagery.[37] As it is used only this one time outside of John 16, this cannot be pressed too far, but it does give at least one example of παροιμία in Johannine vocabulary. The second key, and more germane, is that it is given in contrast to "plainly" (παρρησία). Often translated "boldness," in Johannine

---

[36] Liddell and Scott list the referents as proverbs, maxims, saw, figure, comparison, digression, incidental remark. BDAG defines παροιμία as communication containing truths designed for initiates, veiled saying, figure of speech. To this Hyunsok Doh adds idiomatic expressions and riddles (Hyunsok Doh, "The Johannine *Paroimia*" [Ph.D. diss., Andrews University, 1992], 79). Doh believes that Philo's replacement of παροιμία with αἴνιγμα, announces a shift to a new meaning that is developed in John, i.e., a riddle. The evidence seems rather scant. Tom Thatcher also sees riddles at the heart of the Farewell Discourse. To him the whole of the Farewell Discourse is a "riddling session," marked by ambiguity—misunderstanding—clarification, whereby Jesus never clearly announces his death, propagates ambiguity throughout the discourse and finally the disciples believe at 16:29–31 (Tom Thatcher, *The Riddles of Jesus in John: A Study in Tradition and Folklore*, SBLMS 53 [Atlanta: Society of Biblical Literature, 2000], 197–210). The last two of these keystones are sufficiently problematic to describe the Farewell Discourse as a riddling session.

[37] Andreas J. Köstenberger, "Jesus the Good Shepherd Who Will Also Bring Other Sheep (John 10:16): The Old Testament Background of a Familiar Metaphor," *BBR* 12 (2002): 72.

usage, it carries the force of "openly" or "plainly."³⁸ The use here carries the force of "plainly" as in "easily perceived" because intentional obfuscation on the part of Jesus is unlikely in this context.³⁹ Thus, the word παροιμία must be taken as an antonym of "plainly." So, then, here, like 10:6, it probably signifies symbolic discourse of some sort. Thus, the translation of "figuratively" works well.

But to what does it refer? The assumption that it refers to "A little while and you will no longer see Me" (HCSB) in 16:16 (and subsequently misunderstood in 16:18) does not seem to fit the category as well as the illustration of the woman in labor in 16:21.⁴⁰ The reference, however, probably goes beyond the present vicinity to refer to the entire discourse that is flavored by such metaphorical material.⁴¹ Some choices of words could be understood as figurative on one level (see e.g., 14:6). The allegory of the vine and the branches (15:1–18) and the woman in travail (16:21) both would appropriately be described by the word παροιμία.⁴² Carson rightly describes it: "*En paroimias* (NIV 'figuratively') does not necessarily mean 'in a figure' or 'in a metaphor' or 'in a parable,' but has to do with the obscurity of his utterances."⁴³

It seems best, then, to understand the term as "figurative speech" as opposed to "easily understood speech." The precise referent (i.e., vv. 21 or 18, or the whole discourse) does not affect the meaning of the text a great deal because it announces a new situation that will forego figurative speech and be characterized by clarity.

This yet-to-be situation is the reason for the ambiguity that is unfortunately part of the Farewell Discourse for the disciples. It comes not from any intention on Jesus' part to be elusive but on the inability of the disciples by virtue of their location on the salvation-historical time line. They simply have no point of reference for the information that Jesus is attempting to communicate to them. Analogies and symbolic discourse will only have meaning for them after the resurrection. The contrast between having spoken "in figures of

---

³⁸ In 7:4, 13, 26; 11:54; and 18:20 the sense seems to be "openly," i.e., not in secret. In two other places this translation does not seem to work well. At 10:24 and 11:14 the sense is more surely that of "plainly," i.e., without any elements that could be confused.

³⁹ In 11:24 παρρησία must carry this nuance because it is clear that there is no intentional obfuscation on the part of Jesus implied in the misunderstood words, "Lazarus sleeps."

⁴⁰ Contrary to Ridderbos, *John*, 540.

⁴¹ So Leon Morris, *The Gospel according to John*, NICNT (Grand Rapids: Eerdmans, 1995), 629; Barrett, *John*, 495; and Ridderbos, *John*, 540. It is not necessary then to suppose that this section is the conclusion to the whole discourse.

⁴² Hellenistic usage displays a wide field of semantic meaning. This wide field is attested by its use to translate the Hebrew משׁל in the Old Testament (which is likewise a broad category). It is likely that John, being influenced by the Old Testament (and perhaps purposefully avoiding the term *parable* [παραβολή]) is using the term broadly. Furthermore, the context here may indicate that the term was used broadly (i.e., no specific one referent but a type of discourse).

⁴³ Carson, *John*, 546. See also, Köstenberger, *John*, 478.

speech" (ἐν παροιμίαις) but now "plainly" (παρρησίᾳ) sets up the third advantage for the disciples: direct access to God.

"In that day" (ἐν ἐκείνῃ τῇ ἡμέρᾳ) refers to the period of time after the resurrection as the most likely antecedent (see v. 23). The promise there of efficacious prayer is now expanded to include direct access. Jesus makes clear that asking in his name does not mean using him as an intercessor between them and God in prayer. Through his death on the cross he makes those who approach God through him have a direct access.[44] The reason for this is that the Father loves them. As noted above, it is important not to understand 27b–c as reasons for the Father's love, for that would suggest a treasury of merit that generates the Father's love.[45] Elsewhere the Father's love is clearly given apart from works (cf. 3:16; Rom 5:8). Instead, we should see these as evidences that the disciples can be sure of intimacy with God. That is not to say that Jesus doesn't intercede on our behalf. He certainly does, but he is not an intermediary in prayer. Jesus concludes his point in 16:28 with the affirmation that he is returning to the Father.

The Disciples' Overconfidence (16:29–30)

One of the major characteristics of the Fourth Gospel is the use of misunderstanding. The disciples' response to verse 28 is a clear example of the Johannine use of misunderstanding. The disciples think they understand, but they are mistaken. On cursory examination this concluding exchange appears to be a new topic introduced, but in context it reinforces the present situation that Jesus has just described.

The disciples react to Jesus' comments in confidence. They believe a new era has begun.[46] As they express themselves they seem to say the right things that affirm Jesus' supernatural knowledge. They have forgotten the time sequence of "in that day" and are really no closer to understanding the speech than previously. Jesus told them that the day is coming when he would speak plainly. Because his words were plain to them at that moment, they thought that day was today. Carson rightly points out that the "now" employed by the disciples exposes their error.[47]

---

[44] See Köstenberger, *John*, 478, quoting Brown, *John*, 2:735: "In interceding Jesus will not be a *tertium quid* between the Father and his children. Rather, Jesus' necessary role in bringing men to the Father and Father to men (xiv 6–11) will set up so intimate a relationship of love *in and through Jesus* that Jesus cannot be considered as intervening."

[45] Contrary Morris, *John*, 630. Barrett suggests that this verse is based on 15:13–15 because the disciples are the "friends" (φίλοι) of Jesus (a cognate of the verbs used here). So then, the Father stands within the circle (Barrett, *John*, 496). This would seem to assume a distinction between the verbs for love that we have denied elsewhere.

[46] Most likely based on the plain declaration of Christ in verse 28.

[47] Carson, *John*, 548.

Their problem was not that they were wrong in their facts. Jesus does know all things (16:30b), and yes, he knows their questions before they can ask them (16:30c–d). The problem is preeminently their overconfidence in their ability to follow Jesus now. This is the same overconfidence that Peter expressed in the introduction to the Farewell Discourse, "why can't I follow You now? I will lay down my life for You!" (13:37 HCSB).

The point is subtle, but it can be seen if we connect the dots. All the disciples are in the same boat as Peter—they are overconfident in their abilities. Furthermore, they are simply unable to follow Christ now because "that day" has not arrived. Since we connected Peter's inability in 13:31–38 to 21:15–22, we may do so with the inability of the rest of the disciples as well. 21:15–22 is surely "that day." In that day we must follow him for he has secured that day for us (cf. 13:31–38).

Jesus' Assessment (16:31–32)

Jesus' response, therefore, is not a sigh of relief that the disciples now believe. It is a rhetorical question that must be interpreted like the similar response to Peter's confident assertion in 13:37 (where the same pattern of repeating the overconfident assessment occurs as a response).[48] Jesus denies the validity of the disciples' claim just as he did Peter's. The issue is where they stand in relation to Jesus' work. They stand before the cross. It will only be "in that day" (i.e., after the death, burial, and resurrection) that they will be able to follow Christ. It is a matter of where they stand in salvation history. They do not yet believe nor love him fully. They will, in fact, desert him. Over against the disciples' mistaken self-confidence, verse 32 concludes the section with Jesus' confidence in the Father's presence with him throughout the hour to come.

This final section has been ascending to the conclusion with a series of anaphoras. We have seen that the referent for "I have spoken these things" (ταῦτα . . . λελάληκα) could possibly be verse 21 but surely extends beyond that to the whole discourse. The reference to prayer in Jesus' name in 16:26 reaches back to 14:13; 15:7; and 16:23. The affirmation of the Father's love references 14:21 and probably 15:12–17. Love and faith are repeatedly prescribed in the Farewell Discourse (see especially 14:1, 15, 28–29; and 15:1–11). Jesus' description of his going and coming in 16:28 is an echo of 13:33; 14:3, 12, 18, 25; 15:22, 26; 16:5–7, and 16:22. Jesus' statement that the Father is with him in 16:32 is quite similar to the language of mutual indwelling found in 14:10, 20 and 15:10, but these issues are treated in relation to the main

---

[48] So, Ridderbos, *John*, 544.

topic rather than highlighted back-references. Specific conclusion is not the intent here. 16:33, however, concludes the entirety of the discourse and should be understood as a final propositional cluster in its own right.

Preaching the Text

The structure of the text lends itself to another three-point sermon. Looking at our SSA above, there are three major movements, the REMARK (16:25–28), the COUNTERREMARK (16:29–30), and EVALUATION (16:31–32). The difficulty here is that the second of these movements is not clarified until the third movement. Furthermore, the third movement doesn't stand alone very well. So I suggest a two-movement sermon that combines the last two comments.

The main idea of the text is the third advantage to Jesus' departure. However, the writer is multitasking, for the discourse is closing and he is also making a point about following Jesus based on the Lord's finished work. Therefore, my MIT is "Jesus declared direct access to God in prayer for new covenant believers." As I convert this to the main idea of the message, I want to do more than just put it in the present tense, for the idea is that here is a precious resource available because of Christ's accomplishments. My MIM, then, is "Christians should use the direct access to God made available through Christ's sacrificial death on the cross." My topic is "The Hotline."

SERMON SKETCH

TEXT: John 16:25–32
MIT: Jesus declared direct access to God in prayer for new covenant believers.
MIM: Christians should use the direct access to God made available through Christ's sacrificial death on the cross.
TOPIC: The Hotline

INTRODUCTION

In this last unit of the Farewell Discourse, Jesus has been describing advantages gained through his departure for followers of Christ. The first was the indwelling Holy Spirit, and the second was grief turned into joy. This is the third and final advantage listed here (surely this is not an exhaustive list). For new covenant believers Jesus declared direct access to God in prayer. My objective today is both matter of understanding and practice. You must understand the truth and then apply it in your daily life. Christians should use the direct access to God made available through Christ's sacrificial death on the cross.

OUTLINE

I. What Is the Hotline? (16:25–28)

A. TEXT

"I have spoken these things to you in figures of speech. A time is coming when I will no longer speak to you in figures, but I will tell you plainly about the Father. In that day you will ask in My name. I am not telling you that I will make requests to the Father on your behalf. For the Father Himself loves you, because you have loved Me and have believed that I came from God. I came from the Father and have come into the world. Again, I am leaving the world and going to the Father" (HCSB).

1. "In that day" is after the resurrection.

2. Then, we should ask in his name.

3. The implication is an intimate direct access to God.

> Understand how momentous this is. In the book of Exodus, Moses would enter into the holy of holies and converse with God. In Exodus 33:9 (HCSB) the Scripture states, "When Moses entered the tent, the pillar of cloud would come down and remain at the entrance to the tent, and the Lord would speak with Moses. As all the people saw the pillar of cloud remaining at the entrance to the tent, they would stand up, then bow in worship, each one at the door of his tent. The Lord spoke with Moses face to face, just as a man speaks with his friend." The people on the outside of the tent did not have the same access that Moses had. Jesus declares something more like what Moses experienced than what the people did. Even though they saw the pillar of smoke and fire, it was all external and distant from their innermost beings. It is an advantage to have direct access to God in prayer.

B. TODAY

Three benefits of direct access

1. The person praying with direct access doesn't have to go through someone else.

2. The person praying with direct access doesn't have to wonder if the request got there.

3. The person praying with direct access doesn't have to worry if the message is transmitted correctly.

II. Who Gets to Use It? (16:29–32)

A. TEXT

1. Misunderstanding (vv. 29–30)

"Ah!" His disciples said. "Now You're speaking plainly and not using any figurative language. Now we know that You know everything and don't need anyone to question You. By this we believe that You came from God" (HCSB). The disciples have assumed their status as participants in the new covenant.

2. Jesus corrects them (vv. 31–32).

Jesus responded to them, "Do you now believe? Look: An hour is coming, and has come, when each of you will be scattered to his own home, and you will leave Me alone. Yet I am not alone, because the Father is with Me" (HCSB). Christ affirms that they are in error. They do not believe yet. The evidence is their abandonment of Christ.

3. The implications for the disciples

The indwelling of the Holy Spirit, transformative joy, and now direct access to God are the results of Jesus' sacrificial death. These things are only made available to us through being born again.

B. TODAY

1. Direct access to and intimacy with God is not based on our achievement but Christ's.

2. Direct access is not conditional.

3. This kind of access is unique.

CONCLUSION

The "hotline" to the Kremlin is not the only hotline Washington has. In 2008, the US set up a hotline with China in hopes of developing better communication. The move shows the rise in significance that China plays on the world scene.[49] However, we hope it, like the hotline at the Kremlin, never has to be used. That is, if there is no need to use it, strife between major world powers is not happening.

Quite the opposite is true for the believer's hotline. If we use it, the world is better off. If we use it, our families are better off. If we use it, we are better off. Christ has gained access for us into the holy of holies. We may come, not flippantly, not as if it were not an extreme privilege, but as an honor bought at the expense of the beloved One. We may come not just as servants but as dearly loved children. We may come not just to visit for a while or leave a Christmas wish list, but we may come and love and be loved by our heavenly Father. So come, what are we waiting for?

The Conclusion (16:33)

The final verse of the Farewell Discourse proper announces more than the end of the speech. Jesus announces his victory. His death is not a tragedy he couldn't stop. It is the fulfillment of his purpose in coming to Earth. Furthermore, he also announces our part: to be courageous.

Analyzing the Text

RELATIONAL STRUCTURE	CONTENTS
CONCL ┬ means	(33a) I have spoken these things to you
└ PURP ┬ HEAD	(33b) so that you would have peace in me.
└ amplifi ┬ HEAD	(33c) in the world you have tribulation.
└ CONTR ┬ EXHORT	(33d) but be encouraged
└ grounds	(33e) I have overcome the world.

Structurally, the final section is composed of two sentences, the second of which amplifies the meaning of the first. It could be seen, and often is, as part of the previous paragraph. However, three items hinder this interpretation. First, the cluster shifts dramatically in tone and topic. The topic switches from the fact that Jesus will be abandoned by the disciples to the exhortation that they should be at peace because of Jesus' victory. If a switch in topic is the prerequisite for a paragraph break, this verse meets that requirement.

---

[49] See http://www.bloomberg.com/news/2011-05-13/china-u-s-defense-hotline-shows-gulf.html.

Second, the now-familiar "I have spoken these things" (ταῦτα λελάληκα) does not reference the pronouncement of the disciples' desertion, for its purpose is to give the disciples peace. If it did refer to the pronouncement, the meaning would be strained. Barrett, for example, states that it is possible that it refers to the preceding verse and means something like, "I have foretold your desertion that you may know that it was not unforeseen, and may therefore not be tormented by remorse but have peace."[50] But Barrett himself is not convinced and suggests that it refers to the whole discourse.[51]

Third, 16:33 displays impressive anaphora. This back-referencing, unlike the previous section, is prominent in the main clauses and not subordinate to them. The purpose of the discourse is to bring peace to the disciples. This brings to mind especially 14:1 and serves to clamp together the discourse by way of anaphora. This short cluster also provides back-references to the salient items in the discourse. "In Me" (ἐν ἐμοί) moderately hearkens back to 15:1–11 ("remain in me"; HCSB) but seems to rather presuppose 14:27 ("My peace I give to you"; HCSB) as the kind of peace that is in view here. "You will have suffering in this world" (16:33 HCSB; ἐν τῷ κόσμῳ θλῖψιν ἔχετε) points to the entirety of 15:18–16:4c ("If the world hates you"; HCSB). And finally, "I have conquered the world" (v. 33 HCSB; ἐγὼ νενίκηκα τὸν κόσμον) is reminiscent of 14:30 ("He [the ruler of this world] has no power over Me," HCSB).

Interpreting the Text

In 16:33 Jesus formally closes the discourse. As stated above "these things" refers to the entirety of the discourse. The purpose of speaking this discourse is to deliver peace to his own. As Keener notes, this is not just the stoic philosophy of being unconquered by suffering, "but a promise that evil and suffering do not ultimately prevail for Christ's followers."[52]

In light of this, followers of Jesus should "be courageous" (HCSB; θαρσεῖτε). The Greek word can be used in the sense of "take heart" (as translated in the ESV). Another semantic range of the word is that of courage. In the imperative it would be to "be courageous" (as in the HCSB). The NASB and the NET both take somewhat of a middle ground and translate it "take courage." Admittedly, there is only a slight change of meaning among the renderings. Given that it is in proximity to "overcame" (νενίκηκα), I slightly prefer "be courageous." The latter suggests bold actions on the part of the believer and still incorporates the idea of not losing heart.

---

[50] Barrett, *John*, 498.
[51] Ibid.
[52] Keener, *John*, 2:1049.

We can be bold because Jesus will accomplish through his death the defeat of the world. "World" (κόσμος) is used seventy-eight times in this Gospel. In the Farewell Discourse it is used twenty times.[53] Only twice does it not refer to the hostile forces of lost humanity arrayed against Christ. The world cannot receive the Spirit of truth (14:17). The world no longer sees Jesus (14:19). Jesus does not reveal himself to the world (14:22). Jesus' peace is fundamentally different than the world's peace (14:27). The ruler of this world has no power over Christ (14:30). Jesus' obedience shows the world that he loves the Father (14:31). The world hates Christians (15:18) because they are not *of the world* (15:19). The world will be convicted by the Holy Spirit (16:8). The ruler of this world has been judged (16:11). The world will rejoice over Jesus' death (16:20). Suffering awaits believers in the world (16:33). But Jesus has overcome the world (16:33).

"Overcoming" (νικάω) is a familiar Johannine doctrine. The word is normally translated "overcome." However, that is a bit tame for its meaning. BDAG lists three semantic domains for the word: (1) to win in the face of obstacles, *be victor, conquer, overcome, prevail* (used intransitively); (2) to overcome someone, *vanquish, overcome* (used transitively); and (3) to surpass in ability, *outstrip, excel*. Since in the Johannine context the word is usually transitive, the first option is not a real option, nor is the third, for the meaning is always in a combative setting. It is, then, to vanquish or overcome an enemy. I prefer the term "conquer" in these settings instead of "overcome" when the subject is Christ. "Overcome" seems mild considering the great lengths it took to secure the victory and the magnitude of that victory. However, it seems appropriate for believers, for our struggle has not been completed.

The idea is especially developed in 1 John and Revelation. The relationship between the believer and the world/enemy is victory. Young men have conquered the evil one (2:13–14); believers have conquered the spirits not from God (4:4); everyone who has been born of God overcomes the world (5:4–5). In 1 John it seems that believers have appropriated what Christ has accomplished on the cross.

This is carried over in Revelation where the verb is used seventeen times. Christ continues to be referred to as a conqueror (5:5; 17:14). When referring to believers, the familiar "the ones who are overcoming" in the letters to the seven churches in chapters 2 and 3 are promised a series of gifts related to salvation. Given 1 John, we have to interpret these as promises to those who appropriated Christ's saving work. Believers continue to conquer in Revelation, notably even those who are martyred (12:11 and possibly 15:2). Ultimately, in 21:7 "the ones

---

[53] This is not including the eighteen times it is used in the final prayer of chapter 17!

who are overcoming" inherit the realized salvation. So then, victory is on God's terms. The evil one may persecute, oppress, and kill the believer, but his defeat is secured in what Jesus has accomplished on the cross.

This is the foundation of his peace in the Farewell Discourse. In the world tribulation will happen, perhaps even the ultimate price will be paid. But we are to take courage for he has conquered the world. Because Christ has paid for our sins, nothing can take that away from us. Our victory stands apart from the circumstances of life. It stands apart from health, wealth, or prosperity. It stands apart from any temporary and apparent victories this world may experience. Our victory is because of his victory, and it has been finished.

Preaching the Text

Normally I don't like to preach a sermon on one verse, for such sermons tend to be more topical. However, since 16:33 concludes and to some extent summarizes the entire discourse, it shouldn't be difficult to keep it an expository message. In a series like the Farewell Discourse, a final summary is appropriate.

I see three movements in 16:33 that would lend themselves to unpacking: (1) the purpose of the discourse (v. 33a–b), (2) the declaration of trouble in the world (v. 33c), and finally, (3) our response based on his victory (v. 33d). My MIT is "Jesus declared that his followers can have peace based on his victory." The MIM would be "Believers have peace based on his victory." I call my sermon "The Price of Peace." What follows is a more complete outline than usual to make specific some rather broad movements.

SERMON SKETCH

TEXT: John 16:33
MIT: Jesus declared that his followers can have peace based on his victory.
MIM: Believers have peace based on his victory.
TOPIC: The Price of Peace

INTRODUCTION

There is a different kind of peace that can transcend the fleeting peace of the world. It is an inner peace that only Christ can give. Ultimately, the Farewell Discourse is about our experiencing and enjoying that peace. Jesus began with "Do not let your heart be troubled" (14:1). He will now conclude with "These things I have spoken to you, so that in me you may have peace" (16:33). This is a peace in the midst of turmoil, but it is a peace that is superior to any the world can offer.

The peace that Jesus offers, however, comes with a great price that he paid and we must embrace. The good news is that Jesus declared that his followers could have peace based on his victory. It is my aim today to encourage you that believers have peace based on Christ's victory.

OUTLINE

I. Embrace His Peace (16:33a-b)

"I have told you these things so that in Me you may have peace" (HCSB).

A. TEXT

1. The GOAL is Christ's peace.

2. Embracing peace

   a. The secret to the untroubled heart (John 14 [unit 1])

   Believe in Christ, love/obey him, and the Holy Spirit mediates the presence of Christ in our lives.

   b. Abiding in Christ (John 15 [unit 2])

   Loving obedience, loving one another, and expecting hostility from the world. Our secret weapon is the Spirit working conviction in the world.

   c. The advantages of his departure (John 16 [unit 3])

   The Holy Spirit, grief turned into joy, and direct access to the Father

B. TODAY

1. Peace begins with faith.

2. It continues in loving obedience.

3. It continues in clinging to Christ and others who love him.

Embracing his peace, however, doesn't mean a trouble-free life.

II. Expect Trouble in the World (16:33c)

"You will have suffering in this world" (HCSB).

A. TEXT

1. Expect cosmic hostility.

2. Expect personal hostility.

B. TODAY

1. We should have proper expectations.

   It is a ploy of the Devil for us to expect wealth or health simply because we are believers. It is a ploy of the Devil for us to expect that God's providence means we will never have tribulation. It is the clear word of God that we will. It is, however, neither permanent nor capricious. God has a purpose for our trials, and they are never for nothing.

2. We should pray against the cosmic forces.

   We are in the hands of a loving Father. We are his servants in this war; there is not much more that we can do on the cosmic level other than be obedient in even the smallest details and prayer.

3. We should witness to the people in captivity to the evil one.

   As obedient servants, our chief mission is to worship him in the beauty of holiness and be his voice in testifying to the world.

III. Respond Based on His Victory (16:33d)

"Be courageous! I have conquered the world" (HCSB).

A. TEXT

1. Be courageous.

2. Because he has conquered the world

B. TODAY

Based on his victory we are to be courageous. What would that look like? Among other things, I can think of at least three manifestations of courage in this war between the Lord and the evil one.

1. Boldness in sharing our testimony
2. Intentionality in sharing the gospel
3. Creativity in getting the gospel to the nations

CONCLUSION

For the disciples, Jesus' departure was not good news. But it is what they needed. They needed Jesus to obtain victory over the world. We did as well. Because of Jesus' victory on the cross, we can have a supernatural peace. That does not mean we do not attempt to make our world a better place. What it means is that we attempt it through a variety of means: meeting needs, providing security, and developing infrastructure, among other things that are terribly needed. But what we do most of all is courageously share the gospel, for it is the gospel that brings peace to humanity.

John 16:33, in many ways, is the conclusion to the Farewell Discourse. The speech itself has come to an end. Christ has given his disciples the instructions on how to have an untroubled heart. As I noted in the sermon sketch above, the discourse begins and ends with the promise of peace. Between those declarations, however, Christ outlines what it is to thrive spiritually between his departure and his return. The two matters, peace and discipleship, are intertwined. It would be foolish to expect one without the other. We should expect that believing, loving/obeying Christ, and loving one another would bring the inner peace that Christ promised. The Holy Spirit will mediate his presence, convict the world, and empower believers. What else would we need? On the other hand we should not expect that peace when we fail to nurture these basic issues of following him. So then, 16:33 effectively ends the speech itself. Yet, Christ has more to do before his glorification begins. This is the subject of the last chapter that will encapsulate and enhance much of what Christ has said in his final prayer.

CHAPTER 7

UNIT 4: THE FINAL PRAYER

JESUS concludes his time with his own in prayer. It seems particularly appropriate considering the weight of the moment. Furthermore, it has a ring of truth as at least a summation of a real prayer. I prefer to call this prayer the "final prayer" although it is not the last prayer that Jesus prays in this Gospel. Since the late 1500s (and perhaps earlier) it has often been called the "high priestly" prayer.[1] And, as far as it goes, in that Jesus intercedes for his own, this is correct. However, I feel that labeling it the "final prayer" that concludes the Farewell Discourse is more descriptive without adding unintended baggage. The prayer can be summed up in many ways, and none would be a perfect description. Its content is praise and petition; warmth and chill; concerned and confident; prophetic and priestly; summary and substance; caution and comfort; worship and witness; and we could go on. As Janzen noted, "It is unfathomably rich in its implication and inexhaustible in its potential for explication."[2] We will only scratch the surface.

My explication of the passage will cover all twenty-six verses in one sermon. There are three reasons for this. First, it lets us not bifurcate what is a complete experience. Second, it will help us illustrate the possibility of preaching a much longer text than we have previously shown. Finally, it will give the opportunity for you to contemplate how you would preach the individual petitions that make up this prayer.

---

[1] Rudolf Schnackenburg, *The Gospel according to St. John*, vol. 3 (New York: Crossroad, 1982), 433. Schnackenburg suggests that the term is indebted to David Chytraeus, a disciple of Melanchthon. Barrett notes that the terminology is hinted by Cyril of Alexandria but notes that "high-priestly" prayer, "does not do justice to the full range of the material contained in it" (C. K. Barrett, *The Gospel according to John*, 2nd ed. [Philadelphia: Westminster, 1978], 500).

[2] J. Gerald Janzen, "The Scope of Jesus's High Priestly Prayer in John 17," *Enc* 67 (2006): 1.

Jesus' Last Prayer with His Disciples (17:1–26)

The prayer has many connections to the previous section in the Farewell Discourse. In many ways it summarizes not only the Farewell Discourse but also the whole of the Gospel up to this point.[3] Admittedly this is done in broad-brush strokes (see 17:4, e.g., "I have glorified You on the earth by completing the work You gave Me to do" [HCSB]). Jesus does reference his completed work, choosing of the disciples, and his revelation of God's name. This being so, the connections to the Farewell Discourse are more pronounced and direct. Jesus begins both the discourse and the prayer with a concern over glorifying the Father (13:31–32; 17:1–2). Several other references touch on themes in 13–16: complete joy (17:13/15:11; 16:20–22, and 24); keeping his words/commandments as the essence of discipleship (17:6/14:15, 23–24; 15:10, 20); Jesus having come from the Father (17:8/13:3, 24; 16:5, 10, 17, 28, 30); the hatred of the world (17:14/15:18–19). There is more, but let us finally note that one of the major concerns of Jesus—the unity of believers (17:11, 21–23)—is also a major concern of the discourse through the new commandment in 13:34–35 and 15:12. Thus, in content the final prayer echoes much of the Farewell Discourse, as we would expect with a concluding constituent.

The prayer, however, does more than simply conclude the discourse. Few would describe it simply as a conclusion. The prayer not only anticipates Jesus' completion of his mission and glorification but also the conditions that face the disciples the time after Jesus' departure. But, as we will see, it also describes Jesus' relationship to the Father in trinitarian terms.

Finally, a matter of historical accuracy is in order. Some have suggested that the prayer is fully a Johannine invention.[4] This, however, is not a necessary conclusion from the evidence. Walker has noticed, as have others, quite a few thematic links with the Synoptic model prayer.[5] While the links to the "model prayer" are compelling, Walker's thesis that John 17 is a midrash, adapted and expanded form of the Synoptic prayer is, again, not a necessary conclusion. Instead, Köstenberger is likely correct: "the evidence set forth by Walker at best warrants only the conclusion that both prayers likely were prayed by the same individual."[6] The prayer in John 17 follows a similar pattern as the Synoptic model prayer, following, generally, the same sequence.[7] It is no stretch of

---

[3] D. A. Carson, *The Gospel according to John*, PNTC (Grand Rapids: Eerdmans, 1991), 551.
[4] For a summary see Craig Blomberg, *The Historical Reliability of John's Gospel: Issues and Commentary* (Downers Grove, IL: InterVarsity, 2001), 225.
[5] W. O. Walker Jr., "The Lord's Prayer in Matthew and John," *NTS* 28 (1982): 237–56.
[6] Andreas J. Köstenberger, *John*, BECNT (Grand Rapids: Baker, 2005), 482.
[7] See Blomberg, *Historical Reliability*, 219–27. While the links are compelling, the exact verbal

the imagination that Jesus himself used the pattern of prayer that he instructed his disciples to employ.

Analyzing the Text

Although I will be preparing one sermon sketch on the entirety of John 17, I will be developing and discussing the petitions individually. The first is clearly 17:1–5. The use of "these things" (ταῦτα) with an aorist verb is a common transition in the Gospel of John (see John 2:12; 3:22; 5:1, 14; 6:1; 7:1; 19:28; 21:1). Its use here is not the same as the use at major divisions, for it is missing the characteristic "after" (μετὰ), thus it is still in connection with the Farewell Discourse. However, since the verb is expressed in the aorist (ἐλάλησεν) and not perfect (λελάληκα), it suggests some distance within the connection. In other words, it suggests a new unit has begun.

Furthermore, at almost every significant transition within the discourse movement is expressed or implied. This is typical of Johannine narrative.[8] In 13:30 Judas departs. In 14:31 Jesus' "Get up; let's leave this place" (HCSB; ἐγείρεσθε, ἄγωμεν ἐντεῦθεν) suggests the departure from the table. In 17:1, Jesus "looked up to heaven" (HCSB; ἐπάρας τοὺς ὀφθαλμοὺς αὐτοῦ). And let's also note that 18:1 also indicates movement as it transitions to the Passion Narrative; "He went out with His disciples across the Kidron Valley" (HCSB; Ἰησοῦς ἐξῆλθεν σὺν τοῖς μαθηταῖς αὐτοῦ πέραν τοῦ χειμάρρου τοῦ Κεδρὼν). Clearly, a new unit occurs in 17:1. Just as clearly the Passion Narrative begins when they move out in 18:1 indicating that 17:26 is the concluding boundary for the prayer.

Structurally speaking, this is one of the most difficult passages in the Farewell Discourse to understand. This gives rise to many different opinions among scholarship regarding the overall structure of the prayer. Three-part, four-part, five-part, six-part, and even seven-part divisions have been suggested.[9] However, these differences are often differences of how one perceives the higher-level structures. There is general agreement regarding the petitions offered. They are clearly marked by the grammatical forms and word-choices

---

parallels are few. This would not suggest a rigid adaptation of a written or oral source. It does, however, fit with habitual patterns of an individual.

[8] L. Scott Kellum, *The Unity of the Farewell Discourse: The Literary Integrity of John 13:31–16:33*, JSNTSup 256 (London: T&T Clark, 2005), 230.

[9] Three-part divisions are suggested by, e.g., my colleague David Alan Black, "On the Style and Significance of John 17" *CTR* 3 (1988): 141–59; and Carson, *John*, 53381. Four-part division is suggested by Barrett, *John*, 416–17; and M. Lagrange, *Evangile selon Saint Jean* (Paris: Gabalda, 1925), 436. Five-part division is suggested by D. H. Dodd, *The Interpretation of the Fourth Gospel* (Cambridge: Cambridge University Press, 1953), 417. Six-part division is suggested by Raymond E. Brown, *The Gospel according to John*, AB 29A (New York: Doubleday, 1971), 2:738–81. Borchert suggests a seven-part division arranged in three larger sections (Gerald R. Borchert, *John 12–21*, NAC 25B [Nashville: B&H, 2002], 2:186–88).

employed. We expect imperatives, vocatives, and verbs related to asking to be employed in individual petitions. This is exactly what we get. However, are these to be understood as equally weighted constituents, or are they to be organized by similar features? I believe the latter makes sense regarding this prayer. My own suggestion is that of a three-part division defined by specific petitions arranged according to the people for whom Jesus is praying. Thus, Petition 1, 17:1–5: Jesus prays for himself; Petition 2, 17:6–19, Jesus prays for his present disciples; Petition 3, 17:20–26, Jesus prays for his future disciples. I will deal with the structure of the individual petitions below.

Interpreting the Text
Petition 1 (17:1–5)
Structure

RELATIONAL STRUCTURE	CONTENTS
PETITION 1	
┌HEAD┌EXHORT.───────	(17:1a-e) Father, glorify your Son so that he may glorify you.
│ │ ┌means───	(2a) Because you have given him authority over all flesh
┌HEAD┤ └grounds┌PURPOSE─	(2b) that all you give him he would grant eternal life.
│ └COMM.──────────	(3a-e) Eternal life is to know you, and the Christ you sent.
│ ┌grounds──	(4a-b) I glorified you on the earth, completing my work
└equiv.────┴EXHORT.──	(5a-b) And now, Father glorify me, with your glory

John's employment of "having lifted his eyes" not only indicates movement but also identifies the genre as a prayer. The prayer is introduced in 17:1a–b by introducing the setting of what follows as a prayer. The major structure in our SSA is the typical Orienter-CONTENT employed with speech margins. As such it is not a functionally significant element for meaning (although necessary for structure).

The first petition is introduced by the address to the Father (employing the vocative πάτερ). This will be a repeating pattern in association with other verbs of asking. 17:1c–3e is the major content of the first petition. It describes a simple request framed as an imperative, "glorify." The purpose of the request is a mutual glorification (framed as a Means-PURPOSE relationship in 1d–e). 2a–b forms the grounds for the whole EXHORTATION in 1d–e. The mention of eternal life in 2b triggers the COMMENT defining eternal life in 17:3a–d. 17:4 is a restatement of 17:1c–3e. It adds the new information regarding the completion of his mission and further defines what glorify would mean for Christ.

Comment

The first petition begins with Jesus confessing that his hour had come. Hour (ὥρα) is used twenty-six times in the Fourth Gospel; eight times it refers to his glorification (one of the results of his death, burial, and resurrection).[10] In 2:4, his hour had not come (nor 7:30 or 8:20), but in 12:23, Jesus noted that "the hour has come for the Son of Man to be glorified" (HCSB). From that point forward every reference is that the hour had come. Now, on the very eve of his arrest, his understanding is that the time is upon him. Because of that, the first request is that the Father would glorify the Son so that the Son may glorify him. Keener rightly notes that this "was in effect a request that the Father hasten the cross."[11]

The use of the term, "glorify" (δόξασον) is not simply praising Jesus' gracious sacrifice (as proper as that is). Here the allusions to both his mission and Jesus' final destination suggest something else. He prays later (17:5) to partake of God's glory as he did before the incarnation. The cross, then, in spite of all its horrific details regarding pain, suffering, and the sins of all people being laid on Christ, is necessary for him to be, as Carson puts it, clothed in splendor again.[12]

Surely, however, Jesus' glorification of the Father is not to clothe him in splendor, for it is already his possession. In 17:2 Jesus defines how he will glorify the Father. The Son may glorify the Father because (taking καθώς in a causal sense) the Father granted Jesus authority over human life ("all flesh"; HCSB) to accomplish eternal life. In accomplishing his mission, Jesus will glorify the Father. That is, he will make known the love and generosity of the Father to all who will hear (in this sense it is similar to 14:31). Through his death and resurrection, Jesus will praise and honor God.

The comment in 17:3 is triggered by the mention of eternal life. Some have suggested that the comment is an insertion by John because the use of "Jesus Christ" as a title seems to be anachronistic to the moment of the prayer.[13] The expression is found nowhere else in the Fourth Gospel except on the lips of the narrator in 1:17. However, it seems unnecessary to suppose an insertion by the narrator (although it is possible).[14] The use of "that they may know You" (HCSB), as in a direct address, makes it difficult to assume that anyone but Jesus is making the comment. The use of the third person and Christ as a title may be John putting it in his own words (even this is not necessary) but hardly demands an insertion here.

---

[10] See 2:4; 7:30; 8:20; 12:23, 27; 13:1; and 17:1.
[11] Craig S. Keener, *The Gospel of John: A Commentary* (Peabody, MA: Hendrickson, 2003), 2:1053.
[12] Carson, *John*, 554.
[13] See Blomberg, *Historical Reliability*, 219. So also, Barrett, *John*, 219; Ben Witherington, *John's Wisdom* (Louisville, KY: WJK, 1995), 269; Brown, *John*, 2:741; Schnackenburg, *John*, 3:172.
[14] At other places in the Gospel it is difficult to discern the voice of the speaker or the narrator. See e.g., the most famous of all, John 3:16.

In the comment, Jesus defines eternal life as knowing God and Christ. The description of God as "the only true God" (HCSB; τὸν μόνον ἀληθινὸν θεὸν) does not deter the implication of the deity of Christ as some maintain.[15] Throughout the Gospel John has both repeatedly affirmed the deity of Christ and maintained his independent personhood.[16] The reference to the "only true God" has OT overtones and is a statement aimed at idolatry and not a denial of Jesus' deity. Instead, the definition of eternal life as knowing God and Christ suggests the opposite. The inclusion of Christ on such equal terms is trinitarian in its implications (much like 14:1). The nature of the new covenant is that from the least to the greatest of God's people, all will know him.

In 17:4–5, Jesus reiterates the petition with a significant addition in 17:5. His request to return to his previous glory has impressive implications. The glory, as defined above, is the glory of the splendor of God. It is first of all an indication of his preexistence. It is before the foundation of the world. The glory is with God's own presence, literally "in the presence of yourself" (παρὰ σεαυτῷ). This suggests an intimate sharing. But the most striking feature is that both the content of eternal life and an intimate reciprocal glory are inconsistent with monotheism except in trinitarian terms. See Isaiah 42:8 (HCSB), "I am Yahweh, that is My name; I will not give My glory to another or My praise to idols."

Petition 2 (17:6–19)

Structure

RELATIONAL STRUCTURE	CONTENTS
PETITION 2	
setting — HEAD	(17:6a-e) I manifested your name to the men you gave me
COMM. — CONCL.	(7a-c) They have known that all things are from you
grounds	(8a-g) for they received our words and believed you sent me.
HEAD — EXHORT.	(9a-d) I ask for them and not the world for they are yours.
grounds — HEAD	(10a-c) We hold all things jointly and I am glorified in them.
HEAD 1 — amplifi.	(11a-c) and they are in the world, and I am going to you.
appeal — amplifi — EXHORT.	(11d-e) Holy Father, keep these given men in your name.
grounds — means	(11f) so that they may be one just as we.
PURPOSE	(12a-f) I kept all mine so that the scripture would be fulfilled.
grounds 1	(13a-c) I speak these things so that they may have my joy
HEAD — grounds 2 — RES.	(14a-b) I have given them your word and the world hated them
reason	(14c) because they are not of the world
EXHORT. — HEAD	(15a-b) Do not take them out of the world
HEAD 2 — CONTR.	(15c) but keep them from the evil one.
appeal — HEAD — grounds	(16a-b) Like me, they are not of the world
amplifi — EXHORT.	(17a-b) Sanctify them in the truth which is your word.
amplifi — HEAD	(18a-b) Like you sent me, I also send them.
amplifi	(19a-b) and for them I sanctify myself so they might be sanctified.

---

[15] For a specific discussion regarding cult appropriation of this verse, see Aaron Tuazon Shelenberger, "An Exposition of the Jehovah's Witnesses' Argument in Rejecting Christ's Deity Using John 17:3," *Christian Apologetics Journal* 8 (Fall 2009): 4–20.

[16] See, e.g., John 10:30 where Jesus states the Father and he are "one" and employs the neuter for "one" (ἕν) that must describe unity of essence.

If length is any indication, this is the heart of Jesus' concern as he faces his departure. This section is divided into three main paragraphs. The first extends from 17:6a–8g and creates the setting for the specific requests that follow. The conclusion of the last section with the significant "and now" (καὶ νῦν) signals the conclusion to the previous petition. Furthermore, the shift in verb mood from imperative, "glorify," to indicative "I revealed," and the switch in focus (signified by the objects of the verbs) from Christ to the disciples marks a clear transition. The paragraph sets the stage for the petitions to follow by giving relevant background information for the prayer. Thus, even though it is not a narrative, the communication relation "setting" is appropriate.

In verse 9a Jesus introduces his first petition for his disciples with the verb "I ask" (ἐρωτῶ). This begins an EXHORTATION that extends through the verse. The reset of the proposition cluster is the grounds for the request. This ground extends through 11c. Another related EXHORTATION begins in 11d with the imperative "keep" (τήρησον) in combination with the vocative "Holy Father" (πάτερ ἅγιε). The use of direct address and the imperative form is more prominent than the indicative form used at the previous EXHORTATION. The previous request was not really completed, i.e., ask for what? This request completes and adds the content of the request. I have chosen "amplification," but one could defend "CONTENT" as well. The EXHORTATION in 11c is supported by the ground in 12a–f. Jesus asks for the disciples to be kept by the Father because he will no longer be around to do so. Together, these form the first petition that I have labeled HEAD 1 for it is coequal with the next request. I have given it the clarification "appeal."

The second appeal is marked for development by the use of δέ. Unfortunately, the HCSB declined to translate this conjunction and simply rendered it "Now I am coming to you" (v. 13a). However, the use of δέ here marks a local discontinuity in this context that signals a new paragraph beginning. This paragraph is built by two requests that are in a HEAD-amplification relationship. Linguistically, the lack of any highlighting or prominence markers in 16a suggests close connection to the previous cluster (17:13a–15c). Furthermore, the relatedness of the content of the prayers (here the imperatives "not take but keep" and "sanctify" [ἁγίασον]) associates them together. I think HEAD-amplification represents the meaning well.

Comment

The first paragraph provides the foundation for the two appeals that make up this particular series of requests. The requests that will follow, "keep" and "sanctify," are only appropriate for those who are actually followers of God in Christ. He will not ask for the world in the sense of keeping and sanctifying.

Jesus approaches the discussion mainly from an eternal point of view and not from a human perspective. So, then, humanly speaking there was a time, from the vantage point of the disciples, when they were not following Christ. However, Jesus is not speaking to them. From the point of view of eternity, the disciples have always been God's, "they were Yours" (John 17:6c HCSB; σοὶ ἦσαν—a possessive dative). It is to these men—whom God gave to Jesus—that he revealed God's name.

To reveal God's name is to reveal the essential nature of God to these men.[17] Jesus completed his mission to reveal God to humans. It is, most likely, a summation of his entire ministry.[18] Because some rabbis taught that the name of God was to be revealed in the age to come, there is an eschatological tone to it as well.[19] However, Jesus is emphasizing the disciples' response to it. They have "kept your word." This should not be understood in the sense of "keeping the commandments," for no one is able to do so perfectly. Furthermore, the disciples themselves have not been fully competent in this matter and have been rebuked by Jesus. Instead, it is better to take it in the sense of "they have committed to the message about you."[20]

In contrast, in 8a instead of keeping the words, the disciples are said to have "received them" (HCSB; ἔλαβον). Thus, they not only received Jesus' teaching about God, they have also believed that God sent Christ (17:8). Their faith that Jesus was sent by the Father is another example of meronymy, where the part represents the whole. Not only did they receive Jesus' teaching about God, but they also received his teaching about himself. That they fully understood it or believed in a post-Easter sense is not necessary at this point. Their reception of Christ and God was evidence that God gave them to Christ. Thus, as is typical with John, divine sovereignty and human responsibility are not mutually exclusive but complementary. This will provide the foundation for the appeals to follow.

Jesus prays specifically for the disciples and not the world in 9a–12. This should not be taken as any slight against the world. Jesus' love for the world is not up for debate. He gave himself for the world on the grounds of God's love for it. His prayer, though, is for his own. Due to the reciprocal community between the Father and Son, when the disciples glorify the Son it means that they also glorify the Father. When the Father gives them to Jesus, he has surrendered no ownership of his own, for he and Christ are one. That they have

---

[17] Leon Morris, *The Gospel according to John*, NICNT (Grand Rapids: Eerdmans, 1995), 640; Keener, *John*, 1056.

[18] Carson, *John*, 558.

[19] Dodd, *Interpretation*, 97. "In this age the true name of God is unknown, in the age to come it will be revealed."

[20] Carson notes that the singular "word" often has this connotation in the Fourth Gospel, while "words" usually refers to obeying specific commands (Carson, *John*, 559).

glorified Christ, presumably through the reception of his words, means that they also glorify God. This will be the basis for prayer in 11d.

Jesus addresses his prayer to the "Holy Father." The adjective "holy" is important in this context, for holiness shows up at prominent places in the rest of the prayer. Jesus asks for the disciples' sanctification (17a) and Jesus sanctifies himself (19a) for the sake of their sanctification (19b). All four references (ἅγιε [11a]; ἁγίασον [17a]; ἁγιάζω [19a]; and ἡγιασμένοι [19b]) employ words with the same root (ἁγ-). Jesus' use of the vocative adjective in 11a points to the reason for holiness in humans. It is because of the Father's holiness that we should be holy (a familiar OT theme, cf. Lev 11:44; HCSB, "be holy because I am holy").[21]

The prayer is that the Father would "keep them in your name" (τήρησον αὐτοὺς ἐν τῷ ὀνόματί σου). The phrase "in your name" can suggest that it is the name itself that keeps the disciples (an instrumental use), rendered (as in the HCSB) "by Your name."[22] In this understanding God's essential character forbids him from losing any of his own. This language is certainly used in the OT.[23] So, then, it is certainly a true idea. However, it is not the best option in this passage. In 17:12a–e, Jesus both guarded and protected the disciples with the result that none was lost except Judas (who was not his anyway). This cause-and-effect relationship in 17:12 defines what is meant in 11d. To keep "in your name" is a locative idea.[24] The prayer is for the Father to keep them in fidelity. Thus, the best definition for "keep" is not personal safety. If so, Jesus' prayer was answered, "No," for the disciples were frequently in physical danger. Most, if not all, gave their lives for the sake of the gospel. The "keeping" then is spiritual safety. He will hang on to his own. That Judas was lost indicated that he was never his.[25]

This should in no way be interpreted to mean that it is possible for a disciple to lose his/her salvation. It is not. Jesus' prayer is intended not only for communication with the Father but also with his hearers. He is affirming that it is God's work, not ours, that keeps us. If so we should have nothing but confidence regarding his ability and his will to do so.

The purpose for the keeping is unity (11f). Ridderbos rightly notes, "This last phrase introduces a motif that helps to shape the entire prayer and, while

---

[21] Borchert notes that this verb stem is used here and in 10:36 in the Fourth Gospel (Borchert, *John*, 2:197).

[22] So too, Köstenberger, *John*, 493.

[23] Carson notes Ps 54:1, "God, save me by Your name, and vindicate me by Your might!" (Carson, *John*, 562). See, also, Ps 20:1 and Prov 18:10.

[24] Because it is difficult to adjudicate between the two, some see Johannine double-entendre here and suggest it means both. See e.g., Borchert, *John*, 197, and Brown, *John*, 2:759.

[25] Quite often John 17:5 is a subject of discussion regarding the phrase, "I will keep you from the hour of temptation," found at Rev 3:10. However we read the passage regarding the rapture of the church, one should understand the "keep" there, as here, refers to spiritual safety and not physical safety.

not coming to its full development until vss. 20ff., serves here to define the unity of the disciples as their being taken together into the fellowship of the Father and the Son."[26] Morris notes that this unity is a solidarity that the disciples already have: "Jesus does not pray that they 'become' one but that they may 'continually be' one."[27]

In 13a the final paragraph of this section begins and starts the second appeal that Jesus makes concerning his present disciples. The lines of distinction thematically between this and the previous section are not particularly distinct. The contrast between "when I was with them" and "now I am coming to you" suggests that the sections can be read in a more direct relationship than I have understood the arrangement. However, the use of νῦν δὲ as a temporal point of departure marks the text for discontinuity.[28] Here I see a new proposition cluster beginning that will expand the previous one.

In 17:14 Jesus repeats what he said in 15:18–16:4c: the world has hostility against believers. Jesus' requests reflect the will of God that disciples are not taken out of the world. This would imply a divine purpose for the followers of Christ as they relate to the world. This would of course include evangelism, but we should not limit God's purpose to this alone. The purpose might include a divine demonstration of God's grace through his saints or his church, a demonstration of the judgment to come, or to be the hands of Christ in more social ministries, just to name a few things. Suffice it to say that the purpose is multifaceted and implies a ministry to the world.

Instead, Jesus' prayer is that they would be kept from the evil one (17:15c). His prayer that they would be sanctified is based on the fact that they no longer belong to the world, just like Christ and the Father (17:16b). This sanctification is to be in the truth (17:17a). Previously his Spirit is the Spirit of truth (John 14:17; 15:26; 16:13; see also 1 John 4:6), and he is truth incarnate (14:6). Both the fundamental essence of Christ and the Holy Spirit who guides in all truth seem to be the reference here. Again, the "in truth" may be either locative (in) or instrumental (by). If the usage is locative, truth is the sphere to which Christians are set apart. If it is instrumental, then truth is the means by which one is sanctified. Given that the word is defined as truth in the next clause and that keeping the commands of God is the defining element of sanctification, it seems best to

---

[26] Herman Ridderbos, *The Gospel of John: A Theological Commentary*, trans. J. Vriend (Grand Rapids: Eerdmans, 1991), 553.

[27] Morris, *John*, 644. Morris is playing off the aspectual force of the present subjunctive being verb ὦσιν ("they might be").

[28] δὲ here should not be understood strictly as an adversative (i.e., "but") but a developmental marker. It is marked for development and not close connection.

understand the phrase to be an instrumental use of the preposition. Christ is the embodiment of God's Word; his Spirit guides and promotes holiness in that truth.

Previously the ministry to the world was implied. Now, in 17:18 and 19 it is explicit. Often in John the relationship between the Father and Christ is a model for the relationship between Christ and his followers. This is especially true regarding mission. This is the paradigm that is employed in the present verse. Jesus was "set apart" (the main idea of holiness) and sent into the world with holy orders for the sake of the disciples. They, likewise, are set apart and sent. The sanctification by the truth is, then, for the purpose of mission not simply personal safety or enjoyment.

Jesus' prayer for his disciples on earth is, first, that they would be kept spiritually safe (17:11d). This is not an uncertain prayer but a definite promise of the security of the believer repeated elsewhere in the Gospel (see, e.g., 10:28). This is a word of comfort for the disciples as they face the hostility of the world. The ultimate purpose of this spiritual recognition is the unity of the believers. They are God's gift to Christ individually and corporately. His prayer is, second, that the disciples would employ that spiritual safety in mission to the world. Protection from the evil one does not imply physical safety but an impenetrable wall around the soul of the follower of Christ. They are not raptured out of the world but sent to the world with the truth, guided by the Spirit of truth, who mediates the presence of the One who is truth.

Petition 3 (17:20–26)

Structure

RELATIONAL STRUCTURE	CONTENTS
PETITION 3 — means	(20a-b) I also pray for those who will believe on me
HEAD 1 appeal — HEAD — PURPOSE 1	(21a-b) so that they would be one as we are
— PURPOSE 2	(21c) so that they also would be in us
— PURPOSE 3	(21d-e) so that the world would believe you sent me
amplifi. — means	(22a) and I give them the glory that you gave me.
— PURP. — HEAD	(22b-c) so that they would be one like we are.
amplifi. — means	(23a) I in them and you in me
PURP. 1	(23b) that they would be one,
PURP. 2	(23c-f) that the world would know you sent me and loved them.
HEAD 2 appeal — means	(24a-b) Father, I want mine to be with me.
PURP. — RESULT	(24c-d) so that they would see my glory that you gave me
reason	(24e) because you loved me before the foundation of the world.
CONCL. — HEAD — HEAD	(25a) Righteous Father, the world did not know you,
CONTR.	(25b-d) but I know you and these men know you sent me.
amplifi. — means	(26a-b) And I made your name known to them and continue
PURPs.	(26c-e) so that your love would be in them

The semantic structure of the last three paragraphs is similar to the previous unit. The text features a twofold petition and a conclusion to the whole prayer. The conclusion is present here for pragmatic reasons. The twofold appeal is identified mainly through the persons for whom the prayer is made. The first appeal (17:20–23) is made for future disciples. The second appeal (17:24) is made for all disciples, present and future. Finally, the concluding paragraph (17:25–26) brings the section to a close.

Like in the previous paragraphs, the verb "to ask" (ἐρωτῶ) is employed to introduce another appeal. The appeal is for a threefold purpose—each introduced by ἵνα clauses in 17:21. More information is given regarding the unity of believers that was the content of the first ἵνα clause in 17:21. This is developed in a Means-PURPOSE structure that explains the reason for Jesus' glory given to the disciples: for unity.

The second appeal employs an address to the Father (the vocative πάτερ) and, for the first time, a different verb regarding the act of prayer. Instead of "I ask," here it is "I desire." This is the most general of the appeals in two ways. First, it is directed to all disciples whether present or future. Second, the request itself is rather general in that it is a request for his followers to be with him and enjoy his glory. It is developed in a rather uncomplicated Means-PURPOSE relationship.

The final paragraph contains no appeal and addresses the Father with another vocative that is modified, "Righteous Father." It is developed in a HEAD-amplification that confesses the disciples' belief in Jesus. It also promises a continued ministry by Jesus in revealing the name of God to them.

Comment

In John 17:20 Jesus shifts the object of his request from the disciples to those who believe on him through the ministry of the apostles. The articular participle rendered "those who believe" (HCSB; τῶν πιστευόντων) is a present active participle. It signifies ongoing action contemporaneous with the main verb. Identifying the main verb of the clause is difficult, for it is implied in the text through ellipsis rather than directly expressed and the verbal action associated with the participle is even more offline. It is the preaching of the word that is, for most believers, future in relation to the time of the prayer. The participle expresses ongoing activity contemporaneous with a future event, thus warranting the ESV's rendering of it as a future "those who will believe in me." The further semantic force of the participle refers not to coming to faith but a continual believing on Jesus.

This request is developed in three ἵνα-clauses. The first two deal with the unity of believers and the last the witness to the world. The first two clearly indicate that Jesus is strongly interested in the unity of believers. This is in stark contrast to the disunity evident in the world.[29] In the first clause (21a), he likens the mutuality of believers to his and the Father's mutuality. We can be sure that he is not referring to an ontological oneness like the unity of essence that he and the Father share, but he describes the oneness in love, purpose, and mission. However, the language goes beyond mere unity of purpose. There is an ontological dimension to it: as Christ is in the Father, so too the believer is in Christ (21c).[30] That the same Christ indwells each should create a supernatural harmony if other factors do not get in the way. This view is supported by the second ἵνα-clause (21c), which refers to the type of mutual indwelling between Jesus and believers (cf. 14:20). The final ἵνα-clause (21d) declares the purpose of the believers' unity. It is not for unity's sake but for mission. Unity leads to a closer relationship with the Father and the Son and will then lead to a proclamation to the world.[31] Just as the activity of the Father is in the Son, so too the Son is active in believers. This activity is not merely a privilege of the believer, but it is in service to a broader mission to the world.[32] The point that is often missed is that unity is greatly on the heart of Jesus, but it is not simply unity for the sake of harmony. It is unity with a purpose. As Borchert states, it is a "kerygmatic vehicle in the context of a divided world."[33]

The purpose is also propelled by the supernatural solidarity of the disciples. In 17:23, the unity of the disciples has the purpose of revealing the Father's love for the disciple. This language is not just an emotional reference; it is the language of choice. It is the language of covenant loving-kindness. Thus, unity is for the purpose of demonstrating the divine election of the body of Christ. The heavenly produced unity witnesses to the world that the people of God are constituted in Christ. As God loved Jacob (i.e., chose him, cf. Mal 1:2–3) the world will know of God's choice of the church when the church displays his unity.

In 22a–23f, Jesus amplifies his appeal. The glory that he has given his followers cannot be the preexistent glory that Christ desired to regain.[34] All during the time that the apostles knew Christ, Christ laid aside that glory and was tabernacling among them. This glory must be something else. Jesus' earthly glory is mentioned in 1:14, "The Word became flesh and took up residence

---

[29] Keener, *John*, 2:1062.
[30] Borchert notes, "The petition thus suggests that the oneness of the community is predicated on a direct relationship of the believers with the Godhead" (Borchert, *John*, 2:206).
[31] Morris, *John*, 650.
[32] Köstenberger, *John*, 498. See also Andreas J. Köstenberger, *The Missions of Jesus and the Disciples according to the Fourth Gospel* (Grand Rapids: Baker, 1999).
[33] Borchert, *John*, 2:207. Blomberg notes that it "displays massive evangelistic potential" (Blomberg, *Historical Reliability*, 224).
[34] Köstenberger, *John*, 498.

among us. We observed His glory, the glory as the One and Only Son from the Father, full of grace and truth" (HCSB). In the wilderness God's glory resided in the tabernacle; when he came to earth the glory of God resided among men in Jesus. This glory is the glory of Jesus; it will now reside in the church. The purpose of this indwelling glory is unity. Bearing Jesus' glory comes at a price, however. Jesus' glory was the cross and resurrection (see 7:39; 12:16, 23; 13:31–32). It is this same humble sacrificial service that may lead to hardship that is also part and parcel of glory.

The second appeal (17:24) shifts from interceding for future disciples to interceding for all disciples. The prayer is essentially that the disciples would be with Jesus in heaven. Jesus is rather vague about the exact "location." He refers to "where I am" (ὅπου εἰμὶ ἐγώ). This should not be taken to mean that Jesus does not know the location, for he does not use the indefinite relative pronoun (ὅς εαν, ὅπου ἄν). Instead, the way the sentence is expressed, puts the focus on the presence of Christ himself.[35] The implication is that he is in the presence of God (cf. 17:5).[36] The purpose of believers being with Christ is that they would experience his glory. This is not a heavenly sight-seeing tour. To see his glory is experiential as much as it is observational. The disciples have seen his glory on earth, but they will experience his glory in heaven.[37] The final clause (24e) "because You loved Me before the world's foundation" (HCSB), must be understood as referring to the reason for the glory of Christ and not to the disciples seeing that glory. In other words, the glory of Christ predates creation and stems from an intimate relationship with the Father. That relationship is different than the relationship with any other heavenly being. No angel has ever radiated the heavenly splendor of God. They may only *reflect* the glory of God.[38] This suggests Jesus' deity.

The final two verses of the prayer conclude it and the whole discourse. Furthermore, it sums up the purpose of Christ's mission.[39] Although the world did not know the Father, Jesus did and transferred that to his disciples. Further, the disciples affirm that Jesus was indeed sent by God. As we have seen earlier, this affirmation of the sending is an affirmation that all of the claims of Christ are true. Thus, the knowledge and affirmation of Christ stands between the not knowing of the world and the knowing of the disciples.

---

[35] Cf. Borchert, *John*, 2:209.
[36] Keener, *John*, 2:1063.
[37] F. J. Moloney, *The Gospel of John*, SP 4 (Collegeville, MN: Liturgical, 1998), 475.
[38] See Peter R. Schemm Jr., "The Agents of God: Angels," in *A Theology for the Church*, ed. Daniel L. Akin (Nashville: B&H Academic, 2007), 296. When the angels appear with glory (cf. Luke 1:19), it is the Lord's glory that shines.
[39] Ridderbos, *John*, 566.

The concluding promise is wrapped up in the last four clauses (17:26b–e). That Jesus has made known God's name to the disciples (26b) refers back to 17:6a–b, "I have revealed Your name to the men You gave Me from the world" (HCSB). His revelation to these men is a revelation of God's essential character. The promise that is made is that he will continue to reveal after he's gone. This is accomplished through the indwelling of the Holy Spirit promised earlier (cf. 14:26 and 16:13).

This revelation is so that the love of God would be "in them" (ἐν αὐτοῖς). The phrase may refer to each individual Christian or the church as a whole. If it is the former, and I think it likely, then the latter is still evident. As the love of God is shed abroad in the hearts of individuals, it is also done through the community. As Barrett states, "The church is not a côterie of gnostics [sic] enjoying esoteric knowledge but a community of love."[40] The love that is in the church is the same love that God has for the Son. In other words, this is the highest possible affection. In my opinion this suggests the accomplishment of salvation in the church whereby the righteousness of Christ has been imputed to the disciples. Thus, Christ's address of the Father as "Righteous Father" is no mere platitude but a completely appropriate foundation to Christ's mission and accomplishment.[41]

Finally, the ultimate purpose of Christ's making known the essential character of God is that he would be among them. Here the same phrase translated "in them" previously is employed with much the same nuance. Christ is in the individual through the indwelling of the Spirit, thus in the entirety of the congregation Christ dwells as well. This is the ultimate completion of the hope of the new covenant.[42] As Carson notes, "It is nothing less than the fulfillment of the ancient hope that God would dwell in the midst of his people (cf. 14:20)."[43]

Literarily, the purpose of including this prayer here, before the arrest and passion of Christ, is to explicate clearly the purpose of what is happening to Christ. He voluntarily goes to the cross so that people may know God and have an intimate relationship with the Lord. He leaves, not simply because the job is over, but to reunite and reconcile them all before God. He leaves them briefly so that they can know him eternally. He leaves them physically, where he is limited by space and time, so that he may have an intimate relationship with them all. He leaves them to be permanently united in them—in a fellowship of love. As he walks through the valley of the reality of death to conquer death and the grave, we readers may be able to keep his purpose in mind.

---

[40] Barrett, *John*, 515.
[41] Cf. Morris, *John*, 652.
[42] See Köstenberger, *John*, 501.
[43] Carson, *John*, 570.

Preaching the Text

The structure of the text displays three petitions. These petitions form the major movements within the text with a final conclusion. These are Petition 1 (17:1–5): Jesus prays for himself; Petition 2 (17:6–19): Jesus prays for his present disciples; Petition 3 (17:20–24), Jesus prays for all his disciples, and the Final Word (17:25–26). One could preach a sermon on each of these points. I have treated them individually in the hopes that one would (and possibly that one should!). However, we can easily represent the structure of the text in the sermon with three points based on the object of the prayers. I would describe the MIT as "Jesus prayed for the disciples' protection, unity, and mission." My MIM would then be "Christians should be confident of the Lord's protection and committed to their unity, expressing it in mission."

SERMON SKETCH

TEXT   John 17
MIT: Jesus prayed for the disciples' protection, unity, and mission.
MIM: Christians should be confident of the Lord's protection and committed to their unity, expressing it in mission.
TOPIC: The Lord's Desire for His Flock

INTRODUCTION

John 17, in many ways, is like a last will and testament. It is the longest recorded prayer of Jesus in the Gospels. It shows us what was burdening Jesus' heart as he was preparing to go to the cross. Interestingly enough, it is not merely his upcoming experience for which he prays. His desire is primarily focused on his followers. Jesus prayed for the protection, unity, and mission of his disciples. If these are the things that are on Jesus' mind, then our commitments should be similar. Christians should be confident of the Lord's protection and committed to their unity, expressing it in mission.

OUTLINE

I. The Lord Prayed for Himself (17:1–5)

"Jesus spoke these things, looked up to heaven, and said: Father, the hour has come. Glorify Your Son so that the Son may glorify

You, for You gave Him authority over all flesh; so He may give eternal life to all You have given Him. This is eternal life: that they may know You, the only true God, and the One You have sent—Jesus Christ. I have glorified You on the earth by completing the work You gave Me to do. Now, Father, glorify Me in Your presence with that glory I had with You before the world existed" (HCSB).

A. TEXT

1. Jesus embraced the cross.

    a. The request to glorify the Son is a request to hasten the cross.

    b. His great desire was to accomplish salvation for us.

2. Jesus glorified God by completing his mission.

    He made eternal life possible.

3. Jesus requests to return to his former glory.

    a. This is an indication of deity (cf. Isa 48:2).

    b. This restates his desire to accomplish salvation for us.

B. TODAY

1. Embrace his cross.

    a. We should embrace his cross as the way that we are going to get to heaven.

    b. We should embrace his cross as the way others will get to heaven.

2. Embrace his mission.

    a. Salvation is not our fire insurance.

    b. Actively participate in his mission.

II. Jesus Prays for His Present Disciples (17:6–19)

A. TEXT

1. Jesus prayed for spiritual protection (vv. 9–12).

"I pray for them. I am not praying for the world but for those You have given Me, because they are Yours. Everything I have is Yours, and everything You have is Mine, and I have been glorified in them. I am no longer in the world, but they are in the world, and I am coming to You. Holy Father, protect them by Your name that You have given Me, so that they may be one as We are one. While I was with them, I was protecting them by Your name that You have given Me. I guarded them and not one of them is lost, except the son of destruction, so that the Scripture may be fulfilled" (HCSB).

    a. He prays on the basis of their ownership by God (vv. 9–11).

    b. He prays for their spiritual protection (v. 11).

    c. He prays for their unity (v. 11).

2. Jesus prayed for sanctification for mission (vv. 13–19).

"Now I am coming to You, and I speak these things in the world so that they may have My joy completed in them. I have given them Your word. The world hated them because they are not of the world, as I am not of the world. I am not praying that You take them out of the world but that You protect them from the evil one. They are not of the world, as I am not of the world. Sanctify them by the truth; Your word is truth. As You sent Me into the world, I also have sent them into the world. I sanctify Myself for them, so they also may be sanctified by the truth" (HCSB).

    a. He prays for their joy.

    b. He prays again for their spiritual protection.

    c. He prays for the set-apart-ness for mission.

B. TODAY

1. Embrace your security.

2. Embrace your fellow Christians.

3. Embrace your mission.

III. Jesus Prayed for All His Disciples (17:20–26)

A. TEXT

1. Jesus prayed for his future disciples (vv. 20–23).

   "I pray not only for these, but also for those who believe in Me through their message. May they all be one, as You, Father, are in Me and I am in You. May they also be one in Us, so the world may believe You sent Me. I have given them the glory You have given Me. May they be one as We are one. I am in them and You are in Me. May they be made completely one, so the world may know You have sent Me and have loved them as You have loved Me" (HCSB).

   a. Jesus repeats his request for future disciples to be united (vv. 20–21).
   b. Jesus has given them all they need (his glory) (v. 22).
   c. The purpose is that they would be a witness to the world (v. 23).

2. Jesus prays for all his disciples.

   "Father, I desire those You have given Me to be with Me where I am. Then they will see My glory, which You have given Me because You loved Me before the world's foundation. Righteous Father! The world has not known You. However, I have known You, and these have known that You sent Me. I made Your name known to them and will make it known, so the love You have loved Me with may be in them and I may be in them" (HCSB).

   a. Glory is the ultimate destination of all believers (see previous page vv. 24–25).
   b. Jesus promises to continue to reveal God's name to his own (see previous page vv. 25–26).

B. TODAY

1. Embrace your destination.

Too many believers have nagging doubts about their destination. Some are sure, but they hesitate to declare it. It is not arrogant to be sure of Christ. It is not bragging to know you are going to heaven. It is truth.

2. Continue to abide in Christ.

The continued revelation of God's name comes through the ministry of the indwelling Holy Spirit in the life of the believer. The believer's concern, then, is not to hinder the lines of communication.

CONCLUSION

S. Lewis Johnson, former professor at Dallas Theological Seminary, wrote fourteen expositions of the Farewell Discourse for the *Emmaus Journal*. As he began his treatment of the final prayer, we will conclude it. "When John Knox, the Scottish reformer, was lying on his deathbed in his house on High Street in Edinburgh, he insistently asked that the Bible be read aloud to him. He wanted to hear the fifty-third chapter of Isaiah, and he asked for the Psalms, and he even requested that some of Calvin's sermons be read to him. But above all he asked for his beloved chapter from the Gospel of John, the seventeenth chapter, which he referred to as 'the place where I cast my first anchor.'"[44]

Jesus' prayers here are a declaration of unadulterated truth. Will you cast your anchor here? Will you embrace the cross? Will you embrace your secure position? Will you embrace your brother and sister in Christ? Will you go on mission with Christ? This is the thing that was on Christ's mind immediately before he died for you. Embrace it, and be transformed.

---

[44] S. Lewis Johnson Jr., "Jesus Praying for Himself an Exposition of John 17:1–5," *Emmaus Journal* 7 (1988): 202–3.

Conclusion

AS we conclude our walkthrough of the Johannine Farewell Discourse, two final matters are necessary. First, we need to identify how the Farewell Discourse completes the purpose of the Gospel of John, not only for academic considerations but also to consider how best to express it for our hearers. Second, we must set an agenda to implement our new knowledge in future preaching ministry. Three major topics come to mind as I look beyond this preaching moment: (1) sharpening our mastery of discourse analysis, (2) employing discourse analysis in preaching other genres, and (3) sharpening our use of the original languages.

The Place of the Farewell Discourse in the Rest of John's Gospel

A Brief Sketch of the Farewell Discourse

Peter had declared at 13:31–38 that he was able to follow Jesus wherever and whenever the demand arose. Jesus assured him this was not possible yet. Peter demands to know why he cannot follow Christ now. Jesus assures Peter that he will follow later. "Follow" here seems to have both physical and spiritual dimensions. While the Lord's promise was not enough for Peter, it does set up the rest of the discourse and connects it to the final movements of the Fourth Gospel. Jesus' departure is necessary and provides the means for believers to follow Christ and enjoy his presence after he physically departs. This last point is the first topic developed.

Presence in absence (commands that comfort) (14:1–31). Earlier I described chapter 14 of the Fourth Gospel as "Commands that Comfort." As all titles, it is a bit reductionistic. The command to "not let your heart be troubled" leads to the way that this happens. When a person believes in Christ and loves/obeys Christ, the Lord manifests his presence through the Paraclete. In other words, the Lord promises divine presence even though he is now physically absent. Notice that I said "divine." It is not only his presence but also the Father's that is revealed to the believer who loves/obeys the word of Christ. This, then, is the secret to the untroubled heart. But, it cannot happen until Christ's hour has been completed.

New community (commands that unite) (15:1–16:4c). The highpoint, or peak, of the Farewell Discourse is the vine-and-the-branch allegory of John 15. It is joined to a somber warning about the world's hatred (15:18). I called this section "Commands that Unite." It is built off two commands: (1) abide in Christ and (2) expect the world to hate you. The first is closely connected to the previous chapter through the command to keep his commandments. The essence of abiding in Christ, I argued earlier, is loving Christ. Johannine sanctification, then, is not a list of "dos and don'ts" but one great do—love Christ. The community of those abiding must love one another. This should not be all that difficult for believers, who supposedly love Christ and for whom the Spirit works brotherly love in our hearts (1 John 4:20). Thus, the new community is a body of abiders who also love one another.

By definition, a body of abiders who love Christ must separate from the world that hates Christ. Because of this the world hates the abiders as well. So Jesus warns to expect persecution. In response, Christ provides the Paraclete to enable a bold supernaturally empowered counteroffensive: a witness to the world.

The advantages of his departure (16:4d–33). Like Peter earlier, the disciples proclaim their faith. And, also as with Peter, Jesus is skeptical. But he points to the advantages that wait after his departure. Jesus' death is stated as a necessity for the believers to attain the demands and promises that Jesus has made through this discourse. If he does not depart, the Paraclete will not abide in them, convict the world, and instruct the believers. Their joy and newfound privilege in prayer will be available after his departure.

Jesus' prayer for himself, his present disciples, and his future disciples (17:1–26). The concluding prayer is both priestly and prophetic. He intercedes for his own but also for future believers as well. He prays for himself to be reinstated to his previous glory shared with the Father, prays for his present disciples to be sanctified and unified, and extends that to future followers. So how does this fit in the literary purposes of the Gospel of John? To answer this question we need to look briefly at the rest of the book.

The Closing Movements of the Gospel

I have already given a sketch of the arrest and Passion Narratives (chaps. 18–19) and the resurrection narratives (chap. 20) above. For our purposes in following the flow of thought from the Farewell Discourse through the end of the book, we need merely to note that these narrate the accomplishment of Jesus' hour. Jesus is in full control (18:1–11); he is going to die for the people as Caiaphas predicted (better than he knew) (18:13); his disciples are scattered and Peter denies him. Both happen just as Christ predicted (13:38; 16:32). He is then tried and crucified in fulfillment of Scripture. The resurrection events are told in chapter 20, with the conclusion of the ultimate confession in the Gospel of John made by Thomas—"My Lord and My God!" His hour has come, and he is glorified.

What remains is chapter 21 and, especially, the restoration of Peter. Here I must work in greater detail. If Peter is being restored, what does that entail? In other words, to what is he being restored? Ministry? Discipleship? Abiding? Köstenberger suggests it was to be restored to service.[1] This is, without a doubt true, for the passage points to pastoral service and that Peter would glorify Christ in martyrdom (21:18–19).[2] However, it does seem only to scratch the surface, as "service" is a broad term. Moloney suggests it is to pastoral ministry building off the shepherding language employed.[3]

The address as "Simon, son of John," has gathered much attention over the years. One wonders why he is addressed as such and not as "Peter" or "Simon Peter." The truth is that nowhere except when Jesus changes his name (Matt 16:18; Luke 22:34; John 1:42) does he ever address Simon with the name "Peter."[4] What is significant, then, is not the failure to use "Peter" but the inclusion of the patronymic address "son of John" (Ἰωάννου). There is a formality that borders on stiffness and indicates at least some personal distance between Jesus and Simon Peter. Ridderbos suggests it is because Peter must have a "fresh beginning" with Jesus.[5] I agree, but I think there is a specificity to the restoration that is rarely discussed. Shepherd, discussing the two terms for "love," sets the stage in an eloquent manner:

> In the allusive and psychologically realistic narrative world created by the writer of John's Gospel, it is clear that the most plausible frame of reference—narratively speaking—for what ἀγαπάω and φιλέω mean in the mouths of Jesus and Peter in their first conversation after the resurrection (21:15–17) is what these words meant in their last conversation before the passion (chs. 13–17).[6]

---

[1] Andreas J. Köstenberger, *John*, BECNT (Grand Rapids: Baker, 2005), 595.
[2] So Craig S. Keener, *The Gospel of John: A Commentary* (Peabody, MA: Hendrickson, 2003), 2:1238.
[3] F. J. Moloney, *The Gospel of John*, SP 4 (Collegeville, MN: Liturgical, 1998), 555.
[4] Raymond E. Brown, *The Gospel according to John*, AB 29A (New York: Doubleday, 1971), 1102.
[5] Herman Ridderbos, *The Gospel of John: A Theological Commentary*, trans. J. Vriend (Grand Rapids: Eerdmans, 1991), 665.
[6] David Shepherd, "'Do You Love Me?' A Narrative-Critical Reappraisal of ἀγαπάω and φιλέω in

Many other writers also notice the echo of the Farewell Discourse at John 21:15–19.[7] To understand the restoration that Peter enjoys, recognizing the points of correspondence between Jesus' questions at John 21 and his instruction at John 13:31–16:33 is necessary. I see at least five correspondences with the Farewell Discourse that will illumine the literary purpose of the scene.

First, the situation is virtually a fulfilled prediction by Jesus at 13:36–38. Jesus has predicted his own departure, Peter's lack of love for Christ, and Peter's denial. As Peter stands before Jesus at a charcoal fire, it is difficult not to recall the warning and Peter's failure at a previous charcoal fire (cf. 18:18).

Second, the question posed by Jesus is the backbone of what it is to follow Jesus in the Farewell Discourse. Jesus asks ἀγαπᾷς με? This is the essence of abiding in Christ in the Farewell Discourse. As stated above, abiding in Christ is loving him. It is this very question that Jesus asks Peter at John 21:15–19.[8]

Third, the command, upon Peter's affirmation of love for Christ, is to tend his flock (21:15–17). This is reminiscent of Jesus' new commandment stated at 13:34–35 and reiterated at 15:13–17. In the new community, individuals are to unite through their love for Jesus and each other.

John 21:15–17," *JBL* 129 (2010): 787. Shepherd goes on to defend that, while a formal distinction is not justifiable, a meaning intended by Jesus (that Peter fails to grasp) is that Jesus is demanding a love that is self-sacrificing. While I agree with many of the details, the ultimate premise founders, in my opinion, on the interchangeable use of the words in the Gospel at large. I feel, however, the charge to look to the Farewell Discourse for the ultimate meaning of the pericope quite justified.

[7] See, e.g., J. Ramsey Michaels, *The Gospel of John*, NICNT (Grand Rapids: Eerdmans, 2010), 1042.

[8] In the last century, it was common to assert different levels of love based on the fact that Jesus employs different words for love (φιλέω/ἀγαπάω). Carson's arguments are representative of the basic consensus (Carson, *John*, 676): (1) the verbs are used interchangeably in striking places. Note especially that the phrase "beloved disciple" can employ either word (see 5:20). Furthermore, the phrase "the Father loves the Son," employs both words (3:35; 5:20). Jesus loved Lazarus, employing both verbs (11:5, 36). (2) "No reliable distinction can be based on the LXX. Jacob's preferential love for Joseph is expressed with both verbs (Gn. 37:3, 4).... Despite one verb for 'love' in the Hebrew text of Proverbs 8:17, the LXX uses both *agapaō* and *phileō*" (ibid.). (3) Because φιλέω had taken on the meaning of "kiss," ἀγαπάω was taking over the prominent word for "love" since about the fourth century BC. "In other words, *agapaō* does not come into play because it is a peculiarly sacred word" (ibid.). (4) The word ἀγαπάω is not reserved for higher-level love, Demas loved this present age, Δημᾶς γάρ ... ἀγαπήσας τὸν νῦν αἰῶνα (2 Tim 4:10). In John, "and men loved the darkness rather than light" καὶ ἠγάπησαν οἱ ἄνθρωποι μᾶλλον τὸ σκότος ἢ τὸ φῶς (John 3:19 HCSB). (5) Just because the words are not complete synonyms (i.e., ἀγαπάω can never mean "kiss") does not mean that when the words are used together there is a distinction to be made. When the two words are expressing the same semantic domain they virtually mean the same thing. (6) Those who see a distinction don't agree as to the nature of the distinction. (7) John often uses near synonyms in a context without an observable distinction. In the present passage different words are used for knowing (γινώσκω/οἶδα), feeding (βόσκε/ποιμαίνω), and sheep (ἀρνία/πρόβατον). Especially note 21:17 where the words for knowing are used with the same subject in consecutive order (πάντα σὺ οἶδας, σὺ γινώσκεις ὅτι φιλῶ σε). The parallelism between the two clauses should convince us that John uses the words interchangeably even if we were not already sure that these verbs were roughly equivalent in general usage. Ridderbos notes that Jesus' final use of φιλέω is not a relief to Peter, but that he is grieved by it. It is difficult to suggest that φιλέω has a lesser meaning and not expect Peter to be relieved (Ridderbos, *John*, 666). Furthermore, I would add how odd it would be for Jesus to capitulate his standards to accommodate Peter. This is especially true given the place love has in Johannine discipleship.

Fourth, Peter had adamantly declared his willingness to die for Jesus (13:36–38) as evidence that he was ready to follow Jesus. Jesus rebuked his confidence. But now after Peter has declared his love for Christ three times, he will be given opportunity to show his love for Christ and love for the flock through his own death (21:18–19).

Finally, Jesus commands Peter, "follow me" (ἀκολούθει μοι, 21:19). To follow Jesus was exactly what Peter desired at 13:37 (διὰ τί οὐ δύναμαί σοι ἀκολουθῆσαι ἄρτι). At that time Peter was told he was not ready. Now he is ready. If he loves Jesus, and loves his flock, he may follow Jesus. Peter's ability to follow Jesus does not come from his own resources as if his penitence bought his power for endurance. Rather, since Jesus is returning to the Father, the disciples who are in covenant with him will now have the resources of the Paraclete to help them fulfill their ministry.

Beyond simply a nice gesture for a wayward, struggling disciple, the episode with Peter is the fulfillment of his desires stated at 13:36. Because he loves the Lord, obeys him, and loves his flock, he is in covenant with Christ under the new covenant. Thus, the restoration of Peter embodies the fulfillment of the commands of the Farewell Discourse that describe what it is to follow Jesus and thrive between the advents. I believe it has ramifications for all disciples of the Lord. This then, is what we must notice: the Gospel concludes with an injunction for discipleship. These themes have been interlocked throughout the Book of Glory.

The reason I have gone into the previous discussion is twofold: First, it helps us see the literary purpose of the Fourth Gospel. In doing so, it ought to help us see how the smaller units work together to fulfill the purpose. Second, it forces us to attempt to communicate not only the smaller sections but the overall purpose as well. In the Farewell Discourse, the focus on discipleship ought to be the focus of our sermon series. One of the best ways to develop such a focus is to devise a series title that will help keep our attention on the big picture. Sometimes we get lost in the minute details and lose sight of the larger purposes of a text.

Most of us who preach serially normally attempt a title for the series, but we do not usually have a methodology that informs our description. I believe we should attempt to describe the purpose of the span of text and create maximum interest in the hearer. Before I describe what I think should happen, let me illustrate a few of my own shortcomings. I must admit that I have been all over the map. I have provided titles that have been merely headlines—"The Sermon on the Mount," "The Farewell Discourse of John's Gospel," etc. This is true enough but gathers the same attention as watching paint dry. I have tried to be descriptive—"An Overview of Revelation" or "Jesus' Last Words."

Again, it is true enough but falls short of maximum relevance to the hearers (and the last entry is somewhat of a misnomer). At times I have attempted to be somewhat hip or cool. That always turns out badly and makes me look like the old guy with black socks and Bermuda shorts. It's always best to be ourselves.

To gather the point of the discourse and apply it to the hearer at the same time is sometimes elusive, but let's try something like "John 13–17: Thriving between the Advents." Here, I have attempted to make the point of discipleship personal and not optional by using the verb "thrive." John clearly is not interested in simple survival but flourishing. I refer to "between the advents" to call attention to the eschatological content of the discourse. Christ is clearly preparing us to live in his departure until he comes. So in this way, I hope to peak a sense of neediness in my hearers that matches the purpose of the discourse.

Where to from Here?

Our second matter to wrap up is an agenda to apply these matters in future ministry. I suggest three areas of concern.

Sharpening Our Mastery of Discourse Analysis

"Discourse analysis" is a broad term that covers a wide spectrum of disciplines. We, in essence, are referring to a close inspection of the whole text, that is, a holistic view of the book the author has written. In my mind, it is more than a hermeneutical method but a philosophy of interpretation that is open to several methodologies given the different genres of literature. In this book, we have been discussing the hortatory genre, a text that is trying to get the readers to do something. It is very similar to expository genre—a text arguing a thesis. These are usually found in reported speeches in narratives and in epistles. I find the SSA we employed here to be very helpful.

I believe it is well worth your effort to take the time to become proficient at discourse analysis. To help you do so, let me offer some suggestions. First, dive in. When I look back at my first attempts at discourse analysis, they were a mess. I encourage you to begin your practice of sermon preparation with discourse analysis. In expository or hortatory genres, employ an SSA. You will make mistakes, but we learn the art by doing first. When you do so, you will eventually be able to analyze the text very quickly. So don't get frustrated; just dive in.

My second suggestion is related: practice, practice, practice. Musicians must practice the scales, athletes must do drills, and preachers must work constantly on the craft of sermon preparation. This is also true of the hermeneutical methods you employ. My hope is that you will start looking at the text in holistic terms—not just discreet sections—and, thus, improve your ability to communicate with accuracy. This will take practice.

Employing Discourse Analysis in Preaching Other Genres

The analysis I have proposed is quite appropriate for both hortatory and expository material. So the procedure works well for a large portion of the New Testament, for much of it is expository or hortatory (epistles and speeches/letters in narrative genres). Regarding other genres, I find that a semantic and structural analysis is not as particularly helpful although a close inspection of the text is always valuable.

So what about other genres like narrative or apocalyptic? These are topics of another monograph, but I can make some suggestions. First, my basic theory for an expository sermon is that everything about the text should be reflected in the sermon. The major movements of the text should be the major movements of the sermon (usually called "points"). We should seek to identify the major movements of these texts and form the major movements of our sermon around these points.

In chapter 1 I gave an example from Luke 8, which is a narrative text. You will notice that the outline is structured around the major movements of the text. This was a problem-resolution story, so the story moves in the following order: setting, problem, resolution, sequel.[9] I used these movements to craft the sermon outline. As you explore the different genres of Scripture, this basic philosophy is a good way to craft an expository message.

Sharpening Our Use of the Original Languages

I have taken pains to make this book accessible to readers who are not proficient in Greek. However, let me encourage you to keep your languages fresh or make it a priority to refresh your study. We live in a great day where we have hundreds of translations of the Bible in English. You can do semantic and structural analysis from an English Bible, but you will find that in the translational options the clarity on these matters is often blurred. I have attempted an SSA from the text of both an English and Greek Bible and have found that, depending on the translation and individual text, the SSA often is quite different. Why? There are at least two reasons.

First, there is the problem of specificity. The difference between reading the original and the best English translation is much like the difference between analog and digital television. The clarity and definition are far greater

---

[9] Suggested by Richard Young, *Intermediate Greek: A Linguistic and Exegetical Approach* (Nashville: B&H, 1992), 250. The sequel is a section that "wraps up" the story and often carries the intended point of the story.

in the original. Certain nuances that would constrain us to understand a text in a certain way are often simply not translated in an English text. We noted a few of them in the analysis in this book.

Second, it is my opinion that some translations are aiming for "easy to read" rather than "accurate." This leads to things that obscure some important nuances in the text. For example, consider the following very famous sentence in Greek: πορευθέντες οὖν μαθητεύσατε πάντα τὰ ἔθνη. You may recognize it as Matthew 28:19; it is normally translated, "Go, therefore, and make disciples of all nations." In English you have two commands, "Go" and "make disciples." In Greek, the writer chose not to use two imperative verbs and instead chose to use a participle πορευθέντες "having gone" and an imperative μαθητεύσατε, "make disciples." Matthew's choice was to place the emphasis on "make disciples" and background "go." In English, it would be cumbersome to translate it "having gone, therefore, make disciples of all nations." In English this is not how we say such things, so it is easier to translate it "go." But it obscures the emphasis. We are to go, but making disciples is the issue. This is just one of the many examples. Surely we want to see the emphasis as we communicate Scripture.

I have six suggestions for improving our use of the biblical languages. First, let's remove the angst. American students have little or no experience in foreign languages. For many of us, the study of Greek or Hebrew is a dark cloud over us that we rather dread. We often equate language acquisition to struggle, brute force, and angst. On the other hand, I have had students from other countries who live in multilingual situations; they have no fear of taking on a new language. Let us be more like them. Do not fear.

Second, make every opportunity to expose yourself to the languages. Set aside time each day to study the Word in the original languages. Read the Greek and Hebrew text in church (unless you are preaching, of course!). Use all the senses: see, hear, speak. Pump Greek and Hebrew to your brain.

Third, aim to learn naturally—that is, read whole sentences. I have waged a mini-war against interlinear texts for years. These do not help you read the language. They, in my opinion, never let your brain orient to Greek but to a mashed-up, rearranged English. Constantine Campbell suggests you burn them.[10] I'll bring the marshmallows.

Fourth, do not depend on reading tools too heavily. In the same vein as our approach to interlinear texts, use software with caution. Use it to speed up your translation, not to do your translation for you. If you are forced to look

---

[10] Constantine Campbell, *Keep Your Greek: Strategies for Busy People* (Grand Rapids: Zondervan, 2010), 19.

up a word (and it will happen), find out why. Was it an unknown or forgotten vocabulary word? Was it a difficult or unfamiliar form? Was it the surrounding syntax? Whatever the problem, address it and learn.

Fifth, consider using a "reader's edition" of the Greek New Testament. These provide footnoted lexical information for the lesser-used words in the New Testament. The drawback is that they do not have a textual apparatus, so I would not use it for formal study. If used properly, however, these can help us read more text with efficiency.

Finally, read the Scriptures as your "pure spiritual milk" (1 Pet 2:2). Let Bible study not be a mere academic exercise but your spiritual nourishment. If it becomes an act of love whereby we receive great benefits—and not laborious work—we will be on the path toward loving the exercise.

Final Thoughts

As we conclude, let me offer three final caveats. First, the method I have proposed is *a* way, not *the* way. If the major movements of the text are the major movements of the sermon and if the purpose of the text is the purpose of the sermon (and so forth), then it is an expository message. There are other ways to achieve this. Nor should we think that an occasional topic in biblical theology is improper. There is room for variety if we make it our aim to be thoroughly biblical. I prefer a 90/10 ratio between expository and biblical theology messages.

Second, beware of falling into the twin trap of discouragement and arrogance. When beginning to do discourse analysis it can often be frustrating, but the more you practice the better you get at it. Do not be discouraged; be determined. But as you are growing more confident with the method, beware of the sin of pride.

Finally, do not be discouraged when you produce the occasional boring sermon or study. It happens to us all. If you give your people good content, God can use that in ways you may never dream. Be confident that our Paraclete is working through you to his people. His Word will not return void to him. Set his Word on the wind, and watch the Spirit go where he desires. He requires you to be faithful. Abide in him. May God richly bless your preaching and teaching ministry.

APPENDIX 1

Preparing Your Study

THE Christian exegete should have a ready source of good reference materials. Below I will list ten essential types of reference works and suggest a few standards in the field.[1]

English Bibles

At my last count, there were ninety English Bibles produced in the twentieth century and nine produced in the twenty-first. While I do wish some of the effort was not so commercial and directed obviously for profit, this does put the student who speaks English in a grand position. We have many Bibles in English to reference. The Internet makes available a wide variety of Bible translations at our fingertips if we simply have a computer and an Internet connection.[2]

Regarding English translations there are a wide variety of approaches; suffice it to say that the spectrum has "easy to read" at one end and "accurate" at the other. Each end of the spectrum is valuable to us. Regarding interpretation, "accurate" is preferred. The more free translations often help us see the big picture better and help in personalizing the message. Good interpreters of the Scripture will have several English translations available to them and will consult them readily. The intent, however, is to get a good picture of what the original languages are communicating. This leads us to gathering some good tools for language works.

---

[1] This was inspired and adapted from Paul D. Wegner, *Using Old Testament Hebrew in Preaching: A Guide for Students and Pastors* (Grand Rapids: Kregel, 2009), 29–65, and is a further adaptation of the rough draft I provided for the chapter written for *Invitation to Biblical Hermeneutics* by Köstenberger and Patterson.

[2] See e.g., www.bible.logos.com; www.biblegateway.com; or http://unbound.biola.edu/. These have multiple English Bibles available to the student.

Language Tools

Hebrew and Greek Grammars

Most of us will have a beginning grammar as required by our basic Greek course. In addition, the student should have a more advanced grammar. *Greek Grammar beyond the Basics* by Dan Wallace and *A Greek Grammar of the New Testament and Other Early Christian Literature* by Blass and Debrunner are two standards in the field.[3] A. T. Robertson's advanced grammar, although dated from the first part of the twentieth century, is still a valuable resource and the only advanced Greek grammar regarding *Koinē* Greek on the market.[4]

Lexicons

It pays to have a good lexicon for both Hebrew and Greek. A wide variety of Greek lexicons are available to the student of Scripture. The rule of thumb is that you get what you pay for. The standard in the field regarding Greek is affectionately known as "BDAG," i.e., the Bauer, Danker, Arndt, and Gingrich lexicon.[5] In Hebrew there is the two-volume work affectionately known as "HALOT" and the Brown-Driver-Briggs lexicon ("BDB").[6] Another valuable lexicon is Louw and Nida's lexicon based on semantic domains (i.e., it groups synonyms together); it is invaluable when doing a semantic field study.[7] This kind of study investigates the synonyms and negated antonyms to get a good idea of a biblical concept or theology. A host of shorter lexicons also exist and are helpful when not doing deep linguistic work.[8]

Language-Specific Concordance

A concordance is invaluable in determining where a Greek or Hebrew word is used in the Scriptures because it is impossible to translate a given word with the same English gloss. The standard Greek concordance is Moulton

---

[3] Daniel B. Wallace, *Greek Grammar beyond the Basics* (Grand Rapids: Zondervan, 1996); F. Blass and A. Debrunner, *A Greek Grammar of the New Testament and Other Early Christian Literature*, trans. and ed. Robert W. Funk (Chicago: University of Chicago Press, 1961).

[4] A. T. Robertson, *A Grammar of the Greek New Testament in the Light of Historical Research*, 4th ed. (Nashville: Broadman, 1934).

[5] W. Bauer, F. W. Danker, W. Arndt, and F. W. Gingrich, *A Greek-English Lexicon of the New Testament and Other Early Christian Literature* (Chicago: University of Chicago Press, 2000).

[6] Ludwig, Köehler, Walter Baumgartner, M. E. J. Richardson, and Johann Jakob Stamm, *The Hebrew and Aramaic Lexicon of the Old Testament* (Leiden: E. J. Brill, 1994). Francis Brown, Edward Robinson, S. R. Driver, Charles A. Briggs, and Francis Brown, *The New Brown, Driver, Briggs, Gesenius Hebrew and English Lexicon: With an Appendix Containing the Biblical Aramaic* (Peabody, MA: Hendrickson, 1979). Another nice work is Andreas J. Köstenberger and Raymond Bouchoc, *The Book Study Concordance of the Greek New Testament* (Nashville: B&H, 2003).

[7] J. P. Louw and Eugene Nida, *Greek-English Lexicon of the New Testament: Based on Semantic Domains* (New York: United Bible Societies, 1989).

[8] See e.g., F W. Gingrich, *Shorter Lexicon of the Greek New Testament*, 2nd ed., rev. F. W. Danker (Chicago: University of Chicago Press, 1983).

and Geden, sixth edition.[9] Another valuable resource is Köstenberger and Bouchoc's *Book Study Concordance* that evaluates the lexical stock of each book. For Hebrew, a valuable resource is the *Concordance to the Hebrew Old Testament* by Lisowski, Roost, and Rüger or the less expensive Kohlenberger and Swanson, *The Hebrew English Concordance to the Old Testament*.[10]

Finding where a given word is used in the Scriptures is invaluable in determining the semantic range of a word in a given body of literature. While there are overlaps in English regarding semantic range, it is not always the case in the original languages. In such cases, interpreting that meaning in your context is very important. This is the domain of the theological dictionary.

Theological/Exegetical Dictionary

A theological dictionary is a collection of in-depth word-studies that are designed to show the theological content of a given concept. Although quite valuable, each entry should be critically evaluated. Regarding the NT, the standard in the field is *The Theological Dictionary of the New Testament*, known as "TDNT," and Colin Brown's *Dictionary of New Testament Theology* is also well respected. Regarding the OT, there is a companion volume to the TDNT referred to as TDOT, and Harris, Archer, and Waltke's *Theological Wordbook of the Old Testament* is highly regarded.[11]

Bible Encyclopedia/Dictionary

A good Bible encyclopedia will give solid essay-length treatments of various subjects germane to the biblical world. The standard in the field is the *Anchor Bible Dictionary*. You will find it thorough, although not particularly conservative. I would also recommend the *Zondervan Pictorial Dictionary* for the cost-conscious.[12] These multivolume works are valuable for the exegete, but there are also some one-volume works that are helpful as well.[13]

---

[9] W. F. Moulton, A. S. Geden, and I. Howard Marshall, *Concordance to the Greek New Testament*, 6th ed. (London: T&T Clark, 2002).

[10] Gerhard Lisowksy, Leonhard Rost, Hans Peter Rüger, *Concordance to the Hebrew Old Testament: Konkordanz Zum Hebraischen Alten Testament* (Peabody, MA: Hendrickson, 2010); John R. Kohlenberger and James A. Swanson, *The Hebrew English Concordance to the Old Testament: With the New International Version* (Grand Rapids: Zondervan, 1998).

[11] G. Johannes Botterweck and Helmer Ringgren, *Theological Dictionary of the Old Testament*, 10 vols. (Grand Rapids: Eerdmans, 1977); and R. Laird Harris, Gleason L. Archer, and Bruce K. Waltke, *Theological Wordbook of the Old Testament* (Chicago: Moody, 1980).

[12] David Noel Freedman, ed., *The Anchor Bible Dictionary*, 6 vols. (New York: Doubleday, 1992); and Merrill C. Tenney, ed., *The Zondervan Pictorial Bible Dictionary*, 5 vols. (Grand Rapids: Zondervan, 1975).

[13] See, e.g., Charles W. Draper, Chad Brand, and Archie England, eds., *The Holman Illustrated Bible Dictionary*, rev. edition (Nashville: Holman Reference, 2003). At 1704 pages it is one of the more thorough one-volume dictionaries around.

Bible Atlas

Knowing the geography of a given place at a given time is often quite helpful in exegesis. The juggernaut of Bible Atlases is the *Tübingen Bibelatlas* (it has English subtitles, don't be nervous!).[14] Other well-respected atlases are the *Holman Bible Atlas* and the *Kregel Bible Atlas*.[15]

NT and OT Introductions

Solid, conservative introductions to the Testaments are invaluable tools to the exegete. I am partial to *The Cradle, the Cross, and the Crown* by Köstenberger, Kellum, and Quarles, for obvious reasons.[16] For the OT, B&H has a companion volume by Eugene H. Merrill, Mark Rooker, and Michael Grisanti, *The World and the Word: An Introduction to the Old Testament*.[17] Zondervan's *An Introduction to the Old Testament* is also a standard.[18]

Chart Books

Both Kregel and Zondervan have a series of chart books that summarize chronological, archaeological, thematic, and other very good information in an easy-to-access format. Another good resource is the *Holman Book of Biblical Charts, Maps, and Reconstructions*.[19] Often these are thought-provoking, informative, and a source for visual teaching material.

Commentaries

Commentaries come in a variety of formats, target audiences, and usefulness. Today we have both academic and lay commentaries, preaching commentaries, application commentaries, background commentaries, and ever-further specializations. When buying a commentary, however, I suggest caution. Avoid devotional or preaching commentaries in preparing an exegesis (their place is in application—not interpretation). Most of these commentaries are the sermons of a famous preacher. The danger in reading them first is that you may be unduly influenced by their sermon structure. Academic exegetical

---

[14] Siegfried Mittmann and Götz Schmitt, eds., *Tübinger Bibelatlas* (Stuttgart: Deutsche Bibelgesellschaft, 2001).

[15] Thomas V. Brisco, *Holman Bible Atlas* (Nashville: B&H, 1998); and Tim Dowley, *The Kregel Bible Atlas* (Grand Rapids: Kregel, 2003).

[16] Andreas J. Köstenberger, L. Scott Kellum, and Charles L. Quarles, *The Cradle, the Cross, and the Crown: An Introduction to the New Testament* (Nashville: B&H Academic, 2009).

[17] Eugene H. Merrill, Mark Rooker, and Michael Grisanti, *The World and the Word: An Introduction to the Old Testament* (Nashville: B&H Academic, 2011).

[18] Tremper Longman III, and Raymond B. Dillard, *An Introduction to the Old Testament*, 2nd ed. (Grand Rapids: Zondervan, 2006).

[19] Marsha A. Ellis Smith, *Holman Book of Biblical Charts, Maps, and Reconstructions* (Nashville: Holman Reference, 1993).

commentaries (i.e., commentaries that deal with the original languages verse-by-verse) are the best for our purposes. They will cover the issues and debates that affect exegesis.

However, here the buyer must beware. The value of a commentary is often in the eye of the beholder. Few are written from a solidly evangelical perspective, and some series are mixed in this regard (e.g., the Word Biblical Commentary Series). Furthermore, a commentary series will also invariably be uneven in how well the individual volumes handle the text. It benefits you in this matter to do some research before buying a commentary.[20] In other words, do not necessarily buy sets of commentaries. Think in terms of individual volumes. For example, you should be asking, "What are the five best commentaries on Romans?" rather than completing five sets of commentaries.

Systematic and Biblical Theologies

A systematic theology book with a Scripture index is often a very helpful resource in discerning what matters of theology are germane to your text. This is not a foolproof method but one that will get you thinking about the theological implications of your passage. Sometimes you will discover aspects of your passage that you would not have considered otherwise. A standard in the field is Wayne Grudem's *Systematic Theology* that comes in both an unabridged and abridged versions.[21]

Communicator's Tools

The ultimate job of the exegete is to communicate what he has learned to his hearers. To do this there are a few items that ought to be in your library. The first group is a series of English grammar works. You should have a good English dictionary to help you use words correctly. You should not use an English dictionary to define a biblical word. Nothing is more irritating to me than to hear someone say "*Webster's* defines 'righteousness' as . . ." Use a Greek lexicon for such things, not an English dictionary.

You should also have a good thesaurus to choose the correct word. Again, let's be careful that we do not spend all our time looking for a word that begins

---

[20] I often recommend people just starting to build their academic libraries to begin with D. A. Carson's *New Testament Commentary Survey*. It is now in its sixth edition from Baker at a very reasonable price. There is also an Old Testament version by Tremper Longman III. John Glynn's *Commentary and Reference Survey: A Comprehensive Guide to Biblical and Theological Resources* is also a good reference for a variety of resources.

[21] Wayne Grudem, *Systematic Theology: An Introduction to Biblical Doctrine* (Leicester, England: InterVarsity, 1994); Wayne Grudem and Jeff Purswell, *Bible Doctrine: Essential Teachings of the Christian Faith* (Grand Rapids: Zondervan, 1999).

with "P" to alliterate our points. Good alliteration does not necessarily mean good biblical content.

Finally, since bad grammar is a hindrance to good communication, you should have an English grammar to help you say things correctly. An English grammar is also very helpful to understand the essence of different grammatical references that you will find in your research (e.g., "verbal adjective," "predicate nominative," "hanging nominative," etc.).[22]

Beyond these basic grammar tools, the good wordsmith will also have a series of books, databases, or services that will help him locate illustrative material. Sadly, your hearers will remember your illustrations longer than your sermon content, so illustrate the text. Do not subscribe to the urban-preaching-legend method of getting sermon illustrations. That is, do not simply repeat the things you've heard other preachers say or read in anthologies of their sermons. Verify an illustrative matter as best you can. It is often told in American pulpits that the boxer rebellion in China can be traced to Chinese fury over American plans to tear down the Great Wall of China. These "plans" were actually the invention of four reporters with no real story that week, so they made one up. Thus, the power of the tongue is illustrated with great passion and rhetorical effect. The only trouble is that there is no evidence that the Chinese were ever aware of the story and most consider the connection to be fraudulent.[23] How foolish do we look when we use such illustrations? Above all, preachers of the Word should be committed to the truth. Document your illustrations as best you can.

Electronic Resources

In this age there are numerous electronic resources available to you either on the Internet (in both free and pay varieties) or through applications for your computer. On the Internet, there are quite a few sites that will help you with Hebrew and Greek, but we must be somewhat cautious. For example, one of the most helpful sites on the web regarding the Greek New Testament is the Laparola site.[24] (Yes, it's an Italian website in English about the Greek NT!) At the Greek NT page you have access to and may compare several editions of the GNT including the UBS4, Wescott-Hort, and the Byzantine text-type. Further options include searching for individual Greek and English words and even by Louw and Nida semantic domains. You also have access to the textual

---

[22] Because I didn't listen in English classes in high school, I had two lessons on Greek participles in college without the slightest idea of what a participle was. I found an English grammar was one of my best friends in those years!

[23] See, e.g., http://www.museumofhoaxes.com/hoax/archive/permalink/the_great_wall_of_china_hoax.

[24] See http://www.laparola.net/greco.

variants and a description of the age and text type of each witness through a tool-tip that appears when pulling the cursor over the witness. It is an amazingly sophisticated site. In review, one should consider Laparola like the open-source platforms in other fields—it is constantly being updated and corrected. What we are able to access that otherwise is unavailable in electronic format is amazing (e.g., the Münster textual variants). However, a great number of language works cannot be linked to the website because of copyright limitations. Thus, for example, the lexicons hyperlinked to the individual words are Thayer's and Strong's rather than a better lexicon. It is incredibly helpful but has its limitations.

So when finding these resources, understand the limitations. First, regarding the technical linguistic information, ask, "What is the source of the tagging?" If a program parses a word, it is only as good as the person tagging it with the information. Second, ask, "To what resources is it hyperlinked?" Free lexicons are often outdated. The same may be true for other resources like text-critical information. Third, ask, "What is the faith-background of the authors of the site?" Evangelicals may not agree with non-evangelicals regarding many items that are not straightforward but matters of interpretation. These questions should be helpful in determining how we would employ such sites.

Other Internet sites could easily take the rest of our space and would be obsolete by the time of publication because the technology advances at an incredible pace. I will conclude with a brief set of warnings regarding Internet sources. First, verify all information found on blogs. Furthermore, only a blog from a recognized scholar or a person who has been proven valuable over time should be seriously considered—and then verified. In other words, a non-refereed post can only alert you to information of potential value. Second, avoid websites of individuals who do not provide documentation for their information. Unless it is documented, you have no recourse but to consider it useless. At best, it can help you search for documented verification of the information. Third, sites like Wikipedia, that is, those that rely on user-generated information, are a fine place to begin searching for information but not sufficient to use alone.[25] I would cite two reasons. First, the open interface leaves it open to malicious manipulation and/or error. Much of this is caught immediately; however, the phenomenon suggests we proceed with caution. Second, all such tertiary sources are not valued very highly for formal research.[26] You should be cautious how you use the information on these sites.

---

[25] Wikipedia has become incredibly popular. My children have not been impressed with my publishing record, but they did "geek out" when I showed them a mention in a Wikipedia article on the Farewell Discourse!

[26] As the Wikipedia site admits. See http://en.wikipedia.org/wiki/Reliability_of_Wikipedia.

Sites from trusted sources provide the most valuable information. Some are trusted because of their institutional connections (e.g., www.bible.org and Dallas Seminary). Others are trusted for being useful over a long time (e.g., www.laparola.net/greco) or come from a trusted scholar (e.g., www.reasonablefaith.org and William Lane Craig). The good news is that there are more valuable sites than we could reasonably list here. But for every good site, there are many that should be kept at arm's length or ignored altogether.

Another incredibly valuable source for information is Google Books.[27] At this website you may search the contents of some seven million books. The books in public domain are available to download free through Google Play. Many standards in the field of biblical studies (like the ICC commentary series) are available in this manner. Truly, you could fill your hard drive with the works available to you. But the problem with public domain works is that they are very old (by law). Not only do older works run the danger of being outdated; they will not have the latest linguistic and archaeological discoveries, deal with current debates, and may function from outdated (i.e., mistaken) paradigms. Readers must be discerning about what they find there. Newer books are often accessible as a "limited preview," in which a large portion of the book is available to view online.

While you are spending money for your library, buy a Bible software program. While the investment seems high, you may replace several resources like concordances, atlases, Gospel synopses/harmonies, lexicons, and other reference works with software. Generally for the professional exegete, low-end, low-cost software you see in many general outlets and bookstores is insufficient. These tools simply will not have the resources that will make them very useful to you. Although free resources have a place (especially in the smart-phone market), they will generally be insufficient for the professional exegete who is seriously using the original languages. You should not do exegesis of the original language from a limited (albeit free) smart-phone app. They have their uses, but I doubt they are intended to be the exegetical foundation for a pastor's sermon.

The general rule should be to pay as much as you can afford on your choice of Bible software. Among the commercial programs, *Logos*, *Bibleworks*, and *Accordance* are the major players right now in the premier Bible software category.[28] Expect that number to grow as new programs enter the field. Since it

---

[27] See http://books.google.com.

[28] At the time of writing, they are in version 4 for *Logos*, version 9 for *BibleWorks*, and version 10 for *Accordance*. About every two years or so an upgrade is produced (as is the nature of technology today). Each platform is available in Mac format, and *BibleWorks* and *Logos* are available for PC. All have tablet versions that can be "on the go."

would be impractical to provide a review of programs that could be obsolete by the time of publishing, I will offer some advice for choosing Bible software.

For serious exegesis, a good computer program should provide in-depth grammatical and lexical searches. It should have a concordance function that goes beyond anything a printed concordance can do. For example, searches regarding grammatical constructions, paired words, and semantic domains are difficult if not impossible in a printed concordance. These, often, take less than a second electronically.[29]

Furthermore, a good Bible program should be able to help you diagram sentences; compare text-types, versions, and translations; quickly reference paradigms; hear both modern and Erasmian pronunciation of Greek; parse words immediately; use lexicons at the click of the mouse; quickly look up a grammatical issue in a Hebrew or Greek grammar; use and/or create cross references and notes; connect to external links (like the TLG); do textual criticism; examine major biblical manuscripts (visually and lexically); and browse exegetical resources. The more resources you have—like the apostolic fathers, Second Temple literature, and historical works (like Josephus)—the better the program will be.

When choosing a Bible program (when cost is not a factor), the major question to ask is, "Which philosophy behind the program best suits my needs?" Some programs are basically a library program with a very good Bible module. This is how I would classify *Logos*. It is a massive collection. At the time of writing, the platinum version of *Logos* offers 1,150 e-books with thousands more available to purchase. The philosophy is to be a virtual pastor's study. I often recommend this kind of program to deploying missionaries who then can be on the move without having to transport a library of physical books.

Programs like *BibleWorks*, on the other hand, take a different philosophy. They are more about exegesis and have little interest in serving as a virtual library. You will find digitized books, but usually they are confined to exegetical works like Archer and Chirchino's *Old Testament Quotations in the New Testament*. Programs with an exegetical focus tend to be more streamlined and economical. For those who have no need to be exceedingly mobile or already have a significant library, these kinds of programs are a good choice. E-readers like Kindle or Nook can provide electronic books, but they are not integrated into the *BibleWorks* system. So, if you are studying a passage in Romans, an integrated library can display all references to your passage in all your e-books. Most programs supply this feature, but it will be limited to your integrated resources. This would not be available through an e-reader.

---

[29] Depending on the speed of your computer of course.

The *Accordance* program is somewhat of a middle term between the focused approach of *BibleWorks* and the library of *Logos*. The ultimate version offers a nice set of commentaries and other resources the exegete should find useful. As the other two mentioned, it is a powerful program that the exegete would find very valuable.

Whatever version you choose (and each will have its vigorous proponents), there are several mistakes you should avoid. First, avoid thinking that the programs are perfect. All are dependent on human data entry at some point, thus there can and will be errors in them. A computer program that parses verbs and nouns for you is only as good as the person tagging them. Second, the language tools are useless to you unless you know at least the basics of the grammar (or can look up its significance). The program may facilitate your reading of Hebrew and Greek, not replace it. Third, you must be familiar with the terminology employed by the program. For example, some will describe deponents as "middles" without really denying the existence of deponents. Being unfamiliar with the program's terminology might stimulate some bizarre heresies! Fourth, never be satisfied with one search. The search is only as good as the parameters you set. Think about other options that you might have left out. For example, when searching through a semantic domain, do not neglect to look for negated antonyms. The concept expressed by "not condemned" and "forgiven" is essentially the same thing. Fifth, remember the distinction between formal grammatical constructions and their actual usage. For example, the Greek word "οἶδα" ("I know") is perfect in form, but it is used as a present. Most software will tag it as a perfect because of its form. Always think critically when using such tools. Finally, some programs come in multiple versions with more and more resources available. When you are comparing programs, compare similar versions to get the most for your money.

APPENDIX 2

A SERMON SERIES THROUGH THE FAREWELL DISCOURSE

IN the body of the book I chose to streamline the presentation rather than give sermon manuscripts. However, I thought it helpful also to demonstrate my approach to matters of homiletics—specifically, application and illustration. In this appendix I fill in more application and illustration and weave it into a coherent series. Each sermon in a series should be connected by the purpose of the whole discourse (however large or small). I have identified the purpose of the Farewell Discourse to be authentic discipleship. Our series is titled "John 13–17, Thriving between the Advents."

SERMON 1: JESUS' LAST WISHES

TEXT: John 13:31–38
MIT: As Jesus' death approached, he prepared his disciples for life after his departure.
MIM: In light of our position, Christians should be prepared to live in a way that would glorify God.

Introduction

The last words of people as they are dying are often of great interest to us. There are books and websites devoted to such things.[1] Sometimes these words are ironic. For example, J. M. Barrie (author of *Peter Pan*) said, "I can't sleep,"

---

[1] See, e.g., http://en.wikiquote.org/wiki/Last_words and Laura Ward, *Famous Last Words: The Ultimate Collection of Finales and Farewells* (New York: Sterling, 2004), among many others.

and then did just that and died.[2] Sometimes they are tragic; for example, Confucius is reported to have said to a disciple who offered to pray for him, "I have prayed for a very long time."[3] Or sometimes they may be funny; for example, playwright Oscar Wilde is reported to have said, "Either that wallpaper goes, or I do."[4] Then he went. So what is so important about these last words? I do not think we find so much wisdom or wit or some nugget for life seen in the rearview mirror. Instead, they tell us more about the person.

Our text today is part of Jesus' last teaching to his disciples. Like the last words of mere humans, his last words reveal the person. His concerns reveal his heart. And his heart is all about us. Unlike those of mere humans, his last words are words to live by and a guide to eternity. More than Washington's Farewell Address, or Socrates's, or any other human's last words, we would do well to pay close attention to our Lord's. The entirety of this discourse is about how to spiritually thrive between the advents; between his departure and his return. It is not just about those disciples, then; it is about us. In the next few weeks we will look at John 13–17 and find that as Jesus departs to go to the Father, he does not leave us like orphans, bereft of his presence. Instead, he provides everything we need to thrive in the Spirit's presence.

Jesus' farewell address takes place on Thursday night after the Passover meal, the night before his crucifixion. He has given the example of washing the disciples' feet, and he has both identified Judas as the traitor and dismissed Judas to do the ugly deed. Now, as Jesus' death approached, he prepared his disciples for life after his departure. Three themes are highlighted in 13:31–38. (1) He announced plainly his departure. (2) He gave the New Commandment—to love one another. And (3) in an exchange with Peter, he highlighted the disciple's innate disability apart from divine help (as illustrated by Peter).

These three themes will show up throughout the discourse that follows. In fact, one could argue that Jesus elaborates these themes. In light of our position between his advents, Christians should be prepared to live in a way that would glorify God by addressing Jesus' concerns to our lives.

Outline

I. Live in Light of His Departure (13:31–33)

"When he had gone out, Jesus said, 'Now the Son of Man is glorified, and God is glorified in Him. If God is glorified in Him, God will also glorify Him in Himself and will glorify Him at once. Children, I am with you a little while longer. You will look for Me, and just as

---

[2] Ward, *Famous Last Words*, 16.
[3] W. R. Egbert, *Last Words of Famous Men and Women* (Norristown, PA: Herald, 1898), 39.
[4] Ward, *Famous Last Words*, 27.

I told the Jews, 'Where I am going you cannot come, so now I tell you'" (HCSB).

A. TEXT

1. Jesus' departure is glorification (vv. 31–32).

   a. "Glorification" is expressed in the completion of the hour.

   b. This hour clearly refers to the death on the cross that is soon upon Jesus.

   c. In the cross, Jesus makes the Father's love known (see, e.g., 1:18 where Jesus "exegetes" the Father).

   d. In the cross, the Father makes Jesus' obedience and love known, so that his glorification is "immediately" about to happen.

2. Jesus' departure is temporary (v. 33).

3. Jesus clearly announces his departure.

   He makes an explicit reference to John 7:33–34. That he leaves off 7:34 implies that his dear children will be able to follow him. Thus, the absence is only temporary.

B. TODAY: We need to see Jesus' departure in a similar way.

1. It reveals the glory of the Father and the Son.

2. It leads to a magnificent reunion.

C. ILLUSTRATION

Set in the spring of 1300, Dante's *Magnum Opus* was a story that described hell (*inferno*), purgatory (*purgatorio*), and heaven (*paradiso*). He describes the soul's journey to God with an allegory of his trip through hell, purgatory, and heaven, ultimately to be in the presence of God. He calls his work *the Divine Comedy*. To modern ears this seems to be an odd title, given the serious nature of the contents. The title doesn't seem so odd when we consider that in classical literature the tragedy ended with a funeral, but the comedy ended with a marriage. While Dante's vision is not entirely biblical, I do think he's caught the essence of our journey to God in at least his title. More so,

Jesus' departure is not tragedy ending in a funeral. It is comedy, in the classical sense, ending in a marriage, the marriage feast of the Lamb. Thus, Jesus understands his "hour" not as defeat and death but glory. We should as well. We should live in light of the joy to come.

II. Live Loving One Another (13:34–35)

"I give you a new command: Love one another. Just as I have loved you, you must also love one another. By this all people will know that you are My disciples, if you have love for one another" (HCSB).

A. TEXT

1. The Newness of the Commandment

   a. The command to love your brother is not new (Lev 18:19).

   b. The command is "new" because the people of God are composed in a new way.

2. The Substance of the Commandment

   We love each other as Christ has loved us.

3. The Result of the Commandment

   All men will know that we are his disciples when we love one another.

B. TODAY

Two major issues confront us in the New Commandment:

1. Your relationships with *all* Christians should reflect a Christ-like love.

   Far too often we play favorites, or we have particular trouble with one brother or sister in Christ. The truth is that we should strive to make all our relationships modeled on Christ.

2. Proclamation is dependent on how well you love.

C. ILLUSTRATION

Justin Martyr (I *Apology* xiv) notes the attitude of the early church: "we who formerly delighted in fornication, but now embrace chastity alone; we who formerly used magical arts, dedicate ourselves to the good and unbegotten God; we who valued above all things the acquisition of wealth and possessions, now bring what we have into a common stock, and communicate to everyone in need; we who hated and destroyed one another, and on account of their different manners would not live with men of a different tribe, now, since the coming of Christ, live familiarly with them, and pray for our enemies, and endeavor to persuade those who hate us unjustly to live conformably to the good precepts of Christ, to the end that they may become partakers with us of the same joyful hope of a reward from God the ruler of all."[5]

III. Live Depending on His Resources (13:36-38)

"Lord," Simon Peter said to Him, "where are You going?" Jesus answered, "Where I am going you cannot follow Me now, but you will follow later." "Lord," Peter asked, "why can't I follow You now? I will lay down my life for You!" Jesus replied, "Will you lay down your life for Me? I assure you: A rooster will not crow until you have denied Me three times" (HCSB).

A. TEXT

Through his overconfidence, Peter showed he was not ready to follow Christ.

1. Peter is not concerned with loving his brethren (v. 36).

2. Peter is not ready to hear displeasing news from Christ (v. 37).

B. ILLUSTRATION

Technology advances quickly (as any computer user knows). When World War I began in 1914, the Wright Flier had been invented only eleven years earlier. Yet, due to mainly French innovation, the latest flight technology far outstripped anything that the Wright brothers had produced. When World War II opened in 1939, a scant eleven years after World War I ended, the aircraft being produced in the West far outstripped anything in World War I. The World War I models were "outclassed in

---

[5] Jusin Martyr, *The First Apology XIV* (ANF 1:167).

every type of meaningful flight performance."[6] The West was quite proud and confident in their aircraft. So it was understandable that when Western pilots compared their warplanes to the Japanese Zero they were confident their armored skin and powerful engines could win the day. However, the ones who survived their first encounters with the "Zeke" discovered that the Zero's maneuverability and responsiveness made them deadly foes in the skies. So much so that in the early part of the war the Japanese Zero had the same respect among pilots as the atomic bomb did later. Many a pilot fresh off engaging European heavy fighters gained giant respect for the Zero, if they survived. Needless to say, overconfidence can be a deadly thing. Yet the believer often approaches life as if it were easy.

C. TODAY

Christians often live dependent on themselves.

1. We make choices without seriously seeking God's will.

2. We do not even consider a sacrificial choice.

3. We are willing to believe patently false doctrines and interpretations if they are "beneficial to us."

4. It is a spiritual disaster that may well devastate us.

Conclusion

The Farewell Discourse defines what it is to thrive between his departure and return. Peter is not able to follow him now. However, after Christ is glorified, Peter will be able. In fact, Jesus tells him then, "follow me" (21:19). So now, from this side of Easter, the disciple of Jesus does not have to wait for him to be glorified. The disciple is able; therefore, we must follow in light of what the Lord's departure has accomplished—loving Christ, loving one another, and depending on his resources.

---

[6] Eric M. Bergerud, *Fire in the Sky: The Air War in the South Pacific* (Boulder, CO: Westview, 2001), 161.

SERMON 2: BELIEVE BECAUSE HIS WORD IS TRUE

TEXT: John 14:1–4
MIT: So that they might have untroubled hearts, Jesus commanded his disciples to believe in him because he is faithful to his word.
MIM: To have untroubled hearts, people today should trust Christ because his word is true.

Introduction

The cost of a troubled heart is amazing. Anxiety is expensive in more ways than one. A writer put it this way, "Anxiety is costly. It costs us in physical, emotional, and financial terms. However, it does not stop there. It also incurs huge financial burden for the society as a whole. Anxiety, worry, and stress disrupt relationships, family, and work. Evidently, if you have an issue with anxiety, you incur the cost of having distressed feelings. Anxiety feels awful. You don't have to be a scientist to know that."[7]

The author goes on to list costs to our health, relationships, productivity, and job performance. Anxiety has nothing good and a lot of bad. And yet, it can be common to us all. The Christian is no stranger to anxiety, although he should not be so prone to it. We live in a fallen world with both spiritual and physical enemies all around us. At times it feels like we are all alone. God addresses this in his Word.

On the eve of his departure Jesus had a message for his followers. His desire was that we thrive in Spirit until he returns. The first thing on his mind was that we should grasp the significance and the achievement of his departure. He wants our minds unclouded as we serve till he comes. So his first word is, "Let your heart not be troubled." Perhaps it would not be arrogance to paraphrase it "release your anxiety." The means of this untroubled heart is unfolded in the following chapter. It is twofold: to believe in Christ (14:1–14) and to love/obey him (14:15–31). Over the next few weeks we'll unpack the first of these means to the untroubled heart. Jesus asks us to believe in him. Here it is more than mere affirmation of Jesus. It is even more than coming to him in salvation, although it surely includes both. Here belief is aimed at his disciples. It must be a quiet disposition of trust in the person of Christ.

---

[7] Chistopher Jacoby, "Understanding the Real Cost of Anxiety." Cited 16 January 2014. Online: http://www.healthguidance.org/entry/13872/1/Understanding-the-Real-Cost-of-Anxiety.html.

"Let not your hearts be troubled. Believe in God; believe also in me" (John 14:1 ESV).[8]

In verses 2–14 he will give three reasons to believe in him. Today we will look at the first of these reasons to believe. We should trust Christ to have an untroubled heart because his word is true. So what does he promise?

Outline

I. He Promises Many Rooms (14:2)

"In my Father's house are many rooms. If it were not so, would I have told you that I go to prepare a place for you?" (ESV).

A. TEXT

1. "In my Father's house" indicates the heavenly sanctuary.

2. "Many rooms" indicates a place of intimacy with Christ for his own.

B. TODAY

The promise is powerful because of the implications for our present condition.

1. This world is not a permanent place.

2. Our time here is limited by an act of his grace.

C. ILLUSTRATION

Aubrey de Grey and Michael Rae suggest that aging can be eliminated through science in our lifetime. In their book *Ending Aging* they discuss the elimination of the culprit of aging, the eroding of the "telomere," the end of each DNA strand that shrinks a bit through each replication.[9] This degradation of the molecule causes the aging process and a host of other related health problems. As usual, science are racing ahead without thinking through the ethical issues and perhaps without trying to forecast the unforeseen circumstances. I think there are a host of issues to be solved before embracing such a "breakthrough."

---

[8] Rather than go into all the issues regarding the translation of "ὅτι" in verse 2 that we covered above with a congregation, I usually simply choose a version that is acceptable to me. In this case the ESV does rather nicely.

[9] Aubrey de Grey with Michael Rae, *Ending Aging: The Rejuvenation Breakthroughs That Could Reverse Human Aging in Our Lifetime* (New York: St. Martin's, 2007).

However, let's assume we work out all the wrinkles (pardon the pun) with such a treatment. It only ensures quality of health (to a degree) and not the quality or the permanence of life. All people will still die. To face our journey through the haunted woods we need to know he has a place prepared for us. He does that and more; he promises intimacy with him forever. He promises a room for us in the heavenly sanctuary that he has prepared through his death, resurrection, and ascension into heaven.

II. He Promises a Personal Retrieval (14:3)

"And if I go and prepare a place for you, I will come again and will take you to myself, that where I am you may be also" (ESV).

A. TEXT

1. Retrieval refers to the second coming.

2. It is the purpose of the going away.

B. TODAY

The promise is powerful because . . .

1. It describes the completion of this dysfunctional fallen world.

2. It clearly establishes our resurrection and participation in his majestic return.

C. ILLUSTRATION

It was known as "Operation Gothic Serpent." You might remember it from the 2001 movie *Black Hawk Down*. Michael Durant was the pilot of a Black Hawk helicopter that crashed during the Battle of Mogadishu on October 3, 1993. Its occupants were part of the elite Night Stalkers. In the immediate aftermath of the crash, two Delta Force Snipers who jumped into the site and the helicopter's crew of Bill Cleveland, Ray Frank, and Tommy Field were killed. Durant survived but badly injured his back and had a broken leg. The Somalis broke his nose and paraded the injured pilot through the streets of Mogadishu and held him captive for eleven days with only rudimentary medical assistance. "Ranger, you die Somalia!" was repeatedly screamed at him in the early days. Durant was soon a political pawn, and an obligatory video was made to show he was alive. On the fifth day Durant heard helicopters but figured they were only "signature flights" designed to keep the fleeing warlord jumpy. He soon heard the heavy metal band AC/DC thumping the Somali air with the song "Hell's Bells." And then something marvelous . . . in Durant's own words: "The sound of the rotors grew louder again as the helo made a close pass, and then I heard the voice of some warrior angel, calling out to me from that speaker, so loud and clear. 'Mike Durant . . . Mike Durant . . .' Oh Lord in Heaven, I couldn't believe it. My heart started to pound and the tears just sprang from my eyes. 'Mike Durant . . . Mike Durant . . .' It was Dan's voice. I'd know it anywhere. My good friend Dan Jollota was up there, calling out to me, searching desperately for me. He knew that he was flying above a hornet's nest of RPGs and could get himself shot down at any second, but he just didn't [care]. 'Mike Durant . . . we will not leave without you!' I swallowed hard, my streaming eyes following the sweet drone of that helo's rotors, my ears every syllable of Dan's oath. *I know you won't, Dan.* I tried to reach out to him by telepathy. *I know you won't!* The broadcast and the Blackhawk faded away. I listened hard for a good long minute, but they were gone. Yet I knew they'd be back. They wouldn't give up. Soon enough, they would find me. Soon enough, it would all be over."[10]

Jesus' promise at John 14:2 is like Dan Jollota and the Night Stalkers' loud-speaker message. It is not just a message of hope but a promise to be fulfilled. The Lord Jesus calls to his soldiers, often wounded, some severely so, "I am coming back to receive you unto myself."

III. He Is Confident of a Clear Pathway (14:4)

A. TEXT

"And you know the way to where I am going" (ESV). Jesus is confident they know the way because . . .

1. He is the way, and they know him.

2. He has cleansed them already.

---

[10] Michael J. Durant with Steven Hartov, *In the Company of Heroes* (New York: New American Library, 2003).

B. TODAY

The clear pathway for people today is Jesus Christ.

1. Salvation comes in believing in Jesus.

2. Safekeeping comes in believing in Jesus.

3. Security comes in believing in Jesus.

Conclusion

Belief in Christ begins with acknowledging the facts about him given in the Bible. But that's not the end. Then, we believe to be born-again. That is, we must turn from our sin and make him the Lord of our lives. Finally, we place our trust in what he did on the cross to cover our sin. After that, every day we quietly and confidently trust his providence in our lives. You are somewhere on that continuum today. Christ calls you to progress to that quiet trust. You can begin now.

Sermon 3: Jesus, GPS, and You

TEXT: John 14:5–7
MIT: Jesus is the only way to the Father.
MIM: You ought to believe on Christ because he is the only way to the Father.

Introduction

Map errors have been the bane of travelers since the time of the first map. Today, something fascinating is occurring. We are fast becoming so utterly dependent on GPS devices that we believe them more than our own good sense. The fact of the matter is that who or what directs your path is incredibly important. A flawed guide will not direct you as you expect and may not get you to the destination you anticipate. It matters whom you trust. It matters even more to whom you trust your soul.

Our text today is the second reason one should believe in Jesus. In response to Jesus announcing his departure and his confidence that his own know the way he is going, Thomas declares, "Lord, . . . we don't know where You're going. How can we know the way?" (John 14:5 HCSB). Jesus' response is that he is the only way to the Father. This is perhaps the most important thing you will ever hear. You ought to believe on Christ because he is the *only* way to the Father.

Outline

I. The Lord's Claim Is Comprehensive (14:6)

"I am the way, the truth, and the life."

A. TEXT

1. He is the way.
2. He is the truth.
3. He is the life.

B. TODAY

Humans were created for fellowship with God. The height of satisfaction comes from knowing him. Therefore since Jesus Christ is the way, the truth, and the life . . .

1. Christ should be the object of our study.
2. Christ should be the object of our passions.
3. Christ should be the object of our communication.

II. The Lord's Claim Is Exclusive (14:6)

A. TEXT

B. "No one comes to the Father except through Me."

1. It does not allow for many paths.
2. It does not allow for unintentionally being on the path.

C. TODAY

The implications are critically important.

1. Hopes that you may find eternal life apart from faith in Christ are unfounded.
2. Hope that the people of the world will live eternally apart from faith in Christ is unfounded.
3. Just getting off the wrong path does not ensure salvation.

D. ILLUSTRATION

On June 30, 2012, 150 members of the Mormon Church ("Latter Day Saints" or LDS), met in Salt Lake City, UT, to resign from the church. It is not an easy process. One does not officially leave the church until you submit resignation papers to the church offices. They each had different reasons for leaving, but the one underlying reason was that they no longer believed it to be the true church.[11]

I applaud the decision. I am sure the LDS church—which is not a Christian church—is long on promises and short on truth. But I do have some concerns for these dissidents and others like them. The sometimes oppressive nature of Mormonism has left some of these ex-Mormons gun shy regarding any traditional form of religion, preferring no religion to anything else. That means that their experience in a cult has cut them off from the truth.

---

[11] Jennifer Dobner, "Mormon Group Plans Mass Weekend Resignation from Church." Accessed 29 June 2012. Online: http://www.reuters.com/article/2012/06/29/us-usa-mormons-utah-idUSBRE85S12I20120629.

Yes, it is good that they left the LDS church. Salvation, however, does not occur by leaving a false religion. Nor does it occur when we avoid taking part in a false religion. It occurs when we turn from our sins, make Jesus the Lord of our lives, and trust that what he accomplished on the cross covers our sins. He is the way, the truth, and the life.

III. The Disciple's Certainty (14:7)

"If you know Me, you will also know My Father. From now on you do know Him and have seen Him" (HCSB).

A. TEXT

1. Christ promises intimacy with God.[12] (To know Christ is to know the Father.)
2. Christ is confident of the disciples' relationship to the Father.
   a. They had seen the Father without realizing it.
   b. "From now" is really "certainly" (ἀπάρτι).

B. TODAY

The implications for us today are . . .

1. The way is extraordinarily simple. You simply need to know Jesus.
2. You need no intermediary between you and God. You simply need to know Jesus.

Conclusion

On March 31, 2008, Michael Monsoor posthumously received the Congressional Medal of Honor for his heroic actions at Ramadi, Iraq, on September 29, 2008. Michael and his Navy SEAL team were providing overwatch protection for joint forces. All day long the position was taking some fire, even a rocket-propelled grenade. The Navy SEALs continue the report:

> A couple of hours later, an insurgency fighter closed on the overwatch position and threw a fragment grenade into the overwatch po-

---

[12] In this sermon I will develop the themes of intimacy and confidence (knowledge and certainty). The next passage develops the mutuality of the Father and the Son, so I would only mention it here.

sition which hit Monsoor in the chest before falling in front of him. Monsoor yelled, "Grenade!" and dropped on top of the grenade prior to it exploding. Monsoor's body shielded the others from the brunt of the fragmentation blast and two other SEALs were only wounded by the remaining blast."[13]

What is even more amazing about Monsoor's action was that he was standing at the only exit. The only person who could have safely left the room was Monsoor. Instead, he fell on the grenade.

In fact, the other soldiers noted that Monsoor never looked any where but the grenade. His only move was to jump on the live grenade.

As Kristen Scharnberg of the *Chicago Tribune* summarized in tribute, "The men who were there that day say they could see the options flicker across Michael Monsoor's face: save himself or save the men he had long considered brothers. He chose them."[14]

Something similar but far greater happened on that Friday afternoon in Jerusalem. In an act of complete selflessness Christ took the brunt of our sin. But beyond the scope of Christ's sacrifice, I want you to see the key difference—the "grenade," if you will, before Christ was thrown by us, not the enemy. He died to take our sins away. It is offensive to propose that his is one way among many. It is foolishness to reject it for your own way to God.

---

[13] "Michael Monsoor." Cited 16 January 2014. Online: http://navyseals.com/ns-overview/notable-seals/michael-a-monsoor.
[14] Ibid.

Sermon 4: Seeing God

TEXT: John 14:8–14
MIT: Christ declared that people should believe on him because of his unique relationship to the Father.
MIM: Today we should believe on Jesus because of his unique relationship to the Father.

Introduction

In Jesus' last formal lesson before his disciples, he teaches them about the thing most near to his heart at the moment: how to enjoy his presence, in spite of his absence. This is the essence of thriving spiritually between his going away and coming again. First, he tells us at 14:1 not to have a troubled heart at his departure. Instead he will reveal the "secret" of the untroubled heart. It is to believe in him (14:1–14) and to love/obey him (14:15–25). We have been exploring the concept of believing in him at 14:1–14. We saw that we should believe in him because of his own veracity (14:2–4), because he is the only way to God (14:5–7). Today we will see that we should believe in him because of his unique relationship to the Father at 14:8–14.

The topic is introduced at 14:8 by Philip, who asks Jesus to "show us the Father" (HCSB). This question is at once touching and startling. It is touching because there is no greater desire than to be in the presence of God. It is startling in that Philip asks for a very dangerous thing, for no man can see God and live.

As we listen in to the conversation between Philip and our Lord, I want you to ask yourself a question. "Am I missing that greatest of all desires—to see God—by failure to believe in Jesus?"

Outline

I. The Desire of the Ages: The Longing to See God (14:8–9c)

"Lord," said Philip, "show us the Father, and that's enough for us." Jesus said to him, "Have I been among you all this time without your knowing Me, Philip?" (HCSB).

A. TEXT

   1. Philip's Ambition

The desire to see God is a person's highest ambition.

a. The blessing of the righteous is that they will see God.

"The pure in heart are blessed, for they will see God" (Matt 5:8 HCSB).

b. It was the confidence of Job.

"Even after my skin has been destroyed, yet I will see God in my flesh. I will see Him myself; my eyes will look at Him, and not as a stranger. My heart longs within me" (Job 19:26–27 HCSB).

c. It is noble.

He is not hiding from God like Adam and Eve in the garden. In Philip's case there may very well be a sense of self-indulgence with the request.

2. Philip's Audacity

a. It ignores (or rebukes) Jesus' previous statement.

b. No man can see God and live.

i. A desire to be like Moses? (cf. Exodus 34).

ii. Expecting a special dispensation from God?

3. Philip's Exposure

a. At 14:9 we expect a rebuke from Jesus.

b. Jesus' statement is not a rebuke but a revelation.

It is best understood as "after all these years, you still do not know me."

c. In other words, in Philip's desire to see God he missed perceiving God.

B. ILLUSTRATION

Philip reminds me of a teenager named Icarus. In Greek mythology Daedalus was a first-class engineer. He built the labyrinth at Knossos to enable King Minos of Crete to both subdue the fabled Minotaur and to use it as a weapon for his enemies. As the tale goes, Daedalus fell into disfavor with King Minos and was imprisoned with his son, Icarus. The engineer, however, would not simply waste away, waiting for death. Instead, he planned an escape. He made a pair of wings for himself and his son from feathers and wax.

Daedalus, like a good father, tried his wings first and found them to work. He and his son then made their escape in the skies. However, Daedalus warned his son not to fly either too close to the sea or too near the sun. The sea would wet the feathers and wax, and he would fall into the sea. If he flew too high, the heat from the sun would melt the wax, and the wings would crumble. It both cases Icarus would die if he did not heed his father's warning. Well, you know the story. In his youthful giddiness, Icarus could not restrain himself. He looped too close to the sun and then fell to his death when the wings fell apart. Today, in the Aegean Sea there is an area of water known as the Icarian Sea, near the island of Icaria, both named for the mythic tragedy.

Like Icarus, Philip, in his exuberant desire to see God, misses the very thing that he desired without knowing that he had it all along. Jesus will ask Philip to attain that which he desires, by believing in him because of his unique relationship to the Father.

C. TODAY: A Form of Religion

Philip's problem is that he did not recognize Jesus' union with the Father. Shockingly, then, he's practicing religion without its power. It's far too common today.

1. We desire to do good things but seldom do lasting good.

2. We turn a relationship with God into something for personal gain.

3. We have a form of religion while not knowing the power of it.

   It's time to be done with all that. Jesus' words to Philip are the cure. We must believe.

II. Belief in Christ: The Way to See God (14:9d–10)

A. TEXT

"The one who has seen Me has seen the Father. How can you say, 'Show us the Father'? Don't you believe that I am in the Father and the Father is in Me? The words I speak to you I do not speak on My own. The Father who lives in Me does His works" (HCSB).

Belief in Christ shows we will see God because seeing Jesus is actually seeing the Father.

1. Jesus identifies himself with the Father.

It is a reciprocal (mutual) identification.

2. Jesus commands belief in him (v. 10).

3. The words of Jesus are the Father's works.

The words are the work of the Father who dwells in Christ.

B. TODAY

1. Authentic faith in Jesus identifies him with the Father.
2. Authentic faith in Jesus takes him at his word.

C. ILLUSTRATION

I recently read an accident analysis by the Air Safety Institute. I paraphrase the report: On July 30, 2006, a brand-new Legend Cub airplane had to ditch into Lake Michigan after losing engine power during cruise flight. Two hours into the flight the fuel gauges were showing that the tanks were nearing empty (surprisingly). The pilot argued with his more credentialed copilot that since the instruments were showing a consistent 5.8 gallons per hour the fuel gauges were wrong. Thus, the pilot chose to believe the secondary instruments over the clear reading on the fuel gauges. Sure enough the plane had to ditch into Lake Michigan four minutes later. Because the pilot could not swim he drowned that day. Later investigation showed that the exterior fuel cap was missing. The fuel had siphoned out in flight. The pilot died because he misplaced his trust. He trusted his interpretation of rate of fuel burn rather than the gauges (which were chosen by the manufacturer for their simplicity and reliability).[15] People, every day, make a far worse decision. Some choose to continue in unbelief. Some choose to believe a Jesus after their own making. Some choose to believe the truth about Jesus' person but deny how one comes to salvation. All of these are to misplace trust in secondary interpretations. Go directly to the horse's mouth, if you will: Believe what Jesus said about himself.

D. Belief in Christ: The Way to Glorify God (14:11–14)

"Believe Me that I am in the Father and the Father is in Me. Otherwise, believe because of the works themselves. I assure you: The one who believes in Me will also do the works that I do. And he will do even greater works than these, because I am going to the Father. Whatever you ask in My name, I will do it so that the Father may be glorified in the Son. If you ask Me anything in My name, I will do it" (HCSB).

E. TEXT

1. Believe that Jesus is One with the Father.

    a. Believe because of Jesus' veracity.

    b. Believe because of Jesus' works.

    c. Both point to his messiahship.

2. Believers will do greater works.

    a. Greater works are not more miraculous works.

    b. Greater works are not more numerous works.

    c. Greater works are the works associated with the new covenant.

3. Believers will enjoy effective prayer.

    a. What the promise is not:

        i. The promise is not a promise of a limitless genie.

---

[15] See http://www.aopa.org/asf/epilot_acc/chi06fa224.html.

ii. It is not for personal gain.

The promise assumes many of the caveats elsewhere in Scripture.

b. The promise is the means to glorify the Father.

F. ILLUSTRATION

The website is www.getoutofhellfree.com. They sell a business-card-sized document that states "Last Chance. Get out of Hell Free: the Card. Your salvation courtesy of www.thisistrue.com. This Card may be kept until needed or sold." It features a cartoon of a mustached man drawn in the style of the famous *Monopoly* character. The mustached man is jumping over a small fire pit. The card was made after a reader concluded the owner of the company was going to hell. The reader drew the conclusion that the owner was obviously not a Christian because he wrote a very short article about the Chinese art of feng shui. The owner concluded that if he could be sent to hell by a snap of the mind, he could get people out. Thus the card was born. The card is not designed as a witnessing tool; it is more of a satire from what I can tell (after all the company calls itself GOOHF). The company's motto is "Sin all you want, we'll print more." Hopefully, no one takes the card seriously and trusts it for salvation. But quite a number of people take their conversion to Christ exactly in that way. They claim to be believers but sin all they want because they joined the church, or were baptized, or they think that because their family is comprised of believers they have a "get out of hell free" card that covers it all. On the other hand, there are quite a number of believers who don't seem to get it that their salvation prepares them for works related to salvation. Instead they treat their salvation as if it were their own GOOHF card and don't lift a single finger to change the world. This is not what our Lord describes as greater works.

G. TODAY

1. Jesus expects his followers to do the greater works.

a. Witnessing

    b. Mission trips

    c. Social ministry

 2. Jesus expects his followers to be effective "pray-ers."

    Much of the reason we are not is that we treat salvation as if it were all for us and not to glorify the Father.

Conclusion

Adam walked with God in the cool of the day, but since the fall of humanity, we have not had the same kind of privilege. Humanity is fallen and therefore distant. We hear his voice with difficulty and never see him in the same way. In fact, the fall is so devastating that if we could see God in all his glory, we would die for "no one can see Me and live" (Exod 33:20 HCSB). Yet in Christ, this horrid state of affairs is reversed. When we have seen Jesus, we have seen the Father. Because of his identity with the Father, the results of the fall can be mitigated and ultimately reversed. In Christ, we may see God. Believe in him, for he is God.

Sermon 5: Finding Peace

TEXT: John 14:15–27

MIT: The Paraclete mediates the presence of Christ and produces peace in the hearts of those who love him (expressed in obedience).

MIM: Lovingly obedient believers can expect to experience the presence of God and the peace that passes understanding.

Introduction

So how much is a nickel worth? During the Great Depression, Texas coin dealer B. Max Mehl spent millions of dollars in advertising his *Star Rare Coin Encyclopedia* that listed prices he paid for coins. Mehl offered fifty dollars for the rare 1913 Liberty Head Nickel; only five are known to exist, according to a well-known coin grading service.[16] The 1913, as it came to be known, set off a treasure hunt in the United States. Everyone was looking for the 1913. Streetcar conductors would snarl up traffic while they rifled through their incoming change, looking for the 1913. It represented a virtually free source of wealth. By the way, the last 1913 Liberty Head Nickel went for $3 million.

Today I want to inspire you to hunt for another treasure. This treasure does not really have monetary value, because it can't be bought with money. However, everyone can get it. That being said, it is still quite rare in history and in today's world. The treasure that I am referring to is peace, not world peace or even neighborhood peace. It is not even peace of mind. It's the peace of God. In our text today the Christ calls it "My Peace."

In the Farewell Discourse, Jesus has told us not to have a troubled heart. The first part of not being troubled is faith in him. At John 14:15 he picks up the second step; it comes from the Holy Spirit whom Christ calls the Paraclete. The Paraclete mediates the presence of Christ and produces peace in the heart of those who love him (expressed in obedience). Today I want you to find this priceless treasure. It is the lovingly obedient believer who can expect to experience the presence of God and the peace that passes understanding.

---

[16] See http://www.pcgs.com/News/Pedigree-Of-Five-Known-1913-Liberty-Nickels.

Outline

I. Love and Obedience (14:15–20)

"If you love Me, you will keep My commands. And I will ask the Father, and He will give you another Counselor to be with you forever. He is the Spirit of truth. The world is unable to receive Him because it doesn't see Him or know Him. But you do know Him, because He remains with you and will be in you. I will not leave you as orphans; I am coming to you. In a little while the world will see Me no longer, but you will see Me. Because I live, you will live too. In that day you will know that I am in My Father, you are in Me, and I am in you" (HCSB).

A. TEXT

1. Love and obedience are an expression of a commitment to faithfully follow Christ.

   a. The language of love and obey is covenantal language.

   b. It is closely related to faithfulness.

2. The result is the indwelling of the Spirit.

   a. His presence in Christ's absence.

   b. He is available after the resurrection.

   c. He will produce confidence in the disciples.

B. TODAY

1. Being in the new covenant is not simply believing.

   a. It is a commitment to love him.

   b. Love is defined in terms of a heartfelt obedience.

C. ILLUSTRATION

For years evangelical preachers and teachers have been great moralists. We cry out for obedience. We lift up self-discipline and self-denial. I find this similar to the OT Law. It commanded obedience but did not provide the power of obedience. Self-discipline, self-denial, and self-effort will only go so far. They are not the power of obedience. The power of obedience is love. The prophets recognized this when they denounced an outward obedience that is not generated by faith. When we love Christ, we want to obey him. When we love the Lord, his commands are not burdensome.

II. Presence (14:21–24)

"The one who has My commands and keeps them is the one who loves Me. And the one who loves Me will be loved by My Father. I also will love him and will reveal Myself to him." Judas (not Iscariot) said to Him, "Lord, how is it You're going to reveal Yourself to us and not to the world?" Jesus answered, "If anyone loves Me, he will keep My word. My Father will love him, and We will come to him and make Our home with him. The one who doesn't love Me will not keep My words. The word that you hear is not Mine but is from the Father who sent Me" (HCSB).

A. TEXT

1. The Paraclete mediates the presence of God and Christ to those who love him.

2. Jesus will not manifest himself to the world because the world is not in a covenant relationship with him.

B. TODAY

The implication is that there are three degrees of the presence of Christ in our lives.

1. There is growing in his presence.

   We love him, expressed in obedience. Those who are closest to Christ are the ones who love him in every aspect of life.

2. There is the stagnant Christian.

   We confess love for him, but the truth is that we have let either distraction, pleasure, or convenience choke out our obedience. Our confession of love falls on deaf ears.

3. There are those who don't love or know him.

   It is no wonder that the world struggles to perceive God. Why would he manifest himself to those who refuse to submit in love?

C. ILLUSTRATION

D. G. Fahrenheit invented the alcohol thermometer in 1709 and the now-common mercury thermometer in 1714. Our common "Fahrenheit scale" is essentially the one he made in 1724. Before that time we had what were known as thermoscopes. These could show the increase or decrease of temperature but had no scale to measure it. Can you imagine chemists and other scientists attempting to discuss temperature without a scale or with individual/conflicting scales? It would be Fahrenheit vs. Celsius multiplied! Christians today often measure their love for Christ by their own individual scales: giving, sacrifice, witnessing, teaching, etc. But there is really only one scale to judge your love for Christ: your obedience. Furthermore, there is a one-to-one correspondence between your loving obedience and the experiential presence of God in your life.

III. The Results of the Spirit's Indwelling (14:25–27)

"I have spoken these things to you while I remain with you. But the Counselor, the Holy Spirit—the Father will send Him in My name—will teach you all things and remind you of everything I have told you. Peace I leave with you. My peace I give to you. I do not give to you as the world gives. Your heart must not be troubled or fearful" (HCSB).

A. TEXT

1. The Spirit had a reminding ministry among the disciples.

2. The grand result is peace.

   a. It is a cumulative process.

      i. Belief

      ii. Love/obedience

         (a) Peace is a product of the Holy Spirit.

            (1) It is not an absence of war.

            (2) His peace transcends the earthly realm.

B. TODAY

1. The Spirit has an illuminating ministry among us today.

2. The "peace that passes understanding" is for those who believe in and love Christ.

Conclusion

Sometimes things are not as complicated as they seem. For example, those who accumulate great wealth are not always hyperactive day-traders with big budgets. Grace Groner and her twin sister were orphaned at the age of twelve. The Andersons took them in and educated them at Lake Forest College. Grace graduated Lake Forest and began working as a secretary at a pharmaceutical plant called Abbott Labs. In 1935 she bought $180.00 worth of stock and let it sit for the next forty-three years, always reinvesting her earnings. Through the years she amassed a fortune of more than seven million dollars by making one purchase. When she died she bequeathed it all to Lake Forest College. It was neither complicated nor difficult, but it paid off well.

Likewise, Christ asks you to make an investment. It is to believe in him and love him. It is not complicated. It can be difficult, but the payoff is immense. You receive the indwelling Spirit who will mediate the presence of Christ and bring peace to your heart. Accepting Christ as Lord is an investment well worth making.[17]

---

[17] Aixa Velez, "Secret Millionaire Gives Fortune to Alma Mater." Cited 16 January 2014. Online: http://www.msnbc.msn.com/id/35729174/ns/us_news-giving/t/secret-millionaire-gives-fortune-alma-mater/#.UM-B0KWQHi4.

Sermon 6: Perfect Love

Text: John 14:28–31
MIT: Jesus explained the nature of covenantal love for God.
MIM: Believers should follow Jesus' example of loving obedience.

Introduction

Americans watch a lot of football. The Nielson ratings are divided into three major sections: Prime Broadcast Network TV, Cable Network TV, and Syndication Network TV. One week during the winter shows a great deal about what Americans are watching. Of the top time Prime Broadcast TV positions, the NFL has three (number 4 on the list is a pre-kickoff show!). On cable TV football dominates the first three positions.

In syndication, football takes the top spot.[18] It tells a great deal about what America loves. America loves football! This was particularly telling when a lock-out loomed. The panic that you could hear in the voices of some fans was palpable. In contrast, in 2012–2013, the NHL nearly cancelled its hockey season and much of America yawned. All this is to say that what you love affects what you do and what you say.

Out text today deals with this phenomenon. The disciples' reaction to Jesus' departure reveals a great deal about them. Furthermore, it reveals a great deal about how we should orient our hearts and thoughts. Thus, in our text, Jesus explained the nature of covenantal love for God. As we investigate it we will learn that believers should follow Jesus' example of loving obedience.

Outline

I. Reject an Insufficient Love (14:28)

"You have heard Me tell you, 'I am going away and I am coming to you.' If you loved Me, you would have rejoiced that I am going to the Father, because the Father is greater than I" (HCSB).

A. TEXT

1. The disciples' self-absorbed sorrow

    a. They were sorrowful because he was leaving them.

---

[18] See http://www.nielsen.com/us/en/insights/top10s/television.html.

b. Their grief was for their loss, not Jesus' gain.

2. The sorrow exposes their hearts.

    a. Theirs, at the moment, was a self-absorbed love.

        i. They loved having Jesus with them.

        ii. They wanted the status quo to continue.

        iii. They did not listen to what he was telling them.

B. TODAY

This should cause us to examine why we do what we do, especially in the church. The fundamental fact is that while we may never totally solve the motivation issue, it matters.

1. Why do we serve?

    Do we serve because we love Christ or ourselves? Those who serve out of a sense of duty do not serve for the love of Christ. Perhaps it's guilt that drives us. Or perhaps it is a sense of, "this is what we've always done." If we serve so we won't feel guilty, we are serving because we love ourselves more than Christ. We should serve because we love Christ.

2. Why do we give?

    Do we give to get something from God? The false doctrine that floats around in the health and prosperity circles is that if we give "seed money" God will bless us (usually increase our wealth). This is horrendous. This is self-centered, wealth-obsessed idolatry.

    Some of us give so that we might control the church. If we pay we have say. This, too, is idolatry but of another kind. It is the love of power. The desire to be in control can exist for a number of reasons. Few of them are for the love of Christ.

3. Why do we go?

    Evangelism and mission trips are a great necessity in the church. They are the essence of obedience to Christ. However, some of us go for all the wrong reasons. We go, essentially, for a love of self. We go for a "free" vacation overseas. We go to try and atone for sin, to get right with God through witnessing at home or abroad. Or we might go from a sense of duty or guilt. None of these reasons honor Christ, and they are all about us.

C. ILLUSTRATION

In 2010, I went to Uganda with my then sixteen-year-old son. I taught two classes at the Uganda Baptist Seminary in Jinja, Uganda. It was my second trip to Uganda, and I was very excited about exposing my son to foreign missions. The one thing that caused me trepidation was that two weeks before we landed at Entebbe, militant Islamic terrorists bombed a popular night spot in Kampala. I was going no matter what, but I feared taking my son. I made a few phone calls and decided that, from what we could tell, the bombing was an isolated incident. We had a wonderful trip.

During my teaching with the seminary students, we always stopped to have tea at about 10:00 a.m. It was during one of the tea times that the students expressed their appreciation that I had come to Uganda. Then they added, "We did not expect you to come." "Why?" I asked. "Was it the Kampala bombing?" "Yes," they said with a shaking of their heads. "Have others cancelled their trips?" I asked. "Yes, many." I can't tell you how sad that made me. I'm sure some had legitimate reasons. But most, I am sure, decided the risk was too great. When we ask primarily, "Is it safe?" over "Does God want me to go?" we show that we love our own lives more than Christ.

II. Perfect Love (14:29–31)

"I have told you now before it happens so that when it does happen you may believe. I will not talk with you much longer, because the ruler of the world is coming. He has no power over Me. On the contrary, I am going away so that the world may know that I love the Father. Just as the Father commanded Me, so I do. 'Get up; let's leave this place'" (HCSB).

A. TEXT

Jesus' actions are in direct contrast to the disciples' actions. They love themselves; he loves the Father and expresses it through obedience.

1. Jesus' life is not taken from him; he gives it.
2. It is the demonstration of his love for the Father.
3. He tells the disciples so that they will believe.

B. TODAY

1. We should love Christ more than our own lives.

    This is a constant struggle among believers. God has given us a sense of self-preservation for a good reason: we should choose life. Dead men and women can't serve God on earth. But self-preservation cannot be our highest priority; obeying Christ should be. The good news is that it is rare that God calls on us to give up our lives. But our first question on deciding whether or not we go somewhere should not be "is it safe?" but "is it God's will?" Let us make Revelation 12:11 (HCSB) our highest prayer: "They conquered him by the blood of the Lamb and by the word of their testimony, for they did not love their lives in the face of death."

2. We should demonstrate our love in obedience.

    While it is rare that God calls on his children to be martyrs, it is not rare that he calls on us to be obedient. It is our obedience that will demonstrate our love. Serving should be for the love of Christ. Giving should be for love of Christ. Going should be for the love of Christ. In fact, when we love the Lord, obedience doesn't seem difficult at all.

Conclusion

The Lord is not like us at all. But Jesus illustrates to us both the power for obedience and the greatest expression of obedience. It is love. For us, love for the Lord supplies the ability to obey. It is not burdensome. His yoke is light to those who love him.

Obedience is also the greatest expression of love that we may have for the Lord. Do you want to say significantly to the Lord, "I love you"? Then find what he desires and do it as an expression of worship. Through this first chapter of the farewell Jesus declares his departure, but he also promises his presence to those who believe, that is love/obey through the Holy Spirit. Thus, we can walk with God in his very presence. The grand result is a peace the world cannot provide. As Christians we must embrace it. As an unbeliever you must receive it.

Sermon 7: The Secret of the Vine

TEXT: John 15:1–11
MIT: Jesus commanded his followers to abide in him.
MIM: Believers should abide in Christ.

Introduction

My wife and I bought almost six acres of land in rural Johnston County in North Carolina. It is the culmination of a great desire of ours to get back to being "country folk." We were both raised outside of the great urban areas of the world. On our property we have a great many giant poplar trees. Unfortunately, they have been overrun by giant honeysuckle vines. These vines have so engulfed these trees that they can hardly be seen. While we enjoy the smell of honeysuckle in the spring, these vines have to go.

It would seem a daunting task to remove vines thirty to forty feet up a tree. But I know the truth of the vine. It all grows from one stalk at the base of the tree. When you cut that stalk the branches of the vine die. It's a simple rule of agriculture that is the controlling metaphor of our text today. The branch must be connected to the vine, or it doesn't live.

In John 15:1–11 Jesus will command his disciples to abide in him. It is the single most important thing that a follower of Christ can do. Today we will hear our Lord describe our vital connection with him. He calls it "abiding." Our overall obsession should be abiding in Christ.

Outline

I. Hear a Well-Known Analogy (15:1–2)

"I am the true vine, and My Father is the vineyard keeper. Every branch in Me that does not produce fruit He removes, and He prunes every branch that produces fruit so that it will produce more fruit" (HCSB).

A. TEXT

    1. The allegory

        a. Isaiah 5.

b. The story of the vine in Isaiah is a narrative of disobedience, judgment, and eschatological redemption (Isaiah 27).

 2. The activity of the vinedresser

  a. He removes unfruitful branches.

  b. He prunes fruitful branches.

B. TODAY

 1. The Father's activity is not always pleasant.

 If a grapevine could feel, I'm sure pruning is not fun. The Father's pruning in our lives takes several forms. First, we must learn self-denial. Once we learn to deny bad things, we must move on to denying ourselves good things in favor of the best. Second, prayer is often learned in the crucible of need. Learning the Father is faithful only occurs when we need his intervention. Third, sanctification is learned when we fail and are disciplined by the Lord.

 2. The Father's activity is always necessary.

 The Lord never prunes haphazardly. He never accidentally bruises. He always does what he must to foster our growth. This would include times of distance.

 3. Fruit is dependent on the Father.

 Fruit is what the Father produces in us. It is not a matter of our trying. It is a matter of the believer in Christ abiding in him. You don't see an apple tree trying to pop out apples; it naturally does it when in the right conditions. Your right condition for producing fruit is abiding in Christ.

C. ILLUSTRATION

 Deism arose in the seventeenth and eighteenth centuries. It finds its roots in Enlightenment thinking that tends to reject revelation in favor of reason. Today, there are quite a number of deists—those who hold to deistic thought but call themselves something else (like humanist or secularist). The main tenets of deism are hard to define for every deist was somewhat a religion unto himself. However, one thought did permeate. Yes, there is a Creator, but he set up natural laws and chooses not to intervene in the world. One writer put it this way, "God is thus conceived to be wholly transcendent and never immanent."[19] In deism, God is disinterested in assisting you, although he wants you to be moral. In Christ, we see something else; we see that God not only plants the vine, he continually assists until the day comes. As the children sing, "God's still working on me." I am glad that our heavenly Father is not a clock maker who has wound up the world but the farmer who tends his crop.

II. Understand the Explanation and Application of the Analogy (15:3–10)

A. TEXT

1. The power of abiding (vv. 3–4)

"You are already clean because of the word I have spoken to you. Remain in Me, and I in you. Just as a branch is unable to produce fruit by itself unless it remains on the vine, so neither can you unless you remain in Me" (HCSB).

2. The grounds for abiding (vv. 5–8)

"I am the vine; you are the branches. The one who remains in Me and I in him produces much fruit, because you can do nothing without Me. If anyone does not remain in Me, he is thrown aside like a branch and he withers. They gather them, throw them into the fire, and they are burned. If you remain in Me and My words remain in you, ask whatever you want and it will be done for you. My Father is glorified by this: that you produce much fruit and prove to be My disciples" (HCSB).

3. Abiding defined (vv. 9–10)

"As the Father has loved Me, I have also loved you. Remain in My love. If you keep My commands you will remain in My

---

[19] Richard Comstock Lewis, *A Deist's Love of God and His Natural World: From Cosmic Dust and Solar Gases to Homo Sapiens Sapiens* (np: Xlibris, 2010), 12.

love, just as I have kept My Father's commands and remain in His love" (HCSB).

B. TODAY

1. When we fail to love Christ we forfeit fruit.

   Some of the saddest words are "what could have been." When we fail to abide in Christ we pull ourselves out of fruitful conditions and into the condition of discipline. It is not a smart move at all, but we are "prone to wander."

2. When we bear no fruit, we have reason to doubt.

   Jesus said, "You'll recognize them by their fruit. Are grapes gathered from thornbushes or figs from thistles?" (Matt 7:16 HCSB). The point is the presence or absence of fruit. When professing Christians bear no fruit whatsoever, they have reason to doubt whatever they are calling their experience of salvation.

3. When we sin, we do so because we love ourselves over Christ.

   When we sin we do so because of self-idolatry. We love our convenience more than we love Christ. We love our pleasure more than we love Christ. We love our own self-esteem rather than Christ. Whatever it is in us that led to the sin, it is there because we love ourselves first. This reality is one of the most convicting things about sin.

C. ILLUSTRATION

Wayne Grudem's *Systematic Theology* is a fabulous summation of Christian thought. I suggest you to spend time reading it or the abridged version. However, I found his chapter on sanctification (growing in obedience) interesting. He rightly notes the active role of God in our sanctification and our passive participation in his work (i.e., we get out of the way!). He rightly emphasizes that we should also be active in our sanctification. "The New Testament does not suggest any short-cuts by which we can grow in sanctification, but simply encourages us repeatedly to give ourselves to the old fashioned, time-honored means of Bible reading and mediation . . . prayer . . . worship . . . witnessing . . . Christian fellowship . . . and self-discipline or self-control."[20] Here's my quibble: the power for doing all these things is listed as only one of many things in a section titled "Motives for Obedience." Love for Christ is not one of many motivations. It is the motivation. It is the power for consistency. It is the power for achieving ever-increasing holiness. Without love for Christ, we will fail miserably even if we manage by self-effort to do all the right things.

III. Acquire the Effects of the Analogy (15:11)

"I have spoken these things to you so that My joy may be in you and your joy may be complete" (HCSB).

A. TEXT

1. Christ's joy

2. Maximized joy

B. TODAY

1. Nothing is more joyful than loving Christ.

2. There is no end to the supply of joy.

C. ILLUSTRATION

Let me remind you of the story of Elijah the Tishbite and the widow of Zarephath (1 Kgs 17:10–24). God sends a drought on the land for Israel's disobedience and Elijah must hide in the wilderness. Eventually he is sent to a widow and her son who are starving. They have a little flour and a little oil. She plans to make a couple of "biscuits" for her son and then die. Instead, Elijah makes her a promise, "The flour jar will not become empty and the oil jug will not run dry until the day the LORD sends rain on the surface of the land" (1 Kgs 17:14 HCSB). For her obedience the widow of Zarephath received an endless supply of food. The Christian gets something much better. The result of obedience in the Christian's life is an endless supply of joy.

---

[20] Wayne Grudem, *Systematic Theology: An Introduction to Biblical Theology* (Grand Rapids: Zondervan, 1994), 755.

Conclusion

On October 8, 1984, *Sports Illustrated* published a story on George Foreman on the tenth anniversary of his epic boxing match with Mohammed Ali. The two men met at Ali's mansion in Los Angeles. According to the article, Foreman had come to Los Angeles to receive an award and he felt compelled to see Ali.

They embraced warmly and sat down to talk. Faith quickly became the subject. Ali and Foreman began grading jabs of another kind. Soon Ali suggested Foreman should come visit his mosque in exchange for a promise to visit Foreman's church [where he was pastor].

"I don't want you to come to my church. I want you to join God first. Tell me you love Jesus, Muhammad," Foreman challenged.

"I don't wanna know about Jeeezus. I wanna know about God," Ali answered.

"He's alive. He's not dead. He wants you," Foreman insisted. "Don't fight it."

"I've got peace. The translation of Islam's peace. Come pray with me. I pray five times a day, George."

"But no one answers you," Foreman said. "You've been knocking at the wrong door, champ. There's no one behind your door. Come knock on mine. My God answers me."

"Man, are you for real?" He soon replied. "I'm late, I gotta go." With that, Ali climbed into his car and waved goodbye to Foreman.[21]

Ever since I read that article as a sophomore at Ole Miss, Foreman's words have burned in my ears: "Tell me you love Jesus." Ali left that day without embracing Christ. What will you do? As a believer, orient your life around loving obedience; "Tell me you love Jesus." If you need to come to Christ, take your first steps in love; "Tell me you love Jesus." Abide in Christ and know the joy of the Lord.

---

[21] Adapted from Gary Smith, "After the Fall: Ten Years Ago This Month George Foreman and Muhammad Ali Met in the Ring in Zaïre. While Ali Won that War, It's Foreman Who Has Found Lasting Peace," *Sports Illustrated* (October 8, 1984): 64.

Sermon 8: The Friend of God

TEXT: John 15:12–17
MIT: Christ commanded brotherly love between disciples using his love for his disciples as the premier example.
MIM: Believers must love one another with Christ as their example.

Introduction

It is a bit axiomatic to say that a true friend is hard to find. The truth of the matter is that those who *are* true friends are the ones who *find* true friends. While everyone wants to be liked, and it is far more pleasant to have loved ones around you than a room full of strangers, the believer should not want to be known as a friend of the world. Instead, we should want to be known as the friends of Christ.

Our text today will help us with this concept. At John 15:12–17 Christ commanded brotherly love among disciples using his love for his disciples as the premier example. In this, he commands us to love one another and describes what it is to be the friend of God. Believers must love one another with Christ as their example.

Outline

I. The Friend of Christ Keeps the New Commandment (15:12–13)

"This is My command: Love one another as I have loved you. No one has greater love than this, that someone would lay down his life for his friends" (HCSB).

A. TEXT

1. The new commandment (v. 12)

2. The premier example of love (v. 13)

B. TODAY

What does Christlike brotherly love look like today? We have an inspired description in 1 Corinthians 13.

1. Love is . . . patient, kind, rejoices in the truth, is long suffering, trusting, hopeful, enduring.

2. Love does not practice . . . envy, boasting, conceit, inappropriate things, keeping grudges, or find joy in the hardships of others.

To our shame, Christians often fail to love one another.

3. The secret, however, is abiding in Christ.

Remember, we defined abiding as loving Christ. If we love Christ we will love what he loves. When we look at another believer, we should see them as another who loves Christ. If we love the same thing, how difficult is it to love one another? If you love what I love, how difficult is it for me to love you?

C. ILLUSTRATION

I have a daughter with autism. She's just reaching adult years now, and she's doing fine. As we look back over her early years, there are some people, quite frankly, that we have had to spend time seeking God's help to forgive them for how they've treated her. Kids can be cruel and school administrators can be nitwits. That's life with a disabled child. However, there are those precious individuals who have gone out of their way to love my daughter. Whether it is patience, hugs, gifts, ministry, or just being a friend, these dear people have a special place in my heart. Why? For a variety of reasons, but not the least of which is that they love the person I love. It ought to be the same between believers. If someone loves Christ, we ought to love them because we love Christ.

II. Being the Friend of Jesus (15:14–16)

"You are My friends if you do what I command you. I do not call you slaves anymore, because a slave doesn't know what his master is doing. I have called you friends, because I have made known to you everything I have heard from My Father. You did not choose Me, but I chose you. I appointed you that you should go out and produce fruit and that your fruit should remain, so that whatever you ask the Father in My name, He will give you" (HCSB).

A. TEXT

It was unusual to use the term "friend" in relationship to God in the OT. However, we do see two examples. Abraham is called the friend of God (2 Chr 20:7; Isa 41:8) and God speaks to Moses like a man speaks to his friend (Exod 33:11). Under the new covenant, however, there is a new kind of relationship. We may be his friends.

1. Christ describes his friends.

   a. The Lord's friends are obedient to him.

   b. The Lord's friends are his confidants.

   c. The Lord's friends are not his equals.

2. Christ describes the lives of his friends.

   a. He chose them (not just personal election but in a covenant relationship with Christ).

   b. He appointed them to go and bear lasting fruit.

   c. He gives them access in prayer.

B. ILLUSTRATION

You are probably familiar with Henry Stanley's famous line, "Dr. Livingston, I presume?" In the 1800s, missionary David Livingstone's reports from Africa were so captivating they were bestsellers in England. It is often mentioned that he went to Africa to explore the continent and to end slavery. In fact, he was known as "the Pathfinder." However, his first calling was to be a missionary. His first desire was to go to China. As providence would have it, he heard Dr. Robert Moffatt speak of Africa when Stanley attended a meeting at his boarding house at Aldersgate Street in England. He asked Dr. Moffatt if he should go to Africa. The response: "Yes, if you won't go to an old station, but push on to the vast unoccupied district to the north, where on a clear morning I have seen the smoke of a thousand villages and no missionary has ever been."[22]

David Livingstone's life in Africa was not easy. He broke fingers, endured attacks by beasts and men, suffered disease, and was separated from his wife and two children. Ultimately he buried Mary Livingstone, his spouse, in Africa. He brought much of the

---

[22] Thomas Hughes, *The Life of David Livingstone* (New York: A.L. Burt, 1902), 17.

advances of the West to Africa, but he was supremely pleased to preach the gospel where no Christian had ever been.

He traveled 29,000 miles in Africa, discovered Victoria Falls and four important lakes (Ngami, Nyassa, Moero, and Bangweola), besides several rivers, and added to the known portion of the world about a million square miles of territory. The world may remember him for this achievement, but it happened as a by-product of his service to get the gospel to the nations. He was opening the way for other missionaries.

The Pathfinder died on May 4, 1873. On his last day of life, he was sick and near death, kneeling at a crude cot in prayer. Three delegations had come to request his aid or to offer their help, but each time when they peeked into the hut, he was in this position, praying. At the end of the day they realized that he had died in prayer before God. His body was taken back to England, but his heart was buried in Africa. Indeed this was an appropriate symbol of life.[23] David Livingstone embodied what it is to be a friend of Christ.

C. TODAY

Who is it, then, who is the friend of Christ today?

1. Those who abide in Christ

   If we are friends through obedience, obedience happens when we love him (see John 14:15, 21). The one abiding has more disclosure about what the Lord is doing. We have it through revelation of his Word and through the revelation of his Spirit. It is not full disclosure, but it is often more than what is revealed to those who are not his confidants.

2. Those who are on mission with Christ

   He chose us to go and bear lasting fruit. That means that those who aren't going, those who aren't sharing, those who do not participate in mission are not fulfilling their mission.

3. Those who pray in the Lord's name

---

[23] This information is culled from several links at http://www.wholesomewords.org/biography/biorplivingstone.html.

Can you imagine a friend to whom you never speak? I have lost connection with close friends of my past, and it brings me great sadness. How can we call ourselves friends of Jesus and not pray often? Furthermore, we should be praying in his name. Only this is praying like Jesus, in his authority and likeness. It is praying God's will and not ours. It is praying God's list of wants and desires and not just ours.

Conclusion

We know of Herod the Great mostly from the Bible (especially the birth narratives). He is known as the vicious butcher of Bethlehem. He would probably like it that his name is remembered (even in infamy). He, however, probably would have liked to be remembered in another way. He did many major work projects. After all, the temple in Jerusalem was known as "Herod's Temple." Maybe he would have wanted to be known as a religious man. He also built one to Jupiter elsewhere in Palestine to curry favor with the Gentiles. So, maybe he would want to be known as a tolerant man. He had a man-made harbor installed at Caesarea. On his inscriptions he wrote "Friend of Rome." But even this was not really characteristic of his life. You see, he did all the things as a master politician. He wanted to stay in power. That meant please Rome, keep the masses happy if not skittish, and keep his enemies terrified. He was a friend of Herod and Herod alone. Let us not wear "friend of Christ" t-shirts merely for show or for religious expedience. Let us love him and each other in truth and deed as Christ loved us.

Sermon 9: The Hatred of the World

TEXT: John 15:18–16:4c
MIT: Jesus prepared the disciples for effective testimony in the midst of hostility.
MIM: Christians should be prepared for effective testimony to Christ in the midst of hostility.

Introduction

In Jesus' last speech to his disciples, he is concerned that they will spiritually thrive until he comes. In today's passage he will address an unpleasant dimension of this. He will address the persecution of believers.

We live in a fallen world. Nothing makes it more evident than looking at the kind of violence of which people are capable. We, as a species, are not only capable of grotesque individual violence; we are capable of practicing it in large scales. Some of us are content, rather glad, to eliminate whole races of people for the most trivial of reasons. Perhaps most disturbing is that some are willing to do so in the name of God. Surely this is a gross miscarriage of God's purpose in the world under the new covenant.

Throughout history, Christians have provided examples of both the persecutors and the persecuted. Many of those who lift the sword merely claim Christianity. Many of our evangelical brothers and sisters are bearing hostility even as we speak. And now we in the West are being more and more reviled. Given our text today, I wonder why we are surprised. Jesus warned us that the world would hate us. At John 15:18–16:4c, Jesus prepared the disciples for effective testimony in the midst of hostility. It is not my point to preach a theology that venerates suffering. It is true that there is a special reward for those who pay the ultimate price for the sake of Christ. It is not true that we should venerate it, or manipulate our surroundings to be martyred. Christians in the past have done just that. I find this act repulsive, for it selfishly manipulates someone into murder. It does not matter if you are the victim. Can we say we love someone and then persuade him to commit murder? Surely not. Instead of a morbid culture of suffering and death, Jesus wanted to prepare his disciples for inevitable hostility. My point today is the same. Christians should be prepared for effective testimony to Christ in the midst of hostility.

Outline

I. Expect Persecution (15:18–25)

A. TEXT

1. The world hates Christ and his followers (vv. 18–19).

"If the world hates you, understand that it hated Me before it hated you. If you were of the world, the world would love you as its own. However, because you are not of the world, but I have chosen you out of it, the world hates you" (HCSB).

2. Because the world does not know God (vv. 20–21)

"Remember the word I spoke to you: 'A slave is not greater than his master.' If they persecuted Me, they will also persecute you. If they kept My word, they will also keep yours. But they will do all these things to you on account of My name, because they don't know the One who sent Me" (HCSB).

3. They are without excuse (vv. 22–25).

"If I had not come and spoken to them, they would not have sin. Now they have no excuse for their sin. The one who hates Me also hates My Father. If I had not done the works among them that no one else has done, they would not have sin. Now they have seen and hated both Me and My Father. But this happened so that the statement written in their scripture might be fulfilled: They hated Me for no reason" (HCSB).

B. ILLUSTRATION

The story of Perpetua and Felicitas is about a young noble-born mother and her servant. Perpetua and Felicitas were martyred in the reign of Septimius Severus (c. AD 22).[24] Septimius Severus outlawed conversion to Christianity and Judaism. His persecution was particularly fierce in North Africa where Perpetua lived. I find particularly interesting the account of Vivia Perpetua at chapter 1. She was a catechumen (one being instructed in

---

[24] The full text in English can be found at the following site: http://www.earlychristianwritings.com/text/tertullian24.html.

Christianity), had been arrested by the "persecutors," and was sitting in prison when her father came to visit her. He tried his best to keep her from following through with her confession. After his visit, she consented to baptism and effectively sealed her fate. She came into the faith knowing it would be costly. We know her expectations.

C. TODAY

1. What were you expecting?

   A famous tract claims "God loves you and offers a wonderful plan for your life." It follows up with a definition of the plan: life and life more abundantly (John 10:10).[25] This is true, but unless it is followed up by discipleship, one could get the impression that coming to Christ makes your life easier. It does not. We should expect difficulty in this life.

2. The absence of hostility may be a sign that something is wrong.

   After all, all those who live godly lives in Christ Jesus will suffer persecution (2 Tim 3:12).

3. Nobody needs to "volunteer" for persecution.

   a. By being quarrelsome

   b. By being inappropriate

   c. By being insensitive

   It is enough that you know Christ and live for him; that alone will be enough.

4. We must not think the worst of every non-Christian.

   Few are possessed or lurking for the first opportunity to persecute a believer. Furthermore, we should not look at the world as our enemy but as our mission field. Jesus did the same (John 3:16).

---

[25] See http://www.campuscrusade.com/fourlawseng.htm.

II. Employ the Paraclete's Empowerment (15:26–27)

A. TEXT

The response to the world's hatred (in all its manifestations) is witness. This is an unexpected response. It is not a retreat. It is a bold counteroffensive.

1. The promise and ministry of the Paraclete (v. 26)

"When the Counselor comes, the One I will send to you from the Father—the Spirit of truth who proceeds from the Father—He will testify about Me" (HCSB).

2. The disciple's ministry (v. 27)

"You also will testify, because you have been with Me from the beginning" (HCSB).

B. ILLUSTRATION

Some say the battle of Moscow turned the tide in World War II. While this issue is debated among scholars, most note the importance of Germany's decision to invade Russia.[26] On June 22, 1941, Germany invaded the Soviet Union. Caught completely unaware, the Soviets made a series of blunders that allowed the German forces to make it all the way to Moscow. It is said the Nazis were so close that if they climbed on the roofs of their vehicles, they could see the citizens of Moscow in the streets.[27]

In the face of such a well-armed and battle-hardened enemy sitting literally at Moscow's doorstep, a decision had to be made. Joseph Stalin had made plans to escape by train, to fall back, to give up the capital, and regroup. His personal telegrapher was roused in the middle of the night on October 16, 1941, and was told to wait for Stalin at the train depot. Stalin never came; instead, he decided to fight. He turned over operations to General Zhukov who planned a bold counteroffensive. Supplies and reinforcements were shipped in, but the Russians were still outnumbered. On December 5, 1941, the Soviets launched

---

[26] Lawrence Rees, "What Was the Turning Point of World War II?" (1 June 2010). Cited 16 January 2014. Online: http://www.historynet.com/what-was-the-turning-point-of-world-war-ii.htm.

[27] Tsarevskaya Lyubov, "The Battle That Turned the Course of WW II" (23 December 2011). Cited 16 January 2 http://english.ruvr.ru/radio_broadcast/2249099/62761796.html.

their counteroffensive. They drove off the Wehrmacht and set Germany in a long fight for which they had not planned. The Soviet men loved their country more than their lives, and this fueled their defense. Hitler's defeat kept Japan from joining forces with him.

Our counteroffensive is not so violent, and our warfare is not with flesh and blood. In the light of our hostile environment, however, Jesus calls for our own counteroffensive. He knows no retreat, and he has no train waiting for him. He calls for his followers to love him and to testify to the world about his victory over sin and the Devil.

C. TODAY

We are called to go on the bold offensive with Christ.

1. You are empowered to witness.

   Every believer is indwelled by the Holy Spirit. Just as the Judean leadership was without excuse, you are without excuse. Education helps, training helps, experience helps, but you have the Holy Spirit to help you tell those dead in trespasses and sins about Jesus. The Holy Spirit can use even the most inept in apologetics, rhetoric, or even Bible knowledge as effective evangelists. Trust him.

2. You are commanded to witness.

   There are no qualifications except conversion. If you are converted you are commanded to witness. The monkey is not on your back to convert anybody. You are under obligation to be a witness, to give testimony. Obey him.

III. Evoke His Words (16:1–4c)

A. TEXT

Jesus promises three very real possibilities for the believer:

1. Confidence (v. 1)

   "I have told you these things to keep you from stumbling" (HCSB).

2. Escalation (vv. 2–3)

"They will ban you from the synagogues. In fact, a time is coming when anyone who kills you will think he is offering service to God. They will do these things because they haven't known the Father or Me" (HCSB).

3. Remembrance (v. 4a–c)

"But I have told you these things so that when their time comes you may remember I told them to you" (HCSB).

B. ILLUSTRATION

In 1850 when California became the thirty-first state, the need to get the mail quickly became important. The Pony Express was born. They set up 184 relay stations, five to twenty-five miles apart and hired small, wry boys to carry the mail from station to station. This way they intended to get the mail from St. Joseph, MO to San Francisco, CA in ten days or less.

In the short history of the Pony Express, they lost only one bag of mail. In fact, they lost more riders. The job was arduous and exhausting; one of the boys was murdered by Paiute Indians. All the boys risked hardship, difficulty, and death. Most stuck it out for at least one reason: They knew for what they had signed up. One advertisement for riders was as follows: "Wanted: Young, skinny, wiry fellows not over eighteen. Must be expert riders, willing to risk death daily. Orphans preferred."[28]

Remember, to give your life to Christ is to sign up for the hatred of the world. To give your life to Christ is to take up your cross daily and follow him.

C. TODAY

Our application is straightforward.

1. You can have confidence.

---

[28] Tim McNeese, *The Pony Express: Bringing the Mail to the American West* (New York: Chelsea House, 2009), 50.

Christ has told us ahead of time. But more than that, we have had centuries of seeing this play out in the world.

2. You should not be surprised by an escalation of hostility.

In the West, we have let the moorings slip. Atheism is on the rise, secular humanism rules in our colleges and universities, and our popular media is ruled by the most liberal of the liberal. A thousand tomahawks a day are launched at us. What do you think is next?

When it happens, remember these words.

Conclusion

Bill Wallace was a medical missionary at Wuchow, China, during the communist revolution. His story is one of heroism and faithfulness in the face of strong opposition from the evil one. When the communists came to power, they feared every foreigner and eventually captured Bill Wallace and accused him of espionage. Wallace's days at the prison were days of brutal torture as the communists tried to get a confession of espionage from him. In the blur of sleeplessness and pain they did get a confession that everyone knew was phony. Dr. Wallace probably didn't even know what he signed. What they really wanted was an open confession from Dr. Wallace, so they resorted to brainwashing. Wallace, however, would not succumb. In the days ahead he entered into a battle for his sanity for the sake of Christ. "Interrogations," torture, sleeplessness, all designed to get him to repudiate all that he believed failed. Fearing complete failure, the guards brought long poles to his cell and began thrusting them into his abdomen to make him pass out. But they went too far, and Bill Wallace died having endured torture and brainwashing. He died having kept Christ's word and his own testimony.

What did Wallace do to keep his sanity? His biographer, Jesse C. Fletcher, describes it. "From his cell in the night, Bill sometimes cried out in agony after the battle was over. With pieces of paper and a smuggled pencil, he wrote short affirmations to try and keep his mind centered on things that could anchor him. Some were Scripture passages, others simple denials of guilt, protests of innocence. He stuck these on the walls of his barren room and repeated them to himself in an effort to prepare for the next interrogation."[29]

---

[29] Jesse C. Fletcher, *Bill Wallace of China* (Bloomington, IN: CrossBooks, 2009), 210.

We actually see all three of Christ's commands here lived out. Wallace expected persecution, leaned on the Paraclete's empowerment, and he remembered Christ's words. We should respond to the world's hatred in the same way. We should expect it (but not in a morbid, paranoid way). We should employ the Spirit's empowerment to witness at all times but especially these. We should evoke his words to encourage us to maintain a faithful witness.

SERMON 10: THE BELIEVER'S SECRET WEAPON

TEXT: John 16:4d–15
MIT: The first advantage of Jesus' departure is the sending of the Spirit of truth.
MIM: Every believer should enjoy the advantage of ministry of the Spirit in his or her own ministries.

Introduction

In warfare, if you can develop the secret weapon that no one can defend against you will probably win. The Germans tried to take the technology route in World War II. They developed jet fighters, photosensitive guns, and stealth submarines that could stay submerged indefinitely. The Russians, on the other hand, went low tech. They trained stray dogs to expect food under a tank. Then when the Germans came in their Panzer tanks, they strapped bombs on the back of the poor mutts and let them go. At first, it was highly effective. The practice was ended when a pack ran amuck and caused serious self-inflicted wounds on the Soviets. In like manner, the CIA spent fifteen million dollars on "project acoustic kitty." They surgically implanted listening devices and antennas in the tails of cats and planned to use them to infiltrate the Russians (among others). The project was scrapped when the first cat was deployed. They set it loose, and it promptly ran into the street and was run over by a car.[30] Both tales end in a way that convinces me that the universe is circular after all. Or more precisely, such inhumanity doesn't please the Lord. The desire for the perfect secret weapon led to some poor decisions. However, this does not negate the value of acquiring a powerful secret weapon.

Our text this morning describes the believer's secret weapon. It is the Paraclete whom we have discussed two other times through this series. We have seen that he mediates the presence of the Lord to those who love and obey Christ (14:26 HCSB: "But the Counselor, the Holy Spirit—the Father will send Him in My name—will teach you all things and remind you of everything I have told you"). He will testify about Christ. And now he is promised to be our guide in this world.

In this text, Jesus enumerates several advantages to his departure for the believer. The first advantage of Jesus' departure is the sending of the Spirit

---

[30] See http://www.oddee.com/item_91684.aspx.

of truth. My point today is that every believer should enjoy the advantage of ministry of the Spirit in his or her own ministries.

Outline

I. It Is Better for Us that Jesus Has Departed (16:4d–7)

A. TEXT

1. Jesus' departure filled the disciples with sorrow (16:4d–6).

   "I didn't tell you these things from the beginning, because I was with you. But now I am going away to Him who sent Me, and not one of you asks Me, 'Where are You going?' Yet, because I have spoken these things to you, sorrow has filled your heart" (HCSB).

   a. "Departure" is a euphemism for death.

   b. The disciples had asked before "where are you going?" But now they get it.

   He is going to die. In their experience, death is the chasm that is crossed only one way.

   The thought of being separated from Jesus has filled them with sorrow.

   i. Jesus goes away to benefit us (v. 7).

   "Nevertheless, I am telling you the truth. It is for your benefit that I go away, because if I don't go away the Counselor will not come to you. If I go, I will send Him to you" (HCSB).

   (a) Jesus had to die.

   The Holy Spirit could not come until salvation had been accomplished.

   This was the Father's plan since before the foundation of the world.

   (b) The Paraclete is our "secret weapon."

B. ILLUSTRATION

Secret weapons are only good as long as the secret to the technology is kept safe. After the secret is let out, both sides reach stalemate again. One of the most feared and effective secret weapons of all time was Greek fire. It was invented (at least perfected) by a man named Kallinikos. It was a petroleum mixture that when heated burst into unquenchable flames (said to burn on water). Greek fire could be delivered through large ship-mounted units that employed hoses. The Byzantines had a hand-held and a grenade version of the substance. Their great roaring ships bellowing out streams of unquenchable liquid fire were as much psychological weapons as they were instruments of destruction. The secret of the mixture was considered a gift from God handed down from emperor to emperor. It held Constantinople safe for 781 years, until, for some reason, it was not used in 1453 when the city fell. The Paraclete is our secret weapon in the spiritual battle that we face. He is unseen, omnipotent, omnipresent, and unstoppable.

C. TODAY

1. What they feared, we face.

Although we are on the other side of his death, burial, and resurrection, we too have longed to see, touch, and hear our Lord. We think, at times, they had it better. They did not.

2. Because of the ministry of the Holy Spirit we are advantaged.

II. The Paraclete Leads in Ministry (16:8–11)

A. TEXT

"When He comes, He will convict the world about sin, righteousness, and judgment: About sin, because they do not believe in Me; about righteousness, because I am going to the Father and you will no longer see Me; and about judgment, because the ruler of this world has been judged" (HCSB).

The Paraclete is an advantage to us because he works in the world concerning the gospel.

1. The ministry of the Paraclete involves the conviction of the world.

   a. Sin

   b. Righteousness

   c. Judgment

      i. The ministry of the Paraclete assumes the Christian's involvement in evangelism.

B. TODAY

1. A Christian not involved in evangelism is wasting a precious resource.

2. A Christian not involved in evangelism misses the opportunity to see God work.

3. A Christian involved in evangelism may rest in the Spirit's work. We cannot convict or convert anyone. That is the Spirit's ministry. Ours is simply obedience.

C. ILLUSTRATION

What does God need to convert souls? In the book, *In Their Own Words*, Tom Elliff and Robert G. Witty record the testimony of Rudy Hernandez. His early days were spent in poverty in a single-parent home after his father died. He states, "My sister Ramona had committed to attend a meeting at the Rosillo Street Baptist Mission in west San Antonio. Due to a school schedule, she was unable to keep her commitment. My mom, a firm believer that 'a king's word is never retracted,' reprimanded her, and Mom and I went in her place. I went to church by mistake—a mistake that launched me on the greatest journey of my life. My mother and I attended and enjoyed what we heard and saw. We returned numerous times until on May 26, 1938, as a ten-year-old shoeshine boy, I was sitting on the roughly made pew in the one-car garage converted into a chapel when I felt God speaking to me, 'Jesus loves you, he died for you, take him into your heart.' My heart was breaking. In tears and barefooted, I almost ran, gave my hand to pastor Paul Mason and, repentant of my sins, asked the Lord Jesus Christ into my life.

> Joy was heaped upon joy as Mom followed me down the aisle. She too was asking Christ into her life.
>
> I spotted a blind man, Mr. Martinez, uneasy as if needing to do likewise. I went to him and asked him if he also wanted to trust Jesus as his savior. He replied, 'If you will take me.' Since I had led him by the hand from one place to another, I knew what to do. I literally led him to Christ."[31]

Now understand this: the Holy Spirit used a mistake and a gospel-preaching church to convert a shoeshine boy. That newly converted shoeshine boy, who was simply obedient, led a blind man to Christ. I don't think he needs us at all, but he chooses to use us. But the work of conviction, repentance, and conversion belongs to God. The Paraclete leads us to an empowered ministry.

III. The Paraclete Communicates the Will of God to Us (16:12–15)

A. TEXT

> "I still have many things to tell you, but you can't bear them now. When the Spirit of truth comes, He will guide you into all the truth. For He will not speak on His own, but He will speak whatever He hears. He will also declare to you what is to come. He will glorify Me, because He will take from what is Mine and declare it to you. Everything the Father has is Mine. This is why I told you that He takes from what is Mine and will declare it to you" (HCSB).

1. The Spirit will guide in truth.

    a. Through illumination of God's Word

    b. Through inner promptings

    c. Through godly counsel

2. The Spirit will glorify Christ.

B. ILLUSTRATION

> One of the most amazing things that I have had to deal with as a pastor is people who supposedly claim to be Christians but

---

[31] Tom Elliff and Robert Gee Witty, eds., *In Their Own Words: The Personal Testimonies of Men and Women of Faith* (Nashville: B&H, 2003), 80–81.

have fallen into great sin. The saddest part of this is that many of them claim God told them to do it. Whether it is sexual, financial, or another matter of infidelity to God, some inner prompting had "led them to do it." Most will even say, "I prayed about it." Sometimes they even take something I said in a sermon and use it as an excuse to sin. Beloved, they clearly misidentified to whom they were listening. So, on this side of Easter how should we approach listening to our Guide?

C. TODAY

1. We should not be afraid of the Holy Spirit.

   Far too many believers are afraid of the excesses that we have seen on television. Others fear that they will have to go to some far off land and live as missionaries. Rest assured the Holy Spirit is a gentleman and will not run roughshod over your will. Your desires will conform to his.

2. We should look for him to guide us.

   Far too many believers look to other guides in this life. There are a host of bad choices we can make when we chose counselors other than the Holy Spirit.

   a. Not ungodly "friends"

   They will tell you what you want to hear. They've usually made their lives a shipwreck. Why would you listen to them?

   b. Not TV show "counselors"

   Sources that focus on pop psychology and stunts to get ratings are not always the best places to get good information to guide you. Besides, what good are these counselors when it comes to spiritual issues?

   c. Not self-help gurus

   The latest book on self-improvement may offer some suggestions to lose weight and keep it off, but it is not really helpful in guiding us through life.

3. We should learn how to discriminate his "voice" from other inner influences.

   a. Knowledge of the Word of God

   The Spirit will not lead contrary to God's Word. If we know his Word then any "inner prompting" that goes against it will be more easily identified as your flesh or the ancient chili with the fuzzy green top layer you ate last night.

   b. Knowing what glorifies Christ

   Strong commitment to knowing the Word, knowing what glorifies Christ will help determine the choice to make. You may have to make a choice between two good things. How will you decide? Which one will glorify Christ the most? Once you know that, most often the choice is made.

   c. Experience in walking with him

   Those who have walked with Christ have learned to recognize the voice of his Spirit. Start walking, pay attention, make good choices, learn from the bad choices, and cherish the experience of communion with the Lord.

   d. Know your enemy (Devil, world, and flesh).

   The believer has three enemies. The first is the Devil. Understand that there is a real, literal Devil who wants to destroy your testimony and limit your usefulness. As far as he is concerned, the more "practical atheists" there are, the easier his wickedness will be.

Conclusion

I visited Vietnam in 2012. It was a great experience, and we should be praying for our brothers and sisters in that country. They are doing well, but they are a great minority. The trip over was very long, and at the stop in Hong Kong I noticed that my arrival time had changed, so I texted my hosts that I was going to be later than originally planned. Unfortunately I got there at the original time, and I waited for an hour and a half for my hosts to pick me up (for some reason my phone wasn't working). I got to the airport very early in the morning (around 12 a.m.). I got my bags and went through the concourse to the exit, hoping to see a young local with a sign bearing my name. Due to my own bungling, I saw no one. I was met by a host of "helpful" taxi-cab drivers. "Do you need a ride?" "No, I have friends who will meet me to guide me." The longer I waited the more insistent they got. "Your friends have forgotten you. They are not going to pick you up." I kept saying, "No, my friends are coming." At about the hour mark one taxi driver said, "Do you know Kennedy?" in an angry voice. The reference to the man who led America at the start of the Vietnam conflict made me nervous. I was just about to contemplate employing a guide I did not trust. Finally to my great relief, a young man showed up with a sign that read "Kellum." My guide had arrived! I was no longer lost and confused in a foreign land.

Beloved, you have a guide whom you can trust. Through this foreign and confusing landscape you have a guide—if you love and obey Christ. He has provided the Holy Spirit to indwell you and mediate the presence of Christ for you. He is your secret weapon and your internal guide.

Sermon 11:
The Second Advantage—Complete Joy

TEXT: John 16:16–24
MIT: Jesus promised abiding joy to those who ask in his name because of his completed work.
MIM: Today, abiding followers of Christ may experience complete joy when they ask the Father in Jesus' name.

Introduction

Jefferson included in the Declaration of Independence the famous line that God gave certain inalienable rights to mankind: life, liberty, and the pursuit of happiness. Whether or not government thinks it a right, and even if they don't, mankind has been pursuing happiness with great gusto and sometimes disastrous results. After all, Adam and Eve were pursing happiness when they ate the forbidden fruit. Perhaps the most famous biblical example is the teacher in the OT book of Ecclesiastes. He sets his heart to pursue wisdom, pleasure, laughter, achievement, and possessions, and each one left him empty. He declares them all to be empty: a chasing after the wind. We read the wisdom of the teacher, and yet, as a species, humanity is still seeking happiness. I want to suggest today that what we should be seeking is joy, or else we are chasing after the wind.

In our text today, Christ is in the midst of finishing up his farewell address before his disciples. He is communicating to them (and us) how to spiritually thrive between the advents. Previously we saw that because he has announced his upcoming death (and they seem to understand it), he tells them that there are advantages for them if he departs. The first advantage, we saw last time. It was the gift of the Paraclete. Today we will look at the second advantage: their grief will turn to joy. In our text, Jesus promised abiding joy to those who ask in his name because of his completed work. On this side of Easter, the application to believers is the same, except what was promised to the disciples is a reality for us. Today, abiding followers of Christ may experience complete joy when they ask the Father in Jesus' name. It is this that we will discuss in the moments ahead. This joy begins when the disciples will see him again, that is, in the resurrection.

Outline

I. The Resurrection Is the Foundation for Joy (16:16–19)

"'A little while and you will no longer see Me; again a little while and you will see Me.' Therefore some of His disciples said to one another, 'What is this He tells us: "A little while and you will not see Me; again a little while and you will see Me"; and, "because I am going to the Father"?' They said, 'What is this He is saying, "A little while"? We don't know what He's talking about!' Jesus knew they wanted to question Him, so He said to them, 'Are you asking one another about what I said, "A little while and you will not see Me; again a little while and you will see Me"?'" (HCSB).

A. TEXT

1. Jesus' announcement

   They will see him again after his departure.

2. The disciples' confusion

   They understood "departure" meant death. The statement about seeing them again throws them into confusion.

3. Jesus is announcing his resurrection to his disciples.

B. TODAY

When I was a young Christian most skeptics tried to deny the resurrection in one way or another: Jesus merely swooned, the disciples went to the wrong tomb, they misidentified the gardener, etc. Most of these theories involve deception or confusion.[32] Today, most skeptics don't deny Jesus' unexpected violent death, that the disciples believed they had seen the risen Lord, or that Paul's conversion was due to what he interpreted as a post-resurrection appearance of the Lord. They have moved on to other "solutions" to the belief in the resurrection.

---

[32] The standard popular reference was Josh McDowell, *Evidence That Demands a Verdict*. It is still in print in an updated version. Josh McDowell, *The New Evidence That Demands a Verdict: Evidence I and II Fully Updated in One Volume to Answer Questions Challenging Christians in the 21st Century* (Nashville, TN: Thomas Nelson, 1999).

Some say that we don't know what produced the empty tomb but that a powerful mystical experience in Jerusalem changed the disciples' lives (following Vermes). Others speculate that all involved experienced hallucinations (following Goulder). Still others believe that Peter and others had visions that were the root of a mass ecstasy among other believers (following Lüdemann). Quite popular among certain sectors is that the resurrection was purely a metaphysical (i.e., spiritual) event and that the bodily resurrection did not happen (following Crossan). Finally, some embrace that what actually happened was mass altered states of consciousness (following Craffert).[33] We will not debate the skeptic here except to say that the foundation is on the belief that miracles do not happen. Furthermore, much of what is stated comes across to me as pejorative, elitist, and an attempt to do psychoanalysis on people long dead.

Now, I expect the world to take extraordinary means to defy the resurrection, but why would those in the church do so? In many sectors resurrection might as well be in scare quotes, for it has turned into code-speak for one of the above theories. I understand the enemies of Christ not embracing the bodily resurrection of Christ, but why do those who claim Christianity at times seem embarrassed by the doctrine?

There are no blanket reasons, but let me throw out a few.

1. Some of those who claim Christianity do not embrace Christ. They deny, or redefine, the new birth. We expect them to embrace a non-Christian worldview.

2. Some have drank deep in the wells of modernism, including the belief that miracles do not happen. We expect them to have difficulty with the resurrection.

3. Some are simply afraid of being branded as "unintelligent," "unscientific," or "religious nut" by the world.

4. Some, like Paul's opponents in Galatia, embrace false doctrine so they won't have to endure persecution.

---

[33] This brief sketch is taken from Michael Licona, *The Resurrection of Jesus: A New Historiographical Approach* (Downers Grove, IL: InterVarsity, 2010), 465–610.

Jesus affirmed that he would rise from the dead and that he would appear to his disciples. The born-again believer with courage and insight embraces the resurrection of Christ. But, as we will see, what they gain is joy in what the resurrection represents.

C. Joy Is Available in the Accomplishment of Salvation (16:20–22)

"I assure you: You will weep and wail, but the world will rejoice. You will become sorrowful, but your sorrow will turn to joy. When a woman is in labor she has pain because her time has come. But when she has given birth to a child, she no longer remembers the suffering because of the joy that a person has been born into the world. So you also have sorrow now. But I will see you again. Your hearts will rejoice, and no one will rob you of your joy" (HCSB).

D. TEXT

1. The disciples will be miserable over Jesus' death.
2. Their misery will be forgotten.

   The metaphor of the woman in labor.

3. Their sorrow will be turned into an abiding joy.

   Because the resurrection cannot be taken away, neither can its joy.

E. ILLUSTRATION: "The Agony-of-Defeat Guy"

When I was growing up, ABC's *Wide World of Sports* was a weekly part of life. Jim McKay's narration of the opening sequence is burned into my memory, especially "the agony-of-defeat guy." Ask Yahoo had a nice write up about it:

In the hierarchy of skiing accidents, there are spills, there are falls, and there are catastrophic wipeouts. "The agony of defeat" was definitely a catastrophic wipeout. For years, ABC's *Wide World of Sports* showcased the crash during its introduction:

Spanning the globe to bring you the constant variety of sport! The thrill of victory . . . and the agony of defeat! [insert clip of Bogataj's wipeout] *The human drama of athletic competition! This is ABC's Wide World of Sports!*

The agonized athlete was a Slovene ski jumper by the name of Vinko Bogataj. A respected jumper and a fierce competitor, Bogataj's fate took a turn for the worse at the World Ski Flying Championships in 1970. Midway through his third run, Bogataj felt he was going too fast and tried to slow down. Unfortunately, he lost his balance and tumbled spectacularly over the side of the ramp. Bogataj suffered only a concussion, though apparently he never again jumped with quite the same "abandon." Understandable, if you ask us.

As an interesting side note, Bogataj lived behind the Iron Curtain. As a result, he had no idea how infamous his crash had become in the United States. So it was with great confusion that he accepted an invitation to attend ABC's *Wide World of Sports* anniversary show. Once there, he found himself hounded by fans (including Muhammad Ali) who wanted to shake hands with "the agony of defeat." We call that a minor victory.[34]

Only in America can you win celebrity by becoming "the agony-of-defeat" guy! Because of the resurrection of Christ, believers will never know the agony of defeat but live in the thrill of victory!

F. TODAY

1. Like the disciples, we will know pain and, at times, suffering.

    a. It is part-and-parcel of living in a fallen world.

    When God made the world, he declared that it was good. Then humanity fell. So, now, this world of humanity is no longer good nor permanent. All things are not equal. We live in a fallen world where the sin of others may reach even believers. We are not promised that bad things will not happen. We are promised an inestimable benefit: grace. It is both sustaining grace to make it through such things and delivering grace to rescue us out of some ter-

---

[34] See http://ask.yahoo.com/20060213.html.

rible situations. For the believer, until all is made right, the grace of God is sufficient.

b. In the providence of God, hardship is never for nothing.

There are no pointless exercises in the reign of the Lord. If he asks us to endure suffering of any kind, he does so for a good purpose. All things are not good. But all things work to good for those who love God and are called according to his purpose (Rom 8:28).

c. Jesus himself was no stranger to suffering.

He embraced the cross for the joy that was set before him (Heb 12:2). He was hated for no reason, ridiculed, beaten, and crucified. He was intimately acquainted with the horrors of a fallen world. He is intimately acquainted with the inhumanity of human beings. Yet, he endured for the joy of rescuing us.

2. Unlike the disciples, we live on the other side of the resurrection.

They could only look forward to what Christ promised. We may access the reality of the promise. He has risen from the dead. We cannot explain it away. We dare not deny it. We should not cheapen it in familiarity. We must embrace the reality it secures. He defeated the Devil, paid for our sins, sent the Holy Spirit, and secures our own eventual resurrection. He provides for us the "thrill of victory."

II. Joy Continues in the Relationship that Christ Establishes (16:23–24)

"In that day you will not ask Me anything. I assure you: Anything you ask the Father in My name, He will give you. Until now you have asked for nothing in My name. Ask and you will receive, so that your joy may be complete" (HCSB).

A. TEXT

Jesus describes a new relationship with the Father.

1. A new manner of prayer (v. 23a)

    It is now to the Father in Jesus' name. "Name" suggests the character and authority of Jesus.

2. A familiar promise of prayer (v. 23b–d)

    Three previous times (in every unit of the discourse) a promise regarding effectual prayer has been made. In 14:13–14 asking is connected to loving him, keeping his commands, and bringing him glory. In 15:7 it is connected to abiding in Christ (loving/obeying him) and fruit bearing.

3. A new result of prayer (v. 24)

    At 16:24 nothing new is added except the results. Those who pray to the Father in Jesus' name will have complete joy.

    The purposes of Jesus' coming are fulfilled "in that day." He came to give abundant life (John 10:10, a life rich in the presence of the Holy Spirit and joy). He came to give us streams of living water flowing through us (John 7:38). That can be attained only after his glorification.

    It is dependent, however, upon abiding in Christ. The believer has tremendous potential to experience messianic joy. However, much of that is unrealized in the average Christian.

B. ILLUSTRATION

Unrealized potential is a tragedy of "what could have been" and "if only." On April 17, 2012, the Energy Department released a report of a study that examined the question of how much energy we could get from existing dams if we equipped them to produce hydroelectric power. From the press release, "The report estimates that without building a single new dam, these available hydropower resources, if fully developed, could provide an electrical generating capacity of more than 12 gigawatts (GW), equivalent to roughly 15 percent of current U.S. hydropower capacity. . . . The results indicate that, if fully developed, the nation's non-powered dams could provide enough energy to power over four million households."[35] This energy is clean, renewable, and just sitting there.

This is much like the prayerless, nonabiding, disobedient believer today. He is clean, renewed, and just sitting there. A great tragedy of "what could have been." Let's avoid that tragedy.

C. TODAY

The text hints at a process that I want to make explicit for you who want to meet your potential in Christ.

1. Joy begins with belief.

Faith is the starting point of the Christian life. It is also the matrix in which we operate our lives after we come to Christ. Worry, doubt, and pessimism drown out joy. They do not allow you to be the conqueror that you were born-again to be. Without faith, there will be no abiding joy. There will be fleeting moments of happiness. But these are like a sugar rush—quickly over, when compared to joy.

2. Joy is dependent on the love of/obedience to Christ.

After initial faith and then living faith, one must love Christ as expressed in obedience. We all struggle with our level of obedience. We must all be on an upward climb, not sliding back. If we love Christ, then obeying him comes without even thinking about it.

Conversely, when we are not participating in loving obedience we cannot know joy. In fact, the believer who has unrepentant sin may be the most miserable person alive. He is constantly trying to hide his sin. He is constantly avoiding those who might catch him or point out his sin. He constantly moves back and forth from justifying himself to condemning himself. But foremost, the indwelling Holy Spirit convicts his spirit without end. He lives an existence mired in misery because of rebellion and strife.

---

[35] See http://energy.gov/articles/energy-department-report-finds-major-potential-increase-clean-hydroelectric-power.

What we were made for, what we were born-again for is to know Christ and enjoy his presence, to glorify him, and to have a relationship with him. There is nothing more fulfilling than to lovingly obey Christ. It is not always easy or even pleasant, but it is right and is for what we were redeemed.

3. Ask in Jesus' name.

Finally, we ask in Jesus' name. Such asking implies an intimacy that was previously not available (see 16:24). We ask seeking to glorify God. We ask seeking to lovingly obey him. We ask to bear much fruit. We ask in the authority of Christ based on what he has accomplished in us. When it is his will, we get it. And the result is joy.

4. The result is joy.

Joy is not, strictly speaking, happiness. People can be happy in sin. It gives them pleasure. People can be happy in meaningless, transitory hobbies. People can be happy because the serotonin level is up, or the flowers have bloomed, or the check arrived on time. Joy is something else, something laid on far more secure foundations.

Joy is a spiritual response to the gospel of Jesus Christ. The angel declared to the shepherds at the nativity, "Don't be afraid, for look, I proclaim to you good news of great joy that will be for all the people: Today a Savior, who is Messiah the Lord, was born for you in the city of David" (Luke 2:10–11 HCSB).

It is the delight of the people of God in the presence of God that only redemption in Christ can give us. As such, it rises above the mundane and is the foundation for how we conduct our lives. Through the good, the bad, and the ugly, we can have joy because we have relationship with God through Christ.

Conclusion

Wilhelmus à Brakel (1635–1711) was a Dutch minister who was instrumental in the Dutch Further Reformation that sought to apply Christian doctrine to heart and life. His greatest work, a systematic theology of four volumes and 2,400 pages, is called *The Christian's Reasonable Service*. Where it differs from most of the very dry systematic theologies around is that it, as Paul M. Smalley put it, "throbs with joy."[36] Brakel uses the term or a related word 2,416 times throughout the four volumes. As Smalley summarizes, for Brakel, the gospel is good news of great joy; God is the fullness of joy; man is the seeker of joy; created man was designed for joy; fallen man is excluded from joy; Christ is the mediator of joy; the eternal covenant is the plan of joy; Christ's incarnation to make atonement for us is the embodiment of joy; the church is the community of joy; the congregation is the fellowship of joy; the Lord's Supper is the feast of joy; salvation is the life of joy, begun in conversion which is the return to joy, declared in justification and adoption, the foundation of joy; assurance is the evidence of joy, expressed in love and obedience that is the sacrifice of joy; trials and hope are the training for joy; the seeking of God is the pursuit of joy; ultimate glory is the consummation of joy. Brakel rightly insists that joy is not a byproduct of obedience but is what we were designed to experience in the presence of God. It is the will of God.[37]

So because of what the resurrection represents—the completed work of Christ—ask. Ask to glorify God in Christ. Ask to do his will. Ask to be more fruitful. Ask to lovingly obey him. Ask to have greater faith. Ask and it will be given to you so that your joy will be complete.

---

[36] P. M. Smalley, "Satisfied with the Lord's All-Sufficiency: Wilhelmus à Brakel on Joy," *Puritan Reformed Journal* 3 (2011): 238.

[37] Ibid., 236–66. The English translation is Wilhelmus à Brakel, *The Christian's Reasonable Service*, trans. Bartel Elshout, ed. Joel R. Beeke (Grand Rapids: Reformation Heritage, 1992–94).

Sermon 12: The Hotline

TEXT: John 16:25–32
MIT: Jesus declared direct access to God in prayer for new covenant believers.
MIM: Christians should use the direct access to God made available through Christ's sacrificial death on the cross.

Introduction

After the events of the Cuban missile crisis in October of 1962, a direct line to the Kremlin was established the following July. With nuclear weapons flying around, the US had taken twelve hours to receive and decode Nikita Kruschev's settlement response. Something quicker had to be done. The first hotline was a telegraph machine that can now be found in the Lyndon Johnson museum. It was used once to test the machine and once during the Six-Day War in the Middle East (1967). In 1971 it was upgraded with a telephone and satellite lines. It was used multiple times in various crises. It was upgraded in 1986 again and fax capabilities were added, among other things.[38]

Direct access between these world leaders was a great idea. How disastrous would it be if we had to depend on snail mail or even e-mail? Worse than that, could you imagine the problems created if all correspondence were limited to 140 characters or less? Or could you imagine the White House asking if Putin can Facetime? Listen, the less we have to use this thing, the better off the world is, for it means there are no pending disasters on our horizons.

Another, more important hotline is not like the one in the White House. It is not between equal world leaders. It is not dependent on ever-changing technology. It can never be disconnected. It is an extreme privilege made available from the least of us to the greatest of us. It is the direct access to God made available through Jesus' death on the cross.

In this last unit of the Farewell Discourse, Jesus has been describing advantages gained through Jesus' departure for followers of Christ. The first was the indwelling Holy Spirit; the second was grief turned into joy. This is the third and final advantage listed here (surely this is not an exhaustive list). Jesus declared direct access to God in prayer for new covenant believers. My objective today is both a matter of understanding and practice. You must understand

---

[38] See http://en.wikipedia.org/wiki/Moscow–Washington_hotline.

the truth and then apply it in your daily life. Christians should use the direct access to God made available through Christ's sacrificial death on the cross.

Outline

I. What Is the Hotline? (16:25–28)

A. TEXT

"I have spoken these things to you in figures of speech. A time is coming when I will no longer speak to you in figures, but I will tell you plainly about the Father. In that day you will ask in My name. I am not telling you that I will make requests to the Father on your behalf. For the Father Himself loves you, because you have loved Me and have believed that I came from God. I came from the Father and have come into the world. Again, I am leaving the world and going to the Father" (HCSB).

1. "In that day" is after the resurrection.

2. Then, we should ask in his name.

3. The implication is intimate, direct access to God.

Understand how momentous this is. In the book of Exodus, Moses would enter into the holy of holies and converse with God. At Exodus 33:9–11 (HCSB) the Scripture states, "When Moses entered the tent, the pillar of cloud would come down and remain at the entrance to the tent, and the LORD would speak with Moses. As all the people saw the pillar of cloud remaining at the entrance to the tent, they would stand up, then bow in worship, each one at the door of his tent. The LORD spoke with Moses face to face, just as a man speaks with his friend." The people on the outside of the tent did not have the same access that Moses had. Jesus declares something more like what Moses experienced than what the people experienced. Even though they saw the pillar of smoke and fire, it was all external and distant from their innermost beings. It is an advantage to have direct access to God in prayer.

B. TODAY

Three Benefits of Direct Access

1. The person praying with direct access doesn't have to go through someone else.

   It is always good to have many people praying for you. There is no one who has more access to God than the person with direct access. Jesus' promise cuts out the "middle-man." In this sense it is subversive to organized religion.

2. The person praying with direct access doesn't have to wonder if the request got there.

   Have you ever said, "I don't think my prayers have gotten above the ceiling"? If so, you were terribly wrong. Your prayers are always directly before our heavenly Father. Know that he hears you. Know that he loves your prayers. They are a sweet aroma to him, like that of freshly baked chocolate chip cookies filling the house!

3. The person praying with direct access doesn't have to worry if the message is transmitted correctly.

   The problem with going through an intermediary is that he or she might mess up the message. Miscommunication happens every day, but not with the heavenly Father and one who has direct access.

C. ILLUSTRATION

Helen B. Poole shared the following account about her daughter: "My four-year-old daughter and I would always pray before she went to sleep. One night she volunteered to pray. She prayed and prayed and prayed—her voice getting softer and softer and softer, until only her lips were moving. Then she said, 'Amen.' 'Honey,' I said, 'I didn't hear a word you said.' She answered, 'Mama, I wasn't talking to you.'"[39] If a four-year old can get it, surely there's hope for the rest of us.

---

[39] Edward K. Rowell, ed., *1001 Quotes, Illustrations, and Humorous Stories for Preachers, Teachers, and Writers* (Grand Rapids: Baker, 2006), 503.

II. Who Gets to Use It? (16:29–32)

A. TEXT

1. Misunderstanding (vv. 29–30)

   "Ah!" His disciples said. "Now You're speaking plainly and not using any figurative language. Now we know that You know everything and don't need anyone to question You. By this we believe that You came from God" (HCSB).

   Twice the disciples use the term "now." In essence, it's something like this: "Now you speak clearly. Now we know, thus we believe." They have assumed their status as participants in the new covenant.

2. Jesus corrects them (vv. 31–32).

   "Jesus responded to them, 'Do you now believe? Look: An hour is coming, and has come, when each of you will be scattered to his own home, and you will leave Me alone. Yet I am not alone, because the Father is with Me'" (HCSB).

   Christ affirms that they are in error. They do not believe yet. The evidence is their abandonment of Christ.

3. Implications

   The disciples, on the other side of the cross, say they believe all the right stuff. However, Jesus reveals their deficiency in that they will abandon him. The advantages of his departure, then, are only made available on this side of the cross. The indwelling of the Holy Spirit, transformative joy, and now direct access to God are the results of Jesus' sacrificial death. These things are only made available to us through being born again.

B. TODAY

1. Direct access to and intimacy with God are not based on our achievement but Christ's.

It is the death of Christ that makes us righteous. It is the death of Christ that prepares the way for the indwelling of the Holy Spirit. You do not have to find a tabernacle in which to worship. You are the tabernacle. God dwells in you through the indwelling Holy Spirit. Herein is at least part of the direct access: you are always in the presence of God, because he is always in you through the Holy Spirit. And in this mutual indwelling you enjoy the presence of Christ, the fullness of God.

Paul's prayer at Ephesians 3:16–19 (HCSB) is instructive here. "I pray that He may grant you, according to the riches of His glory, to be strengthened with power in the inner man through His Spirit, and that the Messiah may dwell in your hearts through faith. I pray that you, being rooted and firmly established in love, may be able to comprehend with all the saints what is the length and width, height and depth of God's love, and to know the Messiah's love that surpasses knowledge, so you may be filled with all the fullness of God." It is not that all of God is in you, but that all of you is in God. Think of a teacup in the ocean. It is filled with the ocean, but the ocean cannot be contained in it.

This happens because Christ transferred his righteousness to us. We have direct access to God, through the Holy Spirit, because we are now right enough to stand before him. It is through Christ's faithfulness and his achievement that we can know God and have access to him.

a. Direct access is not conditional.

> Because it is based on Christ's achievement and not ours, there is no condition on the access for believers. You don't have to get clean before you address the Lord. He's already cleaned you. You stand in his righteousness not yours. That does not mean that a backslidden Christian gets everything he requests, or would even particularly enjoy the experience. But he may go directly to God and ask forgiveness and repent, because he does not have to go through anyone to get it.

2. This kind of access is unique.

The question was asked, "Does God hear the prayer of a lost person?" I remember some lively debates on the issue. Looking back I can say that some of the arguments sounded somewhat elitist, as if God were the property of believers. As Paul would say, "may it never be." All people are the property of God by virtue of creation. All people are beloved by God. God hears the prayers of every person who prays to him. How else could we repent? What Christ describes is an intimate access as the child of God and not a stranger's interruption.

C. ILLUSTRATION

Donald Grey Barnhouse pastored a local evangelical reformed church in the French Alps while he was in school. He became friends with the local parish priest who one day asked him why Protestants don't pray to the saints. Barnhouse replied, "Why should we?" The priest replied with an illustration from government. If one wanted to gain an interview with the president, he should go to a lesser department (say, the Ministry of Agriculture) for one of the cabinet ministers might have the clout to get access to the president's office.

Barnhouse replied, "But, Monsieur le Cure, suppose that I were the son of Monsieur Poincare [the French president at the time]? I am living in the Elysee with him. I get up from the breakfast table and kiss him good-bye as he goes off to his office. Then I go down to the Ministry of the Interior and ask the fourth secretary of the second assistant if it is possible for me to see the Minister of the Interior. If I succeed in reaching his office, my request is for an interview with my papa."[40]

How ridiculous! Barnhouse added that he was a child of God, an heir of God and joint-heir with Christ. He had been saved through the death of the Savior and thus had become a son with immediate access to the Father.

---

[40] Donald Grey Barnhouse, *Let Me Illustrate* (Old Tappan, NJ: Fleming H. Revell, 1967), 15–16.

Conclusion

The hotline to the Kremlin is not the only hotline in Washington. In 2008, the US set up a hotline with China in hopes of bettering communications. The move shows the rise in significance that China plays on the world scene.[41] However, like the one to the Kremlin, we hope it never has to be used. That is, if there is no need to use it, strife between our major world powers is not happening.

Quite the opposite is true for the believers' hotline. If we use it the world is better off. If we use it our families are better off. If we use it we are better off. Christ has gained access for us into the holy of holies. We may come, not flippantly, not as if it were not an extreme privilege, but as an honor bought at the expense of the beloved One. We may come, not just as servants, but as dearly loved children. We may not use it just to visit for a while or leave a Christmas wish list, but we may come and love and be loved by our heavenly Father. So come, what are we waiting for?

---

[41] Viola Gienger, "China-U.S. Defense Hotline Shows Gulf Between Nations" (13 May 2011). Cited 16 January 2014. Online: http://www.bloomberg.com/news/2011-05-13/china-u-s-defense-hotline-shows-gulf.html.

Sermon 13: The Reality of Peace

TEXT: John 16:33
MIT: Jesus declared that his followers can have peace based on his victory.
MIM: Believers have peace based on his victory.

Introduction

As Christ finishes explaining how to thrive between the advents to his disciples, his focus is on peace based on his victorious accomplishment on the cross. This is a peace unlike the world gives. The most famous peace from the world was the *Pax Romana* (the Roman Peace), which lasted from 27 BC to AD 180. It was a time when the Mediterranean basin was basically free from war, for Rome had conquered all. It was one of the longest periods of relative peace in the history of the West. Even so, it didn't last. In fact, no such peace has ever lasted. It is estimated that since the beginning of recorded history (since around 3600 BC) there have been only about 300 years of peace. These numbers simply refer to the cessation of war. Most people who write on the subject want more than a cessation of hostilities. They attach to the idea of peace a utopian society of one form or another (however they would define it). Furthermore, the blame for the lack of world peace gets spread around—even Christianity gets blamed for it.

The problem, in my opinion, that undermines a human utopia is not a lack of education, resources, or security. The problem is that we live in a fallen world. As long as there are men and women who aspire to power and selfishness (from the least to the greatest of us), there will be conflict (whether great or small). It arises from those who oppress and steal and consume the resources of another. It's an old story and one that will be replaced ultimately by God.

What does the individual do in this environment before the new creation? There is a different kind of peace that can transcend the fleeting peace of the world. It is an inner peace that only Christ can give. Ultimately, the Farewell Discourse is about our experiencing and enjoying that peace. Jesus began with "Do not let your heart be troubled" (14:1). He will now conclude with "These things I have spoken to you, so that in Me you may have peace" (16:33). It is a peace in the midst of turmoil, but it is a peace that is superior to any the world can offer.

The peace that Jesus offers, however, comes with a great price that he paid and we must embrace. The good news is that Jesus declared that his followers can have peace based on his victory. It is my aim today to encourage you that believers have peace based on his victory.

Outline

I. **The Purpose of the Discourse (16:33a–b)**

   A. TEXT

   1. The goal is Christ's peace.

   2. Embracing peace

      a. The secret to the untroubled heart (chap. 14 [unit 1])

      Believe in Christ, love/obey him, and the Holy Spirit mediates the presence of Christ in our lives.

      b. Abiding in Christ (chap. 15 [unit 2])

      Loving obedience, loving one another, and expecting hostility from the world. Our secret weapon is the Spirit working conviction in the world.

      c. The advantages of his departure (chap. 16 [unit 3])

      The Holy Spirit, grief turned into joy, and direct access to the Father.

   B. ILLUSTRATION

   Sometimes peace comes at a heavy price.

   Monetarily, in 1940 dollars, the estimated cost [of WWII] was *$288 billion*. In 2007 dollars this would amount to approximately *$5 trillion*. In addition, the effects of the war on the U.S. economy were that it decisively ended the depression and created a booming economic windfall. Because the United States mainland was untouched by the war, her economic wealth and prosperity soared as she became the world leader in manufacturing, technology, industry and agriculture. In terms of the costs in American lives lost . . . *295,790.*[42]

Peace seems an astonishingly high price in both dollars and lives. The sad part is that the victory could be wiped out tomorrow from inept leadership, domination, natural disaster, or some other horror. In contrast, Christians have peace that someone else paid for, peace that is permanent. It goes beyond the circumstances of this world. The cost to the Lord goes beyond mere physical pain and suffering (as bad as that was). Placing the sins of billions of people on him—that he became sin for us—is impossible for us to imagine. We have no frame of reference regarding the collision of sinfulness and holiness in the soul of Christ. What we can say is that this, not the prospect of enduring the cross, is what caused the agony in the garden. So how should we respond to the peace he purchased?

C. TODAY

Embrace his peace.

1. It begins with faith.

2. It continues in loving obedience.

3. It continues in clinging to Christ and others who love him.

Embracing his peace, however, doesn't mean a trouble-free life.

D. The Declaration of Trouble in the World (16:33c)

"You will have suffering in this world" (HCSB).

E. TEXT

1. Expect cosmic hostility.

We live in a fallen world that is ruled by the evil one. We should expect a certain amount of hostility from the world that he rules. The influence the Devil has on lost humanity is profound. Behind all the realities that we know, there is a cosmic battle going on between the Lord and the forces of darkness.

---

[42] Paul Calore, "What World War II Cost the United States." Cited 16 January 2014. Online: http://historical.whatitcosts.com/facts-world-war-II-pg2.htm.

Those who don't know Christ are operating against him. Unknowingly (sometimes) they work with the forces of darkness against the Lord and his servants. This battle breaks out around us constantly.

2. The personal dimension

We should not say that every person not a Christian is under the direct sway of the Devil. I hesitate to affirm that. I do affirm, however, that there is a personal dimension that we should understand. There is an element of the message of Christ that many find distasteful. It is known as the scandal of the gospel.

The scandal of the gospel is this: "God now commands all people everywhere to repent" (Acts 17:30 HCSB). That God *commands* all people to repent means that all people *need to repent*. That means that every man, woman, and child on the planet is a sinner and needs a Savior.

F. TODAY

How do we respond?

1. We should have proper expectations.

We will suffer the hatred of the world in one way or another. It is inevitable. It may be as harsh as persecution or as mild as the continued intolerance from our culture. Either way, we should expect such things. Jesus warned us about them (see also 15:18–16:4c). It is a ploy of the Devil for us to expect wealth or health simply because we are believers. It is a ploy of the Devil for us to expect that God's providence means we will never face tribulation. It is the clear word of God that we will. It is, however, neither permanent nor capricious. God has a purpose, and it is never for nothing.

2. We should pray against the cosmic forces.

We are in the hands of a loving Father. We are his servants in this war. There is not much more that we can do on the cosmic level other than be obedient in even the smallest details and prayer.

Obedience in even the small things can possibly have much larger consequences. We never know. We do know that God is at work, and he uses his obedient servants. There is not much more we could do on the cosmic scale. That is his business. We cannot manipulate the world scene to bring about any spiritual reality. We cannot hurry or delay his coming. We cannot hurry or delay the tribulation period before his coming. It is God who does these things; we prayerfully live as obedient servants. How he uses us is up to him.

3. We should witness to the people in captivity to the evil one.

As obedient servants, our chief mission is to worship God in the beauty of holiness and to be his voice in testifying to the world. We are not in hostilities against flesh and blood, as Paul would say. We fight spiritual warfare by doing like the apostles, getting the gospel to as many as people as we can. The rest is up to the Lord.

II. Our Response Based on His Victory (16:33d)
"Be courageous! I have conquered the world" (HCSB).

A. TEXT

1. Be courageous.

2. Because he has conquered the world

B. ILLUSTRATION

In the dictionary, next to the words *willpower* and *tough* are pictures of my brother. He's a year older than I but smaller in frame. But make no mistake, he's the tough one in the family. When he was a two-year-old—before child-proof caps—he climbed up the drawers of the kitchen into the medicine cabinet and consumed a bottle of orange-flavored aspirin. My parents rushed him to the emergency room where the hospital administered not one but two spoonfuls of syrup of ipecac (used to induce vomiting). He, by the force of his will, refused to purge. After dad graphically described "pumping your stomach," he decided to let it go. So, none of us were surprised when, sixteen years later he joined the Army.

On January 16, 1991, Operation Desert Storm kicked off and his duties with Desert Shield changed into combat. I was, of course, nervous for his safety. But because he was a believer we were confident in his ultimate safety. It wasn't until the pictures of captured pilots started showing up on TV that I became really concerned. They had obviously been tortured by Saddam Hussein's regime. Their faces and their voices showed it. My concern flashed back to the young boy with the will of steel. I felt that if my brother had ever been captured they would beat him to a pulp before he said anything other than "name, rank, and serial number." I must have communicated that to him in a letter.

He came through safely, never being harmed or captured. When we got together after he got back, I'll never forget the conversation that we had. He expressed that he was flattered by my high thoughts of his "steel will." However, he said, "They can break anyone, very quickly. It's not the physical pain that will break you; it's that they convince you that it will never end. They break your hope that things will ever change."

You and I are in another war, one that has been waging since the fall of humanity. Our enemy wants you to capitulate. But the truth is that we have a shining beacon of secure hope that anchors us. He has won. Christ has defeated death by his death. Any situation we find ourselves in today is only temporary. They may destroy the body but not the victory. We win because he won. We should never be without hope.

C. TODAY

Based on his victory we are to be courageous. What would that look like? Among other things, I can think of at least three manifestations of courage in this war between the Lord and the evil one.

1. Boldness in sharing our testimony
2. Intentionality in sharing the gospel
3. Creativity in getting the gospel to the nations

Conclusion

For the disciples, Jesus' departure was not good news, but it is what they needed. They needed Jesus to obtain victory over the world. We did as well. Because of Jesus' victory on the cross we can have a supernatural peace. That does not mean we do not attempt to make our world a better place. What it means is that we attempt it through a variety means: meeting needs, providing security, and developing infrastructure, among other things, are terribly needed. But what we do most of all is courageously share the gospel, for it is the gospel that brings peace to humanity.

Sermon 14: The Lord's Desire for His Flock

TEXT: John 17

MIT: Jesus prayed for the disciples' protection, unity, and mission.

MIM: Christians should be confident of the Lord's protection, committed to their unity, and must express it in mission.

Introduction

The essence of thriving between the advents has been given in chapters 13–16. It is believing and loving/obeying Christ—this is the essence of abiding in Christ. Chapter 17 contains Christ's final prayer on earth for his disciples. As we look at it we will find one last encouragement to spiritually thrive until he comes.

When we began this series we noted that a person's last words often tell us about that person. I want to conclude our series with a similar observation. I want you to know that a person's will tells you a lot about that person and what's important to him or her. I found a list of rather strange "last wills and testaments" that I think you would find revealing:

- Ms. Eleanor Ritchey, the unmarried granddaughter of the founder of Quaker State Oil, died in 1968 with an estate worth around $12 million. According to Scott Bieber in *Trusts and Estates* magazine: "Under her will, she left over 1,700 pairs of shoes and 1,200 boxes of stationery to the Salvation Army. The rest of the estate went to the dogs." Real dogs, he means—a pack of 150 strays that Ritchey had adopted as pets. (It tells us she loved her dogs—among other things.)

- When American patriot Patrick Henry died, everything he owned was left to his wife—as long as she never married again. If she did, she forfeited the whole thing. "It would make me unhappy," he explained, "to feel I have worked all my life only to support another man's wife!" She remarried anyway. (It reveals an insecure man.)

- Robert Louis Stevenson, author of *Treasure Island*, tried to leave his birthday. He willed it to a good friend who'd complained that since she was born on Christmas, she never got to have a real birthday celebration. (A kind-hearted and humorous gesture.)

- An Australian named Francis R. Lord left one shilling to his wife "for tram fare so she can go somewhere and drown herself." The inheritance was never claimed. (An unhappy marriage.)

- A woman in Cherokee County, North Carolina, left her entire estate to God. The court instructed the county sheriff to find the beneficiary. A few days later, the sheriff returned and submitted his report: "After due and diligent search, God cannot be found in this county."[43] (No comment; enough said.)

John 17, in many ways, is like a last will and testament. It is the longest recorded prayer of Jesus in the Gospels. It shows us what was burdening Jesus' heart as he was preparing to go to the cross. Interestingly enough, it is not merely his upcoming experience for which he prays. His desire is primarily focused on his followers. Jesus prayed for the protection, unity, and mission of his disciples. If these are the things that are on Jesus' mind, then our commitments should be similar. Christians should be confident of the Lord's protection and committed to their unity, and expressing it in mission.

Outline

I. The Lord Prayed for Himself (17:1–5)

"Jesus spoke these things, looked up to heaven, and said: 'Father, the hour has come. Glorify Your Son so that the Son may glorify You, for You gave Him authority over all flesh; so He may give eternal life to all You have given Him. This is eternal life: that they may know You, the only true God, and the One You have sent—Jesus Christ. I have glorified You on the earth by completing the work You gave Me to do. Now, Father, glorify Me in Your presence with that glory I had with You before the world existed'" (HCSB).

A. TEXT

 1. Jesus embraced the cross.

 a. The request to glorify the Son is a request to hasten the cross.

 b. His great desire was to accomplish salvation for us.

---

[43] Richard Harter, "Bizarre Wills and Testaments" (1 March 2006). Cited 16 January 2014. http://richardhartersworld.com/cri/2006/wills.html.

2. Jesus glorified God by completing his mission.

   He made eternal life possible.

3. Jesus requests to return to his former glory.

   a. This is an indication of deity (cf. Isa 42:8).

   b. This restates his desire to accomplish salvation for us.

B. TODAY

1. Embrace his cross.

   a. We should embrace his cross as the way that we are going to get to heaven.

   No one comes to God another way. It is blasphemous to assume that the agony of the Son is only a way to God. It is the only way.

   i. We should embrace his cross as the way others will get to heaven.

   It is the only way our loved ones will endure eternity. It is the only way for anyone to get to heaven. Far too many today seem almost ashamed of the cross, as if it is good enough for Gentiles but not for Jews. Or perhaps someone, by some quirk of fate or loophole in Scripture, will get to heaven by being sincere, or a good person, or simply by the love of God. God's love is demonstrated in the cross. Embrace it.

2. Embrace his mission.

   a. Salvation is not our fire insurance.

   Once we get it, we can rest at ease. Our soul is taken care of, don't worry. The truth is that just as Jesus embraced his mission, so should we. It is our message. It is our ministry. It is what we do no matter what occupation we are in.

b. Actively participate in his mission.

Participate at church. You should be active in the ministries of your church. You have not done God a favor by attending church today or any day.

C. ILLUSTRATION

When I think of embracing the cross, I think of Arthur Blessitt. Arthur Blessitt from Greenwood, MS, is known as "The Man Who Carried the Cross around the World." From his website:

He has carried on foot a 12 ft. cross for Jesus around the world since 1969. Through wars, deserts, jungles, 321 countries, major island groups and territories, 7 continents, and over 40,195 miles (64,686 km). *The Guinness Book of World Records 1996–2012* lists this as "The World's Longest Walk." This modern day pilgrim has faced a firing squad, been arrested 24 times, been through 54 countries at war, fasted 40 days, ran for President of the United States and has walked with 70,000 people across Poland.[44]

Here is a visual image of a spiritual reality. As much as Mr. Blessitt carried a wooden cross around the world, we should carry the message of the cross wherever we go. God may not call you to such a ministry, but he has called every Christian to embrace the cross and take it to the nations.

II. Jesus Prays for His Present Disciples (17:6–19)

A. TEXT

1. Jesus prayed for spiritual protection (vv. 9–12).

"I pray for them. I am not praying for the world but for those You have given Me, because they are Yours. Everything I have is Yours, and everything You have is Mine, and I have been glorified in them. I am no longer in the world, but they are in the world, and I am coming to You. Holy Father, protect them by Your name that You have given Me, so that they may be one as We are one. While I was with them, I was protecting them by Your name that You have given Me. I guarded

---

[44] See http://www.blessitt.com/MediaPressInfo/MediaPressInfo.html.

them and not one of them is lost, except the son of destruction, so that the Scripture may be fulfilled" (HCSB).

    a. He prays on the basis of their ownership by God (vv. 9–11).

    b. He prays for their spiritual protection (v. 11).

    c. He prays for their unity (v. 11).

        i. Jesus prayed for sanctification for mission (vv. 13–19).

"Now I am coming to You, and I speak these things in the world so that they may have My joy completed in them. I have given them Your word. The world hated them because they are not of the world, as I am not of the world. I am not praying that You take them out of the world but that You protect them from the evil one. They are not of the world, as I am not of the world. Sanctify them by the truth; Your word is truth. As You sent Me into the world, I also have sent them into the world. I sanctify Myself for them, so they also may be sanctified by the truth" (HCSB).

        (a) He prays for their joy.

        (b) He prays again for their spiritual protection.

        (c) He prays for the set-apart-ness for mission.

B. TODAY

1. Embrace your security.

Jesus prayed for our spiritual protection to encourage the disciples. You should also be encouraged. He does not pray because it is not a reality but because it is a reality. He wants the disciples to know they are safe in the Father's hands. They are, and so are you if you know Christ.

2. Embrace your fellow Christians.

Of all people we should be united. Unfortunately, we of all people are terribly disjointed. I personally don't think denominations are particularly evil. I think it is helpful to know the broad contours of theology that a particular church expresses. I do think sectarianism is a bad thing. We may rejoice in another brother or sister in another denomination. If they know Christ there is a supernatural relatedness that should cause us joy.

3. Embrace your mission.

Unity for the sake of unity is a failure to launch. Unity is for the sake of the mission of Christ. When the world sees our unity, they will know that something real is going on. When the world fails to see our unity because we have failed to display it, they believe they have reason to reject the gospel. May this never be.

C. ILLUSTRATION

If there is any doubt that disunity in the church causes problems, all we have to do is look at the book of 1 Corinthians. They had personal attacks against Paul (4:3,15; 9:1–3), abuses at the Lord's table (11:17–34), infamous sexual immorality (5:1–5; 6:12–20), lawsuits among believers (6:1–8), abuse of spiritual gifts (chaps. 12–14), and doctrinal error (esp. regarding the resurrection; chap. 15). Notice, however, that the first problem Paul addresses is the disunity of the believers and the sectarian groups (1 Cor 1:11). Their disunity created or helped create one of the most dysfunctional churches ever recorded.

III. Jesus Prayed for All His Disciples (17:20–26)

A. TEXT

1. Jesus prayed for his future disciples (vv. 20–23).

"I pray not only for these, but also for those who believe in Me through their message. May they all be one, as You, Father, are in Me and I am in You. May they also be one in Us, so the world may believe You sent Me. I have given them the glory You have given Me. May they be one as We are one. I am in them and You are in Me. May they be made completely one, so the world may know You have sent Me and have loved them as You have loved Me" (HCSB).

a. Jesus repeats his request for future disciples to be united (vv. 20–21).

b. Jesus has given them all they need (his glory; v. 22).

c. The purpose is to witness to the world (v. 23).

i. Jesus prays for all his disciples (vv. 24–26).

"Father, I desire those You have given Me to be with Me where I am. Then they will see My glory, which You have given Me because You loved Me before the world's foundation. Righteous Father! The world has not known You. However, I have known You, and these have known that You sent Me. I made Your name known to them and will make it known, so the love You have loved Me with may be in them and I may be in them" (HCSB).

(a) Glory is the ultimate destination of all believers (vv. 24–25).

(b) Jesus promises to continue to reveal God's name to his own (vv. 25–26).

B. ILLUSTRATION

Gary Burge said it well: "This is the essence of Jesus' vision for the church. It is not a community that heals people just so that they will be whole (though healing is important); it is not a community that teaches so that people will be gratified by knowledge (though wisdom is valuable); it is not a community that evangelizes so it will grow its ranks (though its mission to the world is crucial). The church is a community that invites people to touch the glory of God, to be changed by it, and to bear it to the world."[45]

C. TODAY

1. Embrace your destination.

Too many believers have nagging doubts about their destination. Some are sure, but they hesitate to declare it. It is

---

[45] Gary Burge, *John*, NIV Application Commentary (Grand Rapids: Zondervan, 2000), 477.

not arrogant to be sure of Christ. It is not bragging to know you are going to heaven. It is truth. Embrace the truth. Some have nagging doubts that their salvation is sure. Christ has secured it. None will be lost. Embrace your security. What would it look like for a believer to embrace his secure destination? Worry is a thing of the past. Fellowship is easier. Ministry is not hindered (we are often distracted by worry about destination). Witness becomes our concern.

2. Continue to abide in Christ.

The continued revelation of God's name comes through the ministry of the indwelling Holy Spirit in the life of the believer. The believer's concern, then, is not to hinder the lines of communication. The believer who is not abiding in Christ is under the discipline of the Lord, not growing in Christ. He is in no position to hear the voice of the Lord. Keep the lines of communication open through abiding in Christ.

Conclusion

S. Lewis Johnson, former professor at Dallas Theological Seminary, wrote fourteen expositions of the Farewell Discourse for the *Emmaus Journal*. As he began his treatment of the final prayer, we will conclude it. "When John Knox, the Scottish reformer, was lying on his deathbed in his house on High Street in Edinburgh, he insistently asked that the Bible be read aloud to him. He wanted to hear the fifty-third chapter of Isaiah, and he asked for the Psalms, and he even requested that some of Calvin's sermons be read to him. But above all he asked for his beloved chapter from the Gospel of John, the seventeenth chapter, which he referred to as 'the place where I cast my first anchor.'"[46]

Jesus' prayers here are a declaration of unadulterated truth. Will you cast your anchor here? Will you embrace the cross? Will you embrace your secure position? Will you embrace your brother and sister in Christ? Will you go on mission with Christ? This is the thing that was on Christ's mind immediately before he died for you. Embrace it, and be transformed.

---

[46] S. Lewis Johnson Jr., "Jesus Praying for Himself: An Exposition of John 17:1–5," *Emmaus Journal* 7 (1998): 202–3.

SELECT BIBLIOGRAPHY

Akin, Daniel L., Bill Curtis, and Stephen Rummage. *Engaging Exposition*. Nashville: B&H Academic, 2011.
Bammel, John E. "The Farewell Discourse of the Evangelist John and Its Jewish Heritage." *TynBul* 44 (1993): 111–19.
Barrett, C. K. *The Gospel according to John*. 2nd ed. Philadelphia: Westminster, 1978.
Bauckham, Richard. "The Parable of the Vine: Rediscovering a Lost Parable of Jesus." *NTS* 33 (1987): 84–11.
Beasley-Murray, G. R. *John*. WBC 36. Waco, TX: Word, 1987.
Beekman, John, John Callow, and Michael Kopesec. *The Semantic Structure of Written Communication*. 5th revision. Dallas: SIL, 1981.
Blass, F., and A. Debrunner. *A Greek Grammar of the New Testament and Other Early Christian Literature*. Translated and edited by Robert W. Funk. Chicago: University of Chicago Press, 1961.
Blomberg, Craig. *The Historical Reliability of John's Gospel: Issues and Commentary*. Downers Grove, IL: InterVarsity, 2001.
Borchert, Gerald R. *John 12–21*. NAC 25B. Nashville: B&H, 2002.
Boyle, John L. "The Last Discourse (Jn 13,31–16,33) and Prayer (Jn 17): Some Observations on Their Unity and Development." *Bib* 56 (1975): 210–22.
Brodie, Thomas L. *The Gospel according to John: A Literary and Theological Commentary*. New York: Oxford University Press, 1993.
Brown, Colin, ed. *The New International Dictionary of New Testament Theology*. Grand Rapids: Zondervan, 1975.
Brown, Raymond E. *The Gospel according to John*. AB 29A. New York: Doubleday, 1971.
Bryan, Steven M. "The Eschatological Temple in John 14." *BBR* 15 (2005): 187–98.

Bultmann, Rudolf. *The Gospel of John: A Commentary*. Translated by G. R. Beasley-Murray, R. W. N. Hoare, and J. K. Riches. Philadelphia: Westminster, 1971.
Burge, Gary. *John*. NIV Application Commentary. Grand Rapids: Zondervan, 2000.
Carson, D. A. "The Function of the Paraclete in John 16:7–1." *JBL* 98 (1979): 547–66.
———. *The Gospel according to John*. PNTC. Grand Rapids: Eerdmans, 1991.
———. *New Testament Commentary Survey*. 6th ed. Grand Rapids: Baker Academic, 2007.
Chennattu, Rekha M. *Johannine Discipleship as a Covenant Relationship*. Peabody, MA: Hendrikson, 2006.
Coloe, Mary. "Temple Imagery in John." *Int* 63 (2009): 368–81.
Cotterell, Peter, and Max Turner. *Linguistics & Biblical Interpretation*. Downers Grove: IVP Academic, 1989.
Dodd, C. H. *The Interpretation of the Fourth Gospel*. Cambridge: Cambridge University Press, 1953.
Ensor, Peter. "The Glorification of the Son of Man: An Analysis of John 13:31–32." *TynBul* 58 (2007): 229–52.
Erickson, Richard J. "The Damned and the Justified in Romans 5:12–21: An Analysis of Semantic Structure." Pages 282–37 in *Discourse Analysis and the New Testament: Approaches and Results*. Edited by Stanley E. Porter. Sheffield: Sheffield Academic Press, 1999.
Gadamer, Hans-Georg. *Truth and Method*. New York: Seabury, 1975.
Green, Joel B. *The Gospel of Luke*. NICNT. Grand Rapids: Eerdmans, 1997.
Grudem, Wayne. *Systematic Theology: An Introduction to Biblical Doctrine*. Leicester, England: InterVarsity, 1994.
Guthrie, George H. *The Structure of Hebrews: A Text-Linguistic Analysis*. NTSup 73. Leiden: Brill 1997.
Haenchen, Ernst. *A Commentary on the Gospel of John*. 2 vols. Hermeneia. Translated by Robert W. Funk. Philadelphia: Fortress, 1984.
Harris, R. Laird, Gleason L. Archer, and Bruce K. Waltke. *Theological Wordbook of the Old Testament*. Chicago: Moody, 1980.
Hirsch, E. D., Jr. *Validity in Interpretation*. New Haven, CT: Yale University Press, 1967.
Hoskyns, Edwyn Clement. *The Fourth Gospel*. Edited by Francis Noel Davey. 2nd ed. London: Faber & Faber, 1947.
House, H. Wayne, and Daniel G. Garland. *God's Message, Your Sermon: Discover, Develop, and Deliver What God Meant by What He Said*. Nashville: Thomas Nelson, 2007.
Janzen, J. Gerald. "The Scope of Jesus's High Priestly Prayer in John 17." *Enc* 67 (2006): 1–26.

Johnson, S. Lewis, Jr. "Jesus Praying for Himself: An Exposition of John 17:1–5." *Emmaus Journal* 7 (1998): 22–15.
Johnston, George. *The Spirit-Paraclete in the Gospel of John.* SNTSM 12. Cambridge: Cambridge University Press, 1970.
Kaiser, Walter C., Jr. *Toward an Exegetical Theology: Biblical Exegesis for Preaching and Teaching.* Grand Rapids: Baker, 2004.
Keener, Craig S. *The Gospel of John: A Commentary.* 2 vols. Peabody, MA: Hendrickson, 2003.
Kellum, L. Scott. "The Unity of the Farewell Discourse: The Literary Integrity of John 13:31–16:33." Ph.D. diss.. Southeastern Baptist Theological Seminary, 2002.
———. *The Unity of the Farewell Discourse: The Literary Integrity of John 13:31–16:33.* JSNTSup 256. London: T&T Clark, 2005.
Köstenberger, Andreas J., and J. Patterson. *Invitation to Hermeneutics.* Grand Rapids: Kregel, 2011.
Köstenberger, Andreas J., L. Scott Kellum, and Charles L. Quarles. *The Cradle, the Cross, and the Crown: An Introduction to the New Testament.* Nashville: B&H Academic, 2009.
Köstenberger, Andreas. *Encountering John: The Gospel in Historical, Literary, and Theological Perspective.* Encountering Biblical Studies. Grand Rapids: Baker, 1999.
———. *A Theology of John's Gospel and Letters.* Biblical Theology of the New Testament. Grand Rapids: Zondervan, 2009.
———. "Jesus the Good Shepherd Who Will Also Bring Other Sheep (John 10:16): The Old Testament Background of a Familiar Metaphor." *BBR* 12 (2002): 67–96.
———. *John.* BECNT. Grand Rapids: Baker, 2005.
———. "John." Pages 3–216 in *Zondervan Illustrated Bible Backgrounds Commentary.* Edited by Clinton E. Arnold. Grand Rapids: Zondervan, 2001.
———. "The Greater Works of the Believer according to John 14:12." Διδασκαλια (1995): 36–45.
Kruse, Colin G. *John: An Introduction and Commentary.* TNTC. Grand Rapids: Eerdmans, 2003.
Kurz, William S. "Biblical Farewell Addresses." *TBT* 38 (2000): 69–73.
———. "Luke 22:14–38 and Greco-Roman and Biblical Farewell Addresses." *JBL* 14 (1985): 251–68.
Larson, Mildred. *Meaning-Based Translation: A Guide to Cross-Language Equivalence.* 2nd ed. Lanham, MD: University Press of America, 1997.
Levinsohn, Stephen H., and Robert A. Dooley. *Analyzing Discourse: A Manual of Basic Concepts.* Dallas: SIL, 2001.

Levinsohn, Stephen H. *Discourse Features of New Testament Greek: A Coursebook on the Information Structure of New Testament Greek.* 2nd ed. Dallas: SIL International, 2000.

———. "ὅτι *Recitativum* in John's Gospel: A Stylistic or a Pragmatic Device?" Pages 1–14 in *Work Papers of the Summer Institute of Linguistics, University of North Dakota Session,* vol. 43. 1999.

Lightfoot, R. H. *St. John's Gospel: A Commentary.* Oxford: Oxford University Press, 1956.

Lindars, Barnabas. *The Gospel of John.* NCB 34. London: Oliphants, 1972.

Lombard, H. A., and W. H. Oliver. "A Working Supper in Jerusalem: John 13:38 Introduces Jesus' Farewell Discourses." *Neot* 25 (1991): 357–77.

Longacre, Robert E. *The Grammar of Discourse.* 2nd ed. Topics in Language and Linguistics. New York: Plenum, 1996.

———. "Towards an Exegesis of 1 John Based on the Discourse Analysis of the Greek Text." Pages 271–86 in *Linguistics and New Testament Interpretation: Essays on Discourse Analysis.* Edited by David Alan Black, Katherine Barnewell, and Stephen H. Levinsohn. Nashville: B&H, 1992.

Longman, Tremper, III, and Raymond B. Dillard. *An Introduction to the Old Testament.* 2nd ed. Grand Rapids: Zondervan, 2006.

Louw, Johannes P. "Discourse Analysis and the Greek New Testament." *BT* 24 (1973): 11–18.

Maier, Paul L. "Sejanus, Pilate, and the Date of the Crucifixion." *CH* 37 (1968): 3–13.

Marsh, John. *The Gospel of Saint John.* Baltimore: Penguin, 1968.

McCaffrey, James. *The House with Many Rooms: The Temple Theme of John 14:2–3.* Rome: Biblical Institute, 1988.

Merrill, Eugene H., Mark Rooker, and Michael Grisanti. *The World and the Word: An Introduction to the Old Testament.* Nashville: B&H Academic, 2011.

Michaels, J. Ramsey *The Gospel of John.* NICNT. Grand Rapids: Eerdmans, 2010.

Moloney, F. J. *The Gospel of John.* SP 4. Collegeville, MN: Liturgical Press, 1998.

Morris, Leon. *The Gospel according to John.* NICNT. Grand Rapids: Eerdmans, 1995.

Motyer, J. Alec. *The Prophecy of Isaiah: An Introduction and Commentary.* Downers Grove, IL: IVP, 1993.

Olford, Stephen F., with David L. Olford. *Anointed Expository Preaching.* Nashville: B&H, 1998.

Painter, John. *The Quest for the Messiah.* 2nd ed. First American ed. Nashville: Abingdon, 1993.

Ridderbos, Herman. *The Gospel of John: A Theological Commentary.* Translated by J. Vriend. Grand Rapids: Eerdmans, 1991.

Robinson, Haddon. *Biblical Preaching: The Development and Delivery of Expository Messages.* Grand Rapids: Baker, 1980.

Schleiermacher, Friedrich. *Hermeneutics and Criticism: And Other Writings*. Translated and edited by Andrew Bowie. Cambridge: Cambridge University Press, 1998.
Schnackenburg, Rudolf. *The Gospel according to St. John*. 3 vols. New York: Crossroad, 1982.
Schreiner, Thomas R. "A Plea for Biblical Preaching." *SBJT* 3 (1999): 2–3.
Segovia, Fernando F. *The Farewell of the Word: The Johannine Call to Abide*. Philadelphia; Fortress, 1991.
———. *Love Relationships in the Johannine Tradition: Agape/Agapan in 1 John and the Fourth Gospel*. SBLDS 58. Chico, CA: Scholars Press, 1982.
Shelenberger, Aaron Tuazon. "An Exposition of the Jehovah's Witnesses' Argument in Rejecting Christ's Deity Using John 17:3." *Christian Apologetics Journal* 8 (2009): 4–20.
Sheridan, Ruth. "John's Gospel and Modern Genre Theory: The Farewell Discourse (John 13–17) as a Test Case." *ITQ* 75 (2010): 287–299.
Sherman, Grace E., and John C. Tuggy. *A Semantic Structure Analysis of the Johannine Epistles*. Dallas: SIL, 1994.
Smalley, Paul M. "Satisfied with the Lord's All-Sufficiency: Wilhelmus à Brakel on Joy," *Puritan Reformed Journal* 3 (2011): 236–66.
Smith, D. Moody. *The Composition and Order of the Fourth Gospel: Bultmann's Literary Theory*. New Haven: Yale University Press, 1965.
Smith, Marsha A. Ellis. *Holman Book of Biblical Charts, Maps, and Reconstructions*. Nashville: Holman Reference, 1993.
Tasker, R. V. G. *The Gospel according to John: An Introduction and Commentary*. TNTC 4. Grand Rapids: Eerdmans, 1960.
Thatcher, Tom. *The Riddles of Jesus in John: A Study in Tradition and Folklore*. SBLMS 53. Atlanta: Society of Biblical Literature, 2000.
Thomas, Heath. "Building House to House (Isaiah 5:8): Theological Reflection on Land Development and Creation Care." *BBR* 21 (2011): 198.
Unger, Merrill F. "Expository Preaching." *BSac* 111 (1954): 325.
Vanhoozer, Kevin J. *Is There Meaning in This Text? The Bible, the Reader, and the Morality of Literary Knowledge*. Grand Rapids: Zondervan, 1998.
Walker, W. O., Jr. "The Lord's Prayer in Matthew and John." *NTS* 28 (1982): 237–56.
Wallace, D. *Greek Grammar beyond the Basics: An Exegetical Syntax of the New Testament*. Grand Rapids: Zondervan, 1991.
Wegner, Paul D. *Using Old Testament Hebrew in Preaching: A Guide for Students and Pastors*. Grand Rapids: Kregel, 2009.
Wenham, David. "The Enigma of the Fourth Gospel: Another Look." *TynBul* 48 (1997): 149–78.

Whitacre, R. A. "Vine, Fruit of the Vine." Pages 867–88 in *Dictionary of Jesus and the Gospels*. Edited by Joel B. Green, Scot McKnight, and I. Howard Marshall. Downers Grove, IL: IVP, 1992.

Willamson, H. G. M. *Isaiah 1—27: Volume 1 (Isaiah 1—5)*. ICC. London: T&T Clark, 2006.

Witherington, Ben. *John's Wisdom*. Louisville, KY: WJK, 19.

Young, Richard. *Intermediate Greek: A Linguistic and Exegetical Approach*. Nashville: B&H, 1992.

Name Index

Akin, Daniel L. *29, 331*
Archer, Gleason L. *231, 237, 332*
Arndt, W. *230*

Bammel, Ernst *76, 331*
Barnhouse, Donald G. *313*
Barrett, C. K. *70, 82, 91, 93, 100, 110, 117, 139, 150, 173–74, 185–86, 192, 199, 201, 203, 213, 331*
Bauckham, Richard *134, 331*
Bauer, W. *230*
Baumgartner, Walter *230*
Beasley-Murray, G. R. *72, 119, 135, 150, 163, 166, 183, 331*
Becker, Jürgen *119–20, 135, 150, 183*
Beekman, John *21, 51, 57, 61, 131, 331*
Bell, Rob *102*
Bergerud, Eric M. *244*
Beutler, J. *69*
Black, David Allen *201*
Blass, F. *230, 331*
Blomberg, Craig L. *25, 72, 119, 135, 150, 163, 165, 175, 183, 200, 203, 211, 331*
Borchert, Gerald R. *69, 119, 173, 177, 201, 207, 211–12, 331*
Botterweck, G. Johannes *231*
Bouchoc, Raymond *230–31*
Boyle, John L. *72, 331*
Brand, Chad *231*
Briggs, Charles A. *230*

Brisco, Thomas V. *232*
Brodie, Thomas L. *119, 331*
Bromiley, Geoffrey *8*
Brown, Colin *8, 231, 331*
Brown, Francis *230*
Brown, Raymond E. *70, 72, 92, 119, 145, 150, 163, 174, 183, 186, 201, 203, 207, 221, 230, 331*
Bryan, Steven M. *94, 331*
Bultmann, Rudolf *72, 82, 119, 135, 163, 166, 183, 332*
Burge, Gary M. *70, 83, 100, 150, 328, 332*
Callow, John *21, 51, 57, 61, 131, 331*

Campbell, Constatine *226*
Carson, D. A. *70–72, 78, 81, 90–91, 106–7, 110, 117, 119, 125–26, 134–35, 138–39, 150, 163, 165, 173–75, 185–86, 200–201, 203, 206–7, 213, 222, 233, 332*
Carter, Terry G. *34*
Chennattu, Rekha M. *70, 82, 332*
Coloe, Mary *93, 332*
Cotterell, Peter *57–58, 332*
Curtis, Bill *29, 331*

Danker, Frederick W. *81, 230*
Debrunner, A. *230, 331*
Dettwiler, A. *119*
Dillard, Raymond B. *232, 334*
Dodd, D. H. *70, 120, 150, 201, 206, 332*

Doh, Hyunsok *184*
Dowley, Tim *232*
Draper, Charles W. *231*
Driver, S. R. *230*
Durant, Michael J. *247–48*
Duvall, J. Scott *34*

Egbert, W. R. *240*
Elliff, Tom *294*
England, Archie *231*
Ensor, Peter *81, 332*
Erickson, Richard J. *55, 332*

Fee, Gordon *71*
Fletcher, Jesse C. *288*
Freedman, David Noel *231*
Friberg, Timothy *20*
Friedrich, Gerhard *8*

Gadamer, Hans-Georg *13, 332*
Garland, Daniel G. *33, 332*
Geden, A. S. *231*
Gingrich, F. W. *230*
Giurisato, Giorgio *135*
Green, Joel B. *77, 332*
Grey, Aubrey de *246*
Grisanti, Michael *232, 334*
Grudem, Wayne *233, 274–75, 332*
Guthrie, George H. *51, 332*

Haenchen, Ernst *99, 119, 150, 332*
Harris, R. Laird *231, 332*
Hartov, Steven *248*
Hays, J. Daniel *34*
Heidegger, Martin *13*
Hick, John *102*
Hirsch, E. D., Jr. *14, 332*
Hoskyns, Edwyn C. *72, 119, 150, 183, 332*
House, H. Wayne *33, 332*
Hubbard, Robert L., Jr. *25*
Hughes, Thomas *279*

Janzen, J. Gerald *199, 332*
Johnson, S. Lewis Jr. *218, 329, 333*
Johnston, George *72, 150, 333*

Kaiser, Walter C., Jr. *6, 333*

Keener, Craig S. *44, 47, 77, 81, 92, 99–100, 106–7, 111, 119, 125–26, 135, 145, 154, 167, 192, 203, 206, 211–12, 221, 333*
Kellum, L. Scott *iv, 27, 68–69, 74, 201, 232, 333*
Kittel, Gerhard *8*
Klein, William W. *25*
Köehler, Ludwig *230*
Kohlenberger, John R. *231*
Kopesec, Michael *21, 51, 61, 131, 331*
Köstenberger, A. J. *5, 27, 43, 45, 50, 90, 99–101, 107, 110, 120, 125–26, 137, 139, 145, 153, 165, 173, 176, 184–86, 200, 207, 211, 213, 221, 229–32, 333*
Kruse, Colin G. *118, 333*
Kurz, William S. *75–76, 333*

Lagrange, M. L. *69, 119, 201*
Larson, Mildred *24, 51, 57–58, 63–64, 333*
Levinsohn, Stephen *51, 53–54, 70, 109, 133, 333–34*
Lewis, J. P. *27*
Lewis, Richard C. *273*
Licona, Michael *300*
Lightfoot, R. H. *72, 150, 334*
Lindars, Barnabas *119, 150, 334*
Lisowksy, Gerhard *231*
Lombard, H. A. *70, 334*
Longacre, Robert E. *131–34*
Longman, Tremper, III *232–33, 334*
Louw, Johannes P. *55, 230, 234, 334*

Maier, Paul L. *26, 334*
Marshall, I. Howard *231*
Mayo, P. L. *27*
McCaffrey, James *93, 334*
McDowell, Josh *299*
McNeese, TIm *287*
Merrill, Eugene H. *232, 334*
Michaels, J. Ramsey *120, 222, 334*
Miller, Nerva F. *20*
Mittmann, Siegfried *232*
Moloney, F. J. *69, 72, 119, 150, 183, 212, 221, 334*
Morris, Leon *70, 72, 82, 110, 119–20, 125, 140, 144–45, 150, 152–53, 185–86, 206, 208, 211, 213, 334*

Motyer, J. Alec *136–37, 334*
Moulton, W. F. *230–31*

Neugebaur, J. *150*
Nida, Eugene *230, 234*

Olford, David L. *6, 334*
Olford, Stephen F. *6, 29, 334*
Oliver, W. H. *70, 334*

Painter, John *72, 334*
Patterson, J. *5, 229, 333*
Pinnock, Clark *102*
Porter, Stanley E. *51*
Purswell, Jeff *233*

Quarles, Charles L. *27, 232, 333*

Rae, Michael *246*
Rahner, Karl *101*
Richardson, M. E. J. *230*
Ridderbos, Herman *72, 76, 82, 100, 119–20, 126, 135, 140, 153, 164–65, 175–76, 183, 185, 187, 207–8, 212, 221–22, 334*
Ringgren, Helmer *231*
Robertson, A. T. *230*
Robinson, Edward *230*
Robinson, Haddon *5–6, 334*
Rooker, Mark *232, 334*
Rost, Leonhard *231*
Rowell, Edward K. *310*
Rüger, Hans Peter *231*
Rummage, Stephen *29, 331*

Schemm, Peter R. *212*
Schleiermacher, Friedrich *15, 335*
Schmitt, Götz *232*
Schnackenburg, Rudolf *72, 119, 150, 163, 173, 183, 199, 203, 335*
Scholtissek, K. *119*
Schreiner, Thomas R. *7, 335*

Segovia, Fernando F. *67, 72, 75, 119–20, 135, 150, 163, 165, 172, 183, 335*
Shelenberger, Aaron T. *204, 335*
Shepherd, David *221–22*
Sheridan, Ruth *76, 335*
Sherman, Grace E. *133, 335*
Simoens, Y. *69, 72, 150*
Smalley, P. M. *307, 335*
Smith, D. Moody *335*
Smith, Dwight M. *117*
Smith, Gary *143, 276*
Smith, Marsha A. Ellis *232, 335*
Stamm, Johann J. *230*
Stefan, Crinisor *163, 167*
Strauss, David F. *67*
Swanson, James A. *231*

Tasker, R. V. G. *91, 335*
Tenney, Merrill C. *231*
Thatcher, Tom *184, 335*
Thomas, Heath *137, 335*
Tuggy, John C. *133, 335*
Turner, Max *57–58, 332*

Unger, Merrill F. *6–7, 335*

Vanhoozer, Kevin J. *15, 335*
von Ulrich von Hutten, Gespräche *67*

Walker, W. O., Jr. *200, 335*
Wallace, Dan *78, 230, 335*
Waltke, Bruce K. *231, 332*
Ward, Laura *239–40*
Wegner, Paul D. *229, 335*
Whenam, David *27*
Whitacre, Rodney A. *136, 336*
Willamson, Hugh G. M. *136, 336*
Witherington, Ben *72, 135, 203, 336*
Witty, Robert G. *293–94*

York, H. W. *133*
Young, Richard *31, 225, 336*

Subject Index

A

abiding in Christ/abide   73, 93–94, 118, 133–40, 142, 144, 148–49, 159, 178, 218, 220–21, 271–73, 276, 278, 304, 316, 322, 329
anaphora/anaphoric   117, 192
antonyms   140, 185, 230, 238
asyndeton   52

B

background/backgrounding   73, 226
belief in Christ   8, 19, 43–50, 89–125, 138, 151, 159, 166, 170, 182–84, 189–90, 195, 206, 210, 217, 219, 245–60, 264–65, 268–70, 292, 305, 309, 311, 316–17, 327
Bible software   19, 236–38
birkhat ha minim   27
Book of Glory   48–52, 68, 74, 223

Book of Signs   43–48, 50, 68, 74, 100
boundary features   21, 42, 51–53, 65, 70, 151
Bread of Life Discourse   44, 71

C

Caiaphas's "prophecy"   49, 221
Cana Cycle   43–44, 74
canonical context   27–28, 75
chiasm   52, 69
Christ's death   26, 48–50, 69, 70–74, 77–80, 84–89, 92–93, 95–97, 100, 103, 109–10, 112, 125–27, 129, 133, 175, 178, 180, 203, 212–13, 215, 220–22, 239–42, 244–45, 247, 250, 254, 266, 270, 277, 290–92, 298–99, 308, 311–13, 316, 320–21, 324
Christ's deity   44, 46, 125, 204, 212, 324

Christ's hour   48, 69, 79–80, 83–84, 202–3, 220, 241, 323
Christ's resurrection   47–49, 80, 93, 100–101, 110, 118, 203, 212, 221, 247, 262, 292, 298–303, 307, 309, 327
Christian unity (solidarity)   68, 131, 133, 200, 207, 210–11, 214, 216, 220, 222, 277–280, 322, 326, 329
coherence   23, 68, 72, 131, 133
cohesion   131
communication relations   55–74, 205
conjunctions   18, 21, 52–53, 92, 126, 205
conventions   17
conversation   41, 99, 106, 174
crafting conclusions and introductions   34–35

D

deity   111

Devil 126, 171, 208, 286, 288, 296, 303, 317–20, 326
discourse analysis 23, 131, 155, 219, 224–25

E
election 111, 137, 206, 278–79, 294
emphasis 20–21, 23, 49, 76, 79, 82, 226
eschatological temple 94, 97, 100
eternal life 101, 203–4, 251, 323–24
evangelism 77, 217, 259, 264, 267–68, 275, 282, 285–86, 289, 293, 319, 328
expository genre 31, 50, 65, 77
expository preaching 6–8, 12, 65

F
Festival Cycle 44–47
final prayer 200

G
genre 5, 16–17, 69, 131, 219, 224
  embedded 132
  expository 16–17, 224
  hortatory 16–17, 132, 141, 224–25
  narrative 16
  procedural 16–18
glory/glorification 50, 71, 78–81, 84–85, 87, 111, 115, 118, 125, 211–12, 214, 217, 220, 240–41, 257–59, 273, 294, 296, 304, 306–7, 312, 323–25, 327–28
Good Shepherd Discourse 47, 71

H
Herod the Great 26, 149, 281
high-priestly prayer 67, 199
historical context 24–27, 75
historical events 27
Holy Spirit 33, 51, 84, 100, 118, 120–24, 129, 137–38, 149, 154, 157–59, 164–71, 188, 190, 193, 195, 197, 208–9, 213, 220, 261–62, 264, 270, 285–86, 290–97, 303–4, 308, 311–12, 316, 329
hook-words 21, 52, 70, 73
hortatory genres 31, 50, 56–57, 64–65, 68, 77

I
illustrations 39, 234, 241, 243, 246–47, 251, 255, 257–58, 262, 264–66, 268, 271–72, 274–76, 278–79, 281, 283, 285, 287–88, 290, 292–94, 296, 298, 301, 304, 307–8, 310, 313–16, 319, 322–23, 325, 327–29
imbedded genre 41, 47
inclusio 21, 43, 52, 120, 136, 144, 146
indirect speech 92–93

J
John the Baptist 43–44
joy 71, 140, 143, 173, 176, 178, 180–81, 216, 275, 278, 294, 298–99, 301, 303, 305–7, 326
Judas Iscariot 45, 53, 70, 74, 78, 125, 138, 201, 207, 240

K
kingdom of God 153

L
Lazarus 48, 110, 185, 222
literary context 16
location of meaning 13–15

M
macrostructure 21–22, 43, 68–69, 75, 151
markedness 43, 53
MIM (main idea of the message) 28, 30, 32, 35, 37, 84–85, 90, 96, 103, 111–12, 121, 126, 141, 146–47, 155, 168, 178, 188, 194, 214, 245, 250, 253, 261, 266, 271, 277, 282, 290, 298, 308, 315, 322
mindset 25–26
mission 12, 71, 209, 211–12, 214–16, 218, 267–68, 279–80, 285, 295, 319, 322–29
MIT (main idea of the text) 28–30, 32, 35, 37, 84–85, 90, 96, 103, 111–12, 121, 126, 141, 146–47, 155, 168, 177–78, 188, 194, 214, 245, 250, 253, 261, 266, 271, 277, 282, 290, 298, 308, 315, 322

N
new commandment 71, 79, 81–83, 85–87, 135–36, 145–47, 222, 240, 242, 277
new covenant 89, 155, 213, 262, 282
new Moses 89

O
overcoming *193–94*

P
Paraclete *71, 117–21, 123, 154–55, 157, 161–70, 172, 177, 219–20, 223, 263, 285, 289–93, 298*
παροιμία *184–85*
parataxis *162*
participant *52, 54, 79*
participants reference *70*
peak *23, 132–33, 220*
perspective *25–26*
Peter *49–50, 71, 79, 83, 85–87, 89, 125, 219, 221–23, 240, 243–44, 300*
Pharisees *26, 45–48*
point of departure *53–54, 161, 208*
prominence *23, 55, 57, 68, 108, 131–32, 163, 173, 205*
propositions *54*

R
rhetorical questions *21, 52, 54, 83, 93, 95, 106–8, 173, 175*
rhetorical underlining *132*

S
sanctification *140, 208, 220, 272, 274, 326*
semantic and structural analysis (SSA) *23, 54, 65–66, 77–78, 91, 124, 141, 144, 153–54, 161, 168, 172, 183, 188, 202, 224–25*
series' title *223*
sermon development *11, 32–34*
sermon movements *2, 31–32, 66, 121, 141, 155, 168, 177, 225*
setting *31, 58, 79, 116*
SSA *177*
synonyms *230, 238*
syntax *19*

T
tail-head linkage *21*
text-types *18*
  literary *17, 41*
textual criticism *19, 234–35, 237*
textual unity *22, 28*
  coherence *22*
  prominence *22–23*
the Twelve *84, 154*
the world *28, 45–46, 73, 83, 99, 118–20, 133, 152–53, 156–58, 163, 165–66, 170–71, 192–93, 196, 205–6, 209, 211, 216–17, 220, 282–83, 296, 315, 317, 319, 328*
thought-flow (flow of thought) *22, 31, 39, 41, 51, 65–66, 75, 77, 221*
topic *7, 21, 23, 36, 54, 85, 89, 96, 103, 112, 121, 126–27, 135, 188, 214*
translation *18–19, 54–55, 229–30, 246*
Trinity *204*

U
unity of the Farewell Disourse (authorship) *67*

V
vine allegory *53, 72–73, 76, 126, 131–43, 151, 173–278, 185, 220, 271–76*

W
word-order (fronting) *93*
word studies *19, 230–31*

Scripture Index

Genesis
3:6 22
3:14 62
32:30 107
37:3–4 222
48–49 76

Exodus
3:6 107
15:17 94
24:8–11 107
25:9 94
33 107
33:9 189
33:9–11 309
33:11 145, 148, 279
33:18 106
33:19–20 107
33:20 116, 259
34 113, 255

Leviticus
11:44 207
18:19 86, 242
19:18 82

Deuteronomy
4:33 107
5:24 107
5:26 107
7:7–8 146
30:4 94

31:6 90
31:7 77
31:23 90
31–33 75–76
33 77

Joshua
23–24 75

Judges
6:22 107
13:22 107

1 Samuel
12:1–25 75

2 Samuel
7:10 94

1 Kings
17:10–24 275
17:14 275

1 Chronicles
13:6 111
28–29 75

2 Chronicles
20:7 145, 148, 279

Job
9:8 44
19:26–27 113, 254

Psalms
9:2 110

20:1 207
23 47
29:2 110
35:19 153
54:1 207
69:4 153
80:8–18 136
80:14–17 137

Proverbs
8:17 222
18:10 207

Isaiah
5 136, 142, 271
5:1–8 136
5:8 137, 335
6:5 107
9:6 45
13:8 173
21:3 173
26:17–18 173
27 142, 272
27:2–6 136
41:8 145, 148, 279
42:8 204, 324
42:14 173
48:2 215
48:16–19 137
49:1–13 137
61:1–11 137
66:7–13 173

Jeremiah
   2:21   *136*
   4:31   *173*
   6:9   *136*
   6:24   *173*
   12:10–13   *136*
   13:21   *173*
   22:23   *173*
   23:30   *10*
   30:6   *173*
   49:22–24   *173*
   50:43   *173*

Ezekiel
   15:1–8   *136*
   17:5–10   *136*
   19:10–14   *136*

Daniel
   7   *80*
   7:13–14   *80*

Hosea
   10:1–2   *136*
   14:7   *136*

Micah
   4:9–10   *173*

Malachi
   1:2–3   *211*

Matthew
   2   *26*
   2:13   *63*
   5:8   *113, 254*
   7:7–8   *111*
   7:16   *138, 274*
   7:20   *138*
   9:28   *58*
   13:57   *58*
   16:18   *221*
   18:19   *111*
   21:22   *111*
   21:23–25   *59*
   28:18–20   *7*
   28:19   *226*

Mark
   1:14   *58*
   3:7   *52*
   14:58   *94*

Luke
   1:19   *212*
   2:10–11   *306*
   8   *35, 225*
   8:22–23   *37*
   8:22–25   *29, 30–31, 36–37*
   8:23   *32–33*
   8:24   *32, 37*
   8:25   *32*
   9:36   *59*
   12:13–21   *33*
   22:14–38   *75–76*
   22:21–38   *75*
   22:34   *221*

John
   1:1   *43, 52*
   1:1–18   *43, 74*
   1:4   *101*
   1:12   *48*
   1:14   *43, 100, 107, 211*
   1:17   *100, 203*
   1:18   *107*
   1:19   *43*
   1:19–5:47   *74*
   1:19–12:50   *74*
   1:19–51   *43*
   1:39   *79*
   1:42   *221*
   1:51   *80*
   2:4   *79–80, 203*
   2:12   *201*
   2:13–14   *193*
   2:13–22   *43*
   2:16   *93*
   2:23–25   *8, 19, 43, 138*
   3   *8*
   3:2   *8*
   3:3   *84*
   3:5   *84*
   3:13   *80*
   3:14   *80*
   3:14–18   *84*
   3:15   *101*
   3:16   *101, 203, 285*
   3:19   *222*
   3:22   *201*
   3:30   *61*
   3:31–32   *44*
   3:35   *222*
   3:35–36   *44*
   3:36   *101*
   4   *8*
   4:4   *193*
   4:14   *101*
   4:36   *101*
   4:46   *44*
   4:54   *44*
   5:1   *201*
   5:1–7   *136*
   5:4–5   *193*
   5:5   *193*
   5:14   *201*
   5:17   *44*
   5:18   *44*
   5:20   *222*
   5:24   *101*
   5:26   *101*
   5:27   *80*
   5:33   *100*
   5:37   *107*
   5:40   *101*
   5:43   *111*
   6:1   *44, 201*
   6:1–12:50   *74*
   6:16–21   *44*
   6:26   *44*
   6:27   *80, 101*
   6:30   *44*
   6:32   *100*
   6:33   *101*
   6:35   *100–101*
   6:35–40   *45*
   6:40   *101*
   6:41–51   *45*
   6:44   *101*
   6:46   *107*
   6:47   *101*
   6:52–58   *45*
   6:53   *80, 101*
   6:54   *101*
   6:55   *100*
   6:60–71   *45*
   6:62   *80*
   6:63   *101*

6:68   *101*
6:69   *45*
7:1   *44, 201*
7:4   *185*
7:5   *45*
7–8   *45*
7:10   *45*
7:13   *185*
7:14   *45*
7:14–24   *45*
7:16   *100*
7:20   *45*
7:25   *45*
7:26   *185*
7:28   *45*
7:30   *45, 79–80, 203*
7:33   *174*
7:33–34   *80, 241*
7:34   *81*
7:37   *45*
7:38   *181, 304*
7:39   *80, 212*
7:40–44   *45*
7:45–52   *45*
7:52   *45*
8:12   *45, 101*
8:12–59   *80*
8:13–18   *46*
8:14   *80*
8:19–20   *46*
8:20   *79–80, 203*
8:21   *46, 80*
8:28   *46, 80*
8:30   *46*
8:33   *46*
8:39   *46*
8:40   *46*
8:42   *46*
8:44   *46*
8:54   *46, 80*
8:56   *46*
8:58   *46*
9:4   *70*
9:5   *46*
9:22   *47*
9:27   *47*
9:35   *46, 80*
9:35–41   *71*

9:38   *47*
9:39   *47*
9:40   *47*
9:41   *47*
10:1   *47, 101*
10:1–21   *47*
10:2   *47*
10:6   *184*
10:7   *47, 101*
10:9   *47, 101*
10:10   *101, 181, 284, 304*
10:11   *47*
10:14   *47*
10:16   *184*
10:17   *47*
10:20   *47*
10:22   *47*
10:22–39   *47*
10:24   *185*
10:28   *101, 209*
10:30   *204*
10:31   *106*
10:41   *48*
10:42   *44*
11:1–16   *48*
11:5   *222*
11:14   *185*
11:15   *48*
11:17–27   *48*
11:24   *185*
11:26   *48*
11:28–44   *48*
11:36   *222*
11:38–44   *48*
11:40   *48*
11:47–57   *48*
11:48   *26*
11:54   *185*
12:1–11   *48*
12:10   *48*
12:11   *193*
12:12–19   *48*
12:16   *212*
12:19   *48*
12:20–36   *48*
12:23   *79–80, 203, 212*
12:25   *101*

12:27   *79*
12:28   *80*
12:34   *80*
12:35   *174*
12:37   *48, 50*
12:37–43   *48*
12:44–50   *48, 68*
12:50   *69*
13   *69–70*
13:1   *68–69, 71, 79*
13:1–30   *67, 69, 74*
13:3   *70, 200*
13:4–5   *58*
13:16   *152*
13:16–18   *71*
13–17   *48, 67, 74–76, 221, 224, 239–40*
13–20   *74*
13:24   *200*
13:27–30   *70*
13:30   *51, 70, 201*
13:31   *53, 69–70, 74, 80, 212*
13:31–16:33   *67–68, 74–75, 222*
13:31–17   *76*
13:31–17:26   *10, 67*
13:31–18:1   *67*
13:31–32   *71, 78–81, 80–81, 84, 139, 200*
13:31–33   *85, 240*
13:31–38   *69–72, 75, 77–79, 84–85, 87, 125, 152, 187, 219, 239–40*
13:32   *70, 212*
13:33   *78–79, 81, 175, 187*
13:34   *71, 79, 81*
13:34–35   *79, 81–83, 85, 133, 144–45, 200, 222, 242*
13:35   *71, 79, 83*
13:36   *83, 92–93, 164, 175, 223*

13:36–38   71, 79, 83–84, 222–23, 243
13:37   83, 187, 223, 243
13:38   70, 221
13:38–38   86
14   70, 94, 151, 195
14:1   69, 89, 97, 187, 192, 204, 246, 254
14:1–4   96, 245
14:1–14   89–90, 116, 245, 254
14:1–15   162
14:1–16:32   84
14:1–24   119
14:1–31   72, 89, 119, 132, 174, 219
14:1–33   75, 128
14:2   92, 94, 97, 246, 248
14:2–4   90–98, 254
14:2–5   71, 81
14:2–14   90
14:2–31   89
14:3   97, 187, 247
14:4   98, 175, 248
14:5   99, 104, 164, 250
14:5–7   90, 98–104, 103, 250, 254
14:6   100–102, 104, 185, 208, 250–51
14:7   105–6, 252
14:8   254
14:8–9c   254
14:8–14   90, 253–54
14:8–17   71
14:9   107, 125
14:9d–10   256
14:10   187
14:10–11   153
14:11–14   115–123, 257
14:12   110, 187
14:13   111, 139, 173, 187
14:13–14   176
14:14   111

14:15   89, 121, 139, 152, 187, 261, 280
14:15–20   117–18, 122, 262
14:15–24   71
14:15–25   254
14:15–27   89, 261
14:15–31   89, 117, 119, 245
14:16   110, 175
14–17   76
14:17   100, 193, 208
14:17–21   84
14:18   187
14:18–19   71
14:18–20   118
14:19   193
14:19–20   81
14:20   187, 211
14:21   118, 177, 187, 280
14:21–24   118–19, 122, 139, 263
14:22   119, 193
14:23   95
14:25   187
14:25–27   119–21, 123, 264
14:25–31   71
14:26   84, 110, 120, 168, 213
14:27   89, 119–20, 192–93
14:28   120, 125, 127, 164, 175, 187, 266
14:28–31   81, 124–28, 266
14:29   125–26, 187
14:29–31   128, 268
14:30   192–93
14:30–31   126
14:31   68, 72, 126, 193, 201, 203
14:33   74
15   151, 195, 220
15:1   72

15:1–2   134, 136–37, 141, 271
15:1–8   135
15:1–10   135
15:1–11   73, 134–42, 136, 141, 151, 187, 192, 271
15:1–16:4   72–75, 133
15:1–16:4c   220
15:1–16:4d   174
15:1–16:33   72
15:1–17   72, 132
15:1–18   185
15:2   193
15:3–4   142
15:3–8   137
15:3–10   134, 141, 273
15:4   134
15:5   134
15:5–8   142, 273
15:5a   138
15:6   138
15:7   111, 146, 173, 176, 187
15:8   139
15:9   73, 135–36
15:9–10   135, 139, 142, 273
15:9–11   135
15:9–12   145
15:9–16   135
15:9–17   71
15:10   133, 145, 187
15:11   135–36, 140–41, 143, 200, 275
15:12   71, 82, 135, 144–46, 200, 277
15:12–13   147, 277
15:12–17   73, 83, 133, 136, 144–49, 151, 187, 277
15:13   145, 277
15:13–16   144
15:13–17   222
15:14   144
15:14–16   148, 278
15:14–17   145–46
15:15   144

Scripture Index

15:15d–e *146*
15:16 *111, 144, 176*
15:17 *135–36, 146*
15:18 *136, 152, 193, 220*
15:18–16:4 *73, 156, 282*
15:18–16:4c *149, 192, 208*
15:18–19 *156, 200*
15:18–21 *152*
15:18–25 *151–54, 156, 283*
15:19 *152, 193*
15:20–21 *156*
15:20–25 *152*
15:22 *153, 187*
15:22–25 *156*
15:24 *153*
15:26 *84, 100, 187, 208*
15:26–27 *71, 152–53, 157, 285*
15:28 *49*
16 *184, 195*
16:1–4c *152, 154–55, 158, 286*
16:1–7 *54, 164*
16:4 *54, 73*
16:4–5 *164*
16:4–15 *73, 290*
16:4–33 *74–75*
16:4d *151, 162*
16:4d–7 *168–69, 291*
16:4d–15 *162–70*
16:4d–33 *133, 220*
16:5 *73, 151, 172, 175, 200*
16:5–7 *71, 81, 187*
16:7 *168, 172*
16:7–11 *163*
16:7a *164*
16:8 *193*
16:8–11 *165–68, 170, 292*
16:10 *165, 172, 175, 200*
16:11 *193*
16:11a *164*

16:12–15 *166–68, 170, 294*
16:13 *84, 100, 166, 208, 213*
16:14 *139*
16:14–15 *167*
16:15 *161*
16:16 *161*
16:16–18 *174–75*
16:16–19 *177–78, 299*
16:16–22 *81, 187*
16:16–24 *71, 172–80, 298*
16:16a–b *177*
16:17 *175, 200*
16:18 *183, 185*
16:18–33 *132*
16:19 *175–76*
16:19–22 *175–76*
16:19a–24d *177*
16:20 *60, 193, 200*
16:20–22 *180, 301*
16:21 *183, 185*
16:21–22 *175*
16:22 *200*
16:23 *111, 174, 176, 187*
16:23–24 *176–77, 180, 303*
16:23a *176*
16:24 *111, 161, 173, 200*
16:25 *150, 152, 162, 173, 183*
16:25–27 *173*
16:25–28 *184–86, 188–89, 309*
16:25–31 *183*
16:25–32 *173, 182–90, 308*
16:25–33 *177*
16:26 *111, 173, 187*
16:28 *81, 186–87, 200*
16:29 *175*
16:29–32 *83, 190, 311*
16:30 *200*
16:30b *187*
16:31 *54*

16:31–32 *183, 187–88,*
16:32 *187, 221*
16:33 *73, 162, 188, 191–94, 197, 315*
16:33a–b *195, 316*
16:33c *317*
16:33d *319*
17 *74, 77, 199–201, 214, 322–23*
17:1 *74, 139, 201*
17:1–2 *200*
17:1–5 *201–4, 214, 218, 323, 329*
17:1–26 *67, 200–218, 220*
17:1a–b *202*
17:1c–3e *202*
17:2 *101, 203*
17:3 *101, 203–4*
17:4 *139, 200*
17:4–5 *204*
17:5 *139, 203–4, 207, 212*
17:6 *206*
17:6–19 *202, 204–9, 214–15, 325*
17:8 *200, 206*
17:10 *139*
17:11 *200*
17:11d *209*
17:12 *207*
17:13 *200*
17:13a–15c *205*
17:14 *193, 200, 208*
17:15c *208*
17:16b *208*
17:17a *208*
17:18 *209*
17:19 *209*
17:20 *210*
17:20–23 *210*
17:20–24 *214*
17:20–26 *202, 209–10, 217, 327*
17:21 *210*
17:23 *211*
17:24 *210, 212*
17:25–26 *210, 214*

17:26 69, 201
18:1 69, 74, 201
18:1–11 221
18:1–14 49
18:1–27 49
18:9 49
18:11 49
18:13 221
18:15–27 49
18:18 222
18–19 48
18–20 74
18:20 185
18:28–33 49
18:33–38 49
18:37 100
19:1–16 49
19:17–24 49
19:25–27 49
19:28 201
19:28–37 49
19:29–30 186
19:38–42 49
20:1–10 49
20:11–18 49
20:21 48, 139
20:25–29 49
20:28 98
20:29 49
20:30 77
20:30–31 50
20:31 101
21 74, 222
21:1 201
21:1–14 50
21:7 193
21:15 222
21:15–17 221–22
21:15–19 222
21:15–22 187
21:15–23 50
21:16 222
21:17 222
21:18–19 221, 223
21:19 87, 223
21:24–25 50

Acts
7:44 94
7:48 94
8:40–9:1 52
9:2 99
9:31 51
11:28 167
17:24 94
17:30 318
19 99
19:9 99
19:23 99
20:17–38 75
21:10 167
22:4 99
24:14 99
24:22 99

Romans
1:3–4 63–64
1:13 138
1:25 61
3:26 102
5:8 140, 186
5:12–21 55
6:15 52
8:28 303

1 Corinthians
1:11 327
13 147, 277

Galatians
5:22 138

Ephesians
3:2–13 61
3:16–19 312
3:20 38
4:11 7

Philippians
1:11 138
4:7 120

Colossians
2:4 62

1 Thessalonians
4:16–17 95

1 Timothy
2:2 120
6:16 107

2 Timothy
3:12 157, 284
4:10 222

Titus
1:6 19
3:5 62

Hebrews
1:4–5 52
2:3 63
4:12 7
4:13 20
8:5 94
9:11 94
9:24 94
12:2 303

James
1:5–6 111
5:15 111

1 Peter
2:2 227

1 John
1 62
2:1 117
2:5 140
2:6 140
3:21–22 111
4:6 208
4:7–21 133
4:10 133, 140
4:11–12 133
4:16 133
4:20 220
5:14–15 111

Revelation
3:10 207
12:2–5 176
12:11 128, 269

www.ingramcontent.com/pod-product-compliance
Lightning Source LLC
Chambersburg PA
CBHW030519230426
43665CB00010B/682